Lecture Notes in Computer Science 15512

Founding Editors

Gerhard Goos
Juris Hartmanis

Editorial Board Members

Elisa Bertino, *Purdue University, West Lafayette, IN, USA*
Wen Gao, *Peking University, Beijing, China*
Bernhard Steffen⬤, *TU Dortmund University, Dortmund, Germany*
Moti Yung⬤, *Columbia University, New York, NY, USA*

The series Lecture Notes in Computer Science (LNCS), including its subseries Lecture Notes in Artificial Intelligence (LNAI) and Lecture Notes in Bioinformatics (LNBI), has established itself as a medium for the publication of new developments in computer science and information technology research, teaching, and education.

LNCS enjoys close cooperation with the computer science R & D community, the series counts many renowned academics among its volume editors and paper authors, and collaborates with prestigious societies. Its mission is to serve this international community by providing an invaluable service, mainly focused on the publication of conference and workshop proceedings and postproceedings. LNCS commenced publication in 1973.

Hemant Singh · Tapabrata Ray ·
Joshua Knowles · Xiaodong Li · Juergen Branke ·
Bing Wang · Akira Oyama
Editors

Evolutionary Multi-Criterion Optimization

13th International Conference, EMO 2025
Canberra, ACT, Australia, March 4–7, 2025
Proceedings, Part I

Springer

Editors
Hemant Singh (iD)
University of New South Wales
Canberra, NSW, Australia

Joshua Knowles (iD)
SLB Cambridge Research
Cambridge, UK

Juergen Branke (iD)
University of Warwick
Coventry, Warwickshire, UK

Akira Oyama (iD)
Japan Aerospace Exploration Agency
Tokyo, Japan

Tapabrata Ray (iD)
University of New South Wales
Canberra, NSW, Australia

Xiaodong Li (iD)
RMIT
Melbourne, VIC, Australia

Bing Wang (iD)
University of New South Wales
Canberra, NSW, Australia

ISSN 0302-9743   ISSN 1611-3349 (electronic)
Lecture Notes in Computer Science
ISBN 978-981-96-3505-4   ISBN 978-981-96-3506-1 (eBook)
https://doi.org/10.1007/978-981-96-3506-1

This Springer imprint is published by the registered company Springer Nature Singapore Pte Ltd
The registered company address is: 152 Beach Road, #21-01/04 Gateway East, Singapore 189721, Singapore

If disposing of this product, please recycle the paper.

Preface

The International Conference on Evolutionary Multi-criterion Optimization (EMO) is a biennial conference series dedicated to the study of randomized optimization algorithms for addressing problems characterized by having multiple conflicting objectives. Such problems are widely encountered in many disciplines, including (but not limited to) engineering, information science, operations research, and economics. The conference aims to bring together researchers and practitioners in EMO, Multiple Criteria Decision Making (MCDM), and their applications, from across academia, government, and industry, from around the world. The EMO conference was first held in Zürich (Switzerland) in 2001, and up until 2023, it had traveled to four continents. The past hosts include, in chronological order: Faro (Portugal), Guanajuato (Mexico), Matsushima (Japan), Nantes (France), Ouro Preto (Brazil), Sheffield (UK), Guimarães (Portugal), Münster (Germany), East Lansing (USA), Shenzhen (China), and Leiden (Netherlands).

In its 13th edition, EMO 2025 continued to break new ground. For the first time the conference was held in Australia (in its capital, Canberra). Australia, and the Oceania region in general, has a thriving computational intelligence community, including many researchers working in the field of evolutionary computation, optimization, machine learning, and related fields. Hosting EMO 2025 in Australia provided an opportunity for local researchers to participate and potentially expanded the delegate pool and readership of the EMO conference series for future editions. For international delegates, the location also provided an ideal platform to explore a bounty of visitor attractions spanning Australia's rich cultural heritage, natural beauty, and more.

In addition to the main EMO track, the conference program featured two special tracks: one on MCDM and another on Industry applications, to foster collaborations with researchers and practitioners in these areas. For the first time, the call for papers included an option of submitting abstract-only works in the special tracks. The conference received 63 submissions in total, including 57 full papers and 6 abstracts. After a rigorous single-blind peer-review process, 38 full papers and 2 abstracts were selected to appear in the final proceedings. This translates into an acceptance rate of 66.7% for full papers, 33.3% for abstracts, and 63.5% overall. Each full paper was reviewed by three reviewers on average, while each abstract was reviewed by one of the respective track chairs. Three submissions were desk-rejected due to low relevance to the conference. All accepted papers and abstracts were presented in-person, with the exception of a few online presentations made by authors who were unable to travel to the conference. The accepted papers/abstracts had 103 authors from 16 countries, with the top 5 countries of affiliation being UK (20), Australia (15), China (14), Netherlands (10), and USA (9). The accepted papers have been organized into two Springer LNCS volumes that collectively comprise the EMO 2025 proceedings.

Three keynote talks were delivered by pioneering researchers, covering each of the core themes of the conference (EMO, MCDM and Industry). These included *Interactive Multiobjective Optimization from MCDM and EMO Perspectives* by Kaisa Miettinen from University of Jyväskylä, Finland; *Multi-X: Challenges and Opportunities in Optimization for Complex Applications* by Bernhard Sendhoff, CEO of Global Network Honda Research Institutes, Germany; and *Modelling and Set Constraints in Multiobjective Evolutionary Computation* by Qingfu Zhang from the City University of Hong Kong, China.

Especially for the benefit of students and early career researchers, EMO 2025 featured six tutorials on wide-ranging topics. These included *Evolutionary Multi-objective Optimization for Practical Problem Solving* by Kalyanmoy Deb, *Evolutionary Multiobjective Algorithms for Constrained Single-objective Combinatorial Optimization Problems: Theory and Applications* by Aneta Neumann and Frank Neumann, *Difficulties in Fair Performance Comparison of Evolutionary Multi-objective Optimization Algorithms* by Lie Meng Pang and Hisao Ishibuchi, *Multi-objective Algorithm Design using Large Language Models* by Fei Liu, Zhichao Lu, Zhenkun Wang, and Qingfu Zhang, *Dynamic Multi-objective Optimization: Introduction, Challenges, Applications and Future Directions* by Mardé Helbig, and *Interactive Evolutionary Multiobjective Optimization using DESDEO* by Bhupinder Saini and Giomara Lárraga.

We would like to sincerely thank all speakers, authors, attendees, and members of the program committee, organization committee, and steering committee who contributed to the success of EMO 2025. We also thank Springer for providing the platform for publishing the proceedings, the review system (EquinOCS), and sponsorship towards the Outstanding paper awards. Last but not least, we gratefully acknowledge support from the University of New South Wales Canberra in providing the online platforms for managing the registrations and finances of the conference.

We hope that readers will find significant value in the contributions presented in these proceedings and that the ensuing discussions and research opportunities will continue to propel the field forward.

Hemant Singh
Tapabrata Ray
Joshua Knowles
Juergen Branke
Xiaodong Li
Bing Wang
Akira Oyama

Organization

General Chairs

Singh, Hemant   University of New South Wales, Australia
Ray, Tapabrata   University of New South Wales, Australia
Knowles, Joshua   SLB Cambridge Research, UK

Program Chairs

Li, Xiaodong   Royal Melbourne Institute of Technology,
                                 Australia
Branke, Juergen   University of Warwick, UK

Industry Session Chairs

Neumann, Frank   University of Adelaide, Australia
Smith-Miles, Kate   University of Melbourne, Australia

MCDM Chairs

Sarker, Ruhul   University of New South Wales, Australia
Mostaghim, Sanaz   Otto von Guericke University Magdeburg,
                                 Germany

Proceedings Chairs

Wang, Bing   University of New South Wales, Australia
Oyama, Akira   Japan Aerospace Exploration Agency, Japan

Conflict of Interest Chairs

Ishibuchi, Hisao   Southern University of Science and Technology,
                                 China
Pang, Lie Meng   Southern University of Science and Technology,
                                 China

Local Arrangement Chairs

Ahrari, Ali   University of New South Wales, Australia
Elsayed, Saber   University of New South Wales, Australia

Tutorial Chair

Abbass, Hussein   University of New South Wales, Australia

Web Chair

Kenny, Angus   University of New South Wales, Australia

Publicity Chairs

Brockhoff, Dimo   Institut Polytechnique de Paris, France
Coello Coello, Carlos   CINVESTAV-IPN, Mexico
Mei, Yi   Victoria University of Wellington, New Zealand
Neumann, Aneta   University of Adelaide, Australia
Sharma, Deepak   Indian Institute of Technology Guwahati, India
Wang, Handing   Xidian University, China

Program Committee Members

Aguirre, Hernan   Shinshu University, Japan
Allmendinger, Richard   University of Manchester, UK
Bäck, Thomas   Leiden University, The Netherlands
Binois, Mickael   Inria Sophia Antipolis, France
Branke, Juergen   University of Warwick, UK
Brockhoff, Dimo   Institut Polytechnique de Paris, France
Chugh, Tinkle   University of Exeter, UK
Coello Coello, Carlos   CINVESTAV-IPN, Mexico
De Ath, George   University of Exeter, UK
Doerr, Carola   Sorbonne Université, France
Doerr, Benjamin   École Polytechnique, France
Eftimov, Tome   Jožef Stefan Institute, Slovenia
Elarbi, Maha   University of Tunis, Tunisia

Everson, Richard	University of Exeter, UK
Falcón-Cardona, Jesús Guillermo	Tecnológico de Monterrey, Mexico
Fieldsend, Jonathan	University of Exeter, UK
Guha, Ritam	Michigan State University, USA
Guo, Mingyu	University of Adelaide, Australia
Habib, Ahsanul	Murray-Darling Basin Authority, Australia
He, Cheng	Huazhong University of Science and Technology, China
Helbig, Marde	Griffith University, Australia
Ishibuchi, Hisao	Southern University of Science and Technology, China
Kenny, Angus	University of New South Wales, Australia
Knowles, Joshua	SLB Cambridge Research, UK
Kononova, Anna	Leiden University, The Netherlands
Li, Xiaodong	Royal Melbourne Institute of Technology, Australia
Li, Miqing	University of Birmingham, UK
Li, Ke	University of Exeter, UK
Liefooghe, Arnaud	Université du Littoral Côte d'Opale, France
Limmer, Steffen	Honda Research Institute Europe, Germany
Lu, Zhichao	City University of Hong Kong, China
López-Ibáñez, Manuel	University of Manchester, UK
Mei, Yi	Victoria University of Wellington, New Zealand
Mejia-de-Dios, Jesus-Adolfo	Autonomous University of Coahuila, Mexico
Mezura-Montes, Efren	Universidad Veracruzana, Mexico
Mostaghim, Sanaz	Otto von Guericke University Magdeburg, Germany
Neumann, Frank	University of Adelaide, Australia
Neumann, Aneta	University of Adelaide, Australia
Nojima, Yusuke	Osaka Metropolitan University, Japan
Oyama, Akira	Japan Aerospace Exploration Agency, Japan
Pang, Lie	Meng Southern University of Science and Technology, China
Rahi, Kamrul Hasan	University of New South Wales, Australia
Ray, Tapabrata	University of New South Wales, Australia
Rodemann, Tobias	Honda Research Institute Europe, Germany
Rodriguez-Fernandez, Angel	Cinvestav, Mexico
Rojas-Gonzalez, Sebastian	Ghent University, Belgium
Rudolph, Guenter	TU Dortmund University, Germany
Saini, Bhupinder	University of Jyväskylä, Finland
Santoshkumar, Balija	Michigan State University, USA
Sarker, Ruhul	University of New South Wales, Australia

Sato, Hiroyuki	University of Electro-Communications, Japan
Schuetze, Oliver	Cinvestav, Mexico
Shang, Ke	Southern University of Science and Technology, China
Singh, Hemant	University of New South Wales, Australia
Tanabe, Ryoji	Yokohama National University, Japan
Taylor, Kendall	Royal Melbourne Institute of Technology, Australia
Tian, Ye	Anhui University, China
Tušar, Tea	Jožef Stefan Institute, Slovenia
Viet Do, Anh	University of Adelaide, Australia
Volz, Vanessa	Centrum Wiskunde & Informatica, The Netherlands
Wagner, Markus	Monash University, Australia
Walker, David	University of Exeter, UK
Wang, Bing	University of New South Wales, Australia
Wang, Rui	National University of Defense Technology, China
Wang, Handing	Xidian University, China
Wang, Xilu	University of Surrey, UK
Wang, Peng	Zhengzhou University, China
Zhang, Qingfu	City University of Hong Kong, China
Zhang, Xingyi	Anhui University, China
Zhang, Jinyuan	Southern University of Science and Technology, China
Zhong, Jinghui	South China University of Technology, China
Zhou, Aimin	East China Normal University, China

Contents – Part I

Benchmarking

Applications

Contents – Part II

Multi-criteria Decision Support

Short Papers

Algorithm Design

Towards an Efficient Innovation Path Seeking Algorithm Using Directed Domination

Ahmer Khan$^{(\boxtimes)}$ and Kalyanmoy Deb

Michigan State University, East Lansing, MI 48823, USA
{khanahm2,kdeb}@msu.edu
https://www.coin-lab.org

Abstract. In practice, users are often stuck with an existing solution, despite agreeing on the fact that the solution needs a substantial change. The hesitation might stem from the hefty cost or amount of effort required to adopt a new solution or could just be human apathy to large changes. In this regard, a recent preliminary study proposed a step-constrained based bi-objective optimization approach which attempts to discover a set of acceptable intermediate solutions starting from the current solution to the desired target solution leading to an *innovation path* (IP). Intermediate solutions, obtained using a multiobjectivization approach, reduce the amount of change required between two successive steps, thereby facilitating multiple gradual changes more acceptable by the users. In this paper, we propose a directed domination concept to make the IP-seeking algorithm more computationally efficient. Results on a number of test and engineering problems reveal that the proposed new approach reaches closer to the target solution and finds closer to optimally trade-off solutions than the previous IP approach.

Keywords: Innovation Path · Directed Domination · Kaizen Principle

1 Introduction

Instigated by a need to change the existing solution (a design, process or a tool that defines a current implementation of a problem) for achieving a new and a more appropriate goal, users are always skeptical on the extent of change the new optimized solution will cause from the existing solution. In scenarios where the new solution is quite different from the current in-practice solution, implementing the new solution might become undesirable, as it could incur a heavy cost and laborious effort. In such scenarios, a series of solutions is required that leads from the current to the desired solution with a finite number of small gradual changes. Such a series of solutions are referred to as Innovation Path (IP) in recent studies [10,11]. This path is based on the well-known "Kaizen" principle [13,18] which argues that humans are more amenable to accept a few gradually-changed solutions as a sequence of improvements from the current solution,

H. Singh et al. (Eds.): EMO 2025, LNCS 15512, pp. 3–16, 2025.
https://doi.org/10.1007/978-981-96-3506-1_1

rather than one large change, following the so-called "Kaikaku" approach [9]. Traditionally, the Kaizen principle has been used for industrial manufacturing processes [1,2,4,8,15,16], but no generic algorithmic approach is proposed to find intermediate solutions making a gradual change.

The previous IP-seeking algorithm proposed an evolutionary multi-objective optimization approach minimizing two objectives: (i) extent of change and (ii) desired goal(s) for improvement with satisfying user-specified step-constraints which restrict a limiting change desired between two consecutive solutions on the IP. Although the previous IP was able to find a path of solutions satisfying step-constraints, in some problems, the final solution deviated far from the true target solution and in some problems, ended up prematurely with a few intermediate solutions, due to the simplicity adopted in identifying anchor points (which ultimately leads to IP solutions). Moreover, the preliminary idea of identifying the anchor points in a population ignored dominated solutions, which may find themselves to be valid anchor points when the solutions that dominated them became infeasible based on step-constraints by the new anchor points. The simplicity of the anchor point identification also made the process expensive and not particularly efficient.

In this study, in addition to the amplitude of the step, we also consider the direction of such a step toward the next anchor solution that ultimately leads closer to the desired target and is also computationally more efficient. We test the algorithm on a number of test and engineering problems and compare its results with the previous IP-seeking algorithm serving as the baseline method. We additionally test on a few new many-objective problems not considered in the preliminary study [10].

In the remainder of the paper, Sect. 2 presents a brief introduction to the previous IP-seeking algorithm and highlights its shortcomings. Section 3 describes the modified IP-seeking algorithm by defining the directed dominance concept. Section 4 presents extensive results on test and engineering problems. Section 5 concludes this study with possible future extensions.

2   Existing Innovation Path Seeking Algorithms

In recent literature, we have devised a simple technique to find IPs [10]. The method defined a bi-objective problem using the "multiobjectivization" principle proposed by EMO researchers in the past [3,5–7,12,14,17]. The Pareto Front (PF) of this bi-objective problem aims to contain the IP solutions. For a set of M new objectives to be optimized simultaneously as a target, our IP-seeking algorithm always formulates a bi-objective problem, in which one of the objectives is the function $f_{M+1}(\boldsymbol{x})$ as the difference between the variable vector $(\boldsymbol{x})$ and the prescribed current feasible solution $(\boldsymbol{x}^{\mathrm{C}})$, to be minimized:

$$f_{M+1}(\boldsymbol{x}) = \|\boldsymbol{x} - \boldsymbol{x}^{\mathrm{C}}\|_2. \tag{1}$$

While the second objective is the new goal to be optimized in the case of single-objective scenario, a scalarized objective $s(x)$, such as the achievement scalarization function (ASF) [19] with objective preference information in terms of weights ($\boldsymbol{w}$) and an aspiration point ($\boldsymbol{z}$), was proposed in the case of multi- or many-objective scenarios as new goal. To find the PF of the resulting bi-objective problem, the IP-seeking algorithm used the classical domination principle with an added layer of intermediate solutions (anchors) detection in a non-dominated sorted population [10]. Here, anchors are defined as non-dominated solutions satisfying the step-constraints; hence, the algorithm looked for the anchors only in the first non-dominated feasible set. This technique was tested on various single, and multi-objective problems with promising results.

2.1 Shortcomings of the Existing IP-Seeking Algorithm

Though the preliminary algorithms exhibited promising results, it is still limited by its anchor discovery mechanism. Since [10] only looks for anchors in the first non-dominated set, it is unable to find anchors in case where the IP might deviate from the PF given specific step-constraints. Moreover, the anchors are dependent on the solutions available in the front, resulting in incomplete paths or paths with big jumps in between. Figure 1a shows an example of a non-dominated sorted population of 14 solutions with the current solution marked as C and a desired target solution marked as T. Note that the target is not part of the population but is marked to demonstrate the concept. Figure 1b shows the IP found by previous algorithm [10] for the sample population. The IP is found with the following step-constraint:

$$G_1(\boldsymbol{x}, \boldsymbol{x}^{(k)}) \equiv f_{M+1}(\boldsymbol{x}) - f_{M+1}(\boldsymbol{x}^{(k)}) \geq \Delta_1, \tag{2}$$

$$\widehat{G}_1(\boldsymbol{x}, \boldsymbol{x}^{(k)}) = 1 - (f_{M+1}(\boldsymbol{x}) - f_{M+1}(\boldsymbol{x}^{(k)}))/\Delta_1 \leq 0, \tag{3}$$

Here $\boldsymbol{x}$ is the variable vector associated with a population member and $\boldsymbol{x}^{(k)}$ is the previous anchor discovered by the algorithm thus far. To start, $\boldsymbol{x}^{(k)} = \boldsymbol{x}^{C}$ (supplied current point). In this example, $\Delta_1 = 0.1$ such that the two consecutive IP solutions have at least Δ_1 difference in f_{M+1}. For the IP found by [10], seen in Fig. 1b, there is a big jump from solution P1 to P3. as P2 does not satisfy the step-constraint G_1 being at least Δ_1 away from P1. Also, the path stops at P4, whereas solution P10 is closer to the target T. Lastly, since this algorithm moves in increasing value of the diff-obj (f_{M+1}), it selects P1 as the first anchor, where P2 might be a better trade-off choice, as it has a lower $s(x)$ value with a slight loss in diff-obj.

3   Proposed Update for Anchor Selection

In this study, we propose an update to the anchor finding mechanism where the algorithm does not go front by front but considers the ideal direction the path should move from one intermediate solution to the next. The basic characteristics of a new anchor is a solution that is not dominated by previously found anchors and satisfies the step-constraints, but it does not necessarily have to be a solution with minimum diff-obj value. To achieve this we transform all feasible solutions

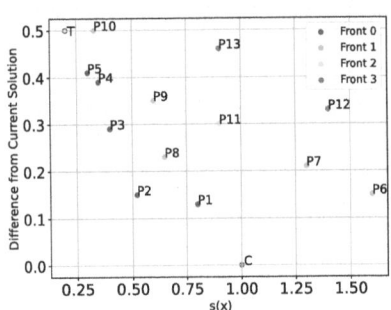

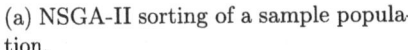

(a) NSGA-II sorting of a sample population.

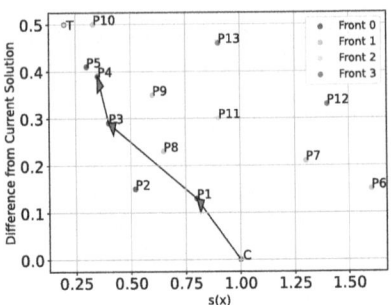

(b) IP (C → P1 → P3 → P4) found by previous approach for sample population.

Fig. 1. ND-sorted sample population of 14 solutions and the IP by the previous approach [10].

to a step-constraint (SC) space, where each axis represents a normalized step-constraint function value and the origin represents the latest found anchor. For L step-constraints, the SC-space is L-dimensional. Solutions are transformed to the SC-space using the following relation:

$$\widehat{S}_l(\boldsymbol{x}, \boldsymbol{x}^{(k)}) = 1 - \widehat{G}_l(\boldsymbol{x}, \boldsymbol{x}^{(k)}), \quad l = 1, 2, \dots, L. \tag{4}$$

For example, the normalized SC function for the G_1 step-constraint defined in Eq. 2 is given below:

$$\widehat{S}_1(\boldsymbol{x}, \boldsymbol{x}^{(k)}) = (f_{M+1}(\boldsymbol{x}) - f_{M+1}(\boldsymbol{x}^{(k)}))/\Delta_1. \tag{5}$$

We always include a default constraint $\widehat{S}_0(\boldsymbol{x}, \boldsymbol{x}^{(k)})$ originating from $G_0(\boldsymbol{x}, \boldsymbol{x}^{(k)})$, as follows:

$$G_0(\boldsymbol{x}, \boldsymbol{x}^{(k)}) \equiv s(\boldsymbol{x}) - s(\boldsymbol{x}^{(k)}) \le 0, \tag{6}$$

$$\widehat{S}_0(\boldsymbol{x}, \boldsymbol{x}^{(k)}) = -1 + s(\boldsymbol{x})/s(\boldsymbol{x}^{(k)}). \tag{7}$$

We use this default constraint realizing that $s(\boldsymbol{x})$ must always be smaller than or equal to the ASF at $\boldsymbol{x}^{(k)}$ (the previous anchor), as our goal is to continuously improve $s(\boldsymbol{x})$ from one anchor to the next in the IP.

Thus, in the presence of the G_1 step-constraint alone, the SC-space is two-dimensional and the current point $\boldsymbol{x}^C$ or the current anchor point $\boldsymbol{x}^{(k)}$ lies at the origin $(0, 0)$ in the SC-space $(\widehat{S}_0, \widehat{S}_1)$. All step-constraint based feasible solutions will lie on the second quadrant of the SC-space (smaller $\widehat{S}_0$ and larger $\widehat{S}_1$) and above the $\widehat{S}_1 = 1$ line, shown in Fig. 2a. For a feasible point P1, we compute the distance D from P1 to a vector joining the origin (location of the current anchor point) to the intersection of two constraints (desired location of the next anchor point): $s(\boldsymbol{x}) = 0$ (or $\widehat{S}_0 = -1$) and $G_1(\boldsymbol{x}, \boldsymbol{x}^{(k)}) = \Delta_1$ (or $\widehat{S}_1 = 1$). The feasible point having the smallest perpendicular distance D is chosen as the next anchor.

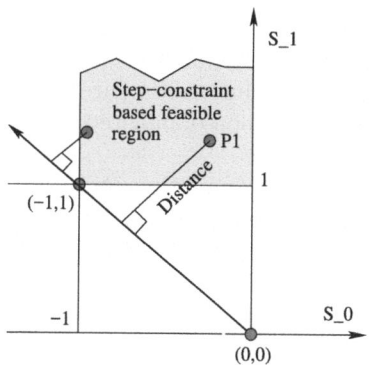 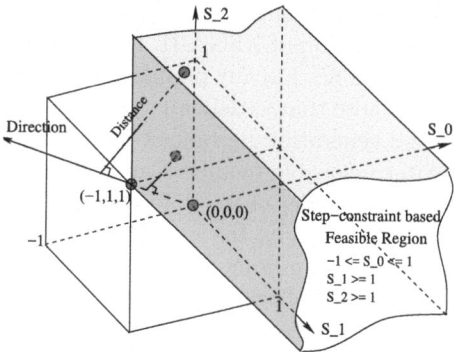

(a) For one supplied step-constraint.   (b) For two supplied step-constraints.

Fig. 2. Proposed anchor finding mechanism in the SC-space.

The above directed domination principle can be extended for more than one supplied step-constraints. To illustrate, let us assume the following two constraints:

$$G_1(\boldsymbol{x}, \boldsymbol{x}^{(k)}) \equiv f_{M+1}(\boldsymbol{x}) - f_{M+1}(\boldsymbol{x}^{(k)}) \geq \Delta_1, \tag{8}$$

$$G_2(\boldsymbol{x}, \boldsymbol{x}^{(k)}) \equiv \|\boldsymbol{x} - \boldsymbol{x}^{(k)}\| \geq \Delta_2. \tag{9}$$

With the default constraint $\widehat{S}_0$, we have a three-dimensional SC space

$$\widehat{S}_0(\boldsymbol{x}, \boldsymbol{x}^{(k)}) = -1 + s(\boldsymbol{x})/s(\boldsymbol{x}^{(k)}),$$
$$\widehat{S}_1(\boldsymbol{x}, \boldsymbol{x}^{(k)}) = (f_{M+1}(\boldsymbol{x}) - f_{M+1}(\boldsymbol{x}^{(k)}))/\Delta_1,$$
$$\widehat{S}_2(\boldsymbol{x}, \boldsymbol{x}^{(k)}) = \|\boldsymbol{x} - \boldsymbol{x}^{(k)}\|/\Delta_2.$$

Note that the current anchor point $(\boldsymbol{x}^{(k)})$ lies at the origin of the SC-space, shown in Fig. 2b. The intersection of three planes, the direction vector and the step-constraint based feasible and improvement space are shown in the figure. It is clear that the intersection point, if exists, will make the shortest perpendicular distance to the line, thereby creating the next anchor point which makes all supplied step-constraints almost active. Interestingly, it can be proven using Karush-Kuhn-Tucker optimality conditions that for both-side bounded step-constraints (for example, $G_1 \geq \Delta_1$ and $G_1 \leq \Delta_2$, the shortest distance from the vector happens for a point making the first constraint ($G_1 \geq \Delta_1$) active. Thus, in such a case, the step-constraint of type $G_1 \leq \Delta_2$ can be ignored for the anchor point identification process.

3.1   Finding Anchors and Sorting Population

As shown in Algorithm 1 we start as in the original NSGA-II with combined population $R_t = P_t \cup Q_t$ (parent (P_t) and offspring (Q_t)). Note that infeasible solutions are excluded for anchor point determination. The current point (which is feasible) is always included in the initial population. Since $f_{M+1}(\boldsymbol{x}^C)$ is zero at the current solution, it is always one of the extreme non-dominated solution at every generation of NSGA-II. It is clear that there is always at least one feasible ND solution (x^C) in any population. Anchor points are solutions that are feasible and are those that satisfy all step-constraints hence, the non-dominated front at the final generation becomes the members of the IP.

After infeasible members are excluded from R_t, the population R_t is sorted in ascending order of the difference function f_{M+1}. The sorted indices are stored in array O. Clearly, the top-most member in the list O is the current solution x^C, having the minimum difference zero from itself. Then, following procedure is repeated in following the sorted list O until all R_t members are considered. If the next member in the list is non-dominated by the already selected anchors its step-constraint violation (SCV) is computed as presented in the algorithm. If SCV is zero, meaning that all step-constraints are satisfied, it is transformed to the SC space and its distance from the ideal direction vector is calculated. The member with minimum distance from the direction vector is selected as the next anchor. If this anchor existed in the previous generation the difference would be calculated as in the algorithm and the count C_{t-1} updated. For our experiments we used $\hat{\delta} = 10^{-4}$. If any of the step-constraints get violated, SCV value will be non-zero and the solution cannot be an anchor point. its normal domination relation with other members of the population is calculated.

Thus, at the end of Algorithm 1, the combined population R_t has defined domination relationships in a matrix where the points not dominated by any other member are the first front and anchors. Similarly others fronts for rest of the population can be found. The Algorithm also provides infeasible set H_t. Figure 3a illustrates how the above procedure determines the anchor point (P_2) in a hypothetical population of 14 points. Figure 3b shows the final found IP for the population. As seen in Fig. 3b the new approach prefers P2 over P1 reducing both the difference between the first and second anchor and improving the tradeoff on the first anchor. Also it includes P_{10} as the final anchor reaching more closer to the target as compared to the approach used in [10].

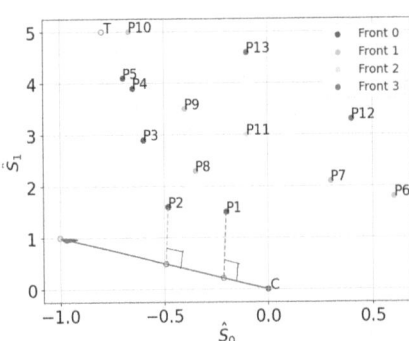

(a) First anchor (P2) discovery. Ortho. dist. from P2 to the direction is shortest.

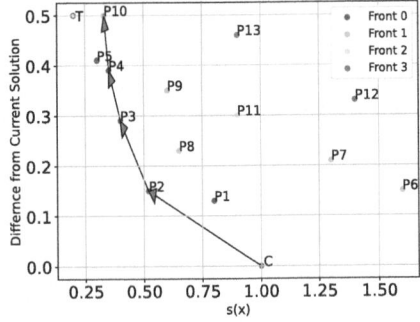

(b) IP (C → P2 → P3 → P4 → P10) determined by the new approach.

Fig. 3. A single step of discovering a new anchor with the proposed approach and the complete IP found using the new approach for the sample population.

Algorithm 1: Identifying Anchor Points

Input: Pop. size N, Pop. R_t with vectors $\boldsymbol{x}^{(i)}$, $i = 1, \ldots, 2N$

1 , normalized problem constraint violation $CV(\boldsymbol{x})$, bi-objective vector

     $\boldsymbol{F}(\boldsymbol{x}) = \{s(\boldsymbol{x}), f_{M+1}(\boldsymbol{x})\}$, normalized step-constraints $\widehat{G}_l(\boldsymbol{x}) \leq 0$,
     normalized transformations $S_l \equiv G_l(\boldsymbol{x}, \boldsymbol{x}^{(k)}) \geq \Delta_l$, anchor set A_{t-1}
     and stability count of anchors $\boldsymbol{C}_{t-1}$. **Output:** Domination relation
     matrix dom_mat, C_t, infeasible pop. H_t

2 $H_t = \{\boldsymbol{x} | CV(\boldsymbol{x}) > 0\}$; // infeasible members;

3 $R_t = R_t \backslash H_t$;

4 $O = \text{Sort}(R_t, \text{'Ascend'})$ using f_{M+1}-objective;

5 $dom\_mat = zeros(|O|, |O|)$;

6 $next\_can, I = 1, golden\_step = (-1, ones(|step|))$;

7 **for** $i = 1, 2, \ldots |O|$ **do**

8   **if** $i = next\_can$ **then**

9          $step\_check = True$;

10         $minimum = \inf$, $dom\_mat(i, :) = 0$;

11   **else**

12         $step\_check = False$;

13   **end**

14   **for** $j = i + 1, i + 2, \ldots |O|$ **do**

15   **if** $\boldsymbol{x}^{O^{(i)}} \prec \boldsymbol{x}^{O^{(j)}}$ **then**

16            $dom\_mat(i, j) = 1$;

17   **else if** $\boldsymbol{x}^{O^{(j)}} \prec \boldsymbol{x}^{O^{(i)}}$ **then**

18            $dom\_mat(j, i) = 1$;

19   **else if** $step\_check$ **then**

20   **if** $SCV = \sum_{l=1}^{L} \langle \widehat{G}_l(\boldsymbol{x}^{O^{(j)}}, \boldsymbol{x}^{O^{(i)}}) \rangle > 0$ **then**

21               $dom\_mat(j, i) = 1$

22   **else**

23               $point = point \cup \widehat{S}_l(\boldsymbol{x}^{O^{(j)}}, \boldsymbol{x}^{O^{(i)}})$, $l = 0, 1, 2, \ldots L$;

24               $distance = \text{perpendicular\_dist}(point, golden\_step)$;

25   **if** $distance < minimum$ **then**

26   **if** $minimum \neq \inf$ **then**

27                     $dom\_mat(next\_can : j, i) = 1$;

28   **end**

29                  $minimum = dist$, $next\_can = j$;

30   **if** $C_{t-1}(I)$ **then**

31   **if** $\| \boldsymbol{F}(A_{t-1}(I)) - \boldsymbol{F}(\boldsymbol{x}^{O^{(j)}}) \|_2 <= \hat{\delta}$ **then**

32                         $C_t(I) = C_{t-1}(I) + 1$;

33   **else**

34                         $C_t(I) = 0$;

35   **end**

36   **else**

37                     $C_t(I).append(0)$;

38   **end**

39                  $I \mathrel{+}= 1$; // update current anchor

40   **end**

41   **end**

42   **end**

43 **end**

3.2   Association, Survival, and Selection Operations

The Association operator is exactly the same as [10], while survival and selection have a slight change in the AnchorSelectProb mechanism used. The anchors from A_t are chosen based a decreasing selection probability $\rho_j = a(1 + (\gamma - 1)(j - 1)/(K - 1))$, where j ($j = 1, 2, \ldots, K$) is the ordering index of anchors, K is the total number of anchor points, and $\gamma < 1$ is a user-defined parameter.

Anchor points are classified into two classes: (i) unstable anchors and (ii) stable anchors, measured by C_t in Lines 33–40 in Algorithm 1. If C_t for an anchor equals or exceeds a threshold ζ ($= 7$ used here), meaning that the anchor does not change its location in the past ζ generations, it is considered stable. Unstable anchors are ordered in increasing f_{M+1} value, so that unstable anchors closer to the current point are assigned more selection probability for stabilizing them to build the foundation for creating more anchor points towards the target point. Stable anchors are ordered in decreasing f_{M+1} value of an anchor, so that a further stable anchor from the current point gets a larger probability value.

4   Results and Discussions

We test the proposed algorithm on various well-known single, multi- and many-objective problems and compare it with the results obtained in [10]. The results obtained in [10] are treated as a baseline and are referred as such in all the plots. Furthermore, for each problem we use the same step-constraints $\widehat{G_l}$ and Δ_l as used in the baseline. The current solution is marked as 'C' in all the plots while the desired target is marked as 'T'. The source code is available at[1].

4.1   Single-Objective Goal

Here we show results on multiple single objective problems and compare with the results achieved in [10]. The different parameter settings for these problems are shown in Table 1. We start with the Himmelblau problem using the G_1 step-constraint, the IP found in the objective space is shown in Fig. 4a, while the IP for G_2 step-constraint in the variable space is shown in Fig. 4b. As seen the

Table 1. Parameter values for problems having a single-objective goal.

	N	T_{max}	γ	Step	Current soln.
Himmelblau	50	100	0.2	(0.5, 1)	[5,5]
Rosenbrock(10)	200	150	0.2	0.3	$w_i = 1.5, \forall i$
G2	100	200	0.25	0.1	[4,6,8,0.8,0.6,1,1,1,1,1]
G4	50	100	0.15	0.2	[100.32, 34.24, 40.47, 42.39, 37.94]

---

[1] https://github.com/Ahmer-khan/Innovation_path/tree/Directed-Domination.

results of the proposed approach are comparable to the baseline for G_1 step-constraint and closer to the target for the G_2 step-constraint. As these results are obtained with half the population size compared to the baseline, it shows the computational efficiency of the proposed approach.

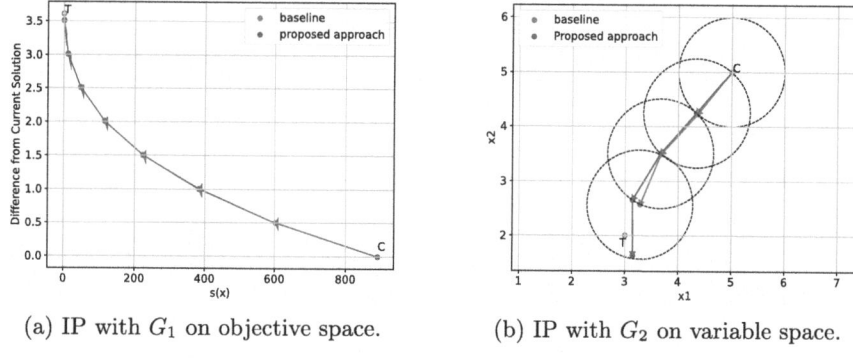

(a) IP with G_1 on objective space.   (b) IP with G_2 on variable space.

Fig. 4. IP with G_1 and G_2 step-constraints for the Himmelblau problem.

Similarly, Fig. 5 shows the IPs found for both the g1 and g2 constrained problem using the G_1 step-constraint.

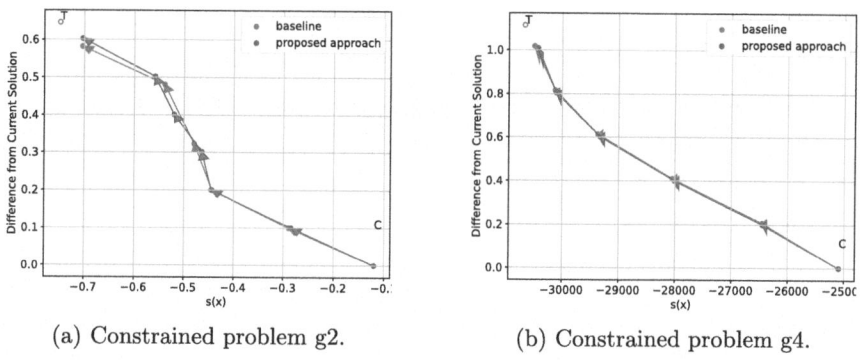

(a) Constrained problem g2.   (b) Constrained problem g4.

Fig. 5. IPs for the constrained g2 and g4 problem using step-constraint G_1.

The proposed approach obtains comparable results to the baseline with a smaller population and fewer generations. Whereas for the 10-var Rosenbrock problem the proposed approach achieve better results, reaching closer to the target as shown in Fig. 7a, in a fewer number of generations. Lastly, our approach achieved better IP for the keyboard configuration (KC) problem with the same setting as in [10]. The goal in the KC problem was to reconfigure keys of the QWERTY keyboard in order to achieve fewer finger movements (a new goal) in typing a large volume of text [11]. As seen in Fig. 7b, although both the new and previous approaches follow a similar trade-off IP, the new approach minimizes the finger movement objective better than that by the previous algorithm (Fig. 6).

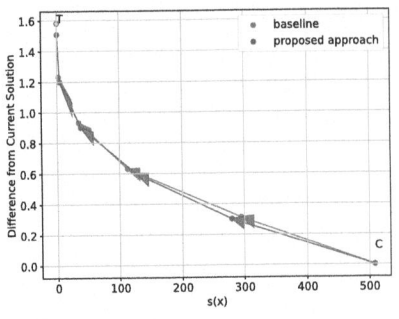

(a) 10-var Rosenbrock problem.

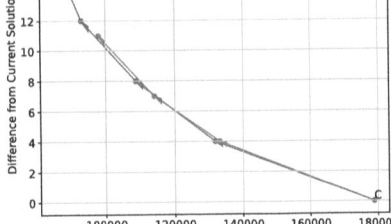

(b) Keyboard configuration problem.

Fig. 6. IPs with step-constraint G_1 for Rosenbrock and keyboard problem.

4.2   Multi-objective Goals

We test and compare our proposed method with the baseline on various well-known multi-objective test and engineering problems. The experimental setup for each problem is shown in Table 2.

Table 2. Parameter values for problems with multi-objective goals.

	N	T_{max}	γ	Step	w	z	Current soln.
ZDT1	100	100	0.2	0.1	[0.75,0.25]	[0,0]	[0.5,0.51,0.002,0.001,0,0,0,0]
ZDT2	100	100	0.2	0.1	[0.75,0.25]	[0,0]	[0.5,0.51,0.002,0.001,0,0,0,0]
ZDT4	100	100	0.2	0.1	[0.75,0.25]	[0,0]	[0.5,0.51,0.02,0.01,0,0,0,0]
ZDT6	100	200	0.2	0.1	[0.75,0.25]	[0,0]	[0.4,0.5,0.002,0.001,0,0,0,0]
OSY	120	100	0.25	0.1	[0.2,0.8]	[-260,0]	[2,4,4,2]
Weld	100	100	0.3	0.1	[0.8,0.2]	[0,0]	[2,4,4,2]

We use the G_1 step-constraint to generate paths for all problems. Figures 7a and 7b shows IP solutions for ZDT4 and ZDT6 problems. The blue point represents the current solution and the green point represents the target. Clearly, the new approach gets closer to the target point T. Figure 8a presents IP solutions for constrained real-world welded beam problem. The results are comparable to the baseline, although the new approach gets closer to the target point.

Innovation Path Deviates from Goal Pareto Front: For certain step-constraints, even with a starting solution on the goal PO front, IP solutions may not lie on the goal PO front. This phenomenon is illustrated in Fig. 8b using a combination of G_1 step-constraint (Eq. 2) and the G_3 step-constraint on ASF values shown in Eq. 11.

$$G_3(\boldsymbol{x}, A^{(k)}) \equiv s(A^{(k)}) - s(\boldsymbol{x}) \leq \Delta_3, \tag{10}$$

$$\widehat{G}_3(\boldsymbol{x}, A^{(k)}) = (s(A^{(k)}) - s(\boldsymbol{x}))/\Delta_3 - 1 \leq 0. \tag{11}$$

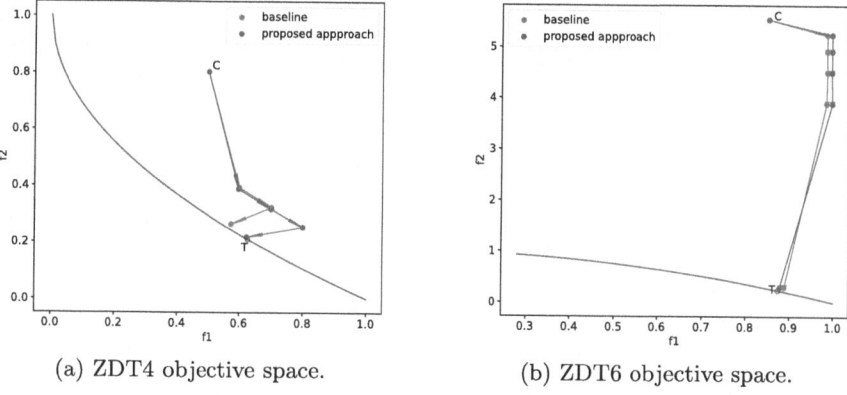

(a) ZDT4 objective space.　　　　(b) ZDT6 objective space.

Fig. 7. IPs for ZDT4 and ZDT6 problems with G_1 step-constraint originating from a non-optimal solution.

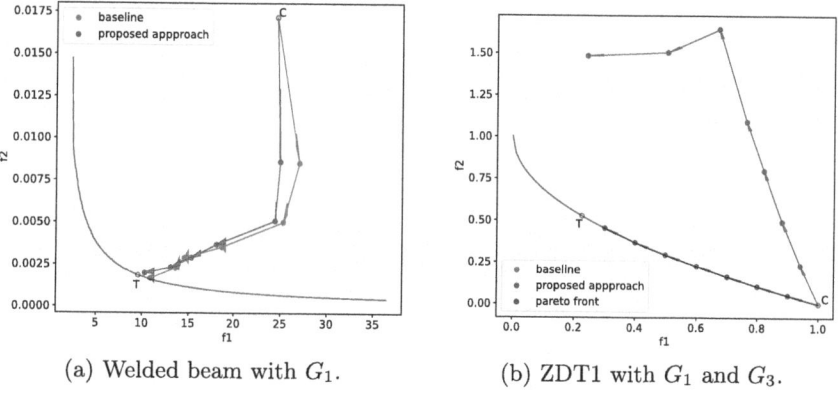

(a) Welded beam with G_1.　　　　(b) ZDT1 with G_1 and G_3.

Fig. 8. IPs with step-constraint(s) for welded beam and PF-deviating problem.

With G_1 alone, IP lies on the goal PF, as shown by the purple path in the Fig. 8b. However, for certain combinations of Δ_1 and Δ_3, all PO solutions of the goal problem become infeasible. Since the baseline only considers anchors in the Non-dominated front it is unable to find a path for this particular problem, whereas the proposed approach can find a valid optimal path diverging away from the PF shown in blue in Fig. 8b.

4.3 Many-Objective Goals

Here we test and compare the proposed approach on three- and five-objective DTLZ2 problems plus the three-objective C2DTLZ2 constrained problem. Though originally the baseline approach has not been tested on many objective problems, we additionally ran the baseline on such problems with the same parameter setting as the proposed approach shown in Table 3.

Table 3. Parameter values for problems with many-objective goals.

	N	$T_{\max}$	γ	Step	w	z	Current solution
DTLZ2-3obj	100	100	0.15	0.2	[0.8,0.1,0.1]	$z_i = 0, \forall i$	$x_1 = 1$ and $x_i = 0.5$ for $i = 2,3,4\ldots12$
DTLZ2-5obj	100	200	0.2	0.2	[0.3,0.3,0.2,0.1,0.1]	$z_i = 0, \forall i$	$x_1 = 1$ and $x_i = 0.5$ for $i = 2,3,4\ldots12$
C2DTLZ2-3obj	200	200	0.15	0.2	[0.1,0.8,0.1]	$z_i = 0, \forall i$	$x_1 = 1$ and $x_i = 0.5$ for $i = 2,3,4\ldots12$

Figure 9a shows the IP found by both approaches for the three-objective DTLZ2 problem. Figure 9b shows the IP found on the five-objective DTLZ2 problem in bi-objective problem space, while Fig. 10 shows the IP found for three-objective C2DTLZ2 constrained problem in the original objective space. Where the proposed approach is comparable to the baseline for three-obj DTLZ2 it does better in the other two problems by reaching closer to the target.

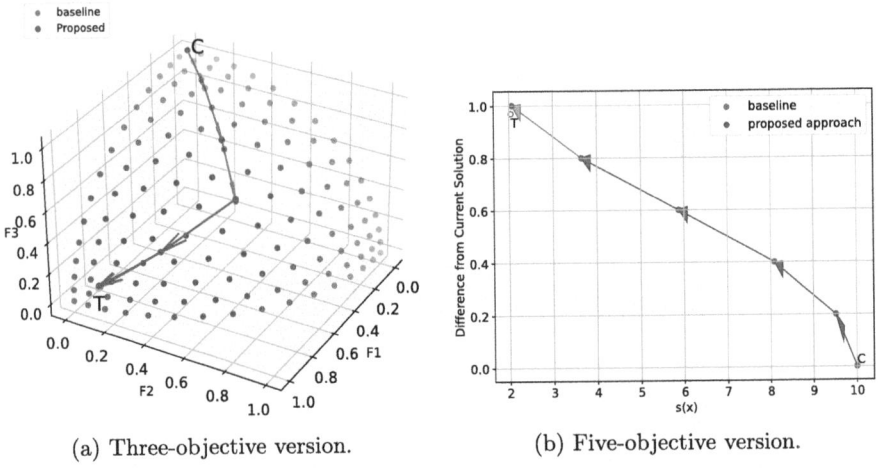

(a) Three-objective version.   (b) Five-objective version.

Fig. 9. IP with G_1 step-constraint for DTLZ2 with three and five objectives.

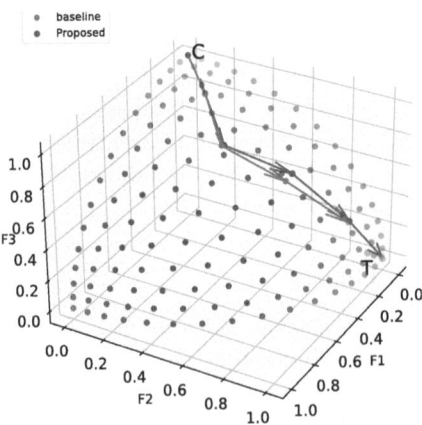

Fig. 10. IP with G_1 step-constraint for C2DTLZ2 problem with three objectives.

5   Conclusions

In this paper, we have proposed a new anchor identification approach based on a concept of directed domination which makes the IP-seeking bi-objective algorithm more computationally efficient compared to the baseline approach proposed earlier. The new approach has been shown to reach closer to the target or achieve comparable results with half the population size and/or using a less number of generations. We have shown these findings on a number of single, multi- and many-objective scenarios. We have also tested the proposed algorithm on new scenarios, where the IP path diverges away for the original PO front due to the peculiarities of the chosen step-constraints. These problems were not possible to be solved by the previous approach. The description of the new directed domination approach and accompanying results show the efficiency and accuracy of the proposed approach.

The IP-seeking procedure requires intermediate solutions to be found one after the other in a serial manner. The efficacy of a population-based EMO approach vis-a-via a point-based optimization approach is worth investigating further in the future. Nevertheless, the algorithmic developments for finding IP solutions is a challenging and useful practical task, which must be pursued and applied further.

References

1. Abdulmouti, H.: The role of kaizen (continuous improvement) in improving companies' performance: a case study. In: 2015 International Conference on Industrial Engineering and Operations Management (IEOM), pp. 1–6. IEEE (2015)
2. Al-Rifai, M.H.: Redesigning and optimizing an electronic device assembly cell through lean manufacturing tools and kaizen philosophy: an application case study. Int. J. Product. Perform. Manag. **73**(4), 1273–1301 (2024)
3. Branke, J., Deb, K., Miettinen, K., Slowinski, R.: Multiobjective Optimization: Interactive and Evolutionary Approaches. Springer-Verlag, Berlin (2008)
4. Carnerud, D., Jaca, C., Bäckström, I.: Kaizen and continuous improvement-trends and patterns over 30 years. TQM J. **30**(4), 371–390 (2018)
5. Coello, C.A.C.: Treating objectives as constraints for single objective optimization. Eng. Optim. **32**(3), 275–308 (2000)
6. Deb, K.: Multi-Objective Optimization Using Evolutionary Algorithms. Wiley, Chichester (2001)
7. Deb, K., Datta, R.: A bi-objective constrained optimization algorithm using a hybrid evolutionary and penalty function approach. Eng. Optim. **45**(5), 503–527 (2012)
8. Ferreira, D.M.C., Saurin, T.A.: A complexity theory perspective of kaizen: a study in healthcare. Prod. Plan. Control **30**(16), 1337–1353 (2019)
9. Gåsvaer, D., von Axelson, J.: Kaikaku - radical improvement in production. In: International Conference on Operations and Maintenance, Singapore, pp. 37–47 (2012)
10. Khan, A., Deb, K.: Innovation path: discovering an ordered set of optimized intermediate solutions from an existing to a desired solution. In: Proceedings of the Genetic and Evolutionary Computation Conference, pp. 529–537 (2024)

11. Khan, A., Deb, K.: Optimizing keyboard configuration using single and multi-objective evolutionary algorithms. In: Proceedings of the Companion Conference on Genetic and Evolutionary Computation, pp. 219–222 (2023)

12. Knowles, J.D., Corne, D.W., Deb, K.: Multiobjective Problem Solving from Nature. Springer Natural Computing Series, Springer-Verlag, Heidelberg (2008)

13. Maurer, R., Hirschman, L.A.: Spirit of Kaizen: Creating Lasting Excellence One Small Step at a Time. McGraw-Hill Professional, New York (2012)

14. Mezura-Montes, E., Coello, C.A.C.: Constraint-handling in nature-inspired numerical optimization: past, present and future. Swarm Evol. Comput. 1(4), 173–194 (2011)

15. Moi, W.A., Sing, S.H.: Application of toyota way incorporating kaizen, kaikaku and 5s in agricultural sector. Int. J. Res. Appl. Sci. Eng. Technol. 9(10), 1565–1579 (2021)

16. Qu, Y., Ming, X., Qiu, S., Liu, Z., Zhang, X., Hou, Z.: Process optimization through closed-loop kaizen with discrete event simulation: a case study in China. Proc. Inst. Mech. Engineers Part B: J. Eng. Manuf. 235(3), 568–579 (2021)

17. Reklaitis, G.V., Ravindran, A., Ragsdell, K.M.: Engineering Optimization Methods and Applications. Wiley, New York (1983)

18. Tozawa, B., Bodek, N.: How to Do Kaizen: A New Path to Innovation: Empowering Everyone to be a Problem Solver. PCS Press, Telford (2009)

19. Wierzbicki, A.P.: The use of reference objectives in multiobjective optimization. In: Fandel, G., Gal, T. (eds.) Multiple Criteria Decision Making Theory and Applications, pp. 468–486. Springer-Verlag, Berlin (1980)

An MaOEA/Local Search Hybrid Based on a Fast, Stochastic BFGS Using Achievement Scalarizing Search Directions

Regina C. L. C. de Sousa[1], Dênis E. C. Vargas[2], Elizabeth Wanner[2,3(✉)], and Joshua Knowles[4]

[1] Federal University of Ouro Preto, Ouro Preto, Brazil
regina_carla@ufop.edu.br
[2] Federal Center of Technological Education, Belo Horizonte, Brazil
denis.vargas@cefetmg.br
[3] Aston University, Birmingham, UK
e.wanner1@aston.ac.uk
[4] SLB Cambridge Research, Cambridge, UK
jknowles2@slb.com

Abstract. We consider the problem of multiobjective and many-objective optimization in the unconstrained, continuous-variable setting. Can modern EAs designed for this setting (such as NSGA-III) that arguably have proven performance be improved by incorporating local search, and can this be achieved in a general way not requiring excessive tuning of parameters? Optimization in this setting is usually found to be increasingly challenging as the number of objectives is increased (albeit some works suggest the contrary) and this is believed to be because of the weakness of selection pressure available from Pareto comparisons, challenges in maintaining diversity and/or, in decomposition-based methods, due to the number of search "directions" that must be managed. To investigate our problem, we propose integrating a many-objective evolutionary algorithm (MaOEA) with local-search techniques based on derivative-free BFGS-like algorithms. This is done in two slightly different ways both using achievement scalarizing functions. Our results on well-known benchmark functions suggest a significant improvement is possible with reasonable assumptions about how to choose the base MaOEA parameters and a principled and general approach to choosing the remaining parameters in the hybrid algorithm. Our findings underline the effectiveness of hybrid methods and suggest powerful algorithms from mathematical programming can be used even without gradients.

Keywords: Multiobjective and Many-Objective Problems · Local Search · Achievement Scalarizing Functions · BFGS

1   Introduction

Optimization is the process of finding the best possible solution within a set of feasible options and plays an important role in addressing real-world problems. Its goal is to identify optimal or near-optimal solutions that satisfy specific criteria [1, 2].

In single-objective optimization problems (SOPs), the focus is on finding solutions that perform well against a single, well-defined objective function. When an optimization problem presents conflicting objectives that cannot be easily aggregated into a single criterion, it is known as a multiobjective optimization problem (MOP) if it has two or three objective functions. If it has more than three objective functions, it is referred to as a many-objective optimization problem (MaOP). MOP and MaOP aim to find a set of solutions, known as the Pareto front, where no solution is superior to another in all objectives [3, 4].

Evolutionary algorithms (EAs) have gained widespread popularity for solving optimization problems. Their adaptability and efficacy make them versatile tools in various domains, mainly those with complex challenges, where traditional methods might not be effective. EAs are inspired by the principles of natural selection and the idea of survival of the fittest. These algorithms iteratively 'evolve' (i.e., update) a population of candidate solutions to a problem by simulating (in simplified form) key processes of biological evolution. Through genetic-like mechanisms such as selection, crossover, and mutation, promising solutions are combined and modified over 'generations', gradually converging toward optimal or near-optimal solutions [5]. When solving MOPs and MaOPs, EAs are known as multiobjective evolutionary algorithms (MOEAs) and many-objective evolutionary algorithms (MaOEAs), respectively [4].

When EAs are combined with local search (to improve convergence or efficiency) they are referred to as Hybrid Local Search algorithms or Memetic Algorithms [6]. Similarly, incorporating local search mechanisms within the evolutionary cycle of MOEAs and MaOEAs, to form hybrid algorithms, might enhance their ability to refine solutions within local neighborhoods, promoting finer convergence toward the true Pareto front, a main challenge as the number of objectives increases. Incorporating local search techniques into MOEAs and MaOEAs has been previously explored in work since the late '90 s.

In [7], the authors proposed a hybrid algorithm for multiobjective optimization combining genetic operations with local search. The algorithm uses a weighted sum of objectives as a fitness function to guide the selection of parent solutions for crossover and mutation. A local search is then applied to each new solution to maximize its fitness value. In [8], authors demonstrated that hybridizing evolutionary multiobjective optimization algorithms with local search improves convergence speed to the Pareto front but increases computation time per generation. Computational experiments on multiobjective scheduling problems highlighted the need to balance genetic and local search for optimal performance.

In [9], the PAES algorithm, a simple (1+1) evolution strategy for Pareto optimization, was introduced. It uses local search from a population of one and

---

Algorithm 1. The Proposed Hybrid Algorithm

Require: f, n, *popsize*, MaxGen, other NSGA-III hyperparameters
 1: Initialize P with *popsize* individuals at random
 2: **while** budget is not met **do**
 3: Run NSGA-III to stagnation   ▷ see Section 3.3
 4: Select $S \subseteq P(t_{end})$ ▷ see Section 4
 5: **for all** $x \in S$ **do**
 6: Choose ASF   ▷ see Section 3.1
 7: Run fastBFGS   ▷ see section 3.2
 8: **end for**
 9: $P_{new} = P(t_{end}) \bigcup$ Local Search Solutions   ▷ see Section 4
10: Run NSGA-III until stopping criterion
11: **end while**

---

a reference archive to generate diverse solutions in the Pareto optimal set. The results suggested that PAES had either superior to or competitive with other population-based methods of the time. In [10], M-PAES, an integration of local search and a population-based evolutionary methods, was proposed and evaluated on a range of benchmark problems from the literature, demonstrating competitive performance compared with other methods.

Although proposed over two decades ago, scalarized local search methods, such as those in [7] and [8], and Pareto-based local search methods, like those in [9] and [10], remain widely used. Both approaches are still relevant, with neither emerging as a definitive best.

In [11] the authors developed an MOP to minimize the total distribution cost and maximize overall customer satisfaction to tackle a collaborative routing problem in the truck-drone system. Additionally, they introduced a hybrid MOEA that integrates a Pareto local search algorithm to solve this problem.

Work reported in [12] established a multiobjective programming model for the multiproduct aggregate production planning problem. The goal is to minimize total production costs and workforce stability. The model addresses the aggregate production planning problem for multiple products, considering both workforce stability and total production costs. The authors also developed a genetic algorithm to solve the model, which is combined with a local search algorithm to improve its search ability.

A new Pareto local search algorithm for MaOPs using three new mechanisms was proposed by [13]. One mechanism is used to select solutions for the exploring their neighborhoods based on the randomly selected weighted Chebycheff scalarizing functions.

In this paper we present a hybrid approach that combines an MaOEA with a local search procedure. The proposed local search is quite general and can be applied to any MaOEA. However, in this paper, we employ the NSGA-III [14] as the baseline MaOEA. The NSGA-III is initially run until a stopping criterion is satisfied, which includes the stagnation of its population. Afterward, a local search method is applied to a subset of solutions from the Pareto front that has been obtained so far. The local search procedure transforms the MOP or MaOP into an SOP using one of the two achievement scalarizing functions (ASFs) discussed in this paper: weighted ASF (W-ASF) [15] and soft ASF (S-ASF) [16].

The ASF has demonstrated its superior effectiveness when compared to the commonly used simple weighted sum of objectives [7,13]. The ASFs are optimized using a stochastic BFGS algorithm (called fastBFGS) [17] for each solution. NSGA-III is rerun with the new population, including local solutions, until another stopping criterion is satisfied. This process iterates continuously until a predefined maximum budget is reached. Algorithm 1 shows the pseudocode of the proposed hybrid approach. For validation of the proposed technique, computational experiments are conducted on well-known DTLZ (1–4) problems with 3, 5, 8, 10, and 15 objectives [18].

The remainder of the paper is organized as follows. Section 2 defines the MOPs, MaOPs and the NSGA-III. Section 3 describes the proposed local search technique. Section 4 shows the computational experiments, the parameter setting, the performance measures, and an analysis of the results. Finally, Sect. 5 presents the conclusions and future work.

2   Multi and Many-Objective Optimization Problems

Mathematically, optimization problems are typically formulated as:

$$
\begin{aligned}
\mathbf{x}^* &= \operatorname{argmin}_{\mathbf{x}} \mathbf{f}(\mathbf{x}), \\
\text{subject to:} &\begin{cases} g_i(\mathbf{x}) \leq 0, \ i = 1, 2, \ldots, r, \\ h_j(\mathbf{x}) = 0, \ j = 1, 2, \ldots, p, \end{cases}
\end{aligned} \tag{1}
$$

where $\mathbf{x} \in \mathbb{R}^n$, $\mathbf{f}(.) : \mathbb{R}^n \to \mathbb{R}^M$, $\mathbf{g}(.) : \mathbb{R}^n \to \mathbb{R}^r$, and $\mathbf{h}(.) : \mathbb{R}^n \to \mathbb{R}^p$. The functions g_i and h_j represent inequality and equality constraint functions, respectively. The vectors $\mathbf{x} \in \mathbb{R}^n$ are named decision variable vectors, constituting the parameter space, while the objective functions, denoted by $\mathbf{f}(\mathbf{x}) \in \mathbb{R}^M$, reside in the objective space. The problem of Eq. (1) is an SOP if $M = 1$, an MOP if $M = 2$ or $M = 3$, and an MaOP if $M \geq 4$.

One well-known state-of-the-art algorithm for handling MOPs and MaOPs is NSGA-III. It sorts the population into nondominated ranks and employs a diversity criterion using a set of reference directions on an $M - 1$-dimensional hyperplane (a unit simplex equally inclined to all objective axes intersecting each axis at 1). The individuals are linked with the nearest reference direction to guarantee a diverse and evenly distributed set of solutions along the Pareto front. More details about NSGA-III can be found in [14]. In this paper, we use a PlatEMO implementation of NSGA-III [19].

3   The Proposed Local Search

Hybrid approaches combine the global exploration power of MOEAs with local search for better solution refinement. Two methods exist in the literature: the serial approach, where MOEAs run until a stopping condition is met before local search is applied, and the concurrent approach, where local search is triggered in each iteration. While serial methods risk disrupting solution distribution due to unclear stopping points, concurrent approaches raise concerns about selection frequency and computational costs. This work adopts the serial approach with an additional criterion to detect the MOEA stagnation.

3.1 Achievement Scalarizing Function

Once an MOEA or an MaOEA has obtained an initial approximation of the Pareto front, local search can be applied in several ways. A possible approach is to employ a single-point method on selected individuals, using any available scalarizing technique. The present work adopts the ASF, proposed by Wierzbicki in [20], as the function to be optimized.

Wierzbicki's main idea is that decision-makers typically don't make decisions by explicitly weighing trade-offs; rather, they tend to set goals or, more precisely, *aspiration levels*. For each objective function $f_1(\cdot)$, $f_2(\cdot)$, ..., $f_m(\cdot)$, if the decision maker establishes corresponding goals z_1^r, z_2^r, ..., z_m^r, these collectively formulate a *reference point* $\mathbf{z}^r = [z_1^r \ z_2^r \ ... \ z_m^r]^T$. Therefore, the MOP or MaOP can be translated as getting as close as possible to this reference point, essentially minimizing some form of distance to it.

The drawback of relying on distances, such as Minkowski distances, for minimization, is that it doesn't ensure Pareto-optimality [21]. Additionally, if the attainable reference point $\mathbf{z}^r$ is not optimal, the solution becomes $\mathbf{z}^r$, contradicting efficiency. Wierzbicki solved this issue by introducing the more intricate ASF denoted as $s(\mathbf{f}(\mathbf{x}), \mathbf{z}^r) : \mathbb{R}^{m \times m} \mapsto \mathbb{R}$, which ensures optimal solutions for any reference point. Consequently, the original MOP or MaOP is transformed into the following scalarized form:

$$\underset{\mathbf{x}}{\text{minimize}} \ s(\mathbf{f}(\mathbf{x}), \mathbf{z}^r) \tag{2}$$

$$\text{subject to} \quad \mathbf{x} \in \mathcal{X}$$

Whenever the ASF is strictly increasing, the solution to (2) is weakly efficient, or efficient if it is unique, for any reference point. Also, if it is strongly increasing, then the solution is always Pareto-optimal[1].

An ASF can take various forms [20,22]. The two most common are: (i) the strictly increasing Chebyshev norm:

$$s(\mathbf{f}(\mathbf{x}), \mathbf{z}^r) = \max_{i \in \{1,2,...,m\}} \lambda_i \{f_i(\mathbf{x}) - z_i^r\}, \tag{3}$$

where λ is the m-vector of non-negative coefficients used for scaling purposes, that is, for normalizing objective functions of different magnitudes; and (ii) the strongly increasing augmented Chebyshev norm:

---

[1] According to [22], an ASF is strictly increasing if $f_i(\mathbf{x}_1) < f_i(\mathbf{x}_2)$, $\forall i = 1, 2, \ldots, m$, implicate $s(\mathbf{f}(\mathbf{x}_1), \mathbf{z}^r) < s(\mathbf{f}(\mathbf{x}_2), \mathbf{z}^r)$ and is strongly increasing if $\mathbf{f}(\mathbf{x}_1) \prec \mathbf{f}(\mathbf{x}_2)$ implicate $s(\mathbf{f}(\mathbf{x}_1), \mathbf{z}^r) < s(\mathbf{f}(\mathbf{x}_2), \mathbf{z}^r)$.

$$s\left(\mathbf{f}(\mathbf{x}), \mathbf{z}^r\right) = \max_{i \in \{1,2,\dots,m\}} \lambda_i \left\{ f_i(\mathbf{x}) - z_i^r \right\} + \rho \sum_{i=1}^{m} \lambda_i \left(f_i(\mathbf{x}) - z_i^r \right), \tag{4}$$

where $\rho > 0$ serves as a positive and small term added to the maximum in the ASF, preventing the occurrence of weakly Pareto-optimal solutions.

Here, for each point selected for the local search and using a reference point given by $z^r = \mathbf{f}(\mathbf{x})$, we use each ASF proposed in [15] (W-ASF) or [16] (S-ASF) to transform the original problem into the following scalarized form as Eqs. (5) and (6), respectively:

$$\underset{\text{subject to } x \in \mathcal{X}}{\text{minimize}} \quad \max_{i=1}^{k} \frac{f_i(x) - z_i^r}{z_i^{\max} - z_i^{\min}} + \rho \sum_{i=1}^{k} \frac{f_i(x) - z_i^r}{z_i^{\max} - z_i^{\min}}, \tag{5}$$

$$\underset{\text{subject to } x \in \mathcal{X}}{\text{minimize}} \quad \frac{1}{a} \ln \left(\sum_{i=1}^{k} e^{a(f_i(x) - z_i^r)} \right) + \rho \sum_{i=1}^{k} (f_i(x) - z_i^r), \tag{6}$$

where $z_i^{\max}$ and $z_i^{\min}$ are the worst and best objective function values available from the currently available non-dominated set, and a controls the quality of the approximation of the "max" function.

3.2   Using the ASF in the Local Search

Once the scalarization method is described, it is easy to include it in the local search procedure. Assume that $P(t_{end})$ contains the individuals of the last iteration of the MOEA or the MaOEA. The approach adopted here is simply: for each $\mathbf{x} \in P(t_{end})$ selected for local search, solve the problem (2) using $\mathbf{x}$ as a starting point and $\mathbf{f}(\mathbf{x})$ as a reference point. For solving the single-objective problem described in (2), we employ mathematical programming techniques as a local solver using a BFGS-like approach [17].

Quasi-Newton methods, in particular BFGS methods, have been the leading optimization algorithm in various fields since the late '60s. BFGS methods, introduced by Broyden, Fletcher, Goldfarb, and Shanno [23], are recognized for their effectiveness in locating local optima of smooth, unconstrained functions through iterative updates of an approximation to the inverse Hessian matrix. Unlike Newton's method, which directly calculate the Hessian matrix of the function, BFGS updates an approximation to the inverse Hessian matrix.

The approach employed here, dubbed as *fastBFGS*, is an accelerated stochastic quasi-Newton method proposed in [17]. The idea is to use sketch-and-project iteration for inverting the Hessian matrix with special sketch operators with an additional caveat: matrix inversion is accelerated and specialized, ensuring symmetric and positive definite matrices as solutions. These approximate solutions can also serve as estimators for the inverse Hessian in the BFGS method, establishing a stochastic quasi-Newton approach. The derivatives have been calculated using the finite derivative method. Further details on this method can be found in [17].

3.3   The Stopping Criteria

The minimization of the ASF guarantees that a Pareto-optimal point is always obtained, even if the initial point is not in a neighborhood of the global optima, provided a global optimizer is used. The important question to be answered is: when should one stop the MOEA/MaOEA and employ the local search procedure?

The idea is to use performance indicators to measure the evolution of the population and stop whenever the indicators reach a threshold or when the evolution becomes stagnated [24]. Two performance indicators are employed in this work: the Moment of Inertia-based-measure [25] and a performance indicator based on the ASF.

The Moment of Inertia is an unary indicator that intends to measure the diversity of the population in the objective space. For a population $\mathcal{P}(t)$, we need to compute the centroid $\mathbf{c} = [c_1 \ c_2 \ \dots \ c_m]^T$ as

$$c_j = \frac{1}{|\mathcal{P}(t)|} \sum_{i=1}^{|\mathcal{P}(t)|} f_j(x_i), \quad \text{for } j = 1, 2, \dots, m \tag{7}$$

wherein $|\mathcal{P}(t)|$ gives the number of points in the population $\mathcal{P}(t)$ at iteration t. The Moment of Inertia indicator will be given by

$$I_M(\mathcal{P}(t)) = \sum_{j=1}^{m} \sum_{i=1}^{|\mathcal{P}(t)|} (f_j(x_i) - c_j)^2. \tag{8}$$

The performance indicator based on the ASF, I_{ASF}, is a binary indicator to measure convergence. Consider two sets, $\mathcal{P}_1$ and $\mathcal{P}_2$. For a given element $\mathbf{x} \in \mathcal{P}_1$, compute the ASF assuming each point $\mathbf{y} \in \mathcal{P}_2$ as a reference point. The indicator value $I_{ASF}(\mathbf{x}, \mathcal{P}_2)$ is given by

$$I_{ASF}(\mathbf{x}, \mathcal{P}_2) = \min_{\mathbf{y} \in \mathcal{P}_2} s(\mathbf{f}(\mathbf{x}), \mathbf{f}(\mathbf{y})). \tag{9}$$

It represents the smallest ASF computed, indicating, for each reference point, the greatest improvement that can be made. For every $\mathbf{x} \in \mathcal{P}_1$, Equation (9) is calculated. To obtain $I_{ASF}(\mathcal{P}_1, \mathcal{P}_2)$, one needs to combine each indicator, taking the minimum of all of them, such that

$$I_{ASF}(\mathcal{P}_1, \mathcal{P}_2) = \min_{\mathbf{x} \in \mathcal{P}_1} I_{ASF}(\mathbf{x}, \mathcal{P}_2). \tag{10}$$

Note that if $\mathcal{P}_1$ represents the current population and $P2$ serves as a reference, the indicator $I_{ASF}(\mathcal{P}_1, \mathcal{P}_2)$ quantifies the optimal improvement achievable. When the value of this indicator stabilizes, it implies that even the best individual within the population is not making sufficient progress. Hence, it is reasonable to infer a stagnation in the population's performance.

In selecting $P2$, we explore two options: using the initial population, $\mathcal{P}(0)$, or the one from the previous iteration, $\mathcal{P}(t-1)$. Based on prior experiments, the indicator $I_{ASF}(\mathcal{P}(t), \mathcal{P}(0))$ provides a comprehensive overview but tends to stagnate quickly when the initial population deviates significantly from the efficient front. Conversely, $I_{ASF}(\mathcal{P}(t), \mathcal{P}(t-1))$ offers a more detailed insight into smaller improvements, yet it may oscillate considerably, potentially resulting in a prematurely horizontal regression line if improvements vary unevenly across iterations. Rather than debating the superiority of one over the other in specific scenarios, we opt to incorporate both indicator variants. This approach allows the strengths of one to compensate for the weaknesses of the other, ensuring a more robust assessment.

After selecting the indicators, we need to define criteria for detecting stagnation and determine how long the indicators should remain stable before assuming stagnation. Then we introduce a *time window* t_w, where at each iteration t, the indicators values from $t - t_w + 1$ to t are analyzed. Stagnation tests are applied within this window and continue at each iteration until they either trigger the termination of the algorithm or a stricter stopping criteria is met, such as exhausting the maximum number of evaluations.

To detect stagnation, we follow the method outlined in [26]. For each window of t_w observations, we fit a regression line $y = \beta_0 + \beta_1 t$ where y is the performance indicator, t is the iteration number, and β_0 and β_1 are the intercept and slope, respectively. Using least squares, we estimate the parameters and check for stagnation by testing if β_1 is approximately zero implying a flat trend. This is done via a hypothesis test on β_1, where the null hypothesis is accepted if the p-value $P \geq \alpha = 0.05$. We use the two indicators and only stop if both simultaneously show stagnation. In this work, a time window of $t_w = 15$ is used.

4   Numerical Experiments

We propose using NSGA-III as the MaOEA with two local search mechanisms. The first uses the W-ASF, and the second uses S-ASF, both solved via the fastBFGS method. These hybrid approaches are called H-NSGA-III-fBFGS-W-ASF and H-NSGA-III-fBFGS-S-ASF, respectively. Numerical experiments compared them to the original NSGA-III in the DTLZ (1–4) problem with 3, 5, 8, 10, and 15 objectives to validate their efficiency. The default parameters for NSGA-III specified in PlatEMO [19] have also been used here.

All algorithms were executed for 21 independent runs. Table 1 shows the population size (PopSize) and maximum number of generations (MaxGen) for each DTLZ (1–4) problem and each number of objective functions utilized by NSGA-III in [14]. To evaluate the algorithms' performance under different budgets, they were executed with three specific maximum numbers of objective function evaluations: (b1) $\dfrac{\text{PopSize} \times \text{MaxGen}}{3}$; (b2) $\dfrac{\text{PopSize} \times \text{MaxGen}}{M}$; and (b3) PopSize $\times$ 150. These budgets were defined to evaluate the algorithms' performance across scenarios with varying budgets, incorporating variations in both problems and dimensions, as recommended in [14]. Furthermore, evaluations were also carried out in scenarios with fixed-size budgets.

The local search is applied to 25% of the current population after NSGA-III reaches a stop criterion, including population stagnation. These 25% individuals are selected based on their nondominated rank (preferring lower ranks) and crowding distance (favoring high values, except infinite crowding distances to prevent local search near the edges of the Pareto front). The stopping criteria for the fastBFGS is when it reaches a maximum of 20 iterations or when the maximum difference in any decision variable between two successive iterations is less than 10^{-6}.

To evaluate the convergence and diversity of Pareto optimal solutions obtained by the algorithms, two performance indicators were adopted: the additive epsilon indicator ($I_{\epsilon+}$) [27] and the inverted generational distance plus (IGD+) [28].

These performance indicators require a reference set, which is defined here as the nondominated solutions of all results by each algorithm in each problem. Statistically significant differences between the results in each indicator $I_{\epsilon+}$ and IGD+ were detected using the nonparametric Wilcoxon rank sum test (with $\alpha = 0.05$).

Performance profiles [29] were used to visualize and interpret the results of IGD+ and $I_{\epsilon+}$. Consider π as a set of problems, S as a set of algorithms, and $t_{p,s}$ as any performance measure evaluated for problem p by algorithm s. The performance profile, for each algorithm s and each positive factor τ, shows the percentage of problems in P where the performance of s is within the best performance achieved by other algorithms. The area under $\rho_s(\tau)$ can be interpreted as a global performance indicator, with a larger area signifying higher algorithm efficiency [30].

Figure 1 displays the performance profile curves using the mean values obtained for each performance indicator in each budget. In addition, Table 2 presents the areas under these performance profile curves (divided by the biggest among them to ensure correct proportionality). Following the approach used in [31], the areas under the performance profile curves can be interpreted as an additional performance indicator to create an overall performance profile. Figure 1 also shows performance profiles for both indicators when the problems having 10 and 15 objective functions are analyzed (subfigures (g) and (h)).

Analyzing Fig. 1, we can see that H-NSGA-III-fBFGS-S-ASF achieved the best results in two budget scenarios tailored to each DTLZ problem (1–4) and each dimension. However, when a fixed budget was considered for all problems in each dimension, H-NSGA-III-fBFGS-W-ASF achieved better solutions. In summary, both results were very similar, indicating that the two ASFs perform equally well.

Considering all budget scenarios, the hybrid algorithms H-NSGA-III-fBFGS-S-ASF and H-NSGA-III-fBFGS-W-ASF consistently outperformed the baseline algorithm, NSGA-III, when the performance was analyzed separately for each number of objective functions. This trend becomes even more pronounced as the number of objective functions increases. Figure 1(g) and (h) illustrate the performance profile curves based on the mean values obtained across all budget levels, focusing exclusively on problems with 10 and 15 objective functions for each performance indicator. The results clearly demonstrate that the H-NSGA-III-fBFGS-S-ASF algorithm achieved superior performance across all indicators. For the $I_{\epsilon+}$ indicator, while H-NSGA-III-fBFGS-S-ASF outperformed H-NSGA-III-fBFGS-W-ASF, the differences between these two algorithms were relatively small. This is evidenced by the area under the Overall Performance Profile, where H-NSGA-III-fBFGS-S-ASF achieves an area of $1 - 10^{-5}$, while H-NSGA-III-fBFGS-W-ASF scores 0.9341. However, when considering the $IGD+$ indicator, the performance gap between the two algorithms becomes more significant. The Overall Performance Profile reveals an area of $> 1 - 10^{-5}$ for H-NSGA-III-fBFGS-S-ASF, compared to 0.7768 for H-NSGA-III-fBFGS-W-ASF, highlighting the stronger performance of H-NSGA-III-fBFGS-S-ASF in this case. In general, the performance profile analysis concluded that coupling NSGA-III with a local search method using both ASFs proved more efficient and reliable in addressing problems than the original NSGA-III.

The Wilcoxon rank-sum test indicates the hybrid NSGA-III algorithms with local search are statistically superior to the original NSGA-III (p-value < 0.05) in most problems, particularly DTLZ (1–4) with 10 and 15 objectives. While differences between H-NSGA-III-fBFGS-S-ASF and H-NSGA-III-fBFGS-W-ASF are fewer, they generally favor H-NSGA-III-fBFGS-S-ASF.

Table 1. Population sizes and maximum number of generation (MaxGen) used in NSGA-III for each problem and each number of objectives in [14].

# of objectives (M)	3	5	8	10	15
PopSize	92	212	156	276	136
MaxGen(DTLZ1)	400	600	750	1000	1500
MaxGen(DTLZ2)	250	350	500	750	1000
MaxGen(DTLZ3)	1000	1000	1000	1500	2000
MaxGen(DTLZ4)	600	1000	1250	2000	3000

Table 2. Areas under the curves of performance profiles: NSGA-III (Alg1), H-NSGA-III-fBFGS-W-ASF (Alg2), and H-NSGA-III-fBFGS-S-ASF (Alg3).

Budget	Indicator	Algorithm 1	Algorithm 2	Algorithm 3
b1	IGD+	0.9211	0.9969	$> 1 - 10^{-5}$
	$I_{\epsilon+}$	0.8964	0.9876	$> 1 - 10^{-5}$
b2	IGD+	0.8944	0.9893	$> 1 - 10^{-5}$
	$I_{\epsilon+}$	0.8051	0.9617	$> 1 - 10^{-5}$
b3	IGD+	0.9134	$> 1 - 10^{-5}$	0.9935
	$I_{\epsilon+}$	0.8358	$> 1 - 10^{-5}$	0.9762
All	IGD+	0.9241	0.9971	$> 1 - 10^{-5}$
	$I_{\epsilon+}$	0.8556	0.9907	$> 1 - 10^{-5}$

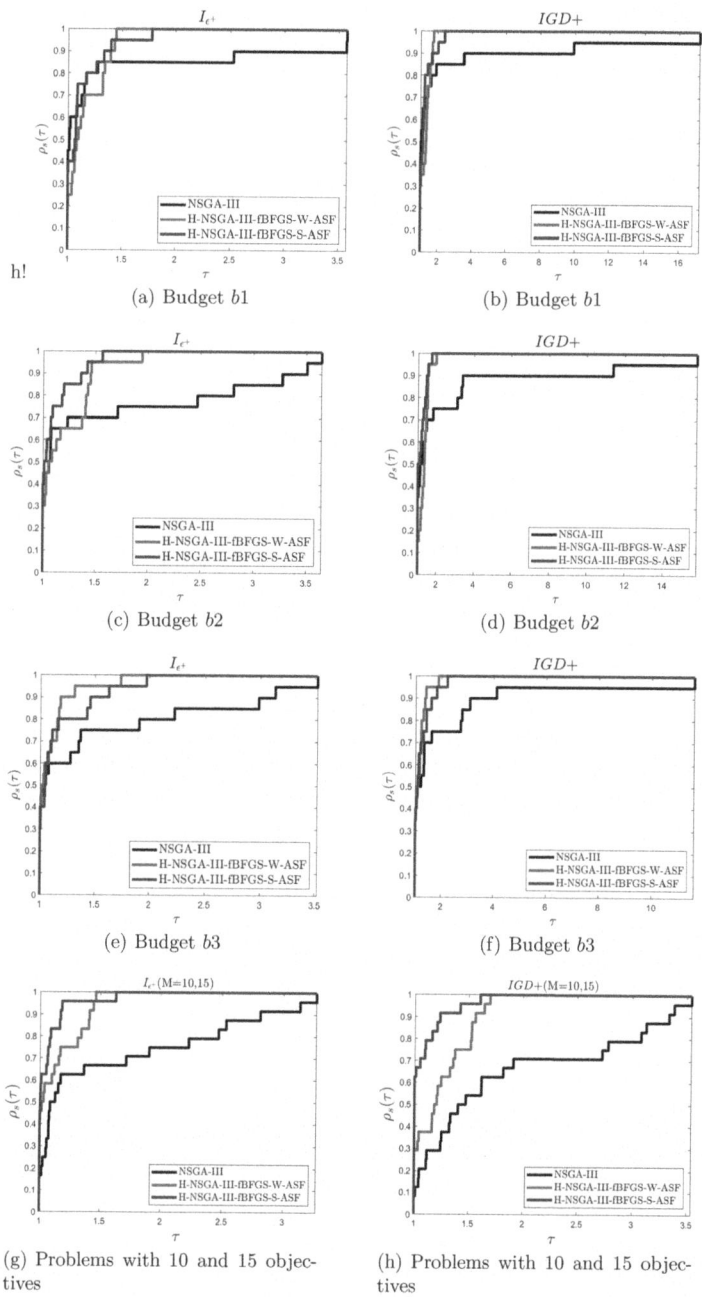

h!

(a) Budget $b1$

(b) Budget $b1$

(c) Budget $b2$

(d) Budget $b2$

(e) Budget $b3$

(f) Budget $b3$

(g) Problems with 10 and 15 objectives

(h) Problems with 10 and 15 objectives

Fig. 1. Performance profile curves using the mean values obtained for each budget and each performance indicator (a-f) and considering problems with 10 and 15 objective functions and each indicator (g-h).

5   Conclusions

Developments in MOEAs and MaOEAs over the past two or three decades have arguably led to steady improvements in performance on benchmarks that it seems evident (from successful applications papers) carries over to their deployment in solving real-world problems. However, while these developments are welcome, it is unclear how much further modern algorithms can be improved, and what procedures are most promising to target for further study. We have taken a modern and well-known MOEA/MaOEA, NSGA-III, and investigated how much improvement can be achieved by incorporating local search, one of the more promising and longstanding routes to making enhancements to EAs. The limitations of such a method in practice might be that the local search has more requirements than the base EA, potentially reducing some of the generality, and/or requiring more of the user's expertise to set up the algorithm correctly. In our work, we partially address these issues by choosing a well-established local search procedure, BFGS, in a form not requiring gradient information or extensive tuning. Nevertheless, BFGS is properly limited to continuous, smooth and unconstrained functions, and so our proposed hybrid is also limited in this way.

Applying a local search derived from single-objective optimization in the multiobjective or many-objective context also presents choices that require careful consideration. The easiest and most direct route is arguably to scalarize the objectives in the local search, the method we chose to pursue here, but that raises the question of the scalarizing method choice. While not definitive, our method and results (where the two variants of our hybrid outperformed NSGA-III consistently across the benchmark functions) seem to indicate that using achievement scalarizing functions might be a good choice due to their well-thought-out mathematical formulation and the resulting ease with which parameters can be chosen to control them. Nevertheless, further investigation concerning whether the local searches are adding to diversity or subtracting from it is needed: we chose one method of generating the ASF ("directions") but other choices are possible that could enhance Pareto front extent, while others may be more appropriate when the expected shape of the Pareto front is partially known.

Tentatively, we can conclude that modern MOEAs and MaOEAs such as NSGA-III can be significantly enhanced with well-chosen local search methods including those from mathematical programming (which have arguably been under-explored). We make the code used in our experiments available to the community for future benchmarking studies.

Acknowledgments. RCLCS, DECV and EW would like to thank the Brazilian Funding Agencies - CAPES, FAPEMIG and CNPq.[1] The authors have no competing interests to declare that are relevant to the content of this article. JK would like to thank SLB for permission to publish this paper.

References

1. Deb, K.: Multi-objective Optimization Using Evolutionary Algorithms, vol. 16. John Wiley & Sons, Hoboken (2001)
2. Coello, C.A.C.: Evolutionary Algorithms for Solving Multi-objective Problems. Springer, Heidelberg (2007)
3. Fleming, P.J., Purshouse, R.C.: Evolutionary algorithms in control systems engineering: a survey. Control. Eng. Pract. **10**(11), 1223–1241 (2002)
4. Li, B., Li, J., Tang, K., Yao, X.: Many-objective evolutionary algorithms: a survey. ACM Comput. Surv. (CSUR) **48**(1), 1–35 (2015)
5. Fogel, D.B.: An introduction to simulated evolutionary optimization. IEEE Trans. Neural Netw. **5**(1), 3–14 (1994)
6. Moscato, P., Cotta, C.: A modern introduction to memetic algorithms. In: International Series in Operations Research & Management Science, pp. 141–183 (2010)
7. Ishibuchi, H., Murata, T.: A multi-objective genetic local search algorithm and its application to flowshop scheduling, IEEE Trans. Syst. Man Cybern. Part C (Appl. Rev.) **28**(3), 392–403 (1998)
8. Ishibuchi, H., Yoshida, T., Murata, T.: Balance between genetic search and local search in memetic algorithms for multiobjective permutation flowshop scheduling. IEEE Trans. Evol. Comput. **7**(2), 204–223 (2003)
9. Knowles, J.D., Corne, D.W.: The Pareto archived evolution strategy: a new baseline algorithm for Pareto multiobjective optimisation. In: Proceedings of the 1999 Congress on Evolutionary Computation, vol. 1, 98–105 (1999)
10. Knowles, J.D., Corne, D.W.: M-PAES: a memetic algorithm for multiobjective optimization. In: Proceedings of the 2000 Congress on Evolutionary Computation, vol. 1, pp. 325–332 (2000)
11. Luo, Q., Wu, G., Ji, B., Wang, L., Suganthan, P.N.: Hybrid multi-objective optimization approach with pareto local search for collaborative truck-drone routing problems considering flexible time windows. IEEE Trans. Intell. Transp. Syst. **23**(8), 13011–13025 (2021)
12. Liu, L.F., Yang, X.F.: Multi-objective aggregate production planning for multiple products: a local search-based genetic algorithm optimization approach. Int. J. Comput. Intell. Syst. **14**(1), 156 (2021)
13. Jaszkiewicz, A.: Many-objective Pareto local search. Eur. J. Oper. Res. **271**(3), 1001–1013 (2018)
14. Deb, K., Jain, H.: An evolutionary many-objective optimization algorithm using reference-point-based nondominated sorting approach, part I: solving problems with box constraints. IEEE Trans. Evol. Comput. **18**(4), 577–601 (2013)
15. Sindhya, K., Sinha, A., Deb, K., Miettinen, K.: Local search based evolutionary multi-objective optimization algorithm for constrained and unconstrained problems. In: 2009 IEEE Congress on Evolutionary Computation, pp. 2919–2926. IEEE (2009)
16. Beck, A., Teboulle, M.: Smoothing and first order methods: a unified framework. SIAM J. Optim. **22**(2), 557–580 (2012)
17. Gower, R., Hanzely, F., Richtárik, P., Stich, S.U.: Accelerated stochastic matrix inversion: general theory and speeding up BFGS rules for faster second-order optimization. Adv. Neural Inf. Process. Syst. **31** (2018)
18. Deb, K., Thiele, L., Laumanns, M., Zitzler, E.: Scalable test problems for evolutionary multiobjective optimization. In: Evolutionary Multiobjective Optimization: Theoretical Advances and Applications, pp. 105–145. Springer, London (2005)

19. Tian, Y., Cheng, R., Zhang, X., Jin, Y.: PlatEMO: a MATLAB platform for evolutionary multi-objective optimization [educational forum]. IEEE Comput. Intell. Mag. **12**(4), 73–87 (2017)

20. Wierzbicki, A.P.: A mathematical basis for satisficing decision making. Math. Model. **3**(5), 391–405 (1982)

21. Emmerich, M., Deutz, A.: Multicriteria optimization and decision making. Leiden university, NL, LIACS (2006)

22. Nikulin, Y., Miettinen, K., Mäkelä, M.M.: A parameterized achievement scalarizing function for multiobjective optimization. TUCS Technical Reports 969, Turku Centre for Computer Science, Turku, Finland (2010)

23. Broyden, C.G.: Quasi-Newton methods and their application to function minimisation. Math. Comput. **21**(99), 368–381 (1967)

24. Wagner, T., Trautmann, H., Martí, L.: A taxonomy of online stopping criteria for multi-objective evolutionary algorithms. In: Takahashi, R.H.C., Deb, K., Wanner, E.F., Greco, S. (eds.) EMO 2011. LNCS, vol. 6576, pp. 16–30. Springer, Heidelberg (2011). https://doi.org/10.1007/978-3-642-19893-9_2

25. Morrison, R.W., De Jong, K.A.: Measurement of population diversity. In: International Conference on Artificial Evolution (evolution artificielle), pp. 31–41. Springer, Heidelberg (2001)

26. Guerrero, J.L., Martí, L., Berlanga, A., García, J., Molina, J.M.: Introducing a robust and efficient stopping criterion for MOEAs. In: IEEE Congress on Evolutionary Computation, pp. 1–8. IEEE(2010,)

27. Zitzler, E., Thiele, L., Laumanns, M., Fonseca, C.M., Da Fonseca, V.G.: Performance assessment of multiobjective optimizers: an analysis and review. IEEE Trans. Evol. Comput. **7**(2), 117–132 (2003)

28. Ishibuchi, H., Masuda, H., Tanigaki, Y., Nojima, Y.: Modified distance calculation in generational distance and inverted generational distance. In: Gaspar-Cunha, A., Henggeler Antunes, C., Coello, C.C. (eds.) EMO 2015. LNCS, vol. 9019, pp. 110–125. Springer, Cham (2015). https://doi.org/10.1007/978-3-319-15892-1_8

29. Dolan, E.D., Moré, J.J.: Benchmarking optimization software with performance profiles. Math. Program. **91**, 201–213 (2002)

30. Barbosa, H.J., Bernardino, H.S., Barreto, A.M.: Using performance profiles to analyze the results of the 2006 CEC constrained optimization competition. In: IEEE Congress on Evolutionary Computation, pp. 1–8. IEEE (2010)

31. Carvalho, J.P.G., Carvalho, É.C., Vargas, D.E., Hallak, P.H., Lima, B.S., Lemonge, A.C.: Multi-objective optimum design of truss structures using differential evolution algorithms. Comput. Struct. **252**, 106544 (2021)

Selective Evaluations for Expediting Multi-objective Bilevel Optimization

Bing Wang$^{(\boxtimes)}$ 🆔, Hemant Kumar Singh 🆔, and Tapabrata Ray 🆔

The University of New South Wales, Canberra, ACT 2600, Australia
{bing.wang,h.singh,t.ray}@unsw.edu.au

Abstract. This study investigates bilevel optimization problems with multiple objectives at both upper and lower levels. For such problems, for every feasible solution at the upper level, there is a corresponding set of Pareto-optimal solutions at the lower level. In typical bilevel evolutionary algorithms, the upper level solution is evaluated for each of these lower level Pareto solutions during the search. This incurs significant computational expense while searching for the overall (upper level) Pareto optimal front. In this study, we aim to reduce this expense by selectively evaluating the upper level solutions with only some of the lower-level solutions during the search. Towards this end, a direction-based selective evaluation scheme is introduced. Numerical experiments demonstrate that the proposed approach improves search accuracy and convergence rate, particularly for problems where the initial search starts far from the Pareto front.

1 Introduction

Bilevel optimization problems (BLOPs) consist of two hierarchically interacting optimization tasks: an upper-level (UL) problem and a lower-level (LL) problem. The UL problem, also known as the leader problem, is constrained by the LL problem, often referred to as the follower problem. Mathematically, a BLOP can be represented as follows:

$$\begin{aligned}
\underset{\mathbf{x}_u \in \mathbb{X}_u}{\text{Minimize}} \quad & F_u(\mathbf{x}_u, \mathbf{x}_l) = F_u^1(\mathbf{x}_u, \mathbf{x}_l), ..., F_u^N(\mathbf{x}_u, \mathbf{x}_l) \\
\text{s.t.} \quad & \mathbf{x}_l = \underset{\mathbf{x}_l \in \mathbb{X}_l}{\text{argmin}} \quad f_l(\mathbf{x}_u, \mathbf{x}_l) = f_l^1(\mathbf{x}_u, \mathbf{x}_l), ..., f_l^M(\mathbf{x}_u, \mathbf{x}_l) \\
& g(\mathbf{x}_u, \mathbf{x}_l) \leq 0; \quad G(\mathbf{x}_u, \mathbf{x}_l) \leq 0
\end{aligned} \quad (1)$$

F^u and f_l refer to the UL problem objectives and LL problem objectives. UL design variables are $\mathbf{x}_u$ sampled from $\mathbb{X}_u$, and LL design variables are $\mathbf{x}_l$ sampled from $\mathbb{X}_l$. Note that in the text that follows, the term 'UL solution' refers to $\mathbf{x}_u$. For evaluating a UL solution, it needs to be combined with the corresponding LL optimal solution(s). N is the number of UL objectives ($N \geq 1$), while M is the number of LL objectives ($M \geq 1$). If both $M = 1$ and $N = 1$, it is called bilevel single objective optimization problem (BLSOP). If $M = 1$ and $N > 1$, the problem is referred to as semi-vectorial bilevel optimization (SVBO)

H. Singh et al. (Eds.): EMO 2025, LNCS 15512, pp. 31–45, 2025.
https://doi.org/10.1007/978-981-96-3506-1_3

problem [14,17]. If $M > 1$, it is called bilevel multi-objective optimization problem (BLMOP). In this study, we're interested in BLMOPs where both $M, N > 1$. $G(\mathbf{x}_u, \mathbf{x}_l)$ and $g(\mathbf{x}_u, \mathbf{x}_l)$ are the constraints for UL problem and LL problem, respectively.

BLOPs have their origins in Stackelberg games from game theory [22], but have since been used to model a range of applications including engineering, policy, transportation, and more [1,7,15,22,23]. As a result, BLOPs have attracted significant attention across various research fields. In this study, we focus on bilevel multi-objective optimization problems (BLMOPs). Both classical and evolutionary methodologies have been proposed in the literature for solving BLMOPs, a recent review of which can be found in [17].

Exact Methods: In classical optimization, specific conditions are often assumed to facilitate finding solutions. For example, in [2], a fuzzy max-min decision model is developed to solve BLMOPs with concave objective functions. In [13], solutions for nonlinear, non-convex BLMOPs (with twice continuously differentiable functions) are first expressed as the set of minimal solutions of a multi-objective optimization problem. The BLMOP is then solved using an iterative process based on sensitivity theorems. The authors of [18] propose an approach for linear BLMOPs by establishing a relationship between the feasible set of upper-level solutions and the Pareto-optimal set of a particular multi-objective programming problem. In [3], a reformulation of BLMOP as a multi-objective mixed 0–1 linear programming problem is proposed.

Evolutionary Methods: Although exact methods can provide solutions to BLMOPs under certain assumptions, many real-world problems are inherently non-linear. This has led to significant interest in heuristic-based methods. One intuitive form of such methods is nested evolutionary search. In a nested search, the number of function evaluations are usually much larger at the LL compared to UL. As a result, a large body of research focuses on reducing the computational cost incurred at LL. Some studies explore the possibility of partially eliminating the LL search. For example, in [21], LL solutions and objectives are predicted using quadratic mapping from UL solutions. This approach allows LL search to concentrate around the target space, reducing resource consumption. Similarly, solution transfer was proposed in [28], where LL search begins from regions closer to the LL Pareto front (PF), reducing the number of LL evaluations. Recently, machine learning-based prediction has been proposed to directly predict LL optimal solutions, enabling the LL search to start even closer to the PF [26,29].

Most existing methods assume that the LL search is the primary consumer of computational resources, because in nested approaches, each UL solution evaluation requires an LL search. However, in some cases, the costs of the two levels may differ, with the UL problem being more expensive than the LL problem [20]. It means that evaluating a single UL solution involves significant cost, which may include physical experiments, financial expenditures, or computational effort. For instance, in the toll price-setting example [22], the UL problem involves a transportation operator aiming to set toll prices to maximize revenue, while the LL problem focuses on individual users' decisions on whether to use the toll road to minimize their travel cost and time. In this case, the LL problem could be relatively simple (only requires one user decisions), but the UL problem may require a high-fidelity model of traffic flow and user demographics for accurate revenue estimation. There have been a few investigations in BLSOP settings that consider expensive problems or varying cost between two levels. Surrogate-assisted optimization and transfer learning have been ap5plied to address expensive BLSOPs [16,27]. Different combinations of evolutionary and surrogate-assisted search has also been explored in [20] for problems with varying costs at UL and LL. However, there has been relatively little work for BLMOPs with expensive UL. In this paper, we specifically focus on BLMOPs where UL evaluations are considered expensive. Thus, the main aim is to reduce the number of function evaluations (FE) at UL to obtain the overall (UL) PF.

2 Motivation and Contributions

In the contemporary solution methods for BLMOPs, when a UL solution $\mathbf{x}_u$ receives its corresponding LL solution set $\{\mathbf{x}_l^*\}$, $\mathbf{x}_u$ is paired with all $\{\mathbf{x}_l^*\}$, and evaluations are performed to determine a set of objective values $\{\mathbf{F}_u\}$. Although all solutions are evaluated, the contribution of each solution in $\{\mathbf{x}_l^*\}$ to the quality of $\{\mathbf{F}_u\}$ is not equal. It is possible that only a subset of $\{\mathbf{F}_u\}$ lies on the non-dominated (ND) front of all $\{\mathbf{F}_u\}$ values, e.g., the gray solutions in the schematic illustration shown in Fig. 1a. The ND solutions in $\{\mathbf{F}_u\}$ may be dominated by the objective set of another UL solution, e.g., green solutions compared to purple solutions in Fig. 1a, or only a subset of this ND front may be on the ND front of the current population, e.g., purple solutions in enclosed purple rectangle in Fig. 1a. Thus, if we can evaluate a small set of LL solutions that are most relevant to the quality of $\{\mathbf{F}_u\}$, there is significant potential to reduce the number of UL FEs. Along these lines, a related recent study identifies knee points of the LL problem [8]. However, without incorporating information

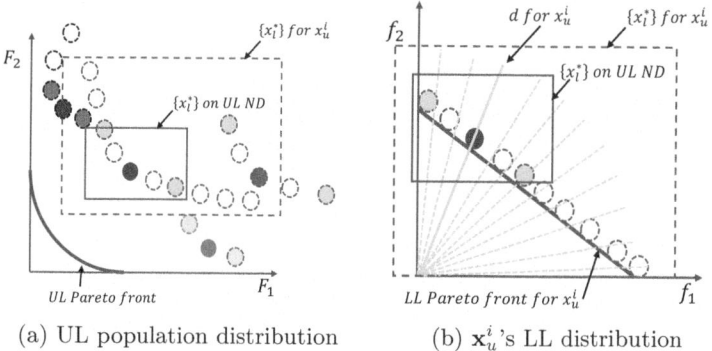

(a) UL population distribution   (b) $\mathbf{x}_u^i$'s LL distribution

Fig. 1. Visualization of LL solution selection

from the UL, it remains unclear whether the LL knee points are preferred at the UL. In this study, we intend to integrate UL information into the LL solution selection process. However, without conducting the UL evaluation, it is not straightforward to accurately determine the exact contribution of each LL solution. Despite this quandary, evolutionary search exhibits a distinction between the early and late stages of the search. In the early stage, the focus is on quickly guiding the population towards the PF, while in the later stage, the emphasis shifts to achieving better coverage of the PF. This characteristic provides an opportunity to heuristically select a small number of LL solutions for each UL solution without requiring high accuracy. To capitalize on this, we propose a direction-based selective evaluation scheme for LL solutions. Specific directions are extracted and marked in the LL objective space to guide the selection of corresponding LL solutions during the early stages of the search. By doing so, only a limited number of LL solutions are paired with the UL solution for evaluation, reducing the computational effort at UL. The contributions of this study are summarized as follows:

- A direction-based LL solution selection scheme is proposed to handle BLMOPs, with particular benefits to the problems with expensive UL evaluations.
- Four variants are constructed to validate the effectiveness of the proposed scheme.
- Experimental results show that the proposed selection scheme performs competitively compared to baseline both in accuracy and convergence.

The remainder of the paper is organized as follows: in Sect. 2 we present the motivation of the proposed approach; Then details of algorithm design is described in Sect. 3; Experimental results and discussion are shown in Sect. 4. Conclusion and future work are discussed in Sect. 5.

3   Proposed Approach

3.1   The Main Idea

The key question this study seeks to address is: when a UL solution receives a set of LL solutions, how can we determine which of these solutions should evaluated at UL? This overarching question can be further broken down into three sub-questions: (1) Which UL objective values (F_u^1, F_u^2) are most preferred for each UL solution? (2) How can the corresponding LL solutions be identified? (3) How can we determine these LL solutions prior to evaluation?

For the first sub-question, the conventional approach would be to evaluate all LL solutions, resulting in a distribution of corresponding $\{\mathbf{F}_u\}$ values in the UL objective space. As shown in Fig. 1a, when UL solution $\mathbf{x}_u^i$ is paired with its set of LL solutions $\{\mathbf{x}_l^{i*}\}$, the resulting objective values form a distribution in the UL objective space (purple circles). A subset of these solutions lies on the population's ND front, shown using purple circles within the solid rectangle. If only one solution is to be evaluated, the solution in the middle of the distribution is a promising candidate (represented by the purple-filled circle). This is because it provides a balance between the two objectives, as well as for convex PFs it is the solution close to the ideal point. For additional diversity, or anticipating non-convex PFs, the extreme solutions are likewise good candidates for evaluation. For a new UL solution, to answer the second sub-question, we need to select some LL solutions for evaluation. We do so by identifying the LL solutions that will yield the UL solutions that correspond to the choices mentioned above for the first sub-question. In order to find them prior to evaluation (as stated in the third sub-question), we utilize two main concepts: solution (knowledge) transfer and reference vector attachment.

As discussed in [28], neighbor UL solutions share some similar characteristics in the LL landscape. Therefore, solutions obtained for one of the UL solutions can inform the LL search for a neighboring UL solution. This idea was used for better seeding of LL population in [28], but we utilize this concept in a different way here. Essentially, corresponding to an existing chosen UL solution for which the PF is available at the LL, we construct uniformly distributed "reference vectors" in the LL objective space. Reference vectors are commonly used in decomposition-based evolutionary algorithms [4,5,9,30] to enhance diversity of the population. Here, we utilize them to identify solution of interest at the LL. The LL objective values are first normalized with their extreme values. Then, reference vectors are generated on the unit hyperplane via the normal-boundary intersection method [25]. In the LL objective space, we attach the solutions to their nearest reference vectors, and check which of them correspond to the solution of interest at the UL (e.g. mid-point or corners). Then, for a newly generated UL solution, we utilize the solution along this reference vector at LL to evaluate the UL objectives. As illustrated in Fig. 1b, the corresponding LL solution of interest is marked by the filled purple circle in the objective space. The reference vector d_t represents the closest reference vector to this purple circle. Thus, given a set of LL solutions, the LL solution whose LL objective value is closest to d_t is the solution of interest for evaluation in the UL objective space. The above approach allows for selective UL evaluations. In the following section, we will combine the aforementioned steps to formulate a complete search algorithm, which provides particular benefits for cases where the UL evaluations are expensive.

3.2 Proposed Algorithm with Direction-Based Selective Evaluation

In Algorithm1, we present the detailed steps of the proposed algorithm. Since the LL search is assumed to be inexpensive and is not the focus of current work, it is not elaborated here. We assume that the LL search can efficiently return Pareto-optimal solutions for LL problems with a satisfactory distribution on the LL PF. The algorithm framework in Algorithm 1 is based on a nested evolutionary search. On the UL, the initial UL population, P_1, is generated using uniform random sampling (Algorithm 1, Line 1). The LL search then returns the corresponding $\{x_l^{i*}\}$ for each x_u^i in P_1. For the first generation, P_1, all solutions in

---

Algorithm 1. Direction-based selective evaluation scheme framework

---

Input: Evolutionary parameters; number of UL population size n^u; number of LL solutions to be evaluated for UL solution; stopping conditions

Output: Final ND front of UL search

1: Initialize population $P_1 = \{\mathbf{x}_u^1, ..., \mathbf{x}_u^i, ...\mathbf{x}_u^{n^u}\}$; Identify LL solutions $\{\mathbf{x}_l^{i*}\}$ for each $\mathbf{x}_u^i$

2: Evaluate $\mathbf{x}_u^i$ with $\{\mathbf{x}_l^{i*}\}$, if LL solutions are feasible. Get population fitness P_1^F.

3: Determine reference vector(s) of interest for each UL solution $\mathbf{x}_u^i$ (Algo. 2)

4: Create ND archive from the first population; $g = 2$

5: **while** termination condition not met **do**

6:    Apply evolutionary operator to P_{g-1} to generate child population $C_g = \{\mathbf{c}_u^1, ..., \mathbf{c}_u^i, ...\mathbf{c}_u^{n^u}\}$

7:    **if** Selective evaluation stopping condition not met **then**

8:       **for each** $\mathbf{c}_u^i$ **do**

9:          Find its nearest neighbor from population P_{g-1}

10:          Inherit its nearest neighbor's evaluation reference vector(s).

11:          Use the reference vector(s) to select LL solution(s) from $\{\mathbf{c}_l^{i*}\}$ for evaluation

12:       **end for**

13:    **else**

14:       **for each** $\mathbf{c}_u^i$ **do**

15:          Evaluate all received $\{\mathbf{c}_l^{i*}\}$

16:       **end for**

17:    **end if**

18:    Get child population fitness C_g^F

19:    Apply feasibility first, non-dominance and crowding distance sorting on $P_{g-1}^F \cup C_g^F$

20:    Incorporate child population into ND archive and update ND archive

21:    Select new population P_g and its fitness P_g^F; $g = g + 1$

22: **end while**

23: Return ND archive

$\{\mathbf{x}_l^{i*}\}$ are evaluated based on the UL objectives. Once all LL solutions are evaluated, they form a knowledge base used to extract which LL solution(s) should be evaluated for each UL solution in the subsequent generations. This decision is made using Algorithm 2, which will be presented in the following section. After such reference vectors are determined for each $\mathbf{x}_u^i$, they are attached to $\mathbf{x}_u^i$ and stored as additional information. A child population is then created using evolutionary operators (Algorithm1, Line 6). Starting with the first child generation, the algorithm switches to a reduced LL solution evaluation mechanism (Algorithm 1, Line 7). In this process, a UL solution, $\mathbf{c}_u^i$, first identifies its nearest neighbor from the parent population (P_{g-1}) using normalized Euclidean distance. Then, $\mathbf{c}_u^i$ borrows its neighbor's reference vector information to determine which LL solution(s) to evaluate (Algorithm1, Line 9-11). Once all the UL solutions in C_g have determined their corresponding LL solutions, the fitness of the child population is finalized, followed by an update of the ND archive. Next, feasibility-first sorting, along with ND and crowding distance (CD) sorting, is applied to the combined population of P_{g-1} and C_g. Finally, environmental selection (Sect. 3.3) is used to retain the surviving population. It is evident that selective evaluation lacks sufficient coverage of the target UL PF. Therefore, at a certain stage, the UL evaluation must switch back to the standard process, where all LL solutions are evaluated (Algorithm 1, Line 15). We use inverted generational distance (IGD) stopping condition as discussed in [6] to determine the switching point. IGD stopping condition monitors the stagnation of the evolving population in terms of convergence and diversity. In short, if over ω generations, the changes on convergence stagnation and diversity stagnation is smaller than a threshold ϵ, then termination is activated. The overall search process continues till a fixed number of UL FE is met (Algorithm 1, Line 5). The ND archive updated through the search is returned as final results.

3.3   Distance Based Subset Selection

In the motivation section, we mentioned that in the UL objective space, the preferred $\mathbf{F}_u$ values are points located in the middle and extreme ends of the distribution (highlighted by purple-filled circles in Fig. 1a). To extract these solutions, we employ distance-based subset selection (DSS) [19]. Originally proposed to maintain solution diversity in evolutionary search, DSS is capable of selecting solutions with near-uniform distribution. DSS selects solutions iteratively, with each selection choosing the solution that has the maximum distance ($d_{\mathbf{v}}$) from the solutions already selected. Suppose $\mathbf{v}_j^s$ refers to solutions already selected, k is the number of solutions already selected. The distance $d_{\mathbf{v}}$ of one solution $\mathbf{v}$ to existing solutions are calculated as Eq. 2. DSS first calculates the pairwise distances between solutions in a set, then randomly selects one from the pair with the maximum distance as the initial solution (one extreme solution). The next selected solution is then the other extreme solution. According to the principle outlined in Eq. 2, the third selection is the solution that lies at the middle of the given solutions. If only one solution is required, we pick this third solution, otherwise we choose the required number as prescribed (three solutions would cover both extremities and center middle point for a bi-objective problem).

$$d_{\mathbf{v}} = min\{d(\mathbf{v}, \mathbf{v}_1^s), ..., d(\mathbf{v}, \mathbf{v}_j^s), ..., d(\mathbf{v}, \mathbf{v}_k^s)\} \qquad (2)$$

3.4   LL Solution Selection Mechanism

The LL solution selection mechanism establishes a link between the preferred UL objective values and the LL reference vectors. These reference vectors are then used to select the preferred LL objectives and, ultimately, the corresponding LL solutions. Algorithm 2 demonstrates the details of the selection.

The input population P first undergoes ND sorting to divide the UL solutions into a non-dominated set S_N and a dominated set S_D. Solutions in these two sets are handled differently. For the dominated set S_D, the preferred direction is calculated independently, without considering other solutions. For each $\mathbf{x}_u^i$, its own objective values $\{\mathbf{F}_u^i\}$ are first sorted using ND sort, and we retain

---

Algorithm 2. LL direction selection

Input: Population $P = \{\mathbf{x}_u^1, \mathbf{x}_u^2, ... \mathbf{x}_u^i, ..., \mathbf{x}_u^n\}$; corresponding LL solutions $\{\mathbf{x}_l^{i*}\}$ of $\mathbf{x}_u^i$
Output: Reference vectors corresponding to LL solutions to be evaluated for each UL solution $\mathbf{x}_u^i$.

1: Apply ND sort to population P
2: Separate solutions in P into ND solutions S_N (size k_N) and dominated solutions S_D (size k_D)
3: **for each** $\mathbf{x}_u^i \in S_D$, $i = 1, ..., k_D$ **do**
4:   Choose all corresponding LL solutions $\{\mathbf{x}_l^{i*}\}$ and corresponding $\{\mathbf{F}_u^i\}$
5:   Apply ND sorting on $\{\mathbf{F}_u^i\}$, keep ND solutions $\{\mathbf{F}_u^{i_N}\}$
6:   Apply DSS selection on $\{\mathbf{F}_u^{i_N}\}$ to select n_t UL objectives $\{\mathbf{F}_u^{i_{Nt}}\}$ and their corresponding LL solution $\{\mathbf{x}_l^{i*t}\}$ and its $\{\mathbf{f}_l^{i*t}\}$
7:   Form m uniform reference vectors on the LL objective space
8:   Normalize LL objectives $\{\mathbf{f}_l^{i*t}\}$ with all $\{\mathbf{f}_l^{i*}\}$
9:   Find closest reference vector $\{d^{i*t}\}$ corresponding to each solution in $\{\mathbf{f}_l^{i*t}\}$ by using vector angle
10:   Attach $\{d^{i*t}\}$ to $\mathbf{x}_u^i$
11: **end for**
12: **for each** $\mathbf{x}_u^j \in S_N$, $j = 1, .., k_N$ **do**
13:   Keep its $\{\mathbf{x}_l^{j*N}\}$ and $\{\mathbf{F}_u^{jN}\}$ located on UL ND front
14:   In $\{\mathbf{F}_u^{jN}\}$, apply DSS selection on objectives to select n_t UL objectives $\{\mathbf{F}_u^{jNt}\}$ and their corresponding LL solutions $\{\mathbf{x}_l^{j*t}\}$
15:   Find the corresponding LL objectives $\{\mathbf{f}_l^{j*t}\}$ of $\{\mathbf{x}_l^{j*t}\}$
16:   Form m uniform reference vectors on the LL objective space
17:   Normalize LL objectives $\{\mathbf{f}_l^{j*t}\}$ with all LL solutions $\{\mathbf{f}_l^{j*}\}$
18:   Find closest directions $\{d^{j*t}\}$ corresponding to $\{\mathbf{f}_l^{j*t}\}$ by using vector angle
19:   Attach $\{d^{j*t}\}$ to $\mathbf{x}_u^j$
20: **end for**

---

its own ND set $\{\mathbf{F}_u^{i_N}\}$ (Algorithm 2, Line 5). This ND set is used to extract target directions. In $\{\mathbf{F}_u^{i_N}\}$, we apply DSS selection to select up to n_t solutions, where $n_t = 1$ *or* 3 as discussed in previous section (Algorithm 2, Line 6). With these n_t solutions selected, we can determine their corresponding LL solutions $\{\mathbf{x}_l^{i*t}\}$. Solutions $\{\mathbf{x}_l^{i*t}\}$ have their corresponding LL objectives $\{\mathbf{f}_l^{i*t}\}$. When we construct a set of uniform reference vectors in the LL objective space (Line 7), we can associate LL solution $\{\mathbf{f}_l^{i*t}\}$ to a reference vector by measuring their vector angle (Algorithm 2, Line 9). When all individuals in $\{\mathbf{f}_l^{i*t}\}$ have found their reference vectors $\{d^{i*t}\}$, this set of vectors are returned to the UL solution $\mathbf{x}_u^i$.

We can see that the association of reference vectors to UL solution are built through 3 steps. First, UL objectives $\{\mathbf{F}_u^{i_{Nt}}\}$ are selected through DSS process. Then, LL solutions $\{\mathbf{x}_l^{i*t}\}$ are determined through $\{\mathbf{F}_u^{i_{Nt}}\}$. LL solutions are then used to find corresponding LL objectives $\{\mathbf{f}_l^{i*t}\}$. With $\{\mathbf{f}_l^{i*t}\}$, the reference vectors $\{d^{i*t}\}$ are finalized and attached to $\mathbf{x}_u^i$.

For the set of UL solutions $\mathbf{x}_u^j$ in ND set S_N, majority of the process is the same, the only difference is that the candidate $\{\mathbf{F}_u^{jN}\}$ changes (Algorithm 2, Line 13). When $\mathbf{x}_u^j$ is on ND front, it is possible that only a subset of its objective values $\{\mathbf{F}_u^j\}$ is on the UL ND front. Take Fig. 1a purple solutions as an example, $\{\mathbf{F}_u^{j_N}\}$ refers to the solutions enclosed by solid purple rectangle. This further narrows down candidate set of LL solutions of interest. With the set of candidate $\{\mathbf{F}_u^{j_N}\}$ exacted, DSS is then applied on it to pick up n_t target objectives $\{\mathbf{F}_u^{j_{N_t}}\}$ and corresponding LL solutions $\{\mathbf{x}_l^{j*t}\}$ (Algorithm 2, Line 14). Then similar to the process described in the last paragraph, with LL solutions $\{\mathbf{x}_l^{j*t}\}$ selected, the corresponding LL objectives $\{\mathbf{f}_l^{j*t}\}$ are also determined (Algorithm 2, Line 15). The reference vectors $\{d^{j*t}\}$ closest to each member of $\{\mathbf{f}_l^{j*t}\}$ are calculated (Algorithm 2, Line 18) and associated to UL solution $\mathbf{x}_u^j$ (Line 19).

4   Numerical Experiments

The DS test problem set is used for the experiments [12]. The theoretical PF can be derived for all problems to validate the performance of the proposed approach. The reference PF is generated using the DSS selection process. For each problem, the PF set contains n points (with $n = 1025$ to ensure a uniform distribution). Initially, $2n$ points are generated on the PF, after which DSS is applied to select n points as the final PF for performance analysis. The performance of the experimental results is measured using the Inverted Generational Distance (IGD) metric [10]. For bilevel optimization problems, the IGD is a more reliable metric for evaluating the final performance of search approaches compared to Pareto-compliant indicators such as Hypervolume (HV), particularly when deceptive problems are involved. In deceptive bilevel problems, if the LL search fails to find the optimal LL solutions, it is possible for the UL evaluations to dominate the true PF, leading to high HV values. In contrast, the IGD metric can capture this issue, revealing that such solutions do not necessarily indicate better performance. Note that in this study, we replace LL search with PS solutions, hence the issue of deceptiveness is not relevant. However, to maintain consistency, we still choose IGD as the performance metric.

The proposed approach employs an evolutionary search method using differential evolution (DE) [24] and polynomial mutation (PM) [11] to generate the child population. The crossover rate for the DE operator is set to 1, and the scaling factor is set to 0.5. For PM, the mutation probability is set to $1/D$ (where D is the number of variables), and the mutation index is set to 20. For all test problems, the LL Pareto set can be theoretically inferred, allowing us to focus on examining the effects of selective LL evaluation by replacing the LL search with theoretical Pareto set solutions. A set of LL solutions (of LL population size) is generated with near uniform distribution on LL PF and returned to the UL. Note that this also eliminates any issues around accuracy of UL evaluation due to sub-optimal LL solutions being returned [28]. The population size of the UL and LL is $10D_u$ (D_u is the number of UL variables) and $10D_l$ (D_l is the number of LL variables), respectively. The UL population is evolved over $10D_u$ generations. The overall stopping condition (Algorithm 1, Line 5) is based on the cumulative UL evaluations. If the UL evaluations exceed ($10D_u \times 10D_l \times 10D_u$), the search terminates. A past study [28] on these problems has shown that this

Table 1. Test problem variable size settings

Problems	S1		S2		S3		Problems	S1		S2		S3	
	D_u	D_l	D_u	D_l	D_u	D_l		D_u	D_l	D_u	D_l	D_u	D_l
DS1	2	2	4	4	10	10	DS4	1	3	1	5	1	9
DS2	2	2	4	4	10	10	DS5	1	3	1	5	1	9
DS3	2	2	4	4	10	10							

setting provides sufficient evaluations to obtain a good approximation of the PF. Therefore, in this study, we adopted the same parameter settings. For the IGD stopping condition (Algorithm 1, Line 7), ω is set to 10 generations, and the threshold ϵ is set to 1×10^{-3}, as suggested in its original paper paper [6]. The size of reference vectors m is set to 100. For a bi-objective problem, it gives a relatively good coverage of the objective space.

Two variations of the proposed approaches are experimented, referred to as Eval1 (1 solution evaluated) and Eval3 (3 solutions evaluated). To verify the efficacy of the proposed selective evaluation, we also create two corresponding variants that use random selection of Pareto solutions from LL. These variants are referred to as Rand1 (1 random solution) and Rand3 (3 random solutions), respectively. Finally, we use the standard nested EA as baseline, where all LL solutions are evaluated. To summarize, the compared algorithms are:

- **Eval1**: One LL solution is selected for evaluation. The selection is based on the middle point of DSS selection.
- **Eval3**: Three LL solutions are selected for evaluation. The first three solution selected by DSS mechanism are evaluated.
- **Rand1**: One random Pareto LL solution is selected for UL evaluation
- **Rand3**: Three random LL Pareto solutions go through UL evaluation
- **Baseline**: Nested EA where all LL Pareto solutions undergo UL evaluation.

To further observe the scalability of the proposed algorithm with respect to number of decision variables, three settings (S1-S3) are constructed as shown in Table 1. For each problem instance, 21 independent runs are conducted using each algorithm. Wilcoxon rank-sum test is used to assess statistical significance.

4.1   Performance (IGD) Comparison

Median IGD results are presented in Table 2 for each problem setting. Statistical test results are indicated by the symbols $\uparrow_i$, $\downarrow_i$, and $\approx_i$ next to the reported IGD values in each column. For brevity, the id i designates the ith approach, where $i = 1, 2, 3$, and 4 for the baseline EA, Eval1, Eval3 and Rand1 respectively.

All four variations of the selective UL evaluation approaches outperform the baseline EA in the majority of test problems and settings. Specifically, Eval1, Rand1, and Rand3 outperform the baseline EA in 9 out of 15 problems, while Eval3 shows superior performance in 10 cases. These results suggest that selective UL evaluation can improve search accuracy in UL search processes, *even when the LL solution(s) are selected at random from the LL Pareto set.*

Table 2. Performance comparison using IGD metric. The symbols $\uparrow_i, \downarrow_i, \approx_i$ denotes that compared to the ith approach, current approach performs significantly better, worse or equivalent, respectively

Problems	Baseline (1)	Eval1 (2)		Eval3 (3)			Rand1 (4)				Rand3				
S1															
DS1	0.0056	0.0040	$\uparrow_1$	0.0042	$\uparrow_1$	$\downarrow_2$	**0.0039**	$\uparrow_1$	$\approx_2$	$\uparrow_3$	0.0039	$\uparrow_1$	$\approx_2$	$\approx_3$	$\approx_4$
DS2	0.0344	**0.0228**	$\uparrow_1$	0.0233	$\uparrow_1$	$\approx_2$	0.0288	$\uparrow_1$	$\downarrow_2$	$\downarrow_3$	0.0289	$\uparrow_1$	$\approx_2$	$\downarrow_3$	$\approx_4$
DS3	0.0259	0.0155	$\uparrow_1$	**0.0139**	$\uparrow_1$	$\uparrow_2$	0.0190	$\uparrow_1$	$\downarrow_2$	$\downarrow_3$	0.0193	$\uparrow_1$	$\downarrow_2$	$\downarrow_3$	$\approx_4$
DS4	**0.0246**	0.0260	$\downarrow_1$	0.0248	$\approx_1$	$\uparrow_2$	0.0267	$\downarrow_1$	$\downarrow_2$	$\downarrow_3$	0.0269	$\downarrow_1$	$\downarrow_2$	$\downarrow_3$	$\approx_4$
DS5	0.0189	0.0195	$\approx_1$	**0.0187**	$\approx_1$	$\approx_2$	0.0190	$\approx_1$	$\approx_2$	$\approx_3$	0.0193	$\approx_1$	$\approx_2$	$\approx_3$	$\approx_4$
S2															
DS1	0.0044	0.0022	$\uparrow_1$	0.0021	$\uparrow_1$	$\approx_2$	**0.0020**	$\uparrow_1$	$\approx_2$	$\approx_3$	0.0022	$\uparrow_1$	$\approx_2$	$\downarrow_3$	$\downarrow_4$
DS2	0.0315	**0.0117**	$\uparrow_1$	0.0119	$\uparrow_1$	$\approx_2$	0.0156	$\uparrow_1$	$\downarrow_2$	$\downarrow_3$	0.0138	$\uparrow_1$	$\downarrow_2$	$\downarrow_3$	$\uparrow_4$
DS3	0.0243	**0.0089**	$\uparrow_1$	0.0090	$\uparrow_1$	$\approx_2$	0.0109	$\uparrow_1$	$\downarrow_2$	$\downarrow_3$	0.0121	$\uparrow_1$	$\downarrow_2$	$\downarrow_3$	$\approx_4$
DS4	**0.0160**	0.0161	$\approx_1$	0.0161	$\approx_1$	$\approx_2$	0.0170	$\downarrow_1$	$\downarrow_2$	$\downarrow_3$	0.0164	$\downarrow_1$	$\approx_2$	$\downarrow_3$	$\uparrow_4$
DS5	0.0138	0.0132	$\approx_1$	0.0132	$\approx_1$	$\approx_2$	**0.0128**	$\approx_1$	$\approx_2$	$\approx_3$	0.0139	$\approx_1$	$\approx_2$	$\approx_3$	$\approx_4$
S3															
DS1	0.0357	**0.0011**	$\uparrow_1$	**0.0011**	$\uparrow_1$	$\approx_2$	**0.0011**	$\uparrow_1$	$\approx_2$	$\approx_3$	**0.0011**	$\uparrow_1$	$\approx_2$	$\approx_3$	$\approx_4$
DS2	0.0790	**0.0082**	$\uparrow_1$	0.0082	$\uparrow_1$	$\approx_2$	0.0118	$\uparrow_1$	$\downarrow_2$	$\downarrow_3$	0.0102	$\uparrow_1$	$\downarrow_2$	$\downarrow_3$	$\uparrow_4$
DS3	0.1007	**0.0093**	$\uparrow_1$	0.0101	$\uparrow_1$	$\downarrow_2$	0.0185	$\uparrow_1$	$\downarrow_2$	$\downarrow_3$	0.0194	$\uparrow_1$	$\downarrow_2$	$\downarrow_3$	$\approx_4$
DS4	0.0108	0.0109	$\approx_1$	**0.0105**	$\uparrow_1$	$\uparrow_2$	0.0111	$\approx_1$	$\approx_2$	$\downarrow_3$	0.0109	$\approx_1$	$\approx_2$	$\downarrow_3$	$\approx_4$
DS5	**0.0085**	0.0086	$\approx_1$	0.0100	$\approx_1$	$\approx_2$	**0.0085**	$\approx_1$	$\approx_2$	$\uparrow_3$	0.0103	$\approx_1$	$\approx_2$	$\approx_3$	$\downarrow_4$
Summary of Wilcoxon rank-sum test results between approaches															
Compared to (1)		$\uparrow_1$ 9/$\downarrow_1$ 1/$\approx_1$ 5		$\uparrow_1$ 10/$\downarrow_1$ 0/$\approx_1$ 5			$\uparrow_1$ 9/$\downarrow_2$ 2/$\approx_1$ 4				$\uparrow_1$ 9/$\downarrow_1$ 2/$\approx_1$ 4				
Compared to (2)				$\uparrow_2$ 3/$\downarrow_2$ 2/$\approx_2$ 10			$\uparrow_2$ 0/$\downarrow_2$ 8/$\approx_2$ 7				$\uparrow_2$ 0/$\downarrow_2$ 7/$\approx_2$ 8				
Compared to (3)							$\uparrow_3$ 2/$\downarrow_3$ 9/$\approx_3$ 4				$\uparrow_3$ 0/$\downarrow_3$ 10/$\approx_3$ 5				
Compared to (4)											$\uparrow_4$ 3/$\downarrow_4$ 2/$\approx_4$ 10				

Between the two evaluation reduction schemes, Eval3 outperforms Eval1 in 3 cases, under-performs in 2 cases, and shows equal performance in the remaining 10 cases. Overall, both approaches have similar performance, with Eval3 holding a slight edge in one instance. Evaluating three solutions on the UL, compared to just one, potentially offers better coverage of the ND front, which could lead to improved accuracy in performance. The current test problem set does not contain problems with non-convex PFs, but it is anticipated that Eval3 might perform better in those cases. This aspect remains unexplored currently due to unavailability of suitable test problems with this feature.

Compared to Eval3, the two random evaluation schemes show a loss in accuracy in the majority of test problems (Rand1 and Rand3 under-perform in 9 and 10 out of 15 problems, respectively). These results demonstrate the efficacy of the proposed selection schemes (Eval1 and Eval3) over the random evaluation schemes. Between the two random schemes, there is no performance difference in 10 out of 15 cases, while Rand3 performs better in 3 cases and Rand1 in 2 cases. Similar to the comparison between Eval1 and Eval3, where Eval3 has a slight advantage, this can likely be attributed to the broader distribution of solutions that evaluating more candidates brings to the search process.

4.2 Convergence Rate Comparison

In Fig. 2, the median IGD convergence plots of all five schemes for each problem are presented. For the selective evaluation schemes, a dot on the convergence plots marks the switching point where the reduced UL evaluation activates the

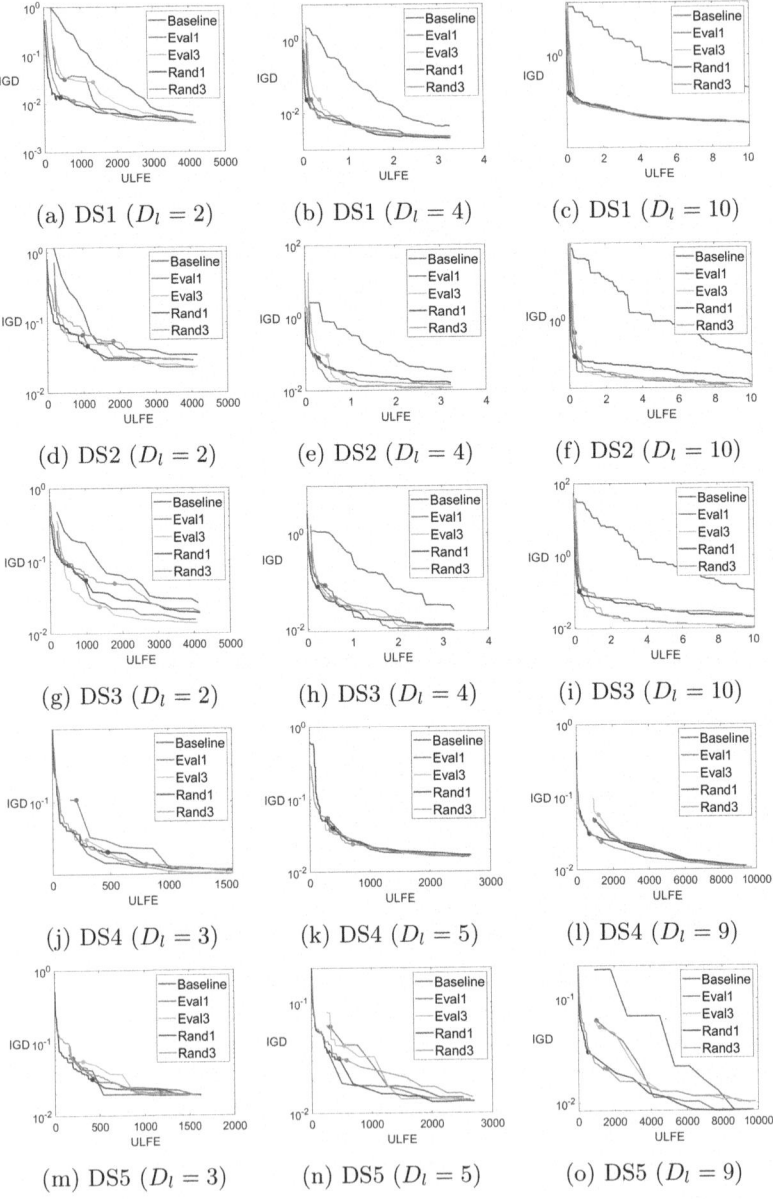

Fig. 2. Convergence plots for median IGD runs (IGD in logarithmic scale)

IGD stopping condition and transitions back to the normal evolutionary search. For DS1-3, it is evident that all four UL evaluation reduction schemes exhibit better convergence rates than the baseline method. By the time the switch to normal evolutionary search occurs, all four variants show better IGD values compared to the baseline, with the exception of the Rand3 scheme on DS2 (the 2-variable version). As the variable size increases, the gap in IGD values also widens. This reflects the primary benefit of the proposed evaluation reduction scheme: it allows the search algorithm to use fewer UL function evaluations to quickly push the search closer to the PF. Then, by switching to normal evaluation, the search can fine-tune and diversify the ND front and achieve a better distribution across the ND front.

When examining the convergence plots for DS4 and DS5, it is interesting to note that the convergence rates of all five approaches are quite similar, the baseline performs very competitively. The reason behind these results is that, for DS4 and DS5, the UL objective values in the first generation are already close to the PF. In this scenario, the focus of the search shifts toward achieving better distribution on the ND front to closely match the true PF, leaving less room for the UL evaluation reduction approach to make a significant impact. However, overall with different problem types, we can see that the UL search with selective evaluation scheme show competitive performance.

5   Conclusion and Future Work

In this paper, we present an approach to expedite the evolutionary search while solving BLMOPs, with particular benefits when the UL evaluation is expensive. The key idea is that during the early phases of the search, substantial proportion of UL evaluations can be saved by evaluating LL Pareto solutions selectively at UL. Our experiments showed that such selective evaluation improves the performance over baseline nested EA even when the selection of LL Pareto solution(s) is done at random. Furthermore, we proposed a more efficient selection scheme for selection, based on identifying a reference vector of interest at LL which corresponds to certain key solution(s) at the UL. Numerical experiments on the widely used DS test problem suite verify the efficacy of the proposed approach over random selection and baseline EA. Significant benefits were observed for problems with large number of UL variables and for problems where the starting solutions are far from the UL PF.

In this paper, the directions associated with LL solutions of interest are determined initially and kept fixed. However, as the search progresses, the LL solutions of interest may shift. Dynamically updating the directions associated with these LL solutions is a promising area for future research.

Acknowledgements. The authors acknowledge the support from Discovery Project DP220101649 from the Australian Research Council.

References

1. Lessin, A.M., B.J.L., Hill, R.R.: A multi-objective, bilevel sensor relocation problem for border security. IISE Trans. **51**(10), 1091–1109 (2019)
2. Abo-Sinna, M.A.: A bi-level non-linear multi-objective decision making under fuzziness. Opsearch **38**, 484–495 (2001)
3. Alves, M.J., Dempe, S., Júdice, J.J.: Computing the pareto frontier of a bi-objective bi-level linear problem using a multiobjective mixed-integer programming algorithm. Optimization **61**(3), 335–358 (2012)
4. Asafuddoula, M., Ray, T., Sarker, R.: A decomposition-based evolutionary algorithm for many objective optimization. IEEE Trans. Evol. Comput. **19**(3), 445–460 (2014)
5. Asafuddoula, M., Singh, H.K., Ray, T.: An enhanced decomposition-based evolutionary algorithm with adaptive reference vectors. IEEE Trans. Cybern. **48**(8), 2321–2334 (2017)
6. Blank, J., Deb, K.: A running performance metric and termination criterion for evaluating evolutionary multi- and many-objective optimization algorithms. In: 2020 IEEE Congress on Evolutionary Computation (CEC), pp. 1–8 (2020)
7. Calamai, P.H., Vicente, L.N.: Generating quadratic bilevel programming test problems. ACM Trans. Math. Softw. (TOMS) **20**(1), 103–119 (1994)
8. Chen, J., Ding, J., Li, K., Chen Tan, K., Chai, T.: A knee point driven evolutionary algorithm for multiobjective bilevel optimization. IEEE Trans. Cybern. **54**(7), 4177–4189 (2024). https://doi.org/10.1109/TCYB.2024.3377272
9. Cheng, R., Jin, Y., Olhofer, M., Sendhoff, B.: A reference vector guided evolutionary algorithm for many-objective optimization. IEEE Trans. Evol. Comput. **20**(5), 773–791 (2016)
10. Coello, C.A.C., Cortés, N.C.: Solving multiobjective optimization problems using an artificial immune system. Genet. Program Evolvable Mach. **6**(2), 163–190 (2005)
11. Deb, K., Pratap, A., Agarwal, S., Meyarivan, T.: A fast and elitist multiobjective genetic algorithm: NSGA-II. IEEE Trans. Evol. Comput. **6**(2), 182–197 (2002)
12. Deb, K., Sinha, A.: An efficient and accurate solution methodology for bilevel multi-objective programming problems using a hybrid evolutionary-local-search algorithm. Evol. Comput. **18**(3), 403–449 (2010)
13. Eichfelder, G.: Multiobjective bilevel optimization. Math. Program. **123**(2), 419–449 (2010)
14. Halter, W., Mostaghim, S.: Bilevel optimization of multi-component chemical systems using particle swarm optimization. In: 2006 IEEE International Conference on Evolutionary Computation, pp. 1240–1247 (2006)
15. Kirjner-Neto, C., Polak, E., Kiureghian, A.D.: An outer approximations approach to reliability-based optimal design of structures. J. Optim. Theory Appl. **98**(1), 1–16 (1998)
16. Lin, L., et al.: Classification model-based assisted preselection and environment selection approach for evolutionary expensive bilevel optimization. Appl. Intell. **53**(23), 28377–28400 (2023)
17. Mejía-De-Dios, J.A., Rodríguez-Molina, A., Mezura-Montes, E.: Multiobjective bilevel optimization: a survey of the state-of-the-art. IEEE Trans. Syst. Man Cybern. Syst. **53**(9), 5478–5490 (2023)
18. Pleume, C.O., Marcotte, P., Fotso, L.P., Siarry, P., et al.: Solving bilevel linear multiobjective programming problems. Am. J. Oper. Res. **1**(4), 214–219 (2011)

19. Singh, H.K., Bhattacharjee, K.S., Ray, T.: Distance-based subset selection for benchmarking in evolutionary multi/many-objective optimization. IEEE Trans. Evol. Comput. **23**(5), 904–912 (2019)
20. Singh, H.K., Islam, M.M., Ray, T., Ryan, M.: Nested evolutionary algorithms for computationally expensive bilevel optimization problems: variants and their systematic analysis. Swarm Evol. Comput. **48**, 329–344 (2019)
21. Sinha, A., Malo, P., Deb, K.: Evolutionary algorithm for bilevel optimization using approximations of the lower level optimal solution mapping. Eur. J. Oper. Res. **257**(2), 395–411 (2017)
22. Sinha, A., Malo, P., Deb, K.: A review on bilevel optimization: from classical to evolutionary approaches and applications. IEEE Trans. Evol. Comput. **22**(2), 276–295 (2018)
23. Sinha, A., Malo, P., Frantsev, A., Deb, K.: Finding optimal strategies in a multi-period multi-leader-follower Stackelberg game using an evolutionary algorithm. Comput. Oper. Res. **41**, 374–385 (2014)
24. Storn, R., Price, K.: Differential evolution-a simple and efficient heuristic for global optimization over continuous spaces. J. Global Optim. **11**(4), 341–359 (1997)
25. Tian, Y., Cheng, R., Zhang, X., Jin, Y.: PlatEMO: a MATLAB platform for evolutionary multi-objective optimization. IEEE Comput. Intell. Mag. **12**(4), 73–87 (2017)
26. Wang, B., Singh, H.K., Ray, T.: Pareto set prediction assisted bilevel multi-objective optimization. arXiv preprint arXiv:2409.03328 (2024)
27. Wang, B., Singh, H.K., Ray, T.: Comparing expected improvement and kriging believer for expensive bilevel optimization. In: 2021 IEEE Congress on Evolutionary Computation (CEC), pp. 1635–1642. IEEE (2021)
28. Wang, B., Singh, H.K., Ray, T.: An evaluation of simple solution transfer strategies for bilevel multiobjective optimization. In: 2023 IEEE Congress on Evolutionary Computation (CEC) (2023), accepted
29. Wang, W., Liu, H.L.: Conditional generative adversarial network-based bilevel evolutionary multiobjective optimization algorithm. IEEE Trans. Evol. Comput. **28**, 1205–1219 (2023)
30. Zhang, Q., Li, H.: MOEA/D: a multiobjective evolutionary algorithm based on decomposition. IEEE Trans. Evol. Comput. **11**(6), 712–731 (2007)

MOAISDX: A New Multi-objective Artificial Immune System Based on Decomposition

Estefania A. Aguilar Arroyo⬩ and Carlos A. Coello Coello⁽✉⁾⬩

Departamento de Computación, CINVESTAV-IPN,
Av. IPN No. 2508, Col. San Pedro Zacatenco, Mexico City 07360, Mexico
carlos.coellocoello@cinvestav.mx

Abstract. From among the many techniques currently available to solve multi-objetive optimization problems (MOPs), an alternative is the use of multi-objective artificial immune systems (MOAISs). This sort of metaheuristic emulates immune processes using computational resources, with the aim of solving MOPs. MOAISs have mechanisms such as the clonal selection principle as well as positive and negative selection, that make them powerful search tools. In recent years, there have been proposals of MOAISs that adopt selection schemes that are more appropriate to deal with many-objective problems (i.e., problems having more than 3 objectives), from which decomposition has been a popular choice. We propose here a new MOAIs called "Multi-objective Artificial Immune System based on Decomposition" (MOAISDX). The performance of our proposed approach is compared with respect to that of NSGA-II and MOEA/D, as well as with respect to four recent MOAISs. The results obtained from this comparative study show that MOAISDX outperforms NSGA-II and obtains results similar to those of MOEA/D in most of the adopted test instances. Furthermore, MOAISDX has better performance than that of the other MOAISs compared, particularly as we increase the number of objectives.

Keywords: Multi-objective optimization · Artificial immune systems · Decomposition

1 Introduction

Multi-objective optimization involves the solution of problems that consist of two or more (often conflicting) objective functions. Assuming minimization, a multi-objective optimization problem (MOP) is defined as:

$$\text{minimize } \vec{f}(\vec{x}) := [f_1(\vec{x}), f_2(\vec{x}), \ldots, f_k(\vec{x})], \tag{1}$$

subject to:

$$g_i(\vec{x}) \leq 0 \quad i = 1, 2, \ldots, m \tag{2}$$

H. Singh et al. (Eds.): EMO 2025, LNCS 15512, pp. 46–59, 2025.
https://doi.org/10.1007/978-981-96-3506-1_4

$$h_i(\vec{x}) = 0 \quad i = 1, 2, \ldots, p \tag{3}$$

where $\vec{x} = [x_1, x_2, \ldots, x_n]^T$ is known as the decision vector, $f_i : \mathbb{R}^n \to \mathbb{R}$, $i = 1, \ldots, k$ are the objective functions and $g_i, h_j : \mathbb{R}^n \to \mathbb{R}$, $i = 1, \ldots, m$, $j = 1, \ldots, p$ are the constraint functions. The goal in multi-objective optimization is to find a set of solutions that represent the best trade-offs among the objective functions. To identify the quality of such solutions we utilize the concept of Pareto dominance. Given two vectors $\vec{x}, \vec{y} \in \mathbb{R}^n$, $\vec{x}$ is said to dominate $\vec{y}$, denoted as $\vec{x} \prec \vec{y}$, if $\vec{f}(\vec{x}) \leq \vec{f}(\vec{y})$ and $\vec{f}(\vec{x}) \neq \vec{f}(\vec{y})$ (given that $\vec{x} \leq \vec{y}$ if $x_i \leq y_i$ for $i = 1, \ldots, n$). A vector $\vec{x}$ is said to be nondominated with respect to $\mathcal{X} \subset \mathbb{R}^n$ if there is no other vector $\vec{y}$ such that $\vec{y} \prec \vec{x}$. We say $\vec{x}$ is a Pareto optimal solution, if $\vec{x}$ is nondominated with respect to the feasible region $\mathcal{F} \subset \mathbb{R}^n$. The set of all Pareto optimal solutions is known as the Pareto optimal set. The set of all $\vec{f}(\vec{x})$ such that $\vec{x}$ is in the Pareto optimal set is called Pareto front.

Multi-objective artificial immune systems (MOAISs) are a metaheuristic inspired on our biological immune system. MOAISs emulate immune processes using computational resources and are oriented to the solution of multi-objective problems. Akin to a multi-objective evolutionary algorithm (MOEA), a MOAIS maintains a population of potential solutions (called antibodies) along the optimization process. The aim is to simulate the immune response subjecting the antibodies to a series of immune operators. In general, a MOIAS undergoes a series of common steps with an indistinct model [14] (Fig. 1):

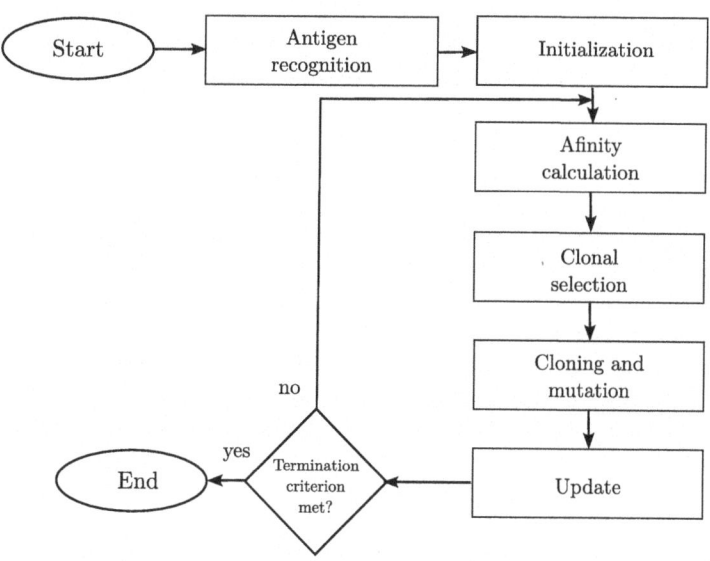

Fig. 1. Steps of a generic MOIAS.

- **Antigen recognition:** The multi-objective problem is recognized as an antigen; in constrained problems the constraint functions are sometimes identified as antigens.
- **Initialization:** A set of randomly initialized potential solutions are designated as the main population, known as antibodies in decision space.
- **Affinity calculation:** The affinity between a pair of antigens and antibodies is calculated at each generation.
- **Clonal selection:** The antibodies with the highest affinities among the population are selected to undergo a proliferation process. In other words, to speed up the convergence of the population, more resources are allocated to more promising areas in the search space.
- **Update:** The parents with the lowest affinities are replaced by antibodies with higher affinities and the resulting population becomes the parents for the next generation.

When the termination criterion is met, the output of a MOAIS is the final population, which contains an approximation of the Pareto optimal set.

MOAISs are called hybrid algorithms when the design includes non immunological operators (e.g., a crossover operator). Hybrid MOAISs are far more popular than pure MOAISs because the lack of crossover severely limits their exploitation capabilities.

MOAISs based on the clonal selection principle [19] aim to identify antibodies with high affinities (i.e., the antibodies that are able to bind with a certain antigen with a high precision) and propagate them, producing a (pre-defined) number of identical copies or clones. The clones are then mutated according to a specific metric, which is normally based on their affinity [4]. This allows to guide the search, changing at higher rates antibodies which are not suitable potential solutions, while keeping or slightly changing the ones that are. In this way, there is no need for an explicit control of the relationship between exploration and exploitation in the search.

Most of the currently available MOAISs are based on Pareto optimality. These approaches use a procedure called nondominated sorting to rank solutions such that all the Pareto optimal solutions found at a certain generation have the same probability of being selected [6]. These approaches normally adopt an additional mechanism (called density estimator) that allows them to maintain diversity in the population over time. This sort of approach quickly loses effectiveness as we increase the number of objectives, which makes them unsuitable for problems having more than three objectives (the so-called many-objective optimization problems). In recent years, there has been some research on the use of decomposition-based approaches into MOAISs [14], obtaining good results. In a decomposition-based approach, the main idea is to transform a MOP into several single-objective problems, which are then solved simultaneously and in a collaborative manner using neighborhood search [21]. A set of search directions (weighted vectors) are used together with a scalarizing function to guide the search [18]. These approaches can be used to solve MOPs with any number of objectives. Although the effectiveness of decomposition-based approaches is based on the scalarizing function adopted, there are several choices which are normally very effective.

Here, we propose a new decomposition-based MOAIS, adopting a cloning operator and a selection mechanism for sub-problem optimization. Our proposed approach is called Multi-objective Artificial Immune System based on Decomposition (MOAISDX).

2   Previous Related Work

Here, we will briefly review some MOAISs representative of the state of the art in the area.

The Nondominated Neighbor Immune Algorithm (NNIA) [9] draws inspiration from the clonal selection principle. The decision of which individuals are to be selected for cloning is made according to the value of their crowding distances. Because of this mechanism, the resulting approximation sets have a good distribution along the Pareto front because the focus is on selecting the nondominated antibodies that lie in less populated areas of the Pareto front. NNIA also maintains an external archive with nondominated solutions found during the search. However, it tends to lose population's diversity and deteriorates its convergence when increasing the number of objectives due to the use of a selection mechanism based on Pareto optimality. NNIA was originally tested on problems with only two and three objectives. Its computational complexity is $O(N^2)$, where N is the population size.

The Novel Immune Clonal Algorithm (NICA) [20] uses an approach similar to NNIA, and it also adopts Pareto optimality to filter out solutions in the population. However, unlike NNIA, NICA incorporates Pareto optimality in its cloning mechanism, since only nondominated solutions undergo the cloning process. In this MOAIS, the number of clones assigned to each selected solution is the same regardless of its affinity. NICA also employs the crowding distance to suppress a nondominated individual at each generation in order to maintain a good distribution in the resulting set. NICA has the same limitations as NNIA because it is also based on Pareto optimality. NICA was evaluated on problems with three objectives, obtaining competitive results. Its computational complexity is $O(N^3)$, where N is the population size.

A Hybrid Evolutionary Immune Algorithm for multiobjective optimization problems (HEIA) [16] is a hybrid framework for artificial immune systems oriented to solve MOPs. HEIA combines immune mechanisms with evolutionary operators to improve the search capabilities of a pure MOAIS. It adopts recombination and mutation schemes in different randomly generated sub-populations trying to find a compromise between proximity and diversity in the final approximation set. Its selection strategy involves categorizing the solutions as dominated and nondominated, as well as removing dominated solutions and sorting the remaining solutions according to their crowding distances. HEIA also keeps an external archive with the nondominated solutions found so far. HEIA is also based on Pareto optimality. HEIA was tested on the ZDT [24], WFG [10], UF

[22] and DTLZ [7] test suites. It was tested on bi-objective and three-objective problems yielding competitive results. It was also reported that HEIA has a computational complexity of $O(N^2)$, where N is the population size.

A Multi-objective Immune Algorithm with Dynamic Population Strategy (MOIAS-DPS) [17] is a hybrid MOAIS which includes a mechanism to dynamically control the population size based on the current state of its external archive of nondominated solutions. The aim is to intensify the exploration capacity by gradually rising the population size when the archive is not full, and decreasing it when it is. MOIAS-DPS was tested on problems having two and three objectives. MOAIS-DPS is also based on Pareto optimality. Its computational complexity was not provided.

The Multi-Objective Immune Algorithm with a Decomposition-based Clonal Selection (MOIA-DCSS) [13] is based on decomposition, so the solutions are associated to a sub-problem and a weighted vector. The number of clones assigned to each individual depends on the improvement of the associated sub-problem through generations. To update the population, the largest relative improvement with regard to the scalarizing function is used to determine if a new solution replaces the current solution. MOIA-DCSS was validated using the F [11], UF and WFG test suites with two and three objectives. Its computational complexity was not provided.

The Vertical Distance-based clonal selection mechanism for MOIAs (VD-MOAI) [12] utilizes a decomposition approach coupled with the Tchebychev scalarizing function. The algorithm makes use of clonal selection based on the vertical distance between a solution and the weighted vector associated to a sub-problem. This method assigns the number of clones to each solution proportional to the vertical distance and it promotes convergence, focusing also on preserving diversity by assigning more clones to solutions with lower vertical distances. VD-MOAI also uses a differential evolution crossover operator. VD-MOAI was originally tested only with problems having two and three objectives. VD-MOIA was tested on the WFG, UF and F test suites. Its computational complexity was not provided.

The Balancing Convergence and Diversity in Multiobjective Immune Algorithm (BCD-MOIA) [15] is a hybrid MOAIS which introduces a cloning operator to balance population convergence and diversity throughout the search. The cloning operator has two parts. Convergence is maintained taking into account the individual's relative improvement. Diversity is kept by establishing which individuals are closer to the associated weighted vector. Both metrics are then combined with a penalty factor which aims to regulate the effect that each value has on the search. BCD-MOIA was tested on the UF and F test suites, which consist of bi-objective and three-objective problems. Its computational complexity was not provided.

3 Our Proposal

Here, we present the details of our proposed algorithm called *Multi-objective Artificial Immune System based on Decomposition* (MOAISDX). The main focus in the design of the algorithm is the role of the clonal selection principle combined with additional mechanisms used to regulate the population's state. Thus, selection is divided into positive selection and negative selection.

Decomposition. The design of our proposed MOAISDX follows the MOEA/D framework [21]. At each generation, MOAISDX maintains:

- a population of antibodies (**Ab**) of size n, which represent potential solutions,
- a set of weighted vectors $(\lambda_1, \lambda_2, \cdots, \lambda_n)$
- a scalarizing function $g^{tch}(\cdot)$
- a neighborhood $B(\cdot)$ of size T
- a population of N_C of clones C
- an affinity function $Aff(\cdot)$

In MOEA/D, each sub-problem is solved in a simultaneous and collaborative manner with the sub-problems within its neighborhood. From the neighboring solutions, parents are chosen for crossover. The offspring y is then mutated and used to update the neighborhood or the general population. The criteria used to decide if the offspring y will replace the current solution x associated to a sub-problem relies on their scalarizing function values. That is if $g^{tch}(y) > g^{tch}(x)$, y will replace x as the solution associated to a sub-problem. To avoid filling the entire population with the same solution, a number of replacements is fixed by the user. MOAIS keeps a population of clones along the optimization process. The clone population is being continuously filled with clones, which are copies of antibodies with the highest affinities. Once this population is full, clones undergo *somatic mutation*. The mutation scheme used in MOAISDX is polynomial-based mutation [5].

Keeping a population of clones is a recurrent mechanism in MOAIS' designs, but the clones are used as a pool of parents that are adopted for crossover [14]. Instead of using a single solution (offspring) for the update process, MOAIS uses the whole population of clones to perform a local or global update. This way, we take advantage of all mutated clones and, to a lesser extent, of identical clones. If $g^{scl}(c_i) < g^{scl}(Ab_i)$ then a clone c_i replaces the solution Ab_i associated to the sub-problem i.

Cloning Operator. Given that we are aiming to keep a solution set with good convergence and diversity at each generation, we are faced with the challenge of selecting solution members that will reflect it. In a decomposition approach, we select solutions with the lowest possible agregation value given a reference vector and a scalarizing function. This selection method alone will ensure that we keep good solutions (according to the scalarizing function of our choice). To make sure that we build a good repertoire of candidate solutions for the selection, we propagate solutions that are close to the related weighted vector. In this paper, we use cosine similarity as an affinity measure. The cosine similarity of two vectors $\vec{x}$ and $\vec{y}$ is given by:

$$\cos(\alpha) = \frac{\vec{x} \cdot \vec{y}}{\sqrt{||\vec{x}||||\vec{y}||}} \tag{4}$$

The cosine similarity value of two vectors reflects how close they are in terms of the angle between them. This value is in the range $[0, 1]$ where 1 indicates the two vectors are in the same direction and 0 that they are orthogonal to each other. Cosine similarity is invariant to scale and works well in higher dimensional spaces.

Linge Li $et\ al.$ [12] used the following expression to assign clones to each individual:

$$c_i = \left\lceil |C| \times \frac{affinity}{\sum_{j=0}^{|C|} affinity} \right\rceil$$

where c_i is the number of assigned clones, $|C|$ is the size of the clone population and $affinity$ is the affinity measure used. In our case, we adopt the value of cosine similarity of the indivual and its corresponding weighted vector as the affinity measure, to propagate individuals closely related. Once the number of clones is calculated, the cloning operator is applied to the selected antibodies. The cloning operator is given by:

$$C = \bigcup_{i=1}^{T} [Ab_i \otimes c_i]$$

where $\otimes$ is the cloning operation, that is, the process used to generate or to replicate an antibody keeping all of its characteristics intact.

Positive and Negative Selection. Once clones are generated, the population of clones undergoes mutation. The role of the affinity function is to generate mutation percentages that correspond to the affinities. Namely, the goal is that the least fit antibodies are subject to a more intensive mutation rate than those who are more fit according to the following expression $pm = \exp(-5.0 * affinity\ value)$ [4]. To avoid loss of diversity, MOAISDX inspects all clones to identify which ones are identical (clones that have not been mutated) and make them candidates to be removed from the population. This is called Negative Selection. The identical clones can be either ignored (become anergic) or replaced by new randomly generated antibodies. The goal is to keep the population of clones as diverse as possible and to take care of convergence by setting a limit on the number of discarded clones.

Positive selection can be interpreted as the process of local/global improvement. That is, each active element in the population of clones C is a candidate to replace elements of the neighborhood or the main population. A clone can become the associated solution to a sub-problem if $g^{scl}(c_i) < g^{scl}(Ab_j)$ and $affinity(c_i) \geq affinity(Ab_j)$ for $i = 1, 2, \cdots, |C|$ and $j = 1, 2, \cdots, N$.

3.1 Our Proposed Algorithm

MOAISDX begins with the initialization where the T closest sub-problems to each sub-problem are computed (neighborhood). At this stage, the main population is initialized by randomly generating N antibodies Ab and their objective values are calculated. In the main loop, we start by updating the reference vector z^*. Subsequently, cloning takes place by selecting antibodies with the highest affinities. For each selected antibody, a fixed number of clones is produced according to its affinity. When cloning is finalized, the clones are mutated. The mutation rate is inversely proportional to their affinity value. Negative selection is then triggered to decrease the number of identical clones, replacing some of them by new randomly generated antibodies. The last stage is related to local/global improvement, where highly fit clone population members take the place of the associated solution to a particular sub-problem. The whole process can be viewed in Algorithm 1. In MOAISDX, recombination is included in a straightforward way: the parents are chosen from the neighborhood and the offspring are incorporated in the population of clones. The computational complexity of MOAISDX depends on the main loop; cloning, negative selection, and mutation each take $O(C)$, where C is the size of the clone population, and the update takes $O(CT)$ where T the size of the neighborhood. The computational complexity of MOAISDX is $O(NCT)$ in each generation, where N is the size of the population.

4 Validation of Our Proposed Approach

The performance of our proposed MOAISDX was compared with respect to that of other state-of-the-art MOAISs and with respect to two MOEAs.

4.1 Experimental Settings

16 test problems were used in our experiments, including 7 problems from the DTLZ test suite (DTLZ1-DTLZ7) and 9 problems from the WFG test suite (WFG1-WFG9). The number of variables for each problem are given in Table 1. In the first experiment, all 16 instances were tested with 3 objectives. In the second experiment, only DTLZ1 was used to explore the capabilities of the algorithm in a high dimensional objective space. Four recent MOAISs were used in our experiments: BCD-MOIA, HEIA, MOIA-DCSS and VD-MOIA. The parameters for each algorithm are those suggested in their original articles. For the MOAISs based on decomposition, the niche size and other decomposition related parameters are given in Table 1. For MOAISDX, N_c was set equal to the niche size and N_R was set to one. The weighted vectors were generated using the Das-Dennis approach [3] for 3, 4 and 7 objectives. For 5, 6, 8, 9 and 10 objectives, the weighted vectors were generated using the Riesz s-Energy method [2].

We adopted the hypervolume indicator [23] to assess performance:

$$I_{HV}(A : \vec{z^{ref}}) = \left\{ \cup \text{volume}(v : \vec{z^{ref}}) | v \in A \right\} \tag{5}$$

Input: MOP, a stopping criterion, N: number of sub-problems, set of weighted
vectors uniformly distributed $\lambda^i, \cdots, \lambda^N$, T : size of the neighborhood,
N_c : or $|C|$ clone population size , N_R : maximum number of
replacements

begin

    Initialization;

    $EP = \emptyset$;

    Compute Euclidean distances between any two weighted vectors and
determine the T closest ones for each vector. For each $i = 1, \cdots, N$, find
$B(i) = \{i_1, \cdots, i_N\}$, where $\lambda^{i_1}, \cdots, \lambda^{i_T}$ are the T closest weighted vectors
to λ^i ;

    Randomly generate an initial population $Ab^1, \cdots, Ab^N$ or by a problem
specific method. $FV^i = F(x^i)$;

    Update;

    while *termination criterion not met* **do**

        for $i = 0$ **to** N **do**

            Reference point update z^*: for each $j = 1, \cdots, k$ if $z_j < f_j(y)$,
then $z_j = f_j(y)$;

            Clone ;

            Mutate ;

            Negative selection;

            Local/global update (positive selection): For each
$i = 1, \cdots, N_C$ and for each index $j \in B(i)$, if
$g^{scl}(C_i|\lambda, z) \leq g^{scl}(Ab_j|\lambda, z)$ and $affinity(C_i) > affinity(Ab_j)$
then $Ab_j = C_i$ y $FV^j = F(C_i)$;

            EP **update**;

        end

    end

end

Algorithm 1: MOAISDX algorithm

where A is the approximation set and z^{ref} is a reference point. For DTLZ1-DTLZ2, DTLZ4-DTLZ6, the reference point was set to $(2, 2, \cdots, 2)$, for DTLZ3 $(4, 4, \cdots, 4)$, for DTLZ7 $(2, 2, \cdots, 2, 8)$ and for the WFG test suite, it was set to $(3, 5, \cdots, 2 * k + 1)$.

For each experiment, we performed 20 independent runs for each algorithm, test instance and number of objectives. MOAISDX, MOEA/D and NSGA-II were implemented in C/C++ in the EMO project framework [1], while BCD-MOIA, HEIA, MOIA-DCSS and VD-MOIA were implemented in Java in the jMetal framework [8].

4.2 Experimental Results

The results of all our experiments were assessed using the Wilcoxon rank sum test with a 95% confidence. In the first experiment, we investigated the performance of MOAISDX with respect to 4 recent MOAISs: BCD-MOIA, HEIA, MOIA-DCSS and VD-MOIA. BCD-MOIA, MOIA-DCSS and VD-MOIA are

Table 1. Parameters values chosen for the experiments

Parameters/ Number of objectives	3	4	5	6	7	8	9	10
Population size (N)		136	166	175	203	210	240	270	290
Niche size		27	33	35	40	42	54	58	60
SBX parameters		$p_c = 1.0, \eta_c = 20, \eta_m = 20$

decomposition-based algorithms while HEIA is a hybrid framework which uses sub-populations, each of which is evolved with a different evolutionary strategy. BCD-MOIA, HEIA and VD-MOIA require fixed mutation rates which were set at $1/n$, where n is the number of variables. BCD-MOIA, MOAI-DCSS and VD-MOIA use differential evolution in the optimization process, while MOAISDX uses SBX and polynomial-based mutation.

In Table 2, we show the comparison of results between our proposed MOAISDX and the other MOAISs and MOEAs adopted for both test suites with three objectives. For the DTLZ test suite, MOAISDX outperformed BCD-MOIA, MOIA-DCSS and VD-MOIA in four out of seven instances and it performed slightly better than HEIA in three out of seven instances. BCD-MOIA, MOIA-DCSS and VD-MOIA outperformed MOAISDX in three out of seven instances and HEIA outperformed MOAISDX in three out of seven instances. MOAISDX shows better perfomance when dealing with problems with multi-modal and disconnected Pareto fronts, while other MOAISs tend to perform better when solving uni-modal problems.

When comparing results with respect to MOEAs in the DTLZ test suite, our proposed MOAISDX outperformed MOEA/D and NSGA-II in 5 and 4 out of 7 instances. NSGA-II outperformed MOAISDX in 3 out of 7 instances, and MOEA/D perfomed similarly to MOAISDX in 2 out of 7 instances. In the WFG test suite, MOAISDX outperformed MOEA/D in 4 out of 9 instances, and it outperformed NSGA-II in 4 out of 9 instances. MOEA/D outperformed MOAISDX in 2 out of 9 instances and NSGA-II outperformed MOAISDX in 3 out of 9 instances. MOAISX shows that it is able to deal with different problem characteristics with moderate success, although its performance is best when dealing with concave, non-separable, parameter-dependent problems.

In the second experiment, as shown in Table 3, we studied the performance of our proposed MOAISDX with respect to other MOAISs and with respect to MOEAs in a high dimensional objective space. Although we performed experiments using the same test problems as before, due to space limitations, we will present here only one test instance with 3 to 10 objectives, but these results are representative of the behavior of the algorithms adopted in our experimental study. We selected DTLZ1. The parameters settings for this experiment are shown in Table 1.

With three, five, six and seven objectives, our proposed MOAISDX outperformed all the other algorithms in the comparasion. With four objectives, MOAISDX outperformed all but one algorithm (HEIA), with respect to which it had a similar performance. With eight and ten objectives, MOAISDX outperformed 5 out of 6 algorithms, showing a similar performance to that of MOEA/D. With nine objectives, MOAISDX outperformed BCD-MOIA, HEIA, MOIA-DCSS, VD-MOIA and NSGA-II. MOAISDX was outperformed by MOEA/D. In general, MOAISDX performs better when dealing with problems with more than 3 objectives in the test problem selected.

Table 2. Comparison of the hypervolume values obtained by MOAISDX and four recent MOIASs and two MOEAs using the DTLZ and WFG test suites with three objectives. The symbols $+, -, \sim$ indicate whether a result is better, worse or similar.

Test problem/ Algorithm	BCD-MOIA	HEIA	MOIA-DCSS	VD-MOIA	MOEA/D	NSGA-II	MOAISDX
DTLZ1	7.64E+00 -	7.97E+00 ~	7.72E+00 -	7.74E+00 -	7.97E+00 ~	7.97E+00 +	7.97E+00
	1.05E+00	5.40E-04	9.17E-01	8.20E-01	1.40E-04	6.07E-04	2.61E-04
DTLZ2	7.42E+00 +	7.39E+00 -	7.42E+00 +	7.42E+00 +	7.39E+00-	7.37E+00-	7.39E+00
	4.47E-04	3.47E-03	5.61E-04	4.73E-04	1.15E-03	2.16E-02	2.11E-03
DTLZ3	5.06E+01 -	6.32E+01 -	4.90E+01 -	4.98E+01 -	6.34E+01 -	6.34E+01 -	6.34E+01
	2.37E+01	9.59E-01	2.40E+01	2.32E+01	9.42E-03	1.10E+00	1.79E-03
DTLZ4	7.42E+00 +	7.39E+00 +	7.42E+00 +	7.42E+00 +	6.47E+00-	7.38E+00 +	7.15E+00
	7.43E-04	4.26E-03	1.41E-02	1.33E+00	1.06E-02	1.42E-02	4.34E-01
DTLZ5	6.08E+00 -	6.10E+00 +	6.08E+00 -	6.08E+00 -	6.09E+00 ~	6.10E+00 +	6.09E+00
	7.37E-05	3.27E-04	7.82E-05	1.03E-04	1.87E-04	3.88E-04	2.07E-03
DTLZ6	6.08E+00 +	6.11E+00 +	6.08E+00 +	6.08E+00 +	5.79E+00 -	5.51E+00 -	5.88E+00
	9.14E-06	5.43E-05	1.17E-05	1.13E-05	7.58E-02	2.55E-01	9.23E-02
DTLZ7	1.70E+01 -	1.72E+01 -	1.67E+01 -	1.50E+01 -	1.73E+01 -	1.73E+01 -	1.73E+01
	9.88E-01	7.16E-01	1.48E+00	2.79E+00	2.14E+00	3.27E-02	1.37E-02
WFG1	4.30E+01-	8.03E+01 -	4.31E+01-	4.34E+01 -	5.42E+01 ~	5.19E+01 -	5.41E+01
	1.02E+00	2.57E+00	1.02E+00	9.65E-01	1.49E+00	1.82E+00	1.47E+00
WFG2	9.67E+01 -	9.97E+01+	9.64E+01-	9.65E+01 -	9.67E+01 -	9.96E+01 +	9.75E+01
	5.39E-01	2.78E-01	6.44E-01	5.81E-01	1.04E+00	2.45E-01	6.68E-01
WFG3	7.20E+01 -	7.46E+01 +	7.15E+01 -	7.16E+01 -	7.35E+01 -	7.49E+01 +	7.39E+01
	6.51E-01	2.70E-01	7.42E-01	5.50E-01	6.27E-01	3.15E-01	5.54E-01
WFG4	6.98E+01 -	7.36E+01 -	6.96E+01 -	6.98E+01 -	7.37E+07 -	7.35E+01 -	7.39E+01
	6.99E-01	4.07E-01	6.81E-01	2.47E+09	4.09E-01	6.13E-01	2.63E-01
WFG5	7.03E+01 -	7.24E+01+	7.02E+01-	7.04E+01-	7.07E+01 -	7.20E+01 +	7.09E+01
	5.34E-01	3.94E-01	5.87E-01	5.44E-01	2.92E-01	3.79E-01	4.21E-01
WFG6	7.15E+01-	7.14E+01-	7.16E+01-	7.17E+01-	7.16E+01 -	7.15E+01 -	7.17E+01
	4.52E-01	1.14E+00	3.65E-01	7.83E-01	6.16E-01	6.54E-01	4.78E-01
WFG7	7.24E+01-	7.42E+01 ~	7.21E+01 -	7.23E+01 -	7.42E+01 ~	7.42E+01 ~	7.42E+01
	3.66E-01	2.49E-01	4.22E-01	3.39E-01	1.22E-01	3.29E-01	2.21E-01
WFG8	6.58E+01 -	6.94E+01 -	6.52E+01 -	6.55E+01 -	7.12E+01~	7.00E+01 -	7.12E+01
	6.94E-01	4.39E-01	9.41E-01	9.21E-01	5.26E-01	4.42E-01	2.54E-01
WFG9	6.99E+01 -	6.92E+01 -	6.92E+01 -	6.88E+01 -	7.14E+01 +	7.08E+01 +	7.03E+01
	1.82E+00	9.07E-01	1.04E+00	1.04E+00	1.63E+00	1.18E+00	1.21E+00

Table 3. Comparison of the hypervolume values between MOAISDX and four recent MOAISs and two MOEAs on DTLZ1 with three to ten objectives. The symbols $+, -, \sim$ indicate whether a result is better, worse or similar.

Dimensionality/Algorithm	BCD-MOIA	HEIA	MOIA-DCSS	VD-MOIA	NSGA2	MOEA/D	MOAISDX
3D	7.64E+00 - 1.05E+00	7.97E+00 ~ 5.40E-04	7.72E+00 - 9.17E-01	7.74E+00 - 8.20E-01	7.97E+00 + 6.07E-04	7.97E+00 ~ 1.40E-04	7.97E+00 2.61E-04
4D	9.46E+00 - 5.22E+00	1.60E+01 ~ 2.45E-02	1.12E+01 - 4.33E+00	9.46E+00 - 5.22E+00	1.55E+01 - 2.19E-02	1.60E+01 - 4.82E-05	1.60E+01 9.85E-04
5D	2.70E+01 - 6.96E+00	3.17E+01 - 2.15E+00	2.93E+01 - 4.95E+00	2.77E+01 - 5.96E+00	0.00E+00 - 0.00E+00	3.19E+01 - 4.28E-02	3.19E+01 2.15E-02
6D	4.46E+01 - 1.58E+01	5.73E+01 - 1.29E+01	5.63E+01 - 1.07E+01	4.34E+01 - 1.26E+01	0.00E+00 - 0.00E+00	6.32E+01 - 4.23E-01	6.37E+01 1.32E-01
7D	3.85E+01 - 4.20E+01	9.28E+01 - 4.21E+01	1.18E+02 - 1.73E+01	3.54E+01 - 4.15E+01	0.00E+00 - 0.00E+00	1.27E+02 - 1.07E+00	1.28E+02 1.99E-01
8D	1.77E+02 - 6.65E+01	1.19E+02 - 9.25E+01	2.40E+02 - 2.61E+01	2.03E+02 - 5.80E+01	0.00E+00 - 0.00E+00	2.56E+02 ~ 4.82E-01	2.56E+02 2.14E-01
9D	3.12E+02 - 1.32E+02	1.14E+02 - 1.53E+02	4.45E+02 - 8.76E+01	3.19E+02 - 1.36E+02	0.00E+00 - 0.00E+00	5.12E+02 + 7.34E-02	5.11E+02 2.74E-01
10D	5.78E+02 - 2.61E+02	2.72E+02 - 3.09E+02	8.94E+02 - 1.76E+02	6.54E+02 - 2.49E+02	0.00E+00 - 0.00E+00	1.02E+03 ~ 2.18E-01	1.02E+03 1.65E-01

5 Conclusions

In this work, we introduced a new multi-objective artificial immune system algorithm based on decomposition (MOAISDX), in which we preserved the immune components through specialized operators and mechanisms. Our proposed cloning operator uses cosine similarity to compute the number of clones or replicas assigned to each member of the population, aiming to produce more copies of those with the highest affinities, that is, the ones that are close to the reference vectors when filling up the population of clones. Positive and negative selection attempt to overcome the loss of diversity that cloning introduces by regulating the number of identical individuals along the search.

Our experimental results showed that our proposed MOAISDX is capable of dealing with complex test problems. MOAISDX shows, in general, a similar or even better performance than NSGA-II and MOEA/D and it outperforms state-of-the-art MOAISs in most of the test problems adopted.

As part of our future work, we are interested in exploring different cloning schemes in which we take into consideration other metrics for clone assignment. We are also interested in studying the role of negative selection in the context of available clone solutions. The role of mutation in MOAISDX is clearly, very important, since it is the main source of diversity in the algorithm and, therefore, studying alternative mutation schemes is also an interesting path for future research.

References

1. Hernández Gómez, R.: Parallel Hyper-Heuristics for Multi-Objective Optimization. Ph.D. thesis, Department of Computer Science, CINVESTAV-IPN, Mexico City, México (2018)
2. Blank, J., Deb, K., Dhebar, Y., Bandaru, S., Seada, H.: Generating well-spaced points on a unit simplex for evolutionary many-objective optimization. IEEE Trans. Evol. Comput. **25**(1), 48–60 (2021)
3. Das, I., Dennis, J.E.: Normal-boundary intersection: a new method for generating the pareto surface in nonlinear multicriteria optimization problems. SIAM J. Optim. **8**(3), 631–657 (1998)
4. De Castro, L.N., Von Zuben, F.J.: Learning and optimization using the clonal selection principle. IEEE Trans. Evol. Comput. **6**(3), 239–251 (2002)
5. Deb, K., Goyal, M., et al.: A combined genetic adaptive search (GeneAS) for engineering design. Comput. Sci. Inf. **26**, 30–45 (1996)
6. Deb, K., Pratap, A., Agarwal, S., Meyarivan, T.: A fast and elitist multiobjective genetic algorithm: NSGA-II. IEEE Trans. Evol. Comput. **6**(2), 182–197 (2002)
7. Deb, K., Thiele, L., Laumanns, M., Zitzler, E.: Scalable Test Problems for Evolutionary Multi-Objective Optimization. Technical Report 112, Computer Engineering and Networks Laboratory (TIK), Swiss Federal Institute of Technology (ETH), Zurich, Switzerland (2001)
8. Durillo, J.J., Nebro, A.J.: jMetal: a java framework for multi-objective optimization. Adv. Eng. Softw. **42**(10), 760–771 (2011)
9. Gong, M., Jiao, L., Du, H., Bo, L.: Multiobjective immune algorithm with nondominated neighbor-based selection. Evol. Comput. **16**(2), 225–255 (2008)
10. Huband, S., Barone, L., While, L., Hingston, P.: A scalable multi-objective test problem toolkit. In: Coello Coello, C.A., Hernández Aguirre, A., Zitzler, E. (eds.) EMO 2005. LNCS, vol. 3410, pp. 280–295. Springer, Heidelberg (2005). https://doi.org/10.1007/978-3-540-31880-4_20
11. Li, H., Zhang, Q.: Multiobjective optimization problems with complicated pareto sets, MOEA/D and NSGA-II. IEEE Trans. Evol. Comput. **13**(2), 284–302 (2009)
12. Li, L., Lin, Q., Li, K., Ming, Z.: Vertical distance-based clonal selection mechanism for the multiobjective immune algorithm. Swarm Evol. Comput. **63**, 100886 (2021)
13. Li, L., Lin, Q., Liu, S., Gong, D., Coello Coello, C.A., Ming, Z.: A novel multi-objective immune algorithm with a decomposition-based clonal selection. Appl. Soft Comput. **81**, 105490 (2019)
14. Li, L., Lin, Q., Ming, Z.: A survey of artificial immune algorithms for multi-objective optimization. Neurocomputing **489**, 211–229 (2022)
15. Li, L., Lin, W., Lin, Q., Ming, Z.: Balancing convergence and diversity in multi-objective immune algorithm. In: 2020 12th International Conference on Advanced Computational Intelligence (ICACI), pp. 102–109 (2020)
16. Lin, Q., et al.: A hybrid evolutionary immune algorithm for multiobjective optimization problems. IEEE Trans. Evol. Comput. **20**(5), 711–729 (2016)
17. Lin, Q., et al.: A multi-objective immune algorithm with dynamic population strategy. Swarm Evol. Comput. **50**, 100477 (2019)
18. Miettinen, K.: Nonlinear Multiobjective Optimization, vol. 12. Springer, Heidelberg (1999)
19. Perelson, A.S., Oster, G.F.: Theoretical studies of clonal selection: minimal antibody repertoire size and reliability of self-non-self discrimination. J. Theor. Biol. **81**(4), 645–670 (1979)
20. Shang, R., Jiao, L., Liu, F., Ma, W.: A novel immune clonal algorithm for MO problems. IEEE Trans. Evol. Comput. **16**(1), 35–50 (2012)

21. Zhang, Q., Li, H.: MOEA/D: a multiobjective evolutionary algorithm based on decomposition. IEEE Trans. Evol. Comput. **11**(6), 712–731 (2007)
22. Zhang, Q., Liu, W., Li, H.: The performance of a new version of MOEA/D on CEC09 unconstrained MOP test instances. In: 2009 IEEE Congress on Evolutionary Computation (CEC'2009), pp. 203–208. IEEE Press, Trondheim (2009)
23. Zitzler, E.: Evolutionary Algorithms for Multiobjective Optimization: Methods and Applications. Ph.D. thesis, Swiss Federal Institute of Technology (ETH), Zurich, Switzerland (1999)
24. Zitzler, E., Deb, K., Thiele, L.: Comparison of Multiobjective Evolutionary Algorithms: Empirical Results. Technical Report 70, Computer Engineering and Networks Laboratory (TIK), Swiss Federal Institute of Technology (ETH) Zurich, Gloriastrasse 35, CH-8092 Zurich, Switzerland (1999)

PAES-25: Local Search, Archiving, and Multi/Many-Objective Pseudo-Boolean Functions

Joshua Knowles[1]([✉]) and Arnaud Liefooghe[2]

[1] SLB, Cambridge, Cambridgeshire, UK
`joshua.knowles@manchester.ac.uk`
[2] LISIC, Université du Littoral Côte d'Opale, Calais, France
`arnaud.liefooghe@univ-littoral.fr`

Abstract. Twenty-five years on from the original Pareto archived evolution strategy (PAES), we present and investigate an updated version (PAES-25), revisiting the algorithmic components of the mutation operator, acceptance criterion, and archiver, focusing on bit-string represented multi- and many- objective optimization problems. The original PAES, particularly the (1+1)-PAES, was intended as a "baseline" algorithm against which EMO algorithms (emerging at the time) with more parameters and the use of a population might be compared. PAES-25, which remains very simple, may serve similar purposes today, and may also help in developing our understanding of local search dynamics on multi-objective landscapes. Using LOTZ as a benchmark, and introducing three multi/many-objective variants, LITZ, sLITZ and FRITZ (up to 8 objectives here), the best performing PAES-25 configuration emerges as one using the multilevel grid archiver, a $1/n$ per-bit standard mutation, and original acceptance criterion (which accepts "neutral" search moves). We find no need for the use of hypervolume-based archiving, which is more computationally expensive, and generally recommend against an unbounded archive. Just as the original (1+1)-PAES has proven useful in developing purely Pareto-based hybrid EMO algorithms, as well as Pareto optimization local search algorithms like simulated annealing and tabu search variants, so should PAES-25, while now benefiting from an archiving component suitable for many-objective problems. We publish our functions, code, and results to facilitate future community benchmarking efforts.

Keywords: PAES · Pareto archived evolution strategy · local search · neighbourhoods · archiving · LOTZ function · benchmarking · many-objective methods

Supplementary Information The online version contains supplementary material available at https://doi.org/10.1007/978-981-96-3506-1_5.

1   Introduction

It is good to take stock periodically and reflect on the progress of the EMO field since its beginnings in 1985 (with VEGA [22]), through later periods of growth, proliferation of algorithms, and then integration, to where we are today. Many early ideas of the field are still found in modern algorithms, but hypothetically there has been development in theory and algorithm design that should result in improved performance—on benchmarks and hopefully in practice. Meanwhile, today's benchmarking studies are more extensive and thorough than in earlier times: they benefit from greater computational power, improvements to performance assessment, and more sophisticated test functions.

So how would an older evolutionary multi-objective optimization (EMO) algorithm fare when using some of the modern infrastructure (both algorithmic components and benchmarking methods) of today? We consider the (1+1)-PAES algorithm developed in 1999–2000 [6,10]. Rather than conducting a large benchmarking study against many of today's algorithms (which we leave for later work or invite others to pursue), we revisit the algorithm in its original form and also explore a small number of the most important potential improvements available today (without detracting from the essential core algorithm).

A key aspect of our study considers modern archiving theory and algorithms for multi-objective optimization. A recent 25-year survey [15] indicates that archiving theory started with PAES and related papers, and has developed gradually since then to have a broad impact. How can modern theory and algorithms inform and explain the performance of PAES when updating the original algorithm to incorporate alternative archivers available today? Additionally, we consider alternatives for the acceptance function in PAES, as well as the mutation (or neighbourhood) operator, drawing insights from recent research.

We call the resulting algorithm framework PAES-25 to mark the 25th anniversary of PAES. The original (1+1)-PAES algorithm was developed primarily as a response to the question, 'what is the simplest, nontrivial equivalent of a random mutation hill climber for multi-objective optimization?'. The origin of this question is less familiar today, especially to younger researchers. At the time, it was something of a preoccupation of the (single-objective) EA field to try to "prove" the advantage of population-based methods (especially with crossover) over simple random mutation hill climbers [19]—and this turned out to be somewhat difficult to do. The authors of the original PAES wondered if the EMO algorithms of the time (MOGA, NPGA, original NSGA) would equally be on firm ground (or not) against a well thought-out simple hill climber for multi-objective problems (if one could be designed). The PAES paper (2000) investigated the (1+1)-PAES against similar algorithms with a population, i.e., $(\mu+\lambda)$ and (μ, λ) PAES variants, and the aforementioned EMO algorithms (also augmented with elitism and archiving). The result was that (1+1)-PAES fared rather well even though it had no mating population, did not ever select from the archive, and used only 1+1 random mutation-based search.

Although (1+1)-PAES performed comparatively well in the original study, it is to be expected that it might not work so well on many-objective optimization problems commonly considered today. Wishing to study the new PAES framework in relatively simple terms to begin with, we focus on discrete pseudo-Boolean functions with well-characterised (or derivable) properties that facilitate empirical analysis. For two-objective problems, we use the LOTZ function [13]. We also introduce new multi- or many-objective generalizations of the function (in Sect. 3). This allows us to study the behaviour of PAES in this more challenging setting and potentially also encouraging (EMO) running time theory, which has developed significantly in the period 2002–present.

Notwithstanding the original question that PAES was designed to answer (i.e., to propose a baseline against which EMO algorithms might be compared), it evidently emerged with several other uses. Hill climbers (or neighbourhood searchers) are components in many other meta-heuristics including tabu search, multi-start and iterated local search, simulated annealing, variable neighbourhood search, and memetic algorithms (a.k.a., hybrid EAs). The first author's PhD thesis [9] proposed and investigated some of these variants of PAES (which uses Pareto comparisons only) for multi-objective optimization. The memetic variant M-PAES [11] was also later published in the literature.

Moreover, as (1+1)-PAES continued to perform rather well even in later studies (e.g., [3]), it serves not only as a baseline method for EMO algorithms to (try to) outperform in benchmarking studies, it also has some relevance as a method for use in practice. It has been included in several third-party software packages such as jMetal [21] or PlatEMO [23]. Arguably, such an algorithm with few parameters to tune and well-understood behaviour can be a useful choice for the "consumer", to complement population-based methods with crossover that might require more tailoring to the target problem, or extensive tuning.

Algorithm 1. PAES-25 (as original (1+1)-PAES but with plug-in archiver and neighbourhood)

Require: MO function $\mathbf{f}$, stopping criterion, neighbourhood
Require: archiver, acceptance rule, archive hyperparameter(s)   ▷ see Sect. 2.1
  $A \leftarrow \emptyset$
  Initialize a single current solution x
  $A \leftarrow A \cup \{(x, \mathbf{f}(x))\}$
  while stopping criterion not met **do**
    $x' \leftarrow \text{neighbour}(x)$ ▷ see Sect. 2.2
    ArchiveUpdate($A, (x', \mathbf{f}(x'))$)
    if x' entered $A \wedge$ optional acceptance condition met **then**   ▷ see Sect. 2.3
      $x \leftarrow x'$
    end if
  end while
  return(A)

---

2   The PAES-25 Algorithm Framework

The PAES-25 framework proposed here in Algorithm 1 is identical to the original (1+1)-PAES provided that: (i) adaptive grid archiving (AGA) is used as the archiver, (ii) mutation is per-bit random mutation, and (iii) the acceptance rule always accepts a solution that has entered the archive. However, PAES-25 expands on this by including alternative choices for the archiver, mutation type, and acceptance rule (defined below).

2.1 Archivers

The primary purpose of archiving is to preserve nondominated solutions. (In PAES, this archive is also used to help make acceptance/rejection decisions). An unbounded archiver (**UNB**) stores all such solutions. However, the archive can grow exponentially with the problem dimensions. To prevent this growth, a bounding mechanism can limit the archive size. Given an archive A and a maximum size μ, a bounded archiver returns a subset $A' \subseteq A$ such that $|A'| \leqslant \mu$; see [8,15,17]. PAES-25 can be used with UNB or with a bounded archiver, the following three being examples we recommend (and later study).

AGA: The adaptive grid archiver defined in [10] for the original (1+1)-PAES algorithm overlays a grid (or hypergrid) over the points in the current PF approximation in the archive. When the archive is full but a new point is nondominated, it admits the new point but removes one from a most-crowded grid cell, breaking ties randomly. AGA was further analysed in [7], where a form of convergence was proved under mild conditions (for bi-objective problems).

HVA: Archiving aimed at maximizing the hypervolume of the PF approximation was first proposed in [7,9] and was the EMO field's first use of hypervolume for selection (here environmental selection) according to Bader [2]. When the archive is full and a new point is nondominated, HVA determines which of the $\mu + 1$ points contributes the least to the hypervolume. If the new point is the smallest contributor, it is discarded. Otherwise, it is admitted to the archive, replacing the least hypervolume contributor.

MGA: The multi-level grid archiver was first proposed in [14] and later analysed theoretically and empirically in [17]. Notably, MGA and HVA are the only known archivers that meet a number of desirable convergence properties (see ibid. for details and also [15]). In particular, they admit solutions outside the objective space region that dominates the current archive. Moreover, their rules ensure that each subsequent archive is at least as good as previous ones in terms of Pareto dominance. HVA and MGA were also considered in [18] for characterizing attraction points in multi-objective local search.

2.2 Mutation or Neighbourhood Operators

As alternative choices of mutation suitable for pseudo-Boolean functions, we consider the following three:

k-flip: Precisely k bits are flipped, chosen uniformly at random and with replacement (i.e., no memory of previous flips is used). We use $k = 1$ here.

rate = 1/n: Standard bit mutation with rate $1/n$; each bit is independently flipped with that probability, allowing for 1 or more bits to be flipped. (We do not allow 0 bits to be flipped in our implementation).

fast: A mixture distribution with heavy tails is used to first select the number k of bits to flip [4]. Then, the k-flip operator is applied. We follow the original setting, using a power-law distribution with $\beta = 1.5$.

2.3 Acceptance Rules

The standard acceptance rule of PAES-25 is to accept a solution if it has entered the archive, even if an equivalent solution (i.e., with same point) already existed in the archive. We call this approach "**neutral**" because it enables movement along neutral fitness plateaus. The alternative is to accept a solution only if it has both entered the archive and is unique within it. We label this "**strict**".

3 Multi/Many-Objective Pseudo-Boolean Test Functions

The use of test functions for the analysis of (proposed) EMO algorithms dates back to at least the mid-90 s (see, e.g., [20]). Test function properties include the coding system used (binary, integer, or continuous variables), the number of objectives, and whether they are of "real-world" origin (e.g., derived from NP-hard problems [5] such as [16]) or of more theoretical interest. For theoretical problems, it is usually possible to establish the complete Pareto front (and Pareto set), allowing close analysis of algorithm performance. Further properties of interest include whether the function is scalable in the number of variables and/or objectives, correlations between objectives [18,24], uni-modality vs. multi-modality, and other specific difficulties the function captures or emphasises (such as search bias).

LOTZ [13]

The LOTZ (Leading Ones Trailing Zeros) function introduced in [13] is a two-objective binary-variable unimodal problem with a scalable variable space. It has known Pareto front and set, and presents the difficulty that the Pareto front size scales linearly with the number of variables. LOTZ is also more complex than a simple counting-ones counting-zeros function where every string is Pareto optimal. It has been a favourite for advancing the theoretical analysis of EMO algorithms. We provide its definition below, closely following its original wording.

Definition 1. *The pseudo-Boolean function* LOTZ $\{0,1\}^n \rightarrow \mathbb{N}^2$ *is computed as:*

$$\text{LOTZ}(\mathbf{x}) = \left(\sum_{i=1}^{n} \prod_{j=1}^{i} x_j, \ \sum_{i=1}^{n} \prod_{j=i}^{n} (1 - x_j) \right) \quad .$$

A multi-objective version of the LOTZ function, mLOTZ [12], works by essentially copy-pasting the original LOTZ function multiple times along the string, i.e., by creating $m/2$ separate (separable) competing pairs of objectives. Interestingly, these pairs of objectives do not actually compete against each other. The function has also been of theoretical interest, even recently [25].

3.1 LITZ

The function we introduce, LITZ (standing for Leading Integers Trailing Zeros), is intended as an alternative multi-objective generalization of LOTZ.

Definition 2. *Assuming there are $m \in 2^p, p > 2$ objectives, then the solution vector $\mathbf{x}$ is interpreted as an integer vector of length n/p, with each contiguous run of p bits defining the integer using standard binary encoding. The objectives are then calculated as follows:*

$$\mathrm{LI}_k(\mathbf{x}) = \sum_{i=1}^{n/p} \prod_{j=1}^{i} \mathrm{I}(\mathrm{bin}_p((x_{j'}) = k)), \quad k = 1, 2, \ldots, 2^p - 1, \quad j' = p \cdot (j-1) + 1 ,$$

where $\mathrm{I}(.)$ is the indicator function, and $\mathrm{bin}_p(x_{j'})$ returns the integer number corresponding to the binary value of the next p bits of $\mathbf{x}$ starting at index j'. The last objective is for trailing zeros:

$$\mathrm{TZ} = \sum_{i=1}^{n/p} \prod_{j=i}^{n/p} \mathrm{I}(\mathrm{bin}_p((x_{j'}) = 0)), \quad j' = p \cdot (j-1) + 1 .$$

The observant reader may notice that LITZ captures some of the essence of LOTZ while having the property that at most one of the "leading integer" objectives can be non-zero for any bit string. We provide further properties of LITZ in Sect. 3.4.

3.2 sLITZ

To overcome the limitation on the number of objectives that can have non-zero values simultaneously (2 for LITZ), we introduce a variation below.

Definition 3. *The function sLITZ (standing for shuffled LITZ) is defined similarly to LITZ, except that the counts for the "leading" integers use a different permutation of the indexes of $\mathbf{x}$ for each objective. To keep the function regular, we choose permutations with starting points (from which to count leading integers) at $sp_k = 1 + n \cdot p \cdot ((k-1)/(m-1))$ on the binary coded string. For example, in a 4-objective sLITZ (which has 3 leading integers), the leading 1s are counted from position 1, but leading 3s are counted after position 2/4 of the way along the string. The remaining indexes shift accordingly modulo n, i.e., the permuted index i' of objective k is $1 + ((i + sp_k - 1) \bmod n)$.*

3.3 FRITZ

We introduce a last function, FRITZ, which stands for "First Run of Integers, Trailing Zeros."

Definition 4. FR_k *for $k \in \{1, \ldots, m-1\}$ is the length of the first run of consecutive integers k encountered, regardless of its starting position. "First" here means counting from the bits encoding the first integer in increasing order. The TZ objective is computed as for LITZ.*

3.4 Analysis of the Pareto Fronts of LITZ, sLITZ and FRITZ

Theorem 1 (PF of LITZ). *The Pareto front of LITZ consists of the following set of points:*

$$\{(0, 0, \ldots, 0, n/p), (1, 0, \ldots, 0, n/p - 1), \ldots, (2, 0, \ldots, 0, n/p - 2),$$
$$\ldots, (n/p, 0, \ldots, 0, 0), (0, 1, \ldots, 0, n/p - 1), \ldots,$$
$$(0, 2, \ldots, 0, n/p - 2), \ldots, (0, n/p, \ldots, 0, 0), \ldots\}$$

Proof. It follows from the Pareto front of LOTZ and the definition of LITZ that each of the $m - 1$ objectives coding for non-zero integers takes the role of the 1 s in LOTZ. Since only one of these objectives can be "leading", all the other $m - 1$ of these has an evaluation of 0.

Theorem 2 (PF of sLITZ). *The Pareto front of sLITZ is a set of points that contains a number of subsets that are easily enumerable. The first such subset is $\{(f_1, \ldots, f_m) \mid \sum_{i=1}^{m} f_i = n/p, \quad \exists i, f_i = n/p\}$, representing each objective's maximum score, with a score of zero for all other objectives. A second subset of the PF comprises all two-objective trade-offs between the first sLI objective and TZ: $\{(f_1, 0, \ldots, 0, f_m) \mid f_1 + f_m = n/p\}$. Also a member of the PF is the "balanced point" $((n/p)/m, (n/p)/m, \ldots, (n/p)/m)$. Other members of the PF depend upon more intricate conflicts between objectives; for example, $f_{m-1} = sLI_{m-1} + f_m = TZ \leq 2 \cdot (n/p)/m$ if $f_{m-1} > 0$ but certain other combinations for the other objectives can make up the sum of objectives to be n/p.*

Proof. Proof is omitted due to length considerations. We have constructed the PF algorithmically for the 96-bit problem and the 4- and 8-objective cases examined below.

Theorem 3 (PF of FRITZ). *The Pareto front of FRITZ is the set of points defined by $\{(k_1, \ldots, k_m) \mid \sum_{i=1}^{m} k_i = n/p, \quad \forall i, k_i \in 0..n/p\}$.*

Proof. It is clear that no run of positive integers or zeros can be greater than n/p, the length of the decoded binary string. Further, any of the positive integers or zero can be repeated throughout the length of the entire string. To obtain a member of the Pareto front starting from the all zeros string, simply substitute some of the zeros with runs of integers, starting from the left of the string, and never repeating a run of an integer already counted. Each substituted zero will be subtracting from the TZ objective while adding one to one of the FRI objectives.

We omit the characterization of the Pareto sets (the decision space pre-image of the PF) of each function due to space limitations.

4   Experimental Study and Results

We run several alternative variants of PAES-25 on a selection of the test functions presented above, as described in Table 1.

Table 1. Key parameter settings of our experiments. We ran all combinations of the settings shown, at different archive sizes (50, 100, 200 and 500), with 30 independent runs on each problem. Results are reported at different time steps, up to 2^{17} evaluations. In all cases, $n = 96$ bits.

Function		archivers	acceptance	mutation
LOTZ	$m = 2$	AGA, MGA, HVA, UNB	strict, neutral	1-flip, rate $= 1/n$, fast
LITZ	$m = 4$	MGA, HVA, UNB	strict, neutral	1-flip, rate $= 1/n$, fast
sLITZ	$m = 4$	MGA, HVA, UNB	strict, neutral	1-flip, rate $= 1/n$, fast
FRITZ	$m = 4$	MGA, HVA, UNB	strict, neutral	1-flip, rate $= 1/n$, fast
LITZ	$m = 8$	MGA, UNB	strict, neutral	1-flip, rate $= 1/n$, fast
sLITZ	$m = 8$	MGA, UNB	strict, neutral	1-flip, rate $= 1/n$, fast
FRITZ	$m = 8$	MGA, UNB	strict, neutral	1-flip, rate $= 1/n$, fast

Figure 1 displays matrix plots of the results for the 2- and 4-objective problems, excluding FRITZ. The columns represent LOTZ, LITZ, and sLITZ, respectively. From top to bottom, the plots show: relative deviation of the current archive from the PF in terms of hypervolume (lower is better, with 0 indicating the entire PF has been found), archive size, number of encountered Pareto-optimal points, number of Pareto-optimal points in the current archive, number of accepted moves, last accepted move, and sum of objectives from the current solution. All statistics are plotted over time, providing a comprehensive view of algorithm performance.

A number of interesting observations emerge from these results. Most notably, the combination of standard $1/n$ mutation and neutral archiving consistently yields the best (or near-best) performance (assessed by hypervolume) across these problems. 1-flip mutation also performs reasonably well, but pairing it with *strict* acceptance appears to be a dangerous choice. This combination apparently gets stuck on local optima plateaus on many of the problems. Interestingly, fast mutation is not indicated on these functions. However, fast mutation (and $1/n$) are less affected by the choice between the neutral or strict acceptance rule, likely because they can inherently flip multiple bits at once and escape neutral plateaus that way.

Turning our attention to the archiver, we find that for these three problems (LOTZ with $m = 2$, and LITZ and sLITZ with $m = 4$), the choice of archiver is irrelevant. This is because the archive never reaches its chosen bound during the run. Consequently, we omit to show the performance of AGA and HVA for these problems, and to focus on a single archive size for ease of presentation.

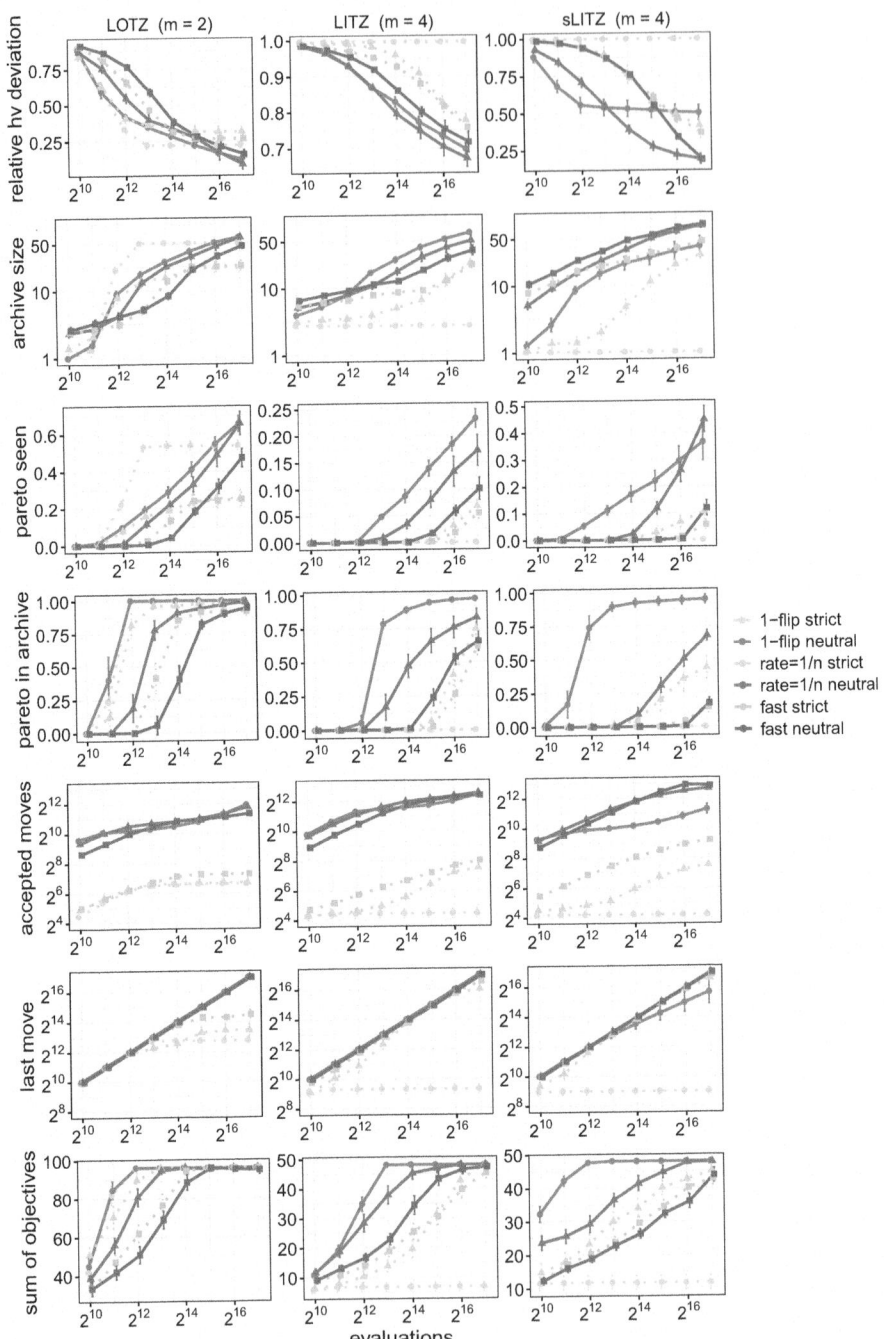

Fig. 1. Mean and 95% confidence intervals from 30 runs for LOTZ (2 objectives), LITZ, and sLITZ (both with 4 objectives) under MGA with a bound of 200.

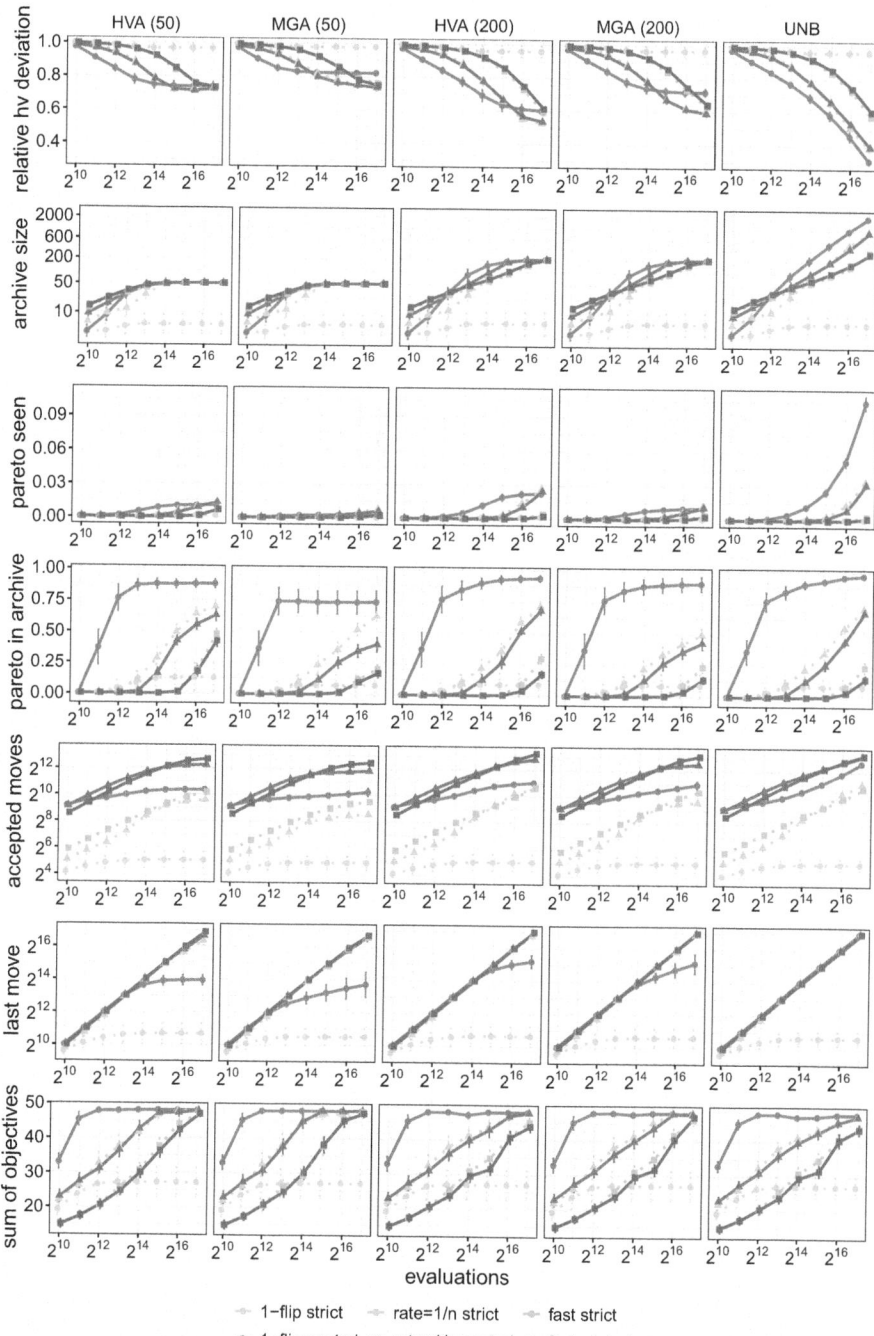

Fig. 2. Mean and 95% confidence intervals from 30 runs for FRITZ with 4 objectives under different archivers and bounds.

However, when looking at Fig. 2 for FRITZ (only) under various archivers and bounds, UNB yields superior performance. We attribute this to the large PF of FRITZ being accessible, especially for 1-flip mutation and neutral acceptance (here 1-flip is best). An unbounded archiver then allows for both a higher number of archived points and larger achieved hypervolumes.

For space reasons, we do not report CPU times for the PAES-25 variants. However, we observed that MGA runs significantly faster than HVA in most problem configurations, even with small archives. The FRITZ problem, in particular, causes substantial overhead for HVA. For the 8-objective problems, we could not complete 30 independent runs after several days, while all other algorithm runs finished within minutes or hours. The UNB archiver is computationally more expensive to update than MGA for FRITZ. This is expected and due to the large number of archived points, which requires numerous Pareto comparisons each time a point is considered for archive entry.

A small sample of the results on the 8-objective problems is given in Fig. 3 under a specific archiver setting. These findings align with previous results, particularly in how 1-flip mutation tends to find more Pareto-optimal solutions than standard mutation, except for sLITZ and FRITZ under larger budgets. A complete set of results are available in the supplementary material at https://doi.org/10.5281/zenodo.13889583.

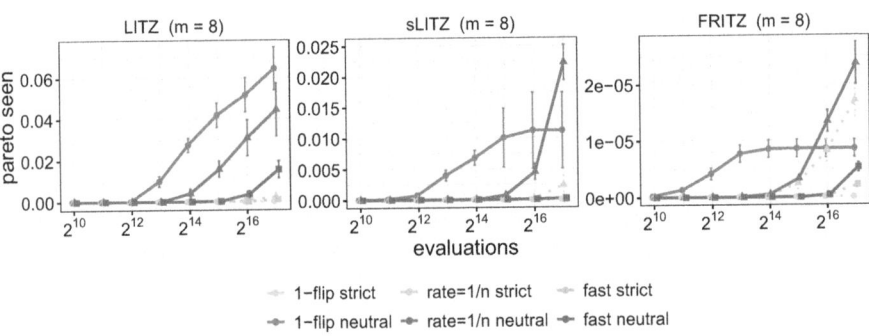

Fig. 3. Mean and 95% confidence intervals from 30 runs for LITZ, sLITZ, and FRITZ with 8 objectives under MGA with a bound of 200.

5   Concluding Discussion

The (1+1)-PAES algorithm [10] was arguably the first multi-objective optimization algorithm designed to work based on local search and Pareto comparisons only [16]. Diversity in the Pareto front approximation is also pursued in PAES through its original archiver (AGA). Its modular design, separating a basic mutation-based hillclimber from comparisons against an archive representing the Pareto front approximation accumulated so far, has since been emulated by many other multi-objective evolutionary and local search algorithms.

Subsequent to the original PAES algorithm, developments in multi-objective evolutionary and local search algorithms have revisited and potentially improved upon some of its components. Meanwhile, there has been increasing interest in so-called many-objective optimization—problems with more than 3 objectives. These developments warrant careful evaluation of progress, which may be facilitated by advances in theory and/or empirical benchmarking methods.

To this end, we have proposed PAES-25, a modular version of PAES that explicitly allows for different choices of archiver, mutation, and acceptance functions. Given this slightly broader framework, how should we select these components? Are these choices straightforward and understandable—at least when properties of the function to be optimized are known?

Our experiments examined simple pseudo-Boolean functions, and even here, the interplay between archiver, mutation and acceptance gave subtly different dynamics depending on the problem. Nevertheless, an overall finding emerged: the combination of a standard $1/n$ mutation and neutral acceptance rule generally provided a stable setting here. A so-called "fast mutation" did not perform well on any of the problems studied here, and this follows expectation. Perhaps the marked drop-off in performance is larger than anticipated, however.

The best choice of archiver is slightly more subtle. AGA was not designed for many objectives, and its convergence proof was only given for the 2-objective case. Arguably, it has been surpassed by later developments, and so we focused on the three other archivers, MGA, HV and UNB. Comparing MGA and HV, we find that MGA performs equally well in interaction with the search process. However, it is significantly less computationally expensive, even when using modern hypervolume computation algorithms.

Between MGA and UNB, the choice seems more a philosophical one—or a personal preference based on context. If you find it acceptable to present potentially billions of solutions to a user, or if you believe that post-processing of a large archive can be done at the end of a run before presenting to a decision maker, then the unbounded archive does sometimes produce better PF approximations than MGA. However, this comes at the cost of increasingly expensive Pareto comparisons as the archive size grows. We did not study here the effect of fast comparison methods that have been proposed elsewhere [1], so this observation needs qualification and further investigation. However, we note that on a function like FRITZ, we did not finish approximating the PF even in 2^{17} function evaluations. Given these considerations, we can tentatively say that MGA seems an excellent compromise and very much aligns with the original PAES algorithm's use of a fast, cell-based archiver to approximate the PF discovered.

Given the popularity and longevity of the original (1+1)-PAES, we believe that this new updated version, PAES-25, may be an important algorithm for future study. We have generalized it, with MGA, to an algorithm that we have demonstrated works on many-objective problems. Our initial findings also show neutral acceptance and standard $1/n$ mutation are good choices generally. This results in an algorithm with very few parameters and low coding complexity.

We hope that PAES-25 will find a place in future theoretical and benchmarking studies as a baseline. We also expect it to be a useful and valuable addition to some of the popular EMO packages (mentioned previously). Facilitating further study, we have made results and benchmarks available at https://doi.org/10.5281/zenodo.13889583.

Acknowledgements. JK wishes to thank SLB for supporting the publication of this work. JK also acknowledges the contributions of David Corne to the original PAES and related work, and thanks him for useful discussions. Both authors gratefully acknowledge the Lorentz center workshop on Benchmarking in Multi-Criteria Optimization (BeMCO 2024), which sparked initial discussions for this paper.

Disclosure of Interests. The authors have no competing interests to declare that are relevant to the content of this article.

References

1. Allmendinger, R., Jaszkiewicz, A., Liefooghe, A., Tammer, C.: What if we increase the number of objectives? theoretical and empirical implications for many-objective combinatorial optimization. Comput. Oper. Res. **145**, 105857 (2022). https://doi.org/10.1016/j.cor.2022.105857
2. Bader, J.M.: Hypervolume-based search for multiobjective optimization: theory and methods. Ph.D. thesis, ETH Zurich (2010)
3. Coello Coello, C.A.: Evolutionary multi-objective optimization: a historical view of the field. IEEE Comput. Intell. Mag. **1**(1), 28–36 (2006)
4. Doerr, B., Le, H.P., Makhmara, R., Nguyen, T.D.: Fast genetic algorithms. In: Proceedings of the Genetic and Evolutionary Computation Conference, pp. 777–784 (2017)
5. Garey, M., Johnson, D.: Computers and intractability: a guide to the theory of NP-Completeness. WH Freeman and Co. (1979)
6. Knowles, J., Corne, D.: The Pareto archived evolution strategy: a new baseline algorithm for pareto multiobjective optimisation. In: Proceedings of the 1999 Congress on Evolutionary Computation-CEC99 (Cat. No. 99TH8406), vol. 1, pp. 98–105. IEEE (1999)
7. Knowles, J., Corne, D.: Properties of an adaptive archiving algorithm for storing nondominated vectors. IEEE Trans. Evol. Comput. **7**(2), 100–116 (2003)
8. Knowles, J., Corne, D.: Bounded pareto archiving: Theory and practice. In: Metaheuristics for multiobjective optimisation, pp. 39–64, Springer, Heidelberg (2004)
9. Knowles, J.D.: Local Search and Hybrid Evolutionary Algorithms for Pareto Optimization. Ph.D. thesis, Department of Computer Science, University of Reading, UK (2002)
10. Knowles, J.D., Corne, D.: Approximating the nondominated front using the Pareto archived evolution strategy. Evol. Comput. **8**(2), 149–172 (2000). https://doi.org/10.1162/106365600568167
11. Knowles, J.D., Corne, D.: M-PAES: a memetic algorithm for multiobjective optimization. In: Proceedings of the 2000 Congress on Evolutionary Computation (CEC'00), pp. 325–332. IEEE Press, Piscataway (2000)

12. Laumanns, M., Thiele, L., Zitzler, E.: Running time analysis of multiobjective evolutionary algorithms on pseudo-boolean functions. IEEE Trans. Evol. Comput. **8**(2), 170–182 (2004)

13. Laumanns, M., Thiele, L., Zitzler, E., Welzl, E., Deb, K.: Running time analysis of multi-objective evolutionary algorithms on a simple discrete optimization problem. In: Guervós, J.J.M., Adamidis, P., Beyer, H.-G., Schwefel, H.-P., Fernández-Villacañas, J.-L. (eds.) PPSN 2002. LNCS, vol. 2439, pp. 44–53. Springer, Heidelberg (2002). https://doi.org/10.1007/3-540-45712-7_5

14. Laumanns, M., Zenklusen, R.: Stochastic convergence of random search methods to fixed size pareto front approximations. Eur. J. Oper. Res. **213**(2), 414–421 (2011)

15. Li, M., López-Ibáñez, M., Yao, X.: Multi-objective archiving. IEEE Trans. Evol. Comput. **28**, 696–717 (2024)

16. Liefooghe, A., Humeau, J., Mesmoudi, S., Jourdan, L., Talbi, E.G.: On dominance-based multiobjective local search: design, implementation and experimental analysis on scheduling and traveling salesman problems. J. Heurist. **18**(2), 317–352 (2012). https://doi.org/10.1007/s10732-011-9181-3

17. López-Ibáñez, M., Knowles, J., Laumanns, M.: On sequential online archiving of objective vectors. In: Takahashi, R.H.C., Deb, K., Wanner, E.F., Greco, S. (eds.) EMO 2011. LNCS, vol. 6576, pp. 46–60. Springer, Heidelberg (2011). https://doi.org/10.1007/978-3-642-19893-9_4

18. López-Ibáñez, M., Liefooghe, A., Verel, S.: Local optimal sets and bounded archiving on multi-objective NK-landscapes with correlated objectives. In: Bartz-Beielstein, T., Branke, J., Filipič, B., Smith, J. (eds.) PPSN 2014. LNCS, vol. 8672, pp. 621–630. Springer, Cham (2014). https://doi.org/10.1007/978-3-319-10762-2_61

19. Mitchell, M., Holland, J., Forrest, S.: When will a genetic algorithm outperform hill climbing? Adv. Neural Inf. Process. Syst. **6** (1993)

20. Murata, T., Ishibuchi, H., et al.: MOGA: multi-objective genetic algorithms. In: IEEE International Conference on Evolutionary Computation, vol. 1, pp. 289–294. IEEE, Piscataway (1995)

21. Nebro, A.J., Durillo, J.J., Vergne, M.: Redesigning the jMetal multi-objective optimization framework. In: Jiménez Laredo, J.L., Silva, S., Esparcia-Alcázar, A.I. (eds.) Proceedings of the Genetic and Evolutionary Computation Conference, GECCO Companion 2015, pp. 1093–1100. ACM Press, New York (2015). https://doi.org/10.1145/2739482.2768462

22. Schaffer, J.D.: Some experiments in machine learning using vector evaluated genetic algorithms. Technical report. Vanderbilt Univ., Nashville, TN (USA) (1985)

23. Tian, Y., Cheng, R., Zhang, X., Jin, Y.: PlatEMO: a MATLAB platform for evolutionary multi-objective optimization [educational forum]. IEEE Comput. Intell. Mag. **12**(4), 73–87 (2017). https://doi.org/10.1109/MCI.2017.2742868

24. Verel, S., Liefooghe, A., Jourdan, L., Dhaenens, C.: On the structure of multiobjective combinatorial search space: MNK-landscapes with correlated objectives. Eur. J. Oper. Res. **227**(2), 331–342 (2013)

25. Zheng, W., Doerr, B.: Runtime analysis for the NSGA-II: proving, quantifying, and explaining the inefficiency for many objectives. IEEE Trans. Evol. Comput., (2023). https://doi.org/10.1109/TEVC.2023.3320278

Weights-Guided Random Bit Climber for Binary Many-Objective Optimization

Yudai Tagawa$^{(\boxtimes)}$, Hernán Aguirre , and Kiyoshi Tanaka

Shinshu University, Wakasato, Nagano, Japan
{23hs252c,ahernan,ktanaka}@shinshu-u.ac.jp

Abstract. In this work, we study a multi-start weights-guided random bit climber (wgRBC). This algorithm selects a random weight from a predefined set, and a simple (1+1) random bit climber uses it to optimize, one bit at a time, the weighted sum of the objective functions of the problem until it reaches a local optimum. A population of non-dominated solutions generated during the climb is kept bounded using the set of weights. The algorithm iterates restarting the climber with a solution chosen randomly from the population of non-dominated solutions and selecting another weight randomly. Thus, the weights are used to provide climbing directions and to maintain a set of non-dominated solutions well-distributed in the reference population. We evaluate the method on subclasses of epistatic problems using MNK-landscapes, varying the number of objectives from 2 to 7 and the number of epistatic interactions from 1 to 20. We show that the simple wgRBC is largely superior to decomposition algorithms like MOEA/D and NSGA-III on this problem class.

Keywords: multi-objective optimization · random bit climber · scalarizing function · MNK-landscapes

1 Introduction

Multi-Objective Evolutionary Algorithms (MOEAs) [6,7] have been widely applied to solve real world multi-objective optimization problems. Various types of algorithms have been proposed, particularly for many-objective optimization [14,16]. Preferred approaches to implement selection in MOEAs are decomposition [8,12,20], performance indicators [4,5,10,13,22], and relaxations of Pareto dominance [1,9,15].

In this study, we focus on decomposition-based algorithms, which decompose the multi-objective problem into a number of single-objective problems using scalarizing functions. The single-objective problems are then solved concurrently. Many different scalarizing functions have been suggested in the literature based on different approaches. These functions require parameters or weights and possibly constraints. In most well-known decomposition MOEAs, the weights associated with the scalarizing functions are usually defined in advance and remain

H. Singh et al. (Eds.): EMO 2025, LNCS 15512, pp. 74–87, 2025.
https://doi.org/10.1007/978-981-96-3506-1_6

fixed during the search. To create a set of weights, we assume a distribution of the Pareto optimal front and the algorithm aims to find good solutions that match our assumptions on this distribution. MOEA/D [20] and NSGA-III [8] are well-known decomposition-based MOEAs. In these algorithms, several critical parameters need to be taken into consideration and set appropriately. Some of these parameters are the number of subproblems, the choice of scalarizing function, the weights generation method, and the size of the overlapping neighborhoods in MOEA/D or the recombination parameters such as the distribution index in the SBX operator of NSGA-III when applied to continuous problems.

We aim to develop simpler and more effective MOEAs for binary multi- and many-objective optimization. MOEA/D and NSGA-III have been applied with some success to binary multi-objective optimization problems, usually keeping their selection mechanism as it is and replacing the recombination and mutation operators used for continuous problems with operators appropriate for binary representations. Another class of effective algorithms for binary optimization are the so-called Random Bit-Climbers (RBCs) algorithms. A canonical RBC is a (1+1) elitist algorithm that applies a one-bit flip mutation operator in a randomly chosen position of the parent to create one offspring. Exploration of different bit positions of the parent continues until it finds an offspring that improves the parent. In this case, the offspring replaces the parent, and exploration continues with the new parent. If no offspring improves the parent after exploring all bit positions, then the RBC has found a one-bit local optimum and restarts the search from a previously found solution that has not been climbed or from a solution randomly created. RBCs are a subclass of the family of hill-climbing algorithms. These algorithms perform best on problems with one local optimum, and unimodal functions in the case of continuous problems, but their performance degrades when the landscape contains multiple local optima, plateaus, or ridges, particularly if no restarts are performed [6]. When an RBC is applied to multi-objective optimization, the algorithm keeps a population of non-dominated solutions collected from the solutions visited by the climber, which at the end of the run is returned as the approximation of the Pareto front found by the optimizer. This population is also used as a reference to select the solution from which to restart climbing once a local optimum has been found.

Various versions of RBCs have been studied for multi-objective optimization, with differences arising from the choice of functions being climbed, the criterion used for parent replacement, the way the reference population of non-dominated solutions is updated, the way the solution for restarts is chosen, and whether one climber searches sequentially from one restart to the next or several climbers are applied concurrently. Among them, moRBC [2] uses Pareto dominance between the offspring and the parent as the criterion to replace the parent. So a solution is a local optimum if there is no one-bit neighbor that dominates it. Also, it uses crowding distance to truncate the non-dominated population if it exceeds its maximum size. moRBC works very well in multi-objective problems, but compared to some decomposition-based algorithms, it does not scale up well to many-objective optimization due to its replacement criterion based on Pareto dominance and its crowding distance-based truncation method of the reference population. Distributed Random Bit Climbers (dRBCs) use a number of RBCs to climb concurrently each of the original M objective functions $f_1, \cdots, f_M$, and an additional scalarizing function f_h that computes the solution hypervolume computed as $f_1 \times \cdots \times f_M$ [17,18]. dRBCs have been implemented to simulate a synchronous concurrent search, where in a given search episode all climbers restart from the same solution randomly chosen from the reference population, and update the non-dominated reference population after all of them have reached a local optimum. dRBCs have been shown to scale up significantly better than moRBC for many-objective optimization across a broad range of epistactic problems. Due to their concurrent nature, RBCs in a dRBC can be applied in parallel, though their effects on synchronous or asynchronous parallel environments have not been studied yet.

In this work, we study a multi-start weights-guided RBC (wgRBC). This algorithm first creates a set of reference weights uniformly distributed in objective space [19]. The weights serve two purposes. The first purpose is to provide climbing directions to the (1+1) RBC. Before the RBC starts a search episode, a weight is randomly selected and passed to the RBC, so it will climb the escalarizing function computed as the sum of the weighted values of the original objective functions of the problem. Once a local optimum is found, the RBC will restart from one of the non-dominated solutions collected so far in the reference population, using a different randomly selected weight to climb in another direction. The second purpose is to maintain a set of well-distributed solutions in the non-dominated reference population when it exceeds its maximum size and truncation is required.

In order to understand the characteristics of the studied approach and evaluate its performance on multi-objective binary problems, we use 100 bits MNK-landscapes [3] as benchmark problems, varying the number of objectives M from 2 to 7 and the number of interacting variables K (epistatic interactions) from 1 to 20. We first compare with various dRBC configurations. Then, we compare results with the decomposition-based MOEA/D and NSGA-III, multi-objective bit climber moRBC. We show that wgRBC is superior to the other MOEAs in all numbers of objectives for $K > 1$. MOEA/D is better only on problems 2 and 3 objectives and epistasis $K = 1$. Overall, this work shows that a simpler wgRBC algorithm can be superior to popular but complex decomposition algorithms for multi-objective binary problems.

2   Proposed Method

The weights-guided Random Bit Climber (wgRBC) is a multi-start algorithm that aims to effectively solve binary multi-objective problems by combining the explorative potential of a number of well-defined search directions provided by a scalarizing function and a set of weights with the exploitative power of a Random Bit Climber (RBC). By randomly switching search directions choosing different weights and restarting from non-dominated solutions in each search episode, it balances an extensive exploration of the objective space with local optimization in decision space.

Algorithm 1 summarizes the main steps of wgRBC, which we describe in more detail below.

Data: max number of evaluation T, max population size S
Result: a subset of non-dominated solutions found by the algorithm P
1   $P \leftarrow \{\}$
2   $W \leftarrow$ CreateReferenceWeights(S)
3   $t \leftarrow 0$
4   **while** $t < T$ **do**
5     $\boldsymbol{x}_i \leftarrow$ InitialSolution(P)
6     $\boldsymbol{w}_i \leftarrow rand(W)$
7     $P_i, t_i \leftarrow$ RBC($\boldsymbol{x}_i, \boldsymbol{w}_i, t, T$)
8     $P \leftarrow$ UpdatePopulation(P, P_i, S, W)
9     $t \leftarrow t + t_i$
10   **end**
11   return P

Algorithm 1: Weight-guided Random Bit Climber

Data: start solution $\boldsymbol{x}_i$, weight $\boldsymbol{w}_i$, evaluations so far t, max number of evaluation T
Result: solutions visited by the RBC P_i, number of evaluations expended t_i
1   $P_i \leftarrow \{\boldsymbol{x}_i\}$ /* i indicates the i-th call to RBC */
2   $t_i \leftarrow 0$
3   $E \leftarrow \{\}$ /* explored bit positions */
4   **while** $length(E) < length(\boldsymbol{x}_i)$ **and** $t + t_i < T$ **do**
5     $j \leftarrow rand(1, length(\boldsymbol{x}_i)) \notin E$
6     $\boldsymbol{x}'_i \leftarrow$ Mutate($\boldsymbol{x}_i, j$)
7   Evaluate($\boldsymbol{x}'_i$) /* Compute the solution's objective values $f_1, \cdots, f_M$ */
8     $P_i \leftarrow P_i \cup \{\boldsymbol{x}'_i\}$
9     $E \leftarrow E \cup \{j\}$
10   **if** $g(\boldsymbol{x}'_i, \mathbf{w}_i) > g(\boldsymbol{x}_i, \mathbf{w}_i)$ **then** /* parent replacement based on scalarized values */
11      $\boldsymbol{x}_i \leftarrow \boldsymbol{x}'_i$
12      $E \leftarrow \{\}$
13   **end**
14    $t_i \leftarrow t_i + 1$
15   **end**
16   return P_i, t_i

Algorithm 2: Random Bit Climber

First, the non-dominated solution set P is initialized to empty (line 1), a set of reference weights W is created using the method described in [19] (line 2),

$$W = \{\mathbf{w}_1, \cdots, \mathbf{w}_j, \cdots, \mathbf{w}_S\} \tag{1}$$

$$\mathbf{w}_j = (w_{j,1}, \cdots, w_{j,M}) \text{ subject to } \sum_{k=1}^{M} w_{j,k} = 1 \qquad (2)$$

and the fitness evaluation counter t is set to 0. Next, the algorithm performs several search episodes using a Random Bit Climber until T fitness evaluations have been spent (lines 4–10), returning a bounded population P of the discovered non-dominated solutions (line 11). In each search episode, an initial solution $\boldsymbol{x}_i$ (line 5) is selected randomly from P and passed together with a weight $\mathbf{w}_i$ randomly chosen from W to the random bit climber RBC (line 7). At the beginning, when P is empty, the solution is created randomly and evaluated. The RBC climbs a weighted sum function of the objective values $f_1, \cdots, f_M$ computed with the objective functions of the problem, i.e.

$$g(\boldsymbol{x}, \mathbf{w}_i) = \sum_{k=1}^{M} w_{i,k} \cdot f_k(\boldsymbol{x}), \qquad (3)$$

until it finds a local optimum and returns the visited solutions P_i. The returned P_i population is used to update the bounded population of non-dominated solutions P (line 10). More precisely, we first compute the set of non-dominated solutions from $P \cup P_i$ and assign it to P. Then, if the updated set P exceeds the maximum population size S, we truncate it to size S, or less, using the set of reference weights W. Here, for each weights vector $\mathbf{w}_j \in W$ (Eq. 1,2), we select for survival the individual from P with maximum scalar value g, expressed by

$$\max_{\boldsymbol{x} \in P} g(\boldsymbol{x}, \mathbf{w}_j) \qquad (4)$$

If the same individual maximizes expression (3) for multiple weights, the individual is selected only once, so there are cases where the number of individuals after truncation selection becomes less than S.

Algorithm 2 shows the main steps of the RBC. In the i-th search episode, the RBC receives a weight $\mathbf{w}_i$, a solution $\boldsymbol{x}_i$ to start climbing, the number of fitness evaluations t spent so far, and the maximum number of evaluations T. The solution $\boldsymbol{x}_i$ is then added to the set P_i of solutions visited by the RBC, a counter t_i of fitness evaluation spent in the i-th search episode is set to 0, and a list E storing the already searched bit positions j of the parent solutions being explored is initialized to empty (lines 1–3). In each step of climbing, the climber randomly determines the bit position j to flip. At this time, previously visited positions in E are not considered (line 5). The new solution $\boldsymbol{x}'$ is generated from $\boldsymbol{x}$ by flipping the bit at position j, evaluated and added to P_i (lines 6–8). Also, the flipped position j is added to E (line 9). If the new solution $\boldsymbol{x}'$ is better than the parent $\boldsymbol{x}$, $\boldsymbol{x}'$ replaces the parent and E is cleared (lines 10–13). At the end, the counter t_i is incremented by +1. When all the positions of the parent have been explored without finding a solution better than the parent, i.e. the length of E equals the length of $\boldsymbol{x}$, a local optimum has been found. In this case, the RBC stops its search (line 4) and returns the explored solutions P_i and the spent number of fitness evaluations t_i (line 16). The climber also stops its search if the total number of fitness evaluations $t + t_i$ reaches the specified maximum number T.

3   MNK-Landscapes

A MNK-Landscape [3] is defined as a vector function $\boldsymbol{f}(\cdot) = (f_1(\cdot), \cdots, f_M(\cdot))$: $\mathcal{B}^N \rightarrow \Re^M$ where M is the number of objectives, $f_i(\cdot)$ is the i-th objective function, $\mathcal{B} = \{0, 1\}$, and N is the bit string length. $K = \{K_1, \cdots, K_M\}$ is a set of integers where K_i $(i = 1, 2, \cdots, M)$ is the number of bits in the string that epistatically interact with each bit in the i-th landscape. Each $f_i(\cdot)$ can be expressed as an average of N functions as follows

$$f_i(\boldsymbol{x}) = \frac{1}{N} \sum_{j=1}^{N} f_{i,j}(x_j, z_1^{(i,j)}, z_2^{(i,j)}, \cdots, z_{K_i}^{(i,j)}) \tag{5}$$

where $f_{i,j} : \mathcal{B}^{K_i+1} \rightarrow \Re$ gives the fitness contribution of bit x_j to $f_i(\cdot)$, and $z_1^{(i,j)}, z_2^{(i,j)}, \cdots, z_{K_i}^{(i,j)}$ are the K_i bits interacting with bit x_j in the string $\boldsymbol{x}$. The fitness contribution $f_{i,j}$ of bit x_j is a number between [0.0, 1.0] drawn from a uniform distribution. Thus, each $f_i(\cdot)$ is a non-linear function of $\boldsymbol{x}$ expressed by a Kauffman's NK-Landscape model of epistatic interactions. For a given N, we can tune the ruggedness of the fitness function $f_i(\cdot)$ by varying K_i. In the limits, $K_i = 0$ corresponds to a model in which there are no epistatic interactions and the fitness contribution from each bit value is simply additive, which yields a single peaked smooth fitness landscape. On the opposite extreme, $K_i = N - 1$ corresponds to a model in which each bit value is epistatically affected by all the remaining bit values yielding a maximally rugged fully random i-th fitness landscape. Varying K_i from 0 to $N-1$ gives a family of increasingly rugged multi-peaked landscapes. Besides defining N and K_i for each $f_i(\cdot)$, it is also possible to arrange the epistatic pattern between bit x_j and the K_i other interacting bits. That is, the distribution D_i of K_i bits among N. Kauffman investigated NK-Landscapes with two kinds of epistatic patterns: (i) *nearest neighbor*, in which a bit interacts with its $K_i/2$ left and right adjacent bits, and (ii) *random*, in which a bit interacts with K_i other randomly chosen bits in the string. Thus, $M, N, K = \{K_1, \cdots, K_M\}$, and $D = \{D_1, \cdots, D_M\}$, completely specify a multi-objective MNK-Landscape and by varying them we can study the effects of the number of objectives, size of the search space, intensity and pattern of epistatic interactions on the performance of multi-objective combinatorial optimization algorithms.

4   Experiments

To understand the characteristics of wgRBC, we solve MNK-landscapes [3] with 100 bits, varying the number of objectives M from 2 to 7 and the number of epistatic interactions K from 1 to 20. We conduct experiments with various dRBC configurations [17,18] to compare with wgRBC. Also, we compare wgRBC with NSGA-III [8], MOEA/D [20], moRBC [2]. The parameters used in these experiments are shown in Tables 1, 2, and 3. The number of weights used in NSGA-III is shown in Table 4. The number of weights used in MOEA/D is the same as the population size. The set of weight vectors for MOEA/D is generated according to the method shown in [19].

In all experiments, results are reported for 30 trials of the algorithms in the same MNK-landscape with different random seeds. All algorithms run until 200,000 fitness evaluations have been completed. We use Hypervolume (HV)

Table 1. MNK-landscapes

parameter	Value
Objectives M	$2, 3, 4, 5, 6, 7$
Variables N	100
Interacting Variables K	$1, 2, 3, 5, 7, 10, 15, 20$
Variables Interaction	random

Table 2. RBCs

parameter	wgRBC	dRBC	moRBC
Evaluations	$200,000$	$200,000$	$200,000$
Reference Population	100	100	100
Number of Weights	100	100	-
Functions to Climb	$g(\boldsymbol{x}_i, \mathbf{w}_i) = \sum_{k=1}^{M} w_{i,k} \times f_k$	$f_{hv}f_1, \cdots, f_M f_1, \cdots, f_M, f_h$	Pareto Dominance
Truncation Method	Weights	Weights	Crowding Distance

Table 3. Other MOEAs

parameter	NSGA-III	MOEA/D
Generations	2000	2000
Population	100	100
Crossover	Two Point	Two Point
Mutation	Bit flip	Bit flip
Number of Weights	Table 4	100
Neighborhood Size	-	20
Scalarizing function	ASF	Tchebycheff

Table 4. Number of Weights in NSGA-III

Objectives	2	3	4	5	6	7
Weights	100	105	120	126	126	112

[21] as the evaluation metric setting the reference point to $(0, \cdots, 0)$. The line plot includes a 95% confidence interval centered on the mean.

We also use Radviz [11] to plot fitness values. RadViz is a visualization technique for multivariate high-dimensional data. A data point is associated with a solution and consists of its evaluation values in all M objective functions $(f_1, \cdots, f_M)$. The M dimensions are positioned as anchors arranged around a circle in a two dimensional plane. Each data point is connected to the anchors by springs, and the data point is placed at the coordinates where the forces of the springs are balanced. In each dimension, a larger value results in a larger objective value (stronger spring force), while a smaller value results in a smaller objective value (weaker spring force).

5   Results and Discussion

5.1   Comparison to Distributed Random Bit Climber

To clarify the differences between dRBC and wgRBC, this section compares the performance of wgRBC and 3 dRBCs. The first configuration of dRBC optimizes the original evaluation functions $f_1, \cdots, f_M$, the second optimizes the solution hypervolume f_h, and the third uses both $f_1, \cdots, f_M$ and f_h. We call these algorithms dRBC$(f_1, \cdots, f_M)$, dRBC(f_h), and dRBC$(f_1, \cdots, f_M, f_h)$. The dRBCs use a RBC per objective function to climb them concurrently. In these configurations, each time a local optimum has been found, all RBCs in dRBC restart their search from the same solution selected randomly from the population of non-dominated solutions.

We compare the algorithms on several subclasses of epistatic problems by varying the values of M and K. Figure 1 plots each approach in terms of the number of epistatic interactions K and HV. Before we discuss in detail this figure it is worth remembering some properties of MNK-landscapes. By enumeration it has been shown that increasing $K > 0$ the landscape becomes rugged and the peak's height increase until medium values of K. Thereafter the peaks remain of similar height for medium to large values of K. The hypervolume of the true Pareto front follows a trend similar to the height of the peaks [3].

Now, looking at Fig. 1, it should be noted that the increase in hypervolume varying K from 1 to 5 for all algorithms is by the properties of the landscapes. However, for $K >= 7$ the hypervolume decreases monotonically with K for most algorithms, which means that the performance of all algorithms drops substantially for $K >= 7$.

From Fig. 1, for $M = 2$ and $K \leq 5$, no significant differences are observed overall, except for dRBC(f_h) whose performance is the worst; however, slight differences can be seen at the HV peak. For problems with three or more objectives, the performance gap between dRBC$(f_1, \cdots, f_M)$ and the others gradually widens, and is eventually overtaken by dRBC(f_h) for $M = 7$ and $K \geq 5$. Additionally, as the number of objectives increases, wgRBC becomes dominant for $M \geq 4$ in all K, with dRBC$(f_1, \cdots, f_M, f_h)$ ranking second.

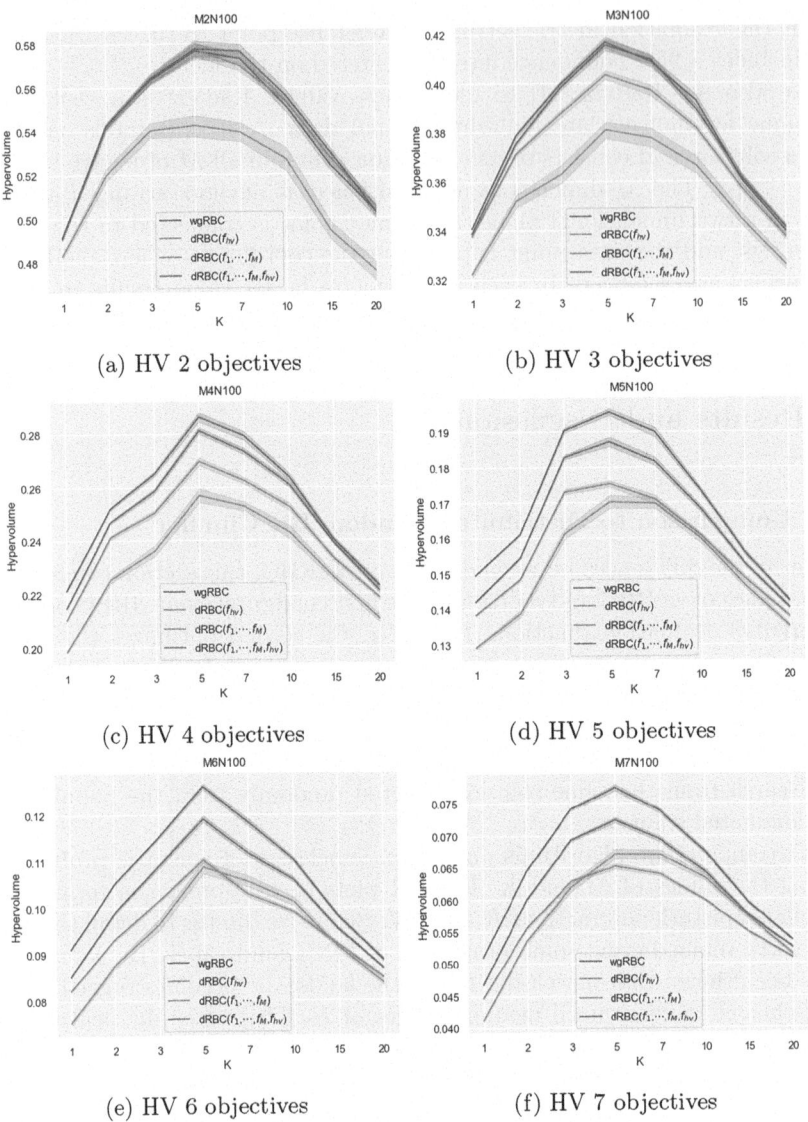

(a) HV 2 objectives

(b) HV 3 objectives

(c) HV 4 objectives

(d) HV 5 objectives

(e) HV 6 objectives

(f) HV 7 objectives

Fig. 1. Comparison of wgRBC with dRBCs

Figure 2a shows the scatter plot in objective space of the solutions found by each dRBC and wgRBC for the 2-objective problem with $K = 7$. In Fig. 1a, for $K = 7$, wgRBC is not superior. This is likely because, as seen in Fig. 2a, wgRBC finds solutions with better convergence near the center but may fail to find extreme solutions. This is due to the fact that, in each search episode, $dRBC(f_1, \cdots, f_M)$ and $dRBC(f_1, \cdots, f_M, f_h)$ always explore the original objective functions, whereas wgRBC only searches for extreme solutions when weights

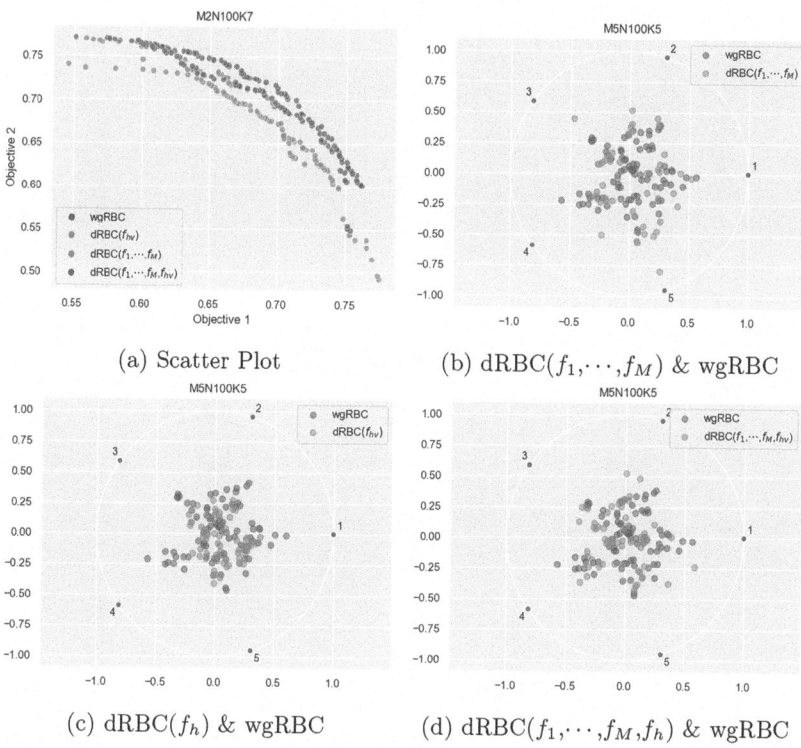

Fig. 2. (a) Scatter Plot of non-dominated solutions by the climbers, $M = 2$ objective problem with $K = 7$. (b)-(d) RadViz of wgRBC compared to other RBCs in $M = 5$ objective problem with $K = 5$

close to the axes are chosen. Additionally, dRBC(f_h) shows the worst convergence and its solutions are dominated by others, which explains its significantly lower HV.

Figure 2b–2d shows the Radviz comparison of wgRBC and RBCs for the 5-objective problem with $K = 5$. In these plots, we show the mutually non-dominated solutions extracted after joining the solutions found by both algorithms to better illustrate their differences. dRBC($f_1, \cdots, f_M$) finds extreme solutions, but there are few solutions near the center, where each objective has average values. In contrast, dRBC(f_h) finds only solutions near the center. The combined dRBC($f_1, \cdots, f_M, f_h$) appears to find both extreme and central solutions to some extent, but many of the solutions are concentrated in similar areas, and it is not as widely distributed as wgRBC. This is likely because in dRBC($f_1, \cdots, f_M, f_h$), the RBCs are biased toward the same direction, as they explore based on the same evaluation functions in every episode, resulting in the generation of similar solutions. On the other hand, wgRBC produces a widely distributed set of solutions, as the randomly chosen weights in each episode alter the search direction.

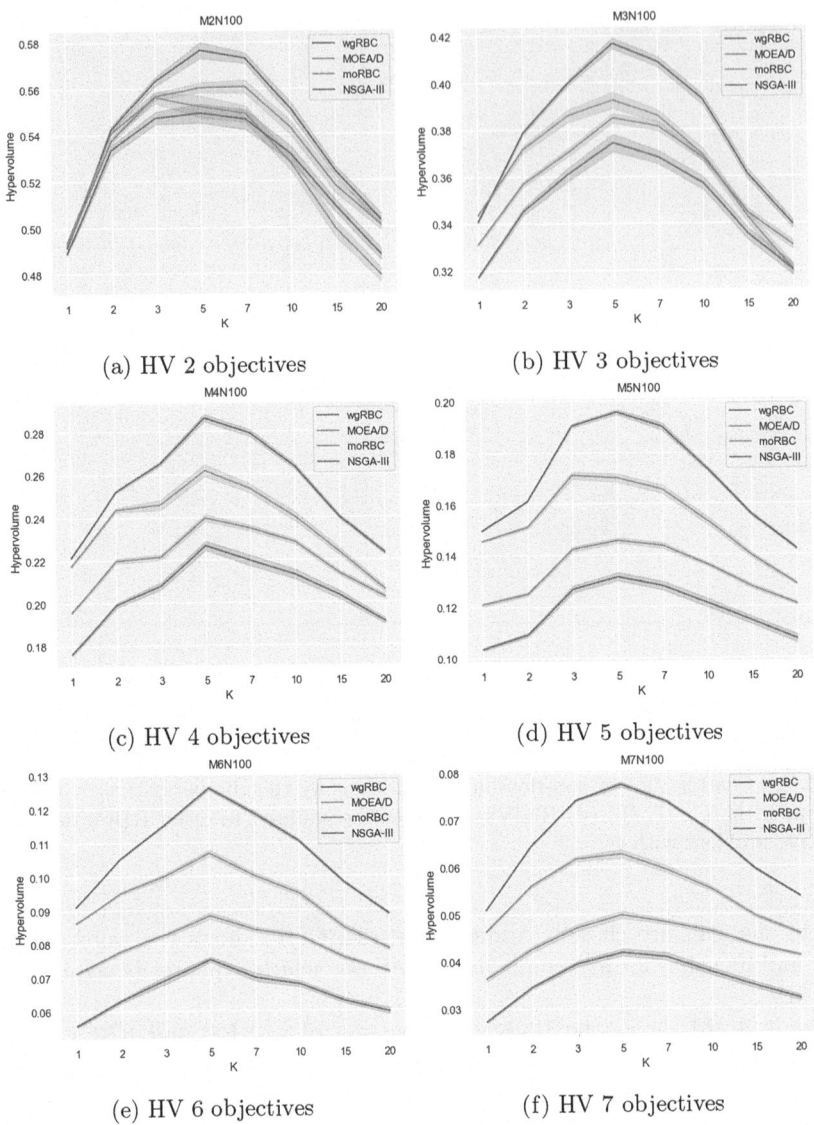

Fig. 3. Comparison of wgRBC with MOEAs

In this work, both the starting solution and the weight are chosen randomly each time the RBC starts a search episode. Further analysis is required to understand the relationship between the chosen weight, the starting solution, and the characteristics of the generated solutions. In addition, a closer examination of the frequency and timing during the search in which the different search directions are explored would provide insights into how to increase the effectiveness of the algorithm even further.

5.2   Comparison to Other MOEAs

We compare the proposed method wgRBC with NSGA-III, MOEA/D, and moRBC running for 200,000 fitness evaluations with a population size of 100. The results of wgRBC are subjected to Welch's t-test, and except for MOEA/D with $M = 2$, $K = 2$ and moRBC with $M = 2$, $K = 20$, all cases show p-values $<$ 0.05. Figure 3 plots the HV over the number of epistatic interactions K, similar to Fig. 1. From Fig. 3, it is clear that wgRBC achieves significantly better HV than the other MOEAs across all M and $K > 1$. Only on 2 and 3 objectives for $K = 1$, MOEA/D performs better than wgRBC. moRBC, which climbs based on Pareto dominance and truncates the reference population based on crowding distance, is a strong algorithm for two objectives problems. However, its performance deteriorates for many objective problems compared to MOEA/D. NSGA-III achieves remarkably low HV. NSGA-III does not emphasize near-parent selection like MOEA/D and other many-objective optimizers do through neighborhoods in objective or decision space. Thus, recombination between parents that are far away becomes too disruptive, making solution search ineffective. NSGA-III in continuous problems relies on SBX with a large distribution index to ensure the offspring is close to the parents. SBX does not work in binary strings, so NSGA-III requires enhancements for binary optimization.

6   Conclusion

In this work, we studied a weights-guided random bit climber (wgRBC) for many-objective optimization of binary problems using MNK-landscapes. We investigated its characteristics comparing with distributed random bit climbers. Also, we verified the effectiveness and scalability of the algorithm. We compared with MOEA/D, NSGA-III and moRBC and showed that the proposed method wgRBC is superior to the other algorithms in all numbers of objectives for $K > 1$. In the future, we would like to use this algorithm for landscape analysis. We would also like to explore adaptive methods to chose the weight that determines the climbing direction for restarts and other methods to diversify the population to support the climbers.

Acknowledgements. This work was supported by JST SPRING, Grant Number JPMJSP2144 (Shinshu University).

Disclosure of Interests. The authors have no competing interests to declare that are relevant to the content of this article.

References

1. Aguirre, H., Oyama, A., Tanaka, K.: Adaptive ϵ-Sampling and ϵ-hood for evolutionary many-objective optimization. In: Purshouse, R.C., Fleming, P.J., Fonseca, C.M., Greco, S., Shaw, J. (eds.) EMO 2013. LNCS, vol. 7811, pp. 322–336. Springer, Heidelberg (2013). https://doi.org/10.1007/978-3-642-37140-0_26

2. Aguirre, H., Tanaka, K.: Random bit climbers on multiobjective MNK-landscapes: effects of memory and population climbing. IEICE Trans. **88-A**, 334–345 (2005)
3. Aguirre, H., Tanaka, K.: Working principles, behavior, and performance of moeas on MNK-landscapes. Eur. J. Oper. Res. **181**, 1670–1690 (2007)
4. Beume, N., Naujoks, B., Emmerich, M.: SMS-EMOA: multiobjective selection based on dominated hypervolume. Eur. J. Oper. Res. **181**(3), 1653–1669 (2007)
5. Brockhoff, D., Wagner, T., Trautmann, H.: R2 indicator-based multiobjective search. Evol. Comput. **23**(3), 369–395 (2015)
6. Coello, C., Carlos, A., Veldhuizen, V., David, A., Lamont, G.: Evolutionary Algorithms for Solving Multi-Objective Problems, Genetic and Evolutionary Computation. Springer, New York (2002)
7. Deb, K.: Multi-Objective Optimization using Evolutionary Algorithms. John Wiley & Sons, Hoboken (2001)
8. Deb, K., Jain, H.: An evolutionary Many-Objective optimization algorithm using Reference-Point-Based nondominated sorting approach, part i: Solving problems with box constraints. IEEE Trans. Evol. Comput. **18**(4), 577–601 (2014)
9. Hadka, D., Reed, P.: Borg: an auto-adaptive many-objective evolutionary computing framework. Evol. Comput. **21**(2), 231–259 (2013)
10. Hansen, M., Jaszkiewicz, A.: Evaluating the quality of approximations to the non-dominated set (1998)
11. Hoffman, P., Grinstein, G., Marx, K., Grosse, I., Stanley, E.: DNA visual and analytic data mining. In: Proceedings. Visualization 1997 (Cat. No. 97CB36155). IEEE (2002)
12. Hughes, E.J.: MSOPS-II: a general-purpose many-objective optimiser. In: 2007 IEEE Congress on Evolutionary Computation, pp. 3944–3951. IEEE (2007)
13. Igel, C., Hansen, N., Roth, S.: Covariance matrix adaptation for multi-objective optimization. Evol. Comput. **15**(1), 1–28 (2007)
14. Ishibuchi, H., Tsukamoto, N., Nojima, Y.: Evolutionary many-objective optimization: a short review. In: 2008 IEEE Congress on Evolutionary Computation (IEEE World Congress on Computational Intelligence), pp. 2419–2426. IEEE (2008)
15. Laumanns, M., Thiele, L., Deb, K., Zitzler, E.: Combining convergence and diversity in evolutionary multiobjective optimization. Evol. Comput. **10**(3), 263–282 (2002)
16. von Lücken, C., Brizuela, C., Barán, B.: An overview on evolutionary algorithms for many-objective optimization problems. Wiley Interdisc. Rev. Data Min. Knowl. Discov. **9**(1), e1267 (2019)
17. Tagawa, Y., Aguirre, H., Tanaka, K.: Simple distributed bit climber for many-objective optimization of binary epistatic problems. In: GECCO 2024 Companion: Proceedings of the Genetic and Evolutionary Computation Conference Companion, pp. 367–370. Association for Computing Machinery, New York (2024)
18. Tagawa, Y., Aguirre, H., Tanaka, K.: Distributed bit climbing algorithm for binary multi-objective optimization. In: 2024 IEEE Congress on Evolutionary Computation (CEC). IEEE (2024)
19. Zapotecas-Martínez, S., Aguirre, H., Tanaka, K., Coello, C.: On the low-discrepancy sequences and their use in moea/d for high-dimensional objective spaces. In: 2015 IEEE Congress on Evolutionary Computation (CEC), pp. 2835–2842 (2015)
20. Zhang, Q., Li, H.: MOEA/D: a multiobjective evolutionary algorithm based on decomposition. IEEE Trans. Evol. Comput. **11**(6), 712–731 (2007)
21. Zitzler, E.: Evolutionary Algorithms for Multiobjective Optimization: Methods and Applications. Ph.D. thesis, ETH Zurich, Switzerland (1999)

22. Zitzler, E., Künzli, S.: Indicator-based selection in multiobjective search. In: Yao, X., Burke, E.K., Lozano, J.A., Smith, J., Merelo-Guervós, J.J., Bullinaria, J.A., Rowe, J.E., Tiňo, P., Kabán, A., Schwefel, H.-P. (eds.) PPSN 2004. LNCS, vol. 3242, pp. 832–842. Springer, Heidelberg (2004). https://doi.org/10.1007/978-3-540-30217-9_84

Bilevel Optimization-Based Decomposition for Solving Single and Multiobjective Optimization Problems

Ankur Sinha[1], Dhaval Pujara[1(✉)], and Hemant Kumar Singh[2]

[1] Brij Disa Centre for Data Science and Artificial Intelligence, Indian Institute of Management, Ahmedabad 380015, Gujarat, India
{asinha,dhavalp}@iima.ac.in
[2] School of Engineering and Technology, University of New South Wales, Canberra, ACT 2610, Australia
h.singh@unsw.edu.au

Abstract. Real world optimization problems contain multiple complexities that are often not tractable if one completely relies on mathematical programming or metaheuristic approaches, as each approach has unique strengths and limitations in dealing with the complexities in optimization problems. For instance, metaheuristic methods have an edge in tackling non-regularities like discontinuity, non-convexity, and discreteness, given that problem has few decision variables (low dimensionality). Contrary to that, mathematical programming based classical methods can efficiently solve high dimensional problems if the problem encompasses regular functions as constraints and objective function. Thus, non-regular and high-dimensional optimization problems pose challenges to both approaches for getting solved using the method explicitly from any one approach. To excel in this situation, this study proposes a difficulties separation approach that enables to convert a single level optimization problem into bilevel optimization problem and solve the problem synergistically by applying methods from both complementary approaches. We demonstrate the benefits of proposed bilevel based decomposition approach on a wide range of single and multiobjective test problems.

Keywords: Bilevel optimization · Separation of difficulties · Decomposition of optimization problem

1 Introduction

In a real-life scenario, optimization practitioners deal with complex optimization problems across various fields of science, engineering, and management. Complexity in the optimization problem arises due to various characteristics of the objective function and feasible region, including but not limited to, non-convexity, discontinuity, non-differentiability, high-dimensionality, etc. A rich literature on optimization consists of studies offering methods to solve such complex optimization problems. Based on the problem solving approach, these methods are broadly classified as mathematical programming based classical methods and

H. Singh et al. (Eds.): EMO 2025, LNCS 15512, pp. 88–102, 2025.
https://doi.org/10.1007/978-981-96-3506-1_7

metaheuristic methods. Classical methods exploit the known characteristics of a problem during the search process and mostly guarantee the optimality of the solution obtained. These methods mainly encompass traditional optimization techniques, for instance, linear programming, mixed-integer programming, and non-linear programming, etc. [18]. On the other hand, the algorithms from the class of metaheuristic methods search for efficient solutions from the solution space by conducting nature inspired or swarm intelligence based region search, but they typically do not guarantee the optimality of the delivered solution. Metaheuristic methods are applicable to a wider range of complex real-life problems, as they do not require the underlying functions to possess specific properties or satisfy particular conditions to ensure specific behavior. However, this flexibility comes at a cost, as metaheuristic methods generally require a large computational cost to arrive at a competitive solution. Simulated annealing, genetic algorithm, and particle swarm optimization are a few examples of metaheuristic algorithms that have shown potential in handling certain classes of optimization problems where the classical methods fall short [12].

The performance of classical and metaheuristic methods largely depends on the complexity associated with the optimization problem at hand. For example, classical methods can effectively solve the problem whose solution space has certain favorable attributes like linearity, convexity, continuity, or differentiability, even when the problem contains a substantial number of variables and constraints [11]. However, their performance deteriorates when they encounter certain non-regularities such as discontinuity, non-convexity, or non-differentiability, where metaheuristic methods yield superior results, albeit for problems with lower dimensionality [7]. Thus, both methods have unique strengths and limitations in terms of solving problems with specific types of complexities. However, real world problems often contain a bunch of complexities such that a problem cannot be handled effectively using a single approach independently.

This study proposes a difficulties separation strategy, wherein we separate each of the decision variables based on the nature of complexity it adds to the problem. It allows us to model the single level optimization problem in the bilevel optimization framework. Later, we solve the derived bilevel problem by handling the upper level and lower level problems using metaheuristic and classical optimization methods, depending on the nature of complexities at each level. We automate the variable separation task by developing a mechanism that dynamically classifies each decision variable into the upper or the lower level of the bilevel problem structure. We embed the difficulties separation strategy into a bilevel optimization algorithm to efficiently solve complex single level optimization problems, which may have single or multiple objectives. We refer to the proposed method as Bilevel Optimization-based Decomposition (BOBD).

The BOBD method is proposed in the study by Sinha et al. [28], and we extend this study with the following contributions: (i) automating the variable classification task within the BOBD framework, (ii) explaining the decomposition of multi objective optimization problems into a bilevel optimization structure, and (iii) evaluating the performance of BOBD on a test suite consisting of seven single objective and three multi objective optimization problems.

The rest of the paper is organized as follows: Sect. 2 presents the proposed decomposition strategy for single objective optimization problems, along with an overview of bilevel optimization. This section also includes the variable classification algorithm designed to automate the difficulty separation task. In Sect. 3, the decomposition strategy is extended for multiobjective optimization problems. Section 4 provides the structure of BOBD method. Section 5 contains the analysis of results obtained by employing multiple optimization methods to solve the test problems. Section 6 presents the concluding remarks and scope for future work.

2   Bilevel Optimization

Bilevel optimization is a special kind of optimization problem comprising of two distinct optimization tasks: the upper level optimization task and the lower level optimization task, interconnected by embedding a lower level optimization task as a constraint into the upper level optimization task [6,20,24]. In practice, the upper level optimization task is referred to as the leader's optimization problem and lower level optimization task is referred to as the follower's optimization problem. In a bilevel optimization setting, leader and follower have individual objectives and constraints. Leader, with the knowledge of follower's potential responses, makes the first move. Considering the leader's actions, follower takes the optimal decision for itself. Thus, for each decision made by leader, the follower's corresponding optimal response becomes a feasible solution for the bilevel optimization problem, provided if the leader's constraints are satisfied. The primary objective is to determine the best possible action plan for leader.

The decision making mechanism in bilevel optimization problem is depicted in Fig. 1, where the set of possible decisions from the leader and follower is shown as the upper level and lower level decision spaces, respectively. The leader's action is symbolized as the upper level decision vector u and the follower's response is represented as the lower level decision vector l. For a specific u^0, the task is to find a corresponding l^0 by performing a parametric optimization at lower level $f(u^0, l)$, where u^0 acts as a parameter. Thus, the pair of decision vectors (u^0, l^0) constitutes a feasible solution for the considered bilevel optimization problem, provided that it satisfies all other constraints inherent in the problem. The aim is to find the best pair of decision vectors (u^*, l^*) that optimizes the upper level objective function $F(u, l)$. With this foundational premise, the bilevel optimization problem is formally defined as follows:

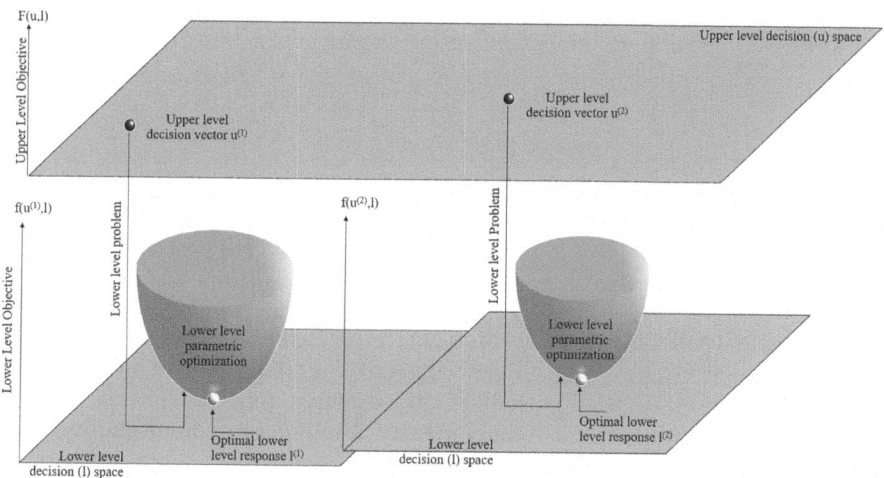

Fig. 1. A hierarchical structure of bilevel optimization problem showing the interconnection between upper level and lower level tasks.

Definition 1. *For the upper-level objective function $F : \mathbb{R}^n \times \mathbb{R}^m \to \mathbb{R}$ and the lower-level objective function $f : \mathbb{R}^n \times \mathbb{R}^m \to \mathbb{R}$, the bilevel problem is given by*

$$\min_{u,l} \quad F(u,l) \tag{1}$$

subject to

$$l \in \underset{l}{\mathrm{argmin}}\{f(u,l) : g_k(u,l) \leq 0, \quad k = 1, \ldots, K,$$

$$h_l(u,l) = 0, \quad l = 1, \ldots, L\} \tag{2}$$

$$G_i(u,l) \leq 0, \quad i = 1, \ldots, I \tag{3}$$

$$H_j(u,l) = 0, \quad j = 1, \ldots, J \tag{4}$$

where $g_k : \mathbb{R}^n \times \mathbb{R}^m \to \mathbb{R}$ and $h_l : \mathbb{R}^n \times \mathbb{R}^m \to \mathbb{R}$ denote the lower level constraints, and $G_i : \mathbb{R}^n \times \mathbb{R}^m \to \mathbb{R}$ and $H_j : \mathbb{R}^n \times \mathbb{R}^m \to \mathbb{R}$ denote the upper level constraints. Variables u and l in the above definition may be real or integers as defined in the problem.

2.1 Separation of Difficulties in Single Level Optimization Problems

Single level optimization problems are the special case of bilevel optimization problems [9]. In this section, we describe a detailed procedure for representing a single level optimization problem in the form of bilevel optimization problem. The procedure involves decomposition of a single level optimization problem by separating the difficulties using the BOBD method.

Definition 2. *We consider a general optimization problem that we want to decompose in the form of bilevel optimization problem to exploit the capabilities* *of two problem-solving approaches simultaneously.*

$$\min_{x} \quad F(x) \tag{5}$$

subject to

$$G_i(x) \le 0, \quad i = 1, \ldots, I \tag{6}$$

$$H_j(x) = 0, \quad j = 1, \ldots, J \tag{7}$$

where $x = (x_1, \ldots, x_n)$ is a solution vector.

The single level optimization problem, presented in Definition 2, has n decision variables $(x_1, \ldots, x_n)$. The complexity in the problem arises when terms with several decision variables, in objective function or constraints, lead to non-regularities such as non-convexity, non-linearity, discontinuity, non-differentiability, discreteness, etc. In addition to that, the presence of a large number of decision variables contributes further to the complexity in the form of high-dimensionality. The classical methods can efficiently solve mathematically well-behaved (regular) high-dimensional problems, but fail very often in solving low-dimensional problems with non-regularities. On the other side, the metaheuristic methods can handle non-regularities in low-dimensional problem effectively, but suffer while solving regular problems with a large number of variables. Thus, both classical methods and metaheuristic methods become less effective while solving complex optimization problems that exhibit non-regularities and high-dimensionality together. However, both methods have their own strengths in tackling high-dimensionality and non-regularities independently, and this observation is used in the BOBD method proposed in this study, which decomposes a single level optimization problem into bilevel optimization using the difficulties separation strategy. The procedure of formulating a single level optimization problem in the form of a bilevel optimization problem is as follows.

From all the decision variables in the considered single level optimization problem (5)–(7), assume that a certain set of variables $x^+ \subseteq x$ introduces a specific type of complexity in objective function or constraints. We classify these variables into the upper level category and group the remaining variables $x^- = x \backslash x^+$ into the lower level category. In this way, we add each of the variables $x_i : i \in 1, \ldots, n$ into x^+ or x^-, based on the complexity caused by respective variable x_i. We refer to this as the difficulty separation procedure. Further, we represent the objective function $F(x)$ and constraints $G_i(x)$, $H_j(x)$ in terms of x^+, x^- as $F(x^+, x^-)$ and $G_i(x^+, x^-)$, $H_j(x^+, x^-)$, respectively. The constraints can also be classified as the upper level or lower level constraints based on the complexity they add. Using a similar procedure as for the variables, we classify the constraints into upper and lower levels and denote them as $G_{i+}(x^+, x^-)/G_{i-}(x^+, x^-)$ and $H_{j+}(x^+, x^-)/H_{j-}(x^+, x^-)$. Accordingly, a single level optimization problem, with decision variables and constraints classified based on the complexities, can be expressed as a bilevel optimization problem as follows:

$$\min_{x^+, x^-} \quad F(x^+, x^-) \tag{8}$$

subject to

$$x^- \in \operatorname*{argmin}_{x^-}\{F(x^+, x^-) : G_{i-}(x^+, x^-) \leq 0,$$

$$H_{j-}(x^+, x^-) = 0\} \tag{9}$$

$$G_{i+}(x^+, x^-) \leq 0 \tag{10}$$

$$H_{j+}(x^+, x^-) = 0 \tag{11}$$

Note that the above formulation would lead to the same optimal solution as the formulation (5)–(7), since the objective functions at both levels are same.

In (8)–(11), assume that x^+ consists of variables causing non-regularities. If the values of these variables are fixed, then the resulting lower level problem needs to be solved only with respect to x^-, which may be a high-dimensional but still a regular problem to solve. In such a scenario, it is convenient to deploy a metaheuristic method for exploring the upper level decision space and a classical method for the search in lower level decision space. While the metaheuristic method performs an intensive search using an intelligent sampling approach, solving the lower level optimization problem for each sample effectively handles high dimensionality and allows convergence to the optimal bilevel solution. Such a solution approach is equivalent to the nested approaches frequently deployed in bilevel optimization [1,17,19,21,25]. Employing the efficient sampling and bilevel mapping exploitation [2,22,23,29], one can solve the bilevel problem more efficiently compared to the nested approach. Surrogate-assisted search [3,14,15], knowledge transfer [8,30], and hybridization [13] are some of the other approaches that can reduce the computational expense.

Numerical Example. Let us consider an example to demonstrate how to delineate and separate the complexities using the BOBD method.

$$\min_{x} \quad F(x) = x_1^{0.6} + x_2^{0.6} + x_3^{0.4} - 4x_3 + 2x_4 + 5x_5 - x_6 - \frac{x_2^2}{16} + \frac{x_3^2}{16}$$

$$- 2\cos(2\pi x_2) - 2\cos(2\pi x_3) + \sum_{p=1}^{20} y_p \cdot x_1^{0.6} \tag{12}$$

subject to

$$x_2 - 3x_1 - 3x_4 = 0; \tag{13}$$

$$x_3 - 2x_2 - 2x_5 = 0; \tag{14}$$

$$4x_4 - x_6 = 0; \tag{15}$$

$$x_1 + 2x_4 \leq 4; \tag{16}$$

$$x_2 + x_5 \leq 4; \tag{17}$$

$$x_3 + x_6 \leq 6; \tag{18}$$

$$\sqrt{(x_1 + x_2 + x_3)} - y_p \leq 0, \ \forall p; \tag{19}$$

$$x_1 \leq 3; \ x_3 \leq 4; \ x_5 \leq 2; \ x_i \geq 0, \ \forall i; \ 1 \leq y_p \leq 5, \ \forall p; \tag{20}$$

The example contains 26 decision variables and encompasses a non-convex objective function, 3 linear equality constraints, 3 linear inequality constraints, 20 non-linear inequality constraints, and bound constraints. Let us manually classify each of the 26 decision variables into the upper or lower level variable category to obtain a bilevel formulation.

Variables x_1, x_2, and x_3 cause non-convexity in objective function and non-linear constraints, so let us classify them into the upper level variable category and keep the remaining variables $(x_4, x_5, x_6, y = \{y_p : p \in 1, \ldots, 20\})$ into the lower level category. As per (8)–(11), $u = (x_1, x_2, x_3)$ and $l = (x_4, x_5, x_6, y)$, we can write a bilevel formulation for (12)–(20) as follows:

$$\min_{u,l} \quad u_1^{0.6} + u_2^{0.6} + u_3^{0.4} - 4u_3 + 2l_1 + 5l_2 - l_3 - \frac{u_2^2}{16} + \frac{u_3^2}{16} - 2\cos{(2\pi u_2)}$$

$$- 2\cos{(2\pi u_3)} + \sum_{p=4}^{23} l_p \cdot u_1^{0.6}$$

subject to

$$l \in \text{argmin} \begin{cases} u_1^{0.6} + u_2^{0.6} + u_3^{0.4} - 4u_3 + 2l_1 + 5l_2 - l_3 - \frac{u_2^2}{16} + \frac{u_3^2}{16} - 2\cos{(2\pi u_2)} \\ -2\cos{(2\pi u_3)} + \sum_{p=4}^{23} l_p \cdot u_1^{0.6} \\ \text{subject to} \\ u_2 - 3u_1 - 3l_1 = 0, \quad u_1 + 2l_1 \leq 4 \\ u_3 - 2u_2 - 2l_2 = 0, \quad u_2 + l_2 \leq 4 \\ 4l_1 - l_3 = 0, \qquad u_3 + l_3 \leq 6 \\ l_1, l_2, l_3 \geq 0, \qquad \sqrt{(u_1 + u_2 + u_3)} - l_p \leq 0, \quad \forall p; \\ l_2 \leq 2, \qquad\qquad 1 \leq l_p \leq 5, \forall p \end{cases}$$

$$u_1 \leq 3, u_3 \leq 4$$

$$u_1, u_2, u_3 \geq 0$$

Note that the chosen decomposition strategy leads to a bilevel optimization problem in which the upper level problem contains a non-linear objective function and no constraints, while the lower level problem becomes a linear program for any given upper level decision. We solve this problem in a nested manner using a genetic algorithm at the upper level and a linear program solver for the lower level. Interestingly, this simple 26-variable problem is intractable, if solved as a single level optimization problem using a genetic algorithm or a non-linear optimization algorithm alone. However, using a bilevel approach explained in this study, we obtained a solution -12.150, which is better compared to the solutions obtained from metaheuristic (-8.450) and classical optimization (-10.778) methods. The solution vector obtained using a bilevel approach is $x = (x_1, x_2, x_3, x_4, x_5, x_6, y_p) = (0, 1.0681, 4, 0.3560, 0.9318, 1.4241, 2.5124)$, where $y_p = 2.5124$, $\forall p = 1, \ldots, 20$.

2.2 Variable Classification Algorithm (VCA)

In the previous Sect. (2.1), we partitioned each decision variable $(x_1, \ldots, x_n)$ in the upper or lower level manually. However, such a manual approach may not work for large scale problems. Therefore, in this section, we propose a Variable Classification Algorithm (VCA) to automate the variable partitioning task. In VCA, we study the behavior of objective function w.r.t. each decision variable. For that, we compute the convexity index of each decision variable, a measure of convexity contributed by decision variable in the objective function, using the characteristics of Hessian matrix related to the objective function. Hessian matrix gives information about the local curvature of the mathematical equation. VCA starts with a seed solution x^s and objective function $F(x)$ passed by the user. x^s is used to form a sample of solutions S consisting of $\frac{(n+1)(n+2)}{2}$ neighbourhood solutions of x^s including x^s. A step-by-step procedure of VCA is provided in Algorithm 1.

Algorithm 1. Variable Classification Algorithm

Input: x^s- seed solution, $F(x)$- objective function
Output: (u, l)- pair of upper and lower level variables vectors

---

Step 1: Form a sample of solutions S using the x^s.
Step 2: Compute the values of $F(x)$ for each solution in S.
Step 3: Fit a quadratic function around the data points of $F(x)$ values.
Step 4: Build a Hessian matrix using the coefficients of quadratic function.
Step 5: Compute the eigenvalues $(\lambda_1, \ldots, \lambda_n)$ and eigenvectors $(e^1, \ldots, e^n)$ of the Hessian matrix. Let $\lambda = (\lambda_1, \ldots, \lambda_n)$ and $\mathbf{E} = [e^1, \ldots, e^n]$.
Step 6: Compute the convexity index of decision variables $(CI_1, \ldots, CI_n) = \mathbf{E}\lambda^T$.
Step 7: Classify each decision variable x_r based on its CI_r:
           $CI_r < 0$: include variable x_r into upper level variable vector u.
           $CI_r \geq 0$: include variable x_r into lower level variable vector l.

In this paper, we compute the convexity index of each decision variable only based on the objective function, but such an index can be computed for each constraint as well and based on these multiple indices, an overall index can be designed for each decision variable for a given optimization problem. Note that the proposed variable classification algorithm is a Hessian-based heuristic and one can design alternative approaches for segregating the variables.

3 BOBD for Multiobjective Optimization Problems

In this section, we extend the difficulties separation approach for the multiobjective optimization problems.

Definition 3. *A single level multiobjective minimization problem with n deci-sion variables and P objective functions can be formulated as follows:*

$$\min_{x} \quad F(x) = (F_1(x), F_2(x), \ldots, F_P(x)) \tag{21}$$

subject to

$$G_i(x) \leq 0, \quad i = 1, \ldots, I \tag{22}$$

$$H_j(x) = 0, \quad j = 1, \ldots, J \tag{23}$$

We decompose the above problem in two levels by following the procedure developed earlier (2.1 and 2.2) for the single objective problem. That is, (i) apply VCA to classify each of the decision variables into the upper level variable category (x^+) or the lower level variable category (x^-) based on the complexities it adds to the problem, (ii) present the objective functions and constraints in the form of upper and lower level variables, (iii) formulate the objective functions for the upper and lower optimization problem, and (iv) classify the constraints into the upper and lower levels, depending on the complexities they hold after the variable classification task. This leads to a bilevel optimization setup for the above single level multiobjective problem, as follows:

$$\min_{w, x^+, x^-} \quad F(x^+, x^-) = \left(F_1(x^+, x^-), F_2(x^+, x^-), \ldots, F_P(x^+, x^-)\right) \tag{24}$$

subject to

$$x^- \in \operatorname*{argmin}_{x^-} \{V\left(F_1(x^+, x^-), F_2(x^+, x^-), \ldots, F_P(x^+, x^-), w\right) :$$

$$G_{i^-}(x^+, x^-) \leq 0,$$

$$H_{j^-}(x^+, x^-) = 0\} \tag{25}$$

$$G_{i^+}(x^+, x^-) \leq 0 \tag{26}$$

$$H_{j^+}(x^+, x^-) = 0 \tag{27}$$

In the above bilevel formulation (24)–(27), we consider a scalarization tech-nique to perform lower level optimization and w represents the preference weights that are treated as UL variables. $V(.)$ represents any suitable scalarization scheme such as weighted sum scalarization [10], weighted Chebyshev [31], conic scalarization [16], or Benson's scalarization [5]. In our experiments in this paper we have chosen the Chebyshev scalarization approach. Also, while performing the variable classification task using VCA, we calculate convexity index for each variable w.r.t. every objective function and then take an average.

4   Implementation of the BOBD Method

The proposed BOBD method combines the VCA algorithm (2.2) with the bilevel problem solving algorithms, BLEAQ-II (Bilevel Evolutionary Algorithm-based on Quadratic Approximations) [22] for single objective and m-BLEAQ [26,27] for multiobjective. We extend the m-BLEAQ algorithm so that it exploits both reaction set mapping and value function mapping as in BLEAQ-II and we refer to it as m-BLEAQ-II. Therefore, m-BLEAQ-II is essentially the BLEAQ-II algorithm with non-dominated sorting and crowding distance used for fitness evaluation at the upper level. The implementation of BOBD method to solve single level optimization problems is provided in Algorithm 2.

Algorithm 2. Bilevel Optimization-based Decomposition

Input: $F(x)$, $G(x)$, $H(x)$- single level optimization problem
Output: x^*- efficient solution of single level optimization problem

Step 1: Generate a population of random initial solutions $\mathcal{P}$.
Step 2: *for* $c = 1$ to C
Step 3: Obtain $(u, l)^c$ using VCA by passing random solution $x \in \mathcal{P}$ and $F(x)$.
Step 4: Formulate a bilevel problem by decomposing the single level problem with respect to $(u, l)^c$.
Step 5: Solve the bilevel problem using BLEAQ-II/m-BLEAQ-II algorithm for k generations.

In VCA, variables are classified based on the behavior of the objective function accessed in a specific region formed by the local data points (i.e., solutions), which allows to examine only the local curvature of the objective function. However, to take the general behavior of the objective function into account, the curvature of objective function must be observed across different regions using the different random samples. Therefore, in BOBD implementation, the given single level optimization problem is reformulated into a bilevel problem multiple times ($C = Number\ Of\ Cycles$). The variable classification algorithm is executed in each cycle to dynamically reformulate different bilevel problems equivalent to the original single level optimization problem.

5   Numerical Experiments

We carry out the performance evaluation of the proposed BOBD method by solving several single and multiobjective test problems from the literature using three approaches: mathematical programming, metaheuristic, and bilevel optimization, and comparing the results obtained from each approach. We select Interior-Point (IP) method from the mathematical programming category [4], a steady state Genetic Algorithm (GA) from the class of metaheuristic algorithms, and the proposed BOBD method following the bilevel optimization approach. In BOBD method, BLEAQ-II or m-BLEAQ-II framework is used to solve the bilevel problem formulated for any given single or multiobjective optimization problem, respectively. In BLEAQ-II/m-BLEAQ-II framework, IP method is used for the lower level optimization and GA is applied at the upper level. This ensures a fair comparison among the methods considered for the numerical experiments. All the methods were encoded in Python and solved in the system with following configuration: 64-bit, 32GB RAM, and 160GB storage. We consider seven single objective optimization problems (TP4-TP10) [28] and three multiobjective optimization problems (ZDT1, ZDT2, ZDT3) [32] as test problems.

In each single objective test problem (TP4-TP10), the objective function and at least one constraint contain terms with the scalable variables y_p and/or z_q (where $y = \{y_p : p \in 1, \ldots, P\}$ and $z = \{z_q : q \in 1, \ldots, Q\}$) to induce high-dimensionality. In BOBD method, we fixed the population size as 30 times the number of variables at the upper level and terminate the algorithm when there is no improvement in the last 100 generations. For GA, we solve each test problem for the same duration as BOBD. In case of IP method, we use the default termination criteria implemented in IPOPT solver. In all test problems, for each equality and inequality constraint, the constraint tolerance was set to 10^{-4}. Further, for test problems TP4-TP10, we execute each algorithm 11 times and report the best feasible solution obtained. In this experimental setup, we evaluate the performance of the IP, GA, and BOBD methods by solving test problems TP4-TP10 under two scenarios: (i) $|y| + |z| = 20$ and (ii) $|y| + |z| = 50$, where $|y| + |z|$ represents the number of scalable variables in each TP. The results for both scenarios are reported in Table 1, which indicates that the proposed BOBD method outperforms the IP and GA methods in terms of solution quality. The IP method provides competitive solutions for all test problems (TP4-TP10), whereas the GA generates comparatively less efficient solutions for most test problems and does not manage to provide feasible solutions for TP4, TP5, TP7, and TP9 in both scenarios.

Table 1. Performance evaluation of BOBD for single objective test problems

Test Problem	$|y| + |z| = 20$			$|y| + |z| = 50$		
	IP	GA	BOBD	IP	GA	BOBD
TP4	−10.778	Infeasible	**-12.150**	−12.151	Infeasible	**-12.161**
TP5	189.923	Infeasible	189.923	264.585	Infeasible	**259.125**
TP6	−321.60	−285.348	**-550**	−541.084	−253.246	**-910**
TP7	−241.44	Infeasible	**-390.124**	−332	Infeasible	**-404.825**
TP8	116.44	−94.952	**-173.479**	−239.765	38.735	**-292.839**
TP9	7064.2	Infeasible	**7053.676**	8176.8	Infeasible	**7048.701**
TP10	74552	78877	74552	232380	245360	**232377.1**

In the case of multiobjective optimization, we solve each test problem (ZDT1, ZDT2, ZDT3) using the BOBD and NSGA-II (Non-dominated Sorting Genetic Algorithm) algorithms. In both methods, the population size and number of generations are set to 100 and 250, respectively. Figure 2 illustrates the Pareto-fronts and the hypervolume scores obtained for each test problem through the application of BOBD and NSGA-II methods. In the computation of hypervolume, the reference points considered for ZDT1, ZDT2, and ZDT3 are (1, 9.37), (1,

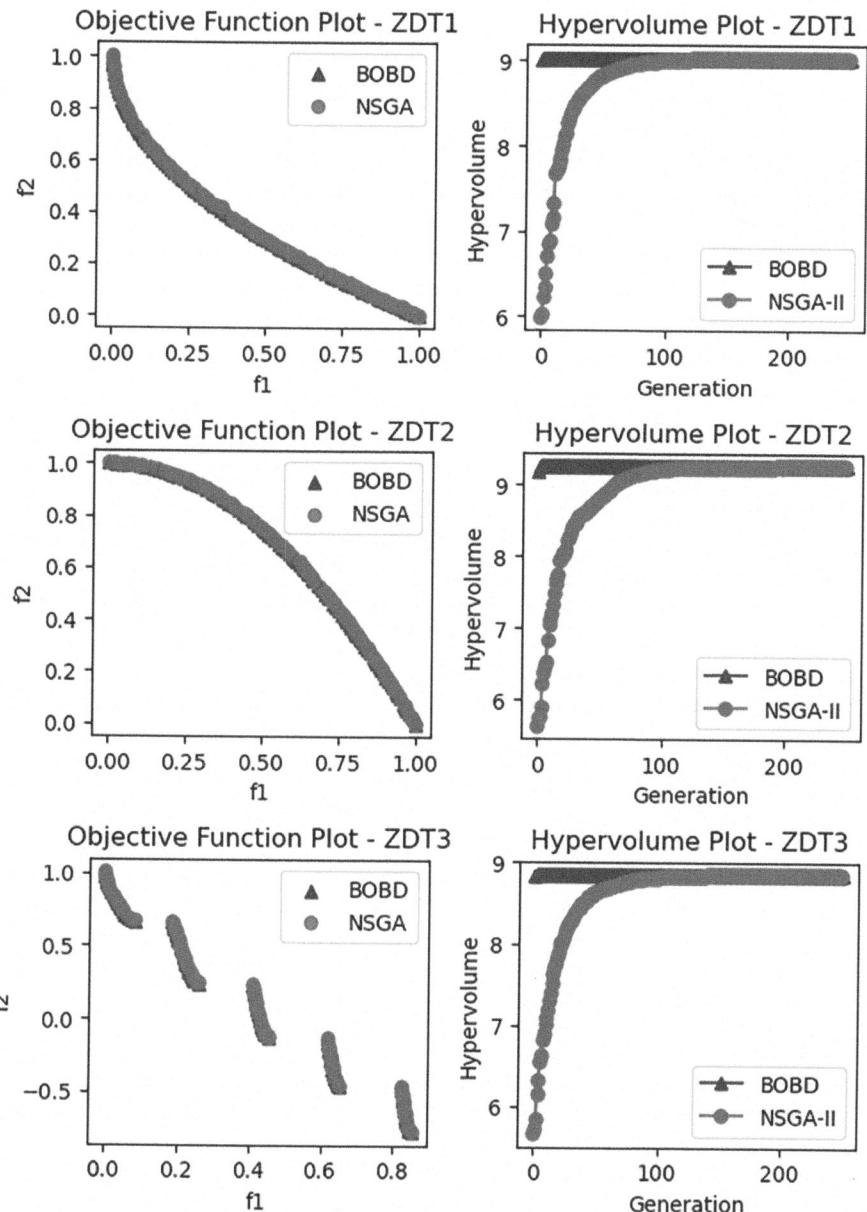

Fig. 2. Performance evaluation of BOBD for multiobjective test problems

9.93), and (1, 8.81), respectively. For all test problems, BOBD method produced marginally efficient Pareto-fronts at high convergence rate.

6   Conclusion

This study proposes an approach for solving complex optimization problems using a Bilevel Optimization-based Decomposition (BOBD) method. This method involves the transformation of single level optimization into a bilevel optimization problem by systematically classifying each decision variable and constraint of a given optimization problem into upper or lower level of bilevel optimization framework. This reformulation enables the application of two suitable approaches to synergistically solve the optimization problem. The proposed bilevel-based approach is useful for solving the optimization problems that are otherwise difficult to solve using classical methods or metaheuristic methods alone.

To evaluate the performance of BOBD, we consider a test suite of 10 test problems consisting of seven single objective and three multiobjective optimization problems. For the single objective test problems, the performance of BOBD is benchmarked against the mathematical programming approach (interior point) and evolutionary approach (genetic algorithm), whereas for the multiobjective test problems, we compare the solutions obtained from BOBD against a popular multiobjective genetic algorithm. In both cases, BOBD consistently outperforms the benchmark methods in terms of solution quality. In the future, it will be interesting to separately study the role and benefits of the reaction set mapping and value function mapping approximations for solving complex single level problems.

References

1. Angelo, J., Krempser, E., Barbosa, H.: Differential evolution for bilevel programming. In: IEEE Congress on Evolutionary Computation(CEC), pp. 70–477 (2013)
2. Angelo, J.S., Krempser, E., Barbosa, H.J.C.: Differential evolution assisted by a surrogate model for bilevel programming problems. In: IEEE Congress on Evolutionary Computation (CEC), pp. 1784–1791 (2014)
3. Angelo, J.S., Krempser, E., Barbosa, H.J.: Performance evaluation of local surrogate models in bilevel optimization. In: International Conference on Machine Learning, Optimization, and Data Science (LOD), pp. 347–359 (2019)
4. Bazaraa, M.S., Sherali, H.D., Shetty, C.M.: Nonlinear Programming: Theory and Algorithms. Wiley & sons (2013)
5. Benson, H.P.: Existence of efficient solutions for vector maximization problems. J. Optim. Theory Appl. **26**, 569–580 (1978)
6. Bracken, J., McGill, J.: Mathematical programs with optimization problems in the constraints. Oper. Res. **21**, 37–44 (1973)
7. Brownlee, J.: Clever Algorithms: Nature-inspired Programming Recipes. Jason Brownlee (2011)

8. Chen, L., Liu, H.L., Tan, K.C., Li, K.: Transfer learning-based parallel evolutionary algorithm framework for bilevel optimization. IEEE Trans. Evol. Comput. **26**(1), 115–129 (2021)

9. Dempe, S.: Foundations of Bilevel Programming. Kluwer Academic Publishers, Secaucus, NJ, USA (2002)

10. Ehrgott, M.: Weighted sum scalarization. In: Multicriteria Optimization, pp. 55–75. Springer (2000)

11. Eiselt, H.A., Sandblom, C.L.: Linear Programming and Its Applications. Springer Science & Business Media (2007)

12. Gendreau, M., Potvin, J.Y.: Handbook of Metaheuristics, vol. 2. Springer (2010)

13. Islam, M.M., Singh, H.K., Ray, T., Sinha, A.: An enhanced memetic algorithm for single-objective bilevel optimization problems. Evol. Comput. **25**(4), 607–642 (2017)

14. Islam, M.M., Singh, H.K., Ray, T.: A surrogate assisted approach for single-objective bilevel optimization. IEEE Trans. Evol. Comput. **21**(5), 681–696 (2017)

15. Islam, M.M., Singh, H.K., Ray, T.: Efficient global optimization for solving computationally expensive bilevel optimization problems. In: IEEE Congress on Evolutionary Computation (CEC), pp. 1–8 (2018)

16. Kasimbeyli, R.: A conic scalarization method in multi-objective optimization. J. Global Optim. **56**, 279–297 (2013)

17. Li, H.: A genetic algorithm using a finite search space for solving nonlinear/linear fractional bilevel programming problems. Ann. Oper. Res. 1–16 (2015)

18. Luenberger, D.G., Ye, Y.: Linear and Nonlinear Programming, vol. 2. Springer (1984)

19. Mathieu, R., Pittard, L., Anandalingam, G.: Genetic algorithm based approach to bi-level linear programming. Oper. Res. **28**(1), 1–21 (1994)

20. Ruuska, S., Miettinen, K., Wiecek, M.M.: Connections between single-level and bilevel multiobjective optimization. J. Optim. Theory Appl. **153**, 60 – 74 (2011). https://api.semanticscholar.org/CorpusID:19555179

21. Singh, H.K., Islam, M.M., Ray, T., Ryan, M.: Nested evolutionary algorithms for computationally expensive bilevel optimization problems: variants and their systematic analysis. Swarm Evol. Comput. **48**, 329–344 (2019)

22. Sinha, A., Lu, Z., Deb, K., Malo, P.: Bilevel optimization based on iterative approximation of multiple mappings. J. Heuristics **26**(2), 151–185 (2020)

23. Sinha, A., Malo, P., Deb, K.: Evolutionary algorithm for bilevel optimization using approximations of the lower level optimal solution mapping. Eur. J. Oper. Res. **257**(2), 395–411 (2017)

24. Sinha, A., Malo, P., Deb, K.: A review on bilevel optimization: from classical to evolutionary approaches and applications. IEEE Trans. Evol. Comput. **22**(2), 276–295 (2018)

25. Sinha, A., Malo, P., Frantsev, A., Deb, K.: Finding optimal strategies in a multi-period multi-leader-follower stackelberg game using an evolutionary algorithm. Comput. Oper. Res. **41**, 374–385 (2014)

26. Sinha, A., Malo, P., Deb, K.: Towards understanding bilevel multi-objective optimization with deterministic lower level decisions. In: Evolutionary Multi-Criterion Optimization: 8th International Conference, EMO 2015, Guimarães, Portugal, March 29–April 1, 2015. Proceedings, Part I 8, pp. 426–443. Springer (2015)

27. Sinha, A., Malo, P., Deb, K., Korhonen, P., Wallenius, J.: Solving bilevel multi-criterion optimization problems with lower level decision uncertainty. IEEE Trans. Evol. Comput. **20**(2), 199–217 (2015)

28. Sinha, A., Pujara, D., Singh, H.K.: Decomposition of difficulties in complex optimization problems using a bilevel approach. In: 2024 IEEE Congress on Evolutionary Computation (CEC), pp. 1–8. IEEE (2024)

29. Sinha, A., Shaikh, V.: Solving bilevel optimization problems using kriging approximations. IEEE Trans. Cybern. **52**(10), 10639–10654 (2021)

30. Wang, B., Singh, H.K., Ray, T.: Investigating neighborhood solution transfer schemes for bilevel optimization. In: IEEE Congress on Evolutionary Computation (CEC), pp. 1–8 (2022)

31. Zadeh, L.: Optimality and non-scalar-valued performance criteria. IEEE Trans. Autom. Control **8**(1), 59–60 (1963)

32. Zitzler, E., Deb, K., Thiele, L.: Comparison of multiobjective evolutionary algorithms: empirical results. Evol. Comput. **8**(2), 173–195 (2000)

A Study on Optimistic and Pessimistic Pareto-Fronts in Multiobjective Bilevel Optimization via δ-Perturbation

Margarita Antoniou[1,3]($\boxtimes$) ![ORCID], Ankur Sinha[2] ![ORCID], and Gregor Papa[1,3] ![ORCID]

[1] Computer Systems Department, Jožef Stefan Institute, Jamova c. 39,
Ljubljana, Slovenia
{margarita.antoniou,gregor.papa}@ijs.si
[2] Operations and Decision Sciences, Indian Institute of Management Ahmedabad,
Gujarat, India
asinha@iima.ac.in
[3] Jožef Stefan International Postgraduate School, Jamova c. 39, Ljubljana, Slovenia

Abstract. In bilevel optimization, an upper level (UL) decision maker seeks to optimize an objective function while considering the optimal solutions of a lower level (LL) optimization problem. This hierarchical structure poses modeling and solution challenges, especially when the LL problem has multiple solutions. In such a case, the UL needs to make assumptions about the LL reaction. In the optimistic approach, the UL assumes that the LL reaction will be favorable, while in the pessimistic approach the opposite is true. In this study, we consider the case of a multiobjective bilevel optimization problem, where the UL has multiple objectives, while the LL has a single objective, but multiple optimal solutions for any given UL decision. Given that the LL can choose any solution from its optimal set, and in case the UL is not aware of the LL choice function, it leads to the possibility of two Pareto-optimal fronts at the UL, i.e. the optimistic and the pessimistic frontiers. To approximate both Pareto-optimal fronts, a δ-perturbation approximation is proposed in this paper, where the LL objective is perturbed by a small δ by utilizing the UL objectives at the LL. The perturbed reformulated bilevel problem is then solved via an extension of m-BLEAQ, an evolutionary bilevel algorithm that can deal with bilevel problems with multiple objectives at the UL and a single objective at the LL. The application of the m-BLEAQ algorithm to the reformulated bilevel problem leads to the identification of the optimistic and pessimistic frontiers for the multiobjective bilevel problem. In this proof-of-concept study, the proposed reformulation strategy is demonstrated on two test problems, showing the effectiveness of the proposal in accurately finding the optimistic and pessimistic frontiers.

Keywords: Multiobjective bilevel optimization · Optimistic approach · Pessimistic approach · Evolutionary multiobjective optimization

H. Singh et al. (Eds.): EMO 2025, LNCS 15512, pp. 103–117, 2025.
https://doi.org/10.1007/978-981-96-3506-1_8

1   Introduction

A bilevel optimization problem (BOP) constitutes a distinctive category of optimization problems, characterized by two interconnected optimization levels: the upper level (UL) and the lower level (LL). The two levels control different sets of variables and have their own objective functions and constraints. Due to its hierarchical nested nature, the LL problem is part of the UL constraints, which requires that every feasible UL solution satisfies the optimality conditions of the LL optimization problem. Related overviews for bilevel optimization can be found in [2,10,26]. In case both or one of the levels have multiple objectives, we have a multiobjective bilevel optimization problem (MBOP). The readers can find a comprehensive review on these problems in [11].

In bilevel optimization problems, when the LL has multiple solutions for each UL solution, it implies that a set of efficient LL decision vectors exists for each given UL vector. This means that for a given UL decision, the optimal LL solution is not a singleton, but a set. This creates ambiguity about which LL solution should be used by the UL while searching for the bilevel optimal solution(s). To address this uncertainty, two approaches are commonly taken: the optimistic and pessimistic approach [26]. When taking an optimistic perspective, the UL assumes that the LL will choose that solution from its optimal set, which is the best for the UL. In the pessimistic approach, the UL aims to optimize their objective by assuming that the LL may make a worst-case choice for the UL.

For most situations, the UL does not have knowledge of the choice function of the LL, meaning the LL may select any solution from its set of optimal solutions for a given UL decision. In the case of multiobjective bilevel optimization, this can result in two distinct Pareto-optimal fronts for the UL and also raises a number of decision making difficulties. These fronts correspond to the best and worst-case scenarios, respectively, for the objectives of the UL, and finding these frontiers is the focus of this study.

In recent years, evolutionary approaches (EAs) have been developed to address the multiobjective bilevel problem, such as [9,12,14]. The authors of [9] suggested an evolutionary local-search algorithm for multiobjective bilevel problems that handles multiple objectives at both levels. The work was an improvement over the older versions of their algorithm [8,22]. Further improvements in multiobjective bilevel solution methods were made in [20] by approximating the LL Pareto-optimal set.

The multiobjective bilevel evolutionary algorithm (m-BLEAQ) was proposed in [24,27] to solve problems with multiple objectives at the UL and a single objective at the LL. A value function, representing the preferences of the LL decision maker, models LL optimization when both levels have multiple objectives. This value function selects a single preferred solution from the LL Pareto front, effectively reducing the multiobjective LL problem to a single-objective one. This reduction assumes that the preference structure of the LL decision maker is known to the UL decision maker. The algorithm's principle relies on estimating LL decisions as a function of UL decisions, utilizing local quadratic approximations to reduce computational costs. Similar bilevel mapping-approximation ideas are used to solve single objective bilevel optimization problems as well [19,21]. In cases of single objective at the LL, if the LL returns a singleton, an optimistic or pessimistic position does not arise.

Most multiobjective methods [9,12] assume an optimistic approach, mostly due to the ease in finding the Pareto-optimal front compared to the pessimistic case. In the context of the pessimistic approach, additional levels of complexity arise from the intricate decision-making interactions between UL and LL. However, the solutions on an optimistic Pareto-optimal frontier are not always realistic since the UL cannot control the choices of the LL. Moreover, the pessimistic Pareto front is essential as it provides a bound for worst-case LL responses. By identifying this front, the decision maker ensures robustness, i.e., by choosing a point from the pessimistic frontier, the UL decision maker's actual realized solution can never be in the region dominated by the frontier, irrespective of the choices of the LL decision maker. In [1], the authors focused on semivectorial[1] bilevel problems and suggested that, apart from optimistic and pessimistic solutions, an UL may also aim for intermediate (moderate) solutions based on the level of risk they are willing to take.

Recently, Deb et al. [7] introduced an evolutionary approach for such hierarchical problem solving, allowing UL decision makers to minimize deviations from their expectations caused by independent LL decisions by identifying a set of pseudopessimistic solutions. To our best knowledge, there is no study that approximates both the optimistic and pessimistic Pareto-optimal fronts of the multiobjective bilevel optimization problem, where the UL contains multiple objectives and the LL contains a single objective with multiple optimal solutions.

In the classical bilevel optimization literature, approximation methods exist for addressing problems with specific mathematical structures- e.g. linearity or convexity- where pessimistic formulations are perturbed and reformulated to facilitate solvability [17,18]. Using an appropriate perturbation strategy for optimistic or pessimistic formulations, it is possible to ensure that the LL problem contains a unique (approximate) optimal solution for any given UL decision. In our previous work [3], we introduced the δ-perturbed formulation for bilevel optimization, designed to handle the challenge of multiple optimal solutions at the LL. This approach modifies the LL objective by incorporating the UL objective by introducing a small perturbation parameter δ. We provided theoretical proofs that establish error bounds and computational results that validate the theoretical findings. The perturbation approach is able to solve bilevel problems with both optimistic and pessimistic formulations by forcing a single optimal solution from the LL optimization problem. The approach thus enables standard bilevel algorithms to be applied to the optimistic as well as the pessimistic formulations.

Building on this foundation, in the present work we extend the δ-perturbed approach for multiobjective bilevel optimization problems that contain multiple objectives at the UL and single objective with multiple optimal solutions at the

---

[1] In semivectorial bilevel optimization, the UL problem is single objective, while the LL problem is multiobjective.

LL. Our contributions lie in reformulating such a bilevel optimization problem in a form so that the LL returns a singleton for optimistic and pessimistic positions. This enables our approach to identify both the optimistic and pessimistic Pareto-frontiers for the problem. In this proof-of-concept study, we use the m-BLEAQ algorithm [24] to solve the reformulated problem, demonstrating the effectiveness of the proposed δ-perturbation method in identifying optimistic and pessimistic Pareto-optimal fronts.

The remainder of this paper is organized as follows: In Sect. 2, we provide definitions of the MBOP and its optimistic and pessimistic Pareto-optimal fronts. Section 3 introduces the proposed δ-perturbation approach for MBOPs. Section 4 presents the evaluation of the proposed method on two test problems. Finally, Sect. 5 concludes the paper and outlines potential directions for future research.

2   Background

In this section, we present the mathematical formulation of the multiobjective bilevel optimization problem. Moreover, we define the optimistic and pessimistic Pareto-optimal fronts.

2.1   Multiobjective Bilevel Optimization Problem

The general mathematical definition of a multiobjective bilevel optimization problem is as follows:

$$\underset{x,y}{\text{``min''}} \, F(x,y) = (F_1(x,y), \ldots, F_M(x,y))$$

subject to

$$y \in \underset{y}{\text{argmin}} \, \{f(x,y) = (f_1(x,y), \ldots, f_N(x,y)) : g_j(x,y) \leq 0, \, j = 1, \ldots, J\}$$

$$G_k(x,y) \leq 0, \, k = 1, \ldots, K$$

$G_k : \mathbb{R}^n \times \mathbb{R}^m \to \mathbb{R}, \, k = 1, \ldots, K$, denotes the kth UL constraint, and $g_j : \mathbb{R}^n \times \mathbb{R}^m \to \mathbb{R}, \, j = 1, \ldots, J$, denotes the jth LL constraint. For simplicity, we do not include equality constraints. Any variable bounds on x and y are included in the inequality constraint set.

In this study, we are interested in the following case of multiobjective bilevel optimization problems, where the UL has multiple objectives while the LL has a single objective:

$$\underset{x,y}{\text{``min''}} \, F(x,y) = (F_1(x,y), \ldots, F_M(x,y)) \tag{1}$$

subject to

$$y \in \underset{y}{\text{argmin}} \, \{f(x,y) : g_j(x,y) \leq 0, \, j = 1, \ldots, J\} \tag{2}$$

$$G_k(x,y) \leq 0, \, k = 1, \ldots, K \tag{3}$$

The problem under consideration in this paper can also be expressed in terms of set-valued mapping, $\Psi : \mathbb{R}^n \rightrightarrows \mathbb{R}^m$ as follows, where $g(x, y)$ and $G(x, y)$ represent vector-valued constraints:

$$\Psi(x) = \underset{y}{\operatorname{argmin}}\{f(x, y) : g(x, y) \leq 0\}$$

The multiobjective bilevel optimization problem, in terms of $\Psi(x)$, can be formulated as a constrained optimization problem in the following manner:

$$\underset{x,y}{\text{"min"}} \, F(x, y) = (F_1(x, y), \ldots, F_M(x, y))$$

subject to

$$y \in \Psi(x), \quad G(x, y) \leq 0$$

Note that we are using quotations in our formulations as we have not yet defined the position that we take, i.e. optimistic or pessimistic, while solving the problem. Without stating the position, the above formulations are ill-posed.

2.2   Optimistic vs. Pessimistic Pareto Front

As discussed, when the LL contains multiple optimal solutions for a given UL decision, we have to make some assumptions. If the UL anticipates that the LL will select that optimal solution from its set that suits the UL, we state that the UL is taking an optimistic position. In such cases, the UL desires to identify an optimistic Pareto-optimal front. The optimistic Pareto-front corresponds to the solution of the following problem.

$$\underset{x,y}{\min} \, F(x, y) = (F_1(x, y), \ldots, F_M(x, y))$$

subject to

$$y \in \Psi^O(x), \quad G(x, y) \leq 0$$

where $\Psi^O(x)$ is a subset of $\Psi(x)$, which provides the optimistic UL feasible solutions and is defined as follows:

$$\Psi^O(x) = \underset{y}{\operatorname{argmin}}\{(F_1(x, y), \ldots, F_M(x, y)) \mid y \in \Psi(x)\}$$

Optimistic Pareto Front Definition: The Pareto front P^O consists of those solutions (x^*, y^*) from $\Omega^O = \{(x, y) : y \in \Psi^O(x), G(x, y) \leq 0\}$ for which there is no solution (x', y') that simultaneously satisfies the following conditions:

$\forall \, i = 1$ to M, $F_i(x', y') \leq F_i(x^*, y^*)$ for $(x^*, y^*) \in \Omega^O, (x', y') \in \Omega^O$

$\exists \, j$ such that $F_j(x', y') < F_j(x^*, y^*)$ for $(x^*, y^*) \in \Omega^O, (x', y') \in \Omega^O$

If the UL anticipates the worst-case from LL, we take the pessimistic approach and converge to the pessimistic Pareto front. The solutions here are:

$$\min_{x,y} F(x,y) = (F_1(x,y), \ldots, F_M(x,y))$$

subject to

$$y \in \Psi^P(x), \quad G(x,y) \leq 0$$

where $\Psi^P(x)$ is a subset of $\Psi(x)$, which provides the pessimistic UL feasible solutions and is defined as follows:

$$\Psi^P(x) = \underset{y}{\mathrm{argmax}}\{(F_1(x,y), \ldots, F_M(x,y)) \mid y \in \Psi(x)\}$$

> **Pessimistic Pareto Front Definition:** The Pareto front P^P consists of those solutions (x^*, y^*) from $\Omega^P = \{(x,y) : y \in \Psi^P(x), G(x,y) \leq 0\}$ for which there is no solution (x', y') that simultaneously satisfies the following conditions:
>
> $$\forall\, i = 1 \text{ to } M,\ F_i(x', y') \leq F_i(x^*, y^*) \quad \text{for } (x^*, y^*) \in \Omega^P, (x', y') \in \Omega^P$$
> $$\exists\, j \text{ such that } F_j(x', y') < F_j(x^*, y^*) \quad \text{for } (x^*, y^*) \in \Omega^P, (x', y') \in \Omega^P$$

The relationship between the objective space (F-space) and the decision space $\Psi(x) - x$ for a multiobjective bilevel optimization problem (two UL objectives and one LL objective with multiple optimal solutions) is shown through Fig. 1. For simplicity, assume that there are no UL constraints, $G(x,y) \leq 0$. On the left, the decision space $\Psi(x) - x$ is shown, where the shaded gray region represents the full set of feasible y for each x. The blue curve represents a subset of optimistic feasible solutions, $\Psi^O(x)$, that contribute to the optimistic Pareto front, while the red curve represents a subset of pessimistic feasible solutions, $\Psi^P(x)$, that contribute to the pessimistic Pareto front. Optimistic and pessimistic solutions for a few x are shown as blue and red circles, respectively. The gray points denote solutions that are part of $\Psi(x)$ but do not lie on either the optimistic or the pessimistic Pareto fronts.

On the right, the objective space is illustrated, where the functions F_1 and F_2 represent the UL objectives. Once again, the blue curve represents the optimistic Pareto front (P^O), and the red curve represents the pessimistic Pareto front (P^P) for a minimization case. The red, blue, and gray points from the left-hand side figure map on to the corresponding points in the right-hand side figure.

The left figure also shows a special UL solution, x^0, for which all the LL optimal solutions are shown in green. On the green line, the blue point corresponds to a solution on the optimistic Pareto front, the red point corresponds to a solution on the pessimistic Pareto front, and the gray point corresponds to neither of the two. All the solutions on the green line in the left figure are mapped to the green curve in the right figure.

It is important to note that in some sense the pessimistic Pareto front can be regarded as an upper bound (in the case of minimization) for the UL decision maker. If a UL decision maker chooses a decision (say (x^0, y')) from the pessimistic Pareto front, then no matter which solution among the multiple optimal solutions is picked up by the LL decision maker (say y'' for x^0), the solution (x^0, y'') will lie somewhere between the pessimistic and optimistic frontiers. The figure illustrates one such scenario using green lines. However, note that it is not necessary that there will always be an optimistic Pareto point corresponding to a UL decision made from the pessimistic Pareto front (as in the case of UL decision x^1 for which LL decisions are shown with yellow lines). Since the realized solution may lie anywhere between the two frontiers, the problem considered in this paper raises a number of decision making difficulties.

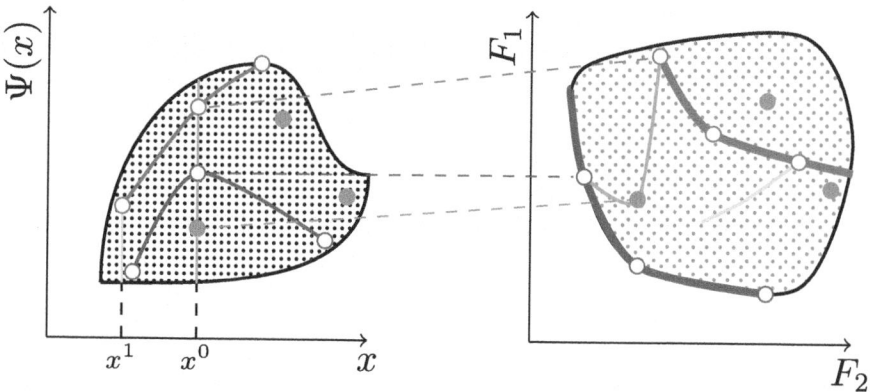

Fig. 1. Illustration of the UL decision space $\Psi(x) - x$ (left) and the UL objective space F (right).

3 δ-Perturbation of MBOPs

In this section, we explain the δ-perturbed formulation of the MBOP. For better understanding, let us first introduce the δ-perturbed formulation of the single-objective bilevel problem,

$$\underset{x,y}{\text{"min"}} \quad F(x,y)$$
$$\text{s.t.} \quad G(x,y) \leq 0$$
$$y \in \operatorname{argmin}\{f(x,y) \mid g(x,y) \leq 0\}$$

which has been thoroughly analyzed in [3]. For a small positive δ, the perturbed optimistic and pessimistic bilevel formulation is obtained by adding or subtracting $\delta F(x,y)$, respectively, as follows:

$$\min_{x,y} \quad F(x,y) \tag{4}$$

$$\text{s.t.} \quad G(x,y) \leq 0 \tag{5}$$

$$y \in \operatorname*{argmin}_{y} \{ f(x,y) \pm \delta F(x,y) \,|\, g(x,y) \leq 0 \} \tag{6}$$

When δ is extremely small, the above formulation leads to an approximate optimistic/pessimistic solution depending on the sign that is chosen. In this paper, we extend this idea for multiobjective bilevel problems where the UL has multiple objectives, while the LL has a single objective but multiple optimal solutions corresponding to a UL decision.

Theorem 1. *For a bilevel optimization problem with multiple objectives at the UL and a single objective at the LL, approximate optimistic and pessimistic Pareto-fronts can be obtained by solving the following bilevel problem with a '+' and '-' sign, respectively.*

$$\min_{x,w,y} \quad F(x,y) = (F_1(x,y), \ldots, F_M(x,y)) \tag{7}$$

$$\text{s.t.} \quad G(x,y) \leq 0 \tag{8}$$

$$y \in \operatorname*{argmin}_{y} \{ f(x,y) \pm \delta V(w, F(x,y)) \,|\, g(x,y) \leq 0 \} \tag{9}$$

where $V(.)$ represents a suitable scalarization scheme such as weighted sum scalarization [13], weighted Chebyshev [28], conic scalarization [16] or Benson's scalarization [5] techniques with w being the preference vector, which is considered to be an UL variable.

Proof. Let us write the problem in (1)–(3) into a single objective problem at the UL for a given preference vector w.

$$\text{``}\min_{x,y}\text{''} \ V(w, F_1(x,y), \ldots, F_M(x,y)) \tag{10}$$

subject to

$$y \in \operatorname*{argmin}_{y} \{ f(x,y) : g_j(x,y) \leq 0, \ j = 1, \ldots, J \} \tag{11}$$

$$G_k(x,y) \leq 0, \ k = 1, \ldots, K \tag{12}$$

Using (4)–(6), one can find the approximated optimistic and the pessimistic solutions for (10)–(12) by solving the following problem.

$$\min_{x,w,y} \quad V(w, F_1(x,y), \ldots, F_M(x,y))$$

$$\text{s.t.} \quad G(x,y) \leq 0$$

$$y \in \operatorname*{argmin}_{y} \{ f(x,y) \pm \delta V(w, F(x,y)) \,|\, g(x,y) \leq 0 \}$$

If the above problem is solved for all possible values of w, it leads to all the (approximate) optimistic and (approximate) pessimistic solutions corresponding to w. Therefore, one can solve the multiobjective problem in (7)–(9) to get an approximation of the entire optimistic and pessimistic Pareto-fronts by choosing the appropriate signs (+/-).

4   Proof-of-Concept Results

In this section, we briefly describe the m-BLEAQ algorithm, the test problems, and the results obtained from applying the proposed approach. It is important to note that the focus of this work is not on developing or testing a new algorithm but rather on reformulating bilevel optimization problems using the δ-perturbation method. The m-BLEAQ algorithm is utilized as an existing solver to demonstrate the feasibility and effectiveness of the reformulated problem.

4.1   m-BLEAQ Algorithm and Experimental Settings

The multiobjective BiLevel Evolutionary Algorithm based on Quadratic approximations, known as m-BLEAQ [24], is a model-based evolutionary method that utilizes insights from parametric optimization theory to reduce computational costs. It is an extension of BLEAQ [21], which was developed for solving single objective bilevel problems and was later extended to BLEAQ-II [19]. BLEAQ utilizes only the reaction set mapping in its implementation, while BLEAQ-II utilizes both the reaction set mapping and value function mapping to solve bilevel problems. In this paper, we employ both the reaction set mapping and value function mapping in our m-BLEAQ implementation, following BLEAQ-II's approach.

With approximations of the mappings in bilevel optimization, the algorithm quickly converges to the Pareto-optimal solutions of the multiobjective bilevel problem. The algorithm has been applied and found to approximate successfully the Pareto fronts to problems with known LL value function in both test problems [24] and applications, such as transportation policy [25] and agricultural policy [4]. Given its capability to handle bilevel problems with multiobjective UL problems and single-objective LL problems, it can serve as a baseline algorithm to validate our proposal in this paper.

The parameters used in m-BLEAQ were maintained at their default settings, with the exception of the population size and generation size, both of which were set to 500. These values were chosen to ensure a sufficiently large population for testing the perturbation method, without any parameter tuning. The perturbation value δ was set to 0.01, chosen as a small enough value based on our previous work [3]. The weighted-sum scalarization technique was used, with the weight parameter w sampled from $[0, 1]$. For each test problem, we conducted 20 independent runs on an Intel(R) Core(TM) i5-8365U CPU @ 1.60GHz with 16 GB of RAM running Windows 10 and MATLAB R2023b.

4.2   Test Problems

The first problem in our study, referred to as Test Problem 1, is taken from [8], where it originally includes two objectives at both the UL and LL. In our formulation, we modify the LL problem to have a single objective with multiple optimal solutions, as shown below:

$$\min_{x,y} \quad F_1(x,y) = (y_1 - 1)^2 + y_2^2 + x^2$$
$$F_2(x,y) = (y_1 - 1)^2 + y_2^2 + (x - 1)^2$$
$$\text{s.t.} \quad y \in \underset{y}{\operatorname{argmin}}\{\sqrt{y_1^2 + y_2^2} + \sqrt{(y_1 - x)^2 + y_2^2} : -1 \le y_1, y_2 \le 2\}$$
$$-1 \le x \le 2$$

The optimistic PF is obtained when $x \in [0.5, 1]$ and $y_1 = x, y_2 = 0$. In contrast, the pessimistic PF is derived for $x \in [0, 1]$ and $y_1 = y_2 = 0$.

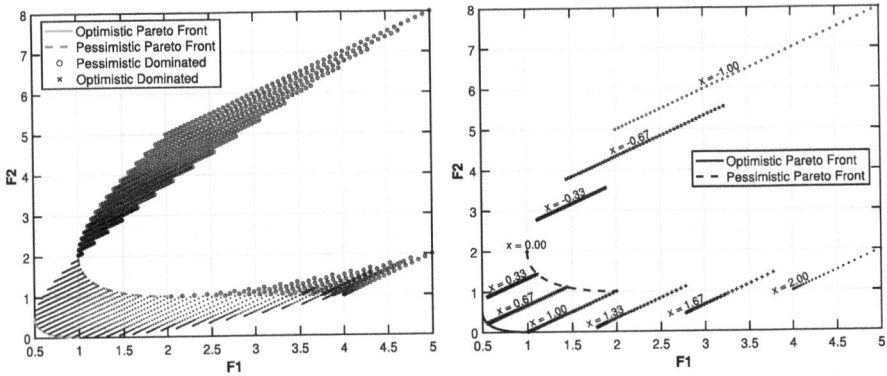

(a) Optimistic and pessimistic Pareto fronts in the UL objective space.

(b) Optimal LL solutions for various x by varying y_1 and keeping $y_2 = 0$.

Fig. 2. Illustration of the optimistic and pessimistic feasible solutions in the UL objective space for Test Problem 1.

We illustrate the characteristics of Test Problem 1 through Fig. 2, which shows the relationship between optimistic and pessimistic solutions in the UL objective space. If for any fixed x, the LL has multiple optimal solutions to choose from, then we refer to the non-dominated solution(s) with respect to the UL objectives as optimistic solution(s). Conversely, for that x, the solutions in the subset of pessimistic feasible space are referred to as pessimistic solution(s), with the non-dominated solutions among them forming the pessimistic Pareto front. For certain problems, for any given x, the optimistic/pessimistic solution(s) may coincide. Our objective is to find the best (with respect to UL objectives) optimistic and pessimistic fronts, i.e. optimistic and pessimistic Pareto fronts. Figure 2a shows the optimistic and pessimistic feasible solutions in the UL objective space. The solid line represents the optimistic Pareto front, while the dashed line corresponds to the pessimistic Pareto front. The black points represent pessimistic-dominated solutions, while the 'x' markers denote optimistic-dominated solutions. Naturally, all pessimistic solutions, including both the Pareto front and the dominated solutions, are dominated by the optimistic Pareto front. Figure 2b illustrates the range of LL optimal solutions for a fixed value of x in the UL decision space. The multiple LL optimal solutions for any x can be generated by fixing $y_2 = 0$ and varying y_1.

The second problem considered in our study is Test Problem 2, which combines modified SMD1 at the UL and SMD6 at the LL [23]. SMD6 is selected for the LL due to its multimodal structure. The description of Test Problem 2 is as follows:

$$\min_{x,y} \quad F_1(x,y) = x_1^2 + y_1^2 + y_2^2 + x_2^2 + (x_2 - y_3)^2$$
$$F_2(x,y) = 1 - |x_1| + x_2^2 + y_1^2 + y_2^2 + (x_2 - y_3)^2$$
$$\text{s.t.} \quad y \in \underset{y}{\operatorname{argmin}}\{x_1^2 + (y_2 - y_1)^2 + (x_2 - y_2)^2 : -5 \le y_1, y_2 \le 10\}$$
$$-5 \le x_1, x_2, x_3 \le 10$$

The optimistic PF is obtained when $x_1 \in [-5, 10]$ and $x_2 = y_1 = y_2 = y_3 = 0$, while the pessimistic PF is derived for $x_1 \in [-5, 10]$ and $x_2 = y_3 = 0, y_1 = y_2 = 10$.

4.3 Results and Discussion

To evaluate the performance of the algorithm, it is essential to choose an appropriate performance indicator to assess the quality and diversity of the solutions obtained. Commonly used indicators in multiobjective EAs include hypervolume (HV) [29], inverted generational distance (IGD) [6], and others. While using EAs with a perturbation strategy, the Pareto-optimal solutions obtained are an approximation of the true optima. Therefore, a better Pareto front in terms of HV may not necessarily indicate superior algorithm performance, as an inaccurate solution at the LL may provide an artificially better UL solution. Instead, IGD calculates the sum of distances between each point of the true Pareto front and the nearest non-dominated set found by the algorithm. Smaller IGD values indicate that the approximated points are closer to the Pareto front of the problem. IGD+ [15], a Pareto-compliant alternative, modifies IGD by incorporating dominance relationships to exclude dominated solutions, ensuring a more accurate assessment. Both IGD and IGD+ are used in this study to analyze the quality of the approximated Pareto front.

We report four IGD values, IGD_O, IGD_{O+}, IGD_P, and IGD_{P+}, for the optimistic and pessimistic Pareto fronts in Table 1, calculated as the median of 20 runs. For the first problem, all values are of the order 0.001, while for the second problem, they are of the order 0.01. This difference can be attributed to the higher dimensionality and complexity of the second problem. In all cases, $IGD+$ values are slightly higher than IGD due to the exclusion of dominated solutions, which can artificially improve IGD by reducing the apparent distance to the true Pareto front. Both results demonstrate that the algorithm effectively approximates the true Pareto fronts.

To further illustrate the performance, we display in Fig. 3 the true optimistic (blue line) and pessimistic (red line) Pareto fronts, alongside the final population solutions (blue and red) and the Pareto fronts derived from these solutions for

Table 1. Median IGD and IGD+ values for the Test Problems over 20 runs.

	IGD_O	IGD_{O+}	IGD_P	IGD_{P+}
Test Problem 1	2.218e-03	2.699e-03	2.652e-03	2.653e-03
Test Problem 2	6.097e-02	6.30e-02	5.930e-02	6.091e-02

the two Test Problems after one run. The black circles indicate the pessimistic-nondominated solutions from the final population, while the black crosses show the optimistic-nondominated solutions. In Fig. 3a, which corresponds to Test Problem 1, the solutions found are densely distributed and spread well, closely approximating the true Pareto fronts. In Fig. 3b, which corresponds to Test Problem 2, the solutions are less densely distributed, which aligns with the slightly higher IGD values observed above.

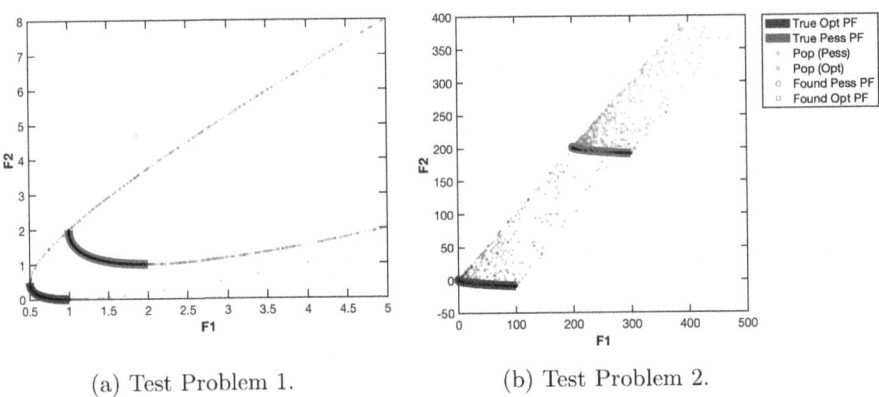

(a) Test Problem 1.   (b) Test Problem 2.

Fig. 3. True and algorithm-obtained Pareto fronts for optimistic and pessimistic cases and algorithm's final population. (Color figure online)

For both test problems, the optimistic and pessimistic Pareto fronts can become valuable tools for decision-makers. For example, in both test problems, the optimistic and pessimistic solutions deviate significantly. From a decision-maker's perspective, the risk of adopting the optimistic assumption may result in surprises and substantial costs to the UL decision maker. This makes such a kind of analysis critically important. Also note that identifying the optimistic and pessimistic Pareto fronts does not completely solve the decision making challenges for these problems.

As a final remark, it is important to highlight that, as previously mentioned, we used the weighted sum scalarization, and it worked well since the specific Pareto fronts are convex. In the case of nonconvexity, other suitable methods should be selected.

5   Conclusion and Future Work

In this paper, we investigated the multiobjective bilevel optimization problem, where the UL has multiple objectives, and the LL has a single-objective but multiple optimal solutions for any given UL decision. We first defined the problem, introducing both optimistic and pessimistic Pareto-fronts in the context of multiobjective bilevel problems. To approximate these fronts, we developed a perturbation technique that perturbs the lower-level objective by a small δ based on the weighted values of the UL objectives. The reformulated bilevel problem was then addressed using m-BLEAQ, an evolutionary algorithm capable of handling multiple objectives at the UL. The effectiveness of the proposed method was demonstrated through tests on two benchmark problems, successfully capturing both optimistic and pessimistic Pareto fronts.

As part of our ongoing research, we plan to extend this work by testing the proposed approach on a wider range of benchmark problems and exploring real-world applications. Additionally, a theoretical investigation of the δ-perturbation method, including the derivation of error bounds, will be valuable for further refinement. We also aim to expand this approach to scenarios where both levels involve multiobjective optimization, potentially offering decision-makers richer, more informed solution landscapes in multiobjective bilevel problems.

Acknowledgements. The authors acknowledge the financial support from the Slovenian Research Agency (research core funding No. P2-0098). This work was also partially funded by the European Union's Horizon Europe research an innovation programme under Grant Agreement No 101077049 (CONDUCTOR).

References

1. Alves, M.J., Antunes, C.H., Costa, J.P.: New concepts and an algorithm for multiobjective bilevel programming: optimistic, pessimistic and moderate solutions. Oper. Res. Int. Journal **21**(4), 2593–2626 (2021)
2. Antoniou, M., Korošec, P.: Multilevel optimisation. Optim. Under Uncertainty Appl. Aerosp. Eng. 307–331 (2021)
3. Antoniou, M., Sinha, A., Papa, G.: δ-perturbation of bilevel optimization problems: an error bound analysis. Oper. Res. Perspect. 100315 (2024)
4. Barnharta, B., et al.: Handling practicalities in agricultural policy optimization for water quality improvements coin report number 2017007
5. Benson, H.P.: Existence of efficient solutions for vector maximization problems. J. Optim. Theory Appl. **26**, 569–580 (1978)
6. Coello Coello, C.A., Reyes Sierra, M.: A study of the parallelization of a coevolutionary multi-objective evolutionary algorithm. In: Monroy, R., Arroyo-Figueroa, G., Sucar, L.E., Sossa, H. (eds.) MICAI 2004. LNCS (LNAI), vol. 2972, pp. 688–697. Springer, Heidelberg (2004). https://doi.org/10.1007/978-3-540-24694-7_71
7. Deb, K., et al.: Minimizing expected deviation in upper-level outcomes due to lower-level decision-making in hierarchical multi-objective problems. IEEE Trans. Evol. Comput. (2022)

8. Deb, K., Sinha, A.: Solving bilevel multi-objective optimization problems using evolutionary algorithms. In: International Conference on Evolutionary Multi-criterion Optimization, pp. 110–124. Springer (2009)

9. Deb, K., Sinha, A.: An efficient and accurate solution methodology for bilevel multi-objective programming problems using a hybrid evolutionary-local-search algorithm. Evol. Comput. **18**(3), 403–449 (2010)

10. Dempe, S., Kalashnikov, V., Pérez-Valdés, G.A., Kalashnykova, N.: Bilevel programming problems. Energy Syst.**10**, 978–3 (2015)

11. Mejía-de Dios, J.A., Rodríguez-Molina, A., Mezura-Montes, E.: Multiobjective bilevel optimization: a survey of the state-of-the-art. IEEE Trans. Syst. Man Cybern. Syst. (2023)

12. Eichfelder, G.: Solving nonlinear multiobjective bilevel optimization problems with coupled upper level constraints (2007). https://api.semanticscholar.org/CorpusID: 211008773

13. Gass, S., Saaty, T.: The computational algorithm for the parametric objective function. Naval Res. Logistics Q. **2**(1–2), 39–45 (1955)

14. Halter, W., Mostaghim, S.: Bilevel optimization of multi-component chemical systems using particle swarm optimization. In: 2006 IEEE International Conference on Evolutionary Computation, pp. 1240–1247 (2006). https://api.semanticscholar. org/CorpusID:22916372

15. Castro, O.R., Pozo, A.: Using hyper-heuristic to select leader and archiving methods for many-objective problems. In: Gaspar-Cunha, A., Henggeler Antunes, C., Coello, C.C. (eds.) EMO 2015. LNCS, vol. 9018, pp. 109–123. Springer, Cham (2015). https://doi.org/10.1007/978-3-319-15934-8_8

16. Kasimbeyli, R.: A conic scalarization method in multi-objective optimization. J. Global Optim. **56**, 279–297 (2013)

17. Lampariello, L., Sagratella, S., Stein, O.: The standard pessimistic bilevel problem. SIAM J. Optim. **29**(2), 1634–1656 (2019)

18. Loridan, P., Morgan, J.: Weak via strong stackelberg problem: new results. J. Global Optim. **8**, 263–287 (1996)

19. Sinha, A., Lu, Z., Deb, K., Malo, P.: Bilevel optimization based on iterative approximation of multiple mappings. J. Heuristics **26**(2), 151–185 (2020)

20. Sinha, A., Malo, P., Deb, K.: Approximated set-valued mapping approach for handling multiobjective bilevel problems. Comput. Oper. Res. **77**, 194–209 (2017)

21. Sinha, A., Malo, P., Deb, K.: Evolutionary algorithm for bilevel optimization using approximations of the lower level optimal solution mapping. Eur. J. Oper. Res. **257**(2), 395–411 (2017)

22. Sinha, A., Deb, K.: Towards understanding evolutionary bilevel multi-objective optimization algorithm. IFAC Proc. Volumes **42**(2), 338–343 (2009)

23. Sinha, A., Malo, P., Deb, K.: Test problem construction for single-objective bilevel optimization. Evol. Comput. **22**(3), 439–477 (2014)

24. Sinha, A., Malo, P., Deb, K.: Towards understanding bilevel multi-objective optimization with deterministic lower level decisions. In: Gaspar-Cunha, A., Henggeler Antunes, C., Coello, C.C. (eds.) EMO 2015. LNCS, vol. 9018, pp. 426–443. Springer, Cham (2015). https://doi.org/10.1007/978-3-319-15934-8_29

25. Sinha, A., Malo, P., Deb, K.: Transportation policy formulation as a multi-objective bilevel optimization problem. In: 2015 IEEE Congress on Evolutionary Computation (CEC), pp. 1651–1658. IEEE (2015)

26. Sinha, A., Malo, P., Deb, K.: A review on bilevel optimization: from classical to evolutionary approaches and applications. IEEE Trans. Evol. Comput. **22**(2), 276–295 (2017)

27. Sinha, A., Malo, P., Deb, K., Korhonen, P., Wallenius, J.: Solving bilevel multi-criterion optimization problems with lower level decision uncertainty. IEEE Trans. Evol. Comput. **20**(2), 199–217 (2015)
28. Zadeh, L.: Optimality and non-scalar-valued performance criteria. IEEE Trans. Autom. Control **8**(1), 59–60 (1963)
29. Zitzler, E., Thiele, L.: Multiobjective evolutionary algorithms: a comparative case study and the strength pareto approach. IEEE Trans. Evol. Comput. **3**(4), 257–271 (1999)

Cumulative Step Size Adaptation
for Adaptive SEMO in Integer Space

Günter Rudolph[1] and Markus Wagner[2(✉)]

[1] Department of Computer Science, TU Dortmund University, Dortmund, Germany
guenter.rudolph@tu-dortmund.de
[2] Department of Data Science and AI, Monash University, Clayton, Australia
markus.wagner@monash.edu

Abstract. Parameter control involves dynamically adjusting the parameter values of the evolutionary algorithm throughout the optimization process, including parameters like mutation rate and operator selection. Self-adaptation can improve the performance and robustness of the algorithm, however, parameter control mechanisms themselves need to be designed and configured carefully. In this article, we review the cumulative step size adaptation method originally proposed for single-objective optimization over continuous variables and recast it for deployment in multiobjective optimization over unbounded integer space. We contribute a systematic investigation of its hyperparameters which shows that while (1) the very best configurations remain problem-specific, (2) the performance of the algorithm is largely independent of the self-adaptation scheme's parameterization and initial configuration.

Keywords: step size adaptation · integer search space

1 Introduction

Multi-objective optimization (MOO) focuses on solving problems with multiple conflicting objectives that require simultaneous optimization. It is widely applied in fields like science, engineering, economics, and logistics, where solutions often involve balancing trade-offs among various criteria. Evolutionary computation, a key method in MOO, uses population-based search to approximate the Pareto frontier—the set of nondominated solutions representing optimal trade-offs. The field of evolutionary multi-objective optimization (EMO) has seen substantial research, leading to a diverse range of algorithms [4,13].

Many EMO methods require parameterization, such as setting population sizes and variation operator probabilities, which are often adjusted to enhance performance and robustness. According to Eiben et al. [8], parameters can be set either through offline optimization ("parameter tuning") or dynamically via online optimization ("parameter control"). The latter includes: (1) deterministic approaches, which assume consistent patterns in optimal settings; (2) adaptive

H. Singh et al. (Eds.): EMO 2025, LNCS 15512, pp. 118–131, 2025.
https://doi.org/10.1007/978-981-96-3506-1_9

approaches, which use feedback from the optimization process; and (3) self-adaptive approaches, where individuals themselves adjust parameters. However, the terms "adaptive" and "self-adaptive" can vary widely in usage, influenced by concepts from fields like "self-adaptive software systems" or "self-driving cars."

Self-adaptive approaches enjoy a long history and popularity, for example, with that of Abbass [1] being one of the first and with that of Igel et al. [10] being one that is based on self-adaptive, single-objective evolution strategies. Many works in this area often describe mechanisms and test a single parameterization on standard benchmarks, typically aiming to surpass the state-of-the-art rather than exploring design choices in depth.

Systematic investigations of (self-)adaptive algorithms are relatively rare, often focusing on single objectives and convergence in continuous settings [15], or bitstrings for computational complexity analysis. For instance, Doerr et al. introduced a simple $(1+1)$ EA with success-based multiplicative mutation rate adjustments and explored the influence of the adaptation scheme's initial values [6,7]. The only theoretical work we know of on self-adaptation in single-objective problems with integer decision spaces is also by Doerr et al. [5].

The SEMO algorithm, originally proposed for multiobjective evolutionary optimization over binary variables [12], was later adapted for unbounded integer space with an adaptive mutation step size in [18], leading to the ASEMO (adaptive SEMO) algorithm. ASEMO's adaptation was steered by a success-based rule at population level, i.e., the same step size was applied to every member of the population. Here, we replace this by an individual-based adaptation.

For this purpose, we review the *cumulative step size adaptation* (CSA) method originally proposed for step size control in evolutionary algorithms (EAs) for single-objective optimization over continuous variables [16] and recast it for use in evolutionary multiobjective optimization over unbounded integer space.

Section 2 introduces the mutation distributions over integers whereas Sect. 3 develops the CSA method for integer variables. We then evaluate the new method for some test problems in Sect. 4. We summarize our findings in Sect. 5 and point out observations warranting further research.

2   Adaptive SEMO in Integer Space

Since the representation of the individuals of the adaptive SEMO (ASEMO) are unbounded integer values gathered in an n-tuple, we need a mutation distribution with support $\mathbb{Z}^n$. The mutations are drawn from a *Discrete Laplace distribution* [11,17] with p.m.f.

$$\mathsf{P}\{Z = k\} = \frac{q}{2-q}(1-q)^{|k|} \tag{1}$$

with $q \in (0,1) \subset \mathbb{R}$ for $k \in \mathbb{Z}$ and moments

$$\mathsf{E}[Z] = 0, \quad \mathsf{V}[Z] = \frac{2(1-q)}{q^2} \quad \text{and} \quad \mathsf{E}[|Z|] = \frac{2(1-q)}{q(2-q)}. \tag{2}$$

We denote the 1-dimensional distribution with $DLap(q)$ and the n-dimensional distribution with $DLap(p,q)$ where parameter $p \in (0,1]$ is the probability to draw a random number $Z \sim DLap(q)$ independently in each dimension, i.e., $Z_k = Z$ with probability p and $Z_k = 0$ otherwise for $k = 1, \ldots, n$. Here, we will only consider *sub-dimensional* mutation $(p = 1/n)$ and *full-dimensional* mutation $(p = 1)$.

3   Cumulative Step Size Adaptation

The method *cumulative step size adaptation* (CSA) has been proposed in [16] for continuous variables, multinormal distributed mutations and single-objective optimization. It is based on the idea that the length of the path consisting of consecutive accepted steps can serve as an indicator of the appropriateness of the current step size if it is compared to the length of the path travelled by a random walk. If the path of the EA is much shorter than that of a random walk, then the EA most likely cycles around a (local) optimum and we should decrease the step size. If the path of the EA is much longer, then the EA most likely moves in a suitable direction and we might increase the step size.

In the following we explain the approach in general form before we instantiate variables and mutations: first as in [16] with variables in $\mathbb{R}^n$ and multinormal mutations (Sect. 3.2), and then with variables in $\mathbb{Z}^n$ and discrete Laplace mutations (Sect. 3.3).

3.1   General Case

Let $X^{(t)}$ be an individual and $s^{(t)}$ be the step size at step $t \geq 0$. An offspring $Y^{(t)}$ is created via

$$Y^{(t)} = X^{(t)} + s^{(t)} \cdot D^{(t)} \cdot Z^{(t)} \tag{3}$$

where $D^{(t)}$ is a positive diagonal matrix, which we set to the unit matrix $D^{(t)} \equiv I_n$ for $t \geq 0$ (to keep things simple). We note that after several offspring have been generated via (3) and the best of them has been selected then the path update rule (4) only takes into account the directional information Z^+ of the best offspring whereas the applied step size is ignored.

The estimation of the EA's path length is realized by a cumulative weighted average of the accepted steps. Let $\hat{Z}^{(t)}$ be the current estimated path length at iteration $t \geq 0$, then the updated estimator is

$$\hat{Z}^{(t+1)} = (1 - c) \cdot \hat{Z}^{(t)} + c \cdot Z^+ \tag{4}$$

where $c \in (0,1) \subset \mathbb{R}$ and Z^+ is the last accepted mutation vector.

For the comparison with the path length of the random walk we need the length of the vector $\bar{Z}$ after m iterations of

$$\bar{Z}^{(t+1)} = (1 - c) \cdot \bar{Z}^{(t)} + c \cdot Z^{(t)} \tag{5}$$

for $t \geq 0$ where $\bar{Z}^{(0)} = Z^{(0)}$ and the sequence $Z^{(0)}, Z^{(1)}, \ldots$ is i.i.d. with zero expectation and bounded variance.

The solution of the recurrence in (5) is

$$\bar{Z}^{(t)} = (1 - c)^t Z^{(0)} + c \sum_{i=0}^{t} (1 - c)^i \cdot Z^{(t-1-i)}. \tag{6}$$

Clearly, $\mathsf{E}[\bar{Z}^{(t)}] = 0$ for $t \geq 0$. We assume that the mutation vectors are constructed by i.i.d. random variables for each dimension. As a consequence, we can determine the variance of $\bar{Z}^{(t)}$ per dimension $k = 1, \ldots, n$ via

$$\mathsf{V}[\bar{Z}_k^{(t)}] = (1 - c)^{2t} \mathsf{V}[Z_k^{(0)}] + c^2 \sum_{i=0}^{t-1} (1 - c)^{2i} \mathsf{V}[Z_k^{(t-1-i)}] \tag{7}$$

$$= (1 - c)^{2t} \mathsf{V}[Z_k] + c^2 \mathsf{V}[Z_k] \sum_{i=0}^{t-1} (1 - c)^{2i} \tag{8}$$

$$= \mathsf{V}[Z_k] \left((1 - c)^{2t} + c^2 \frac{1 - (1 - c)^{2t}}{1 - (1 - c)^2} \right) \tag{9}$$

$$\to \mathsf{V}[Z_k] \frac{c}{2 - c} \quad \text{(monotone decreasing)} \tag{10}$$

as $t \to \infty$, where we exploited stochastic independence in (7) and identical distributions in (8). Now we leave the general case and distinguish between continuous and discrete mutations.

3.2 Continuous Mutations

In the original work [16] each dimension of the random vector was realized by a standard normal random variable. Owing to the addition theorem for independent normal r.v.s we obtain $\bar{Z}_k \sim N(0, \sigma^2)$ in (6) with variance σ^2 as given in (9), or asymptotically $\bar{Z}_k \sim_a N(0, \frac{c}{2-c})$, given that $Z_k \sim N(0, 1)$. In the following the asymptotic expression (10) is used to get rid of the dependence on the iteration counter t.

In [16] they made use of the fact that in case of normally distributed random numbers $\bar{Z}_k \sim N(0, \frac{c}{2-c}))$ the Euclidean length of the normal random vector $\bar{Z} = (\bar{Z}_1, \ldots, \bar{Z}_n)$ is $\chi_n((\frac{c}{2-c})^{\frac{1}{2}})$-distributed with expectation $\mathsf{E}[\|\bar{Z}\|_2] \approx_a (\frac{cn}{2-c})^{\frac{1}{2}}$ for sufficiently large n.

After these preparations the rule for cumulative step size adaptation can be formulated:

$$s^{(t+1)} = s^{(t)} \cdot \exp \left(\frac{\|\hat{Z}^{(t)}\|_2}{\mathsf{E}[\|\bar{Z}\|_2]} - 1 \right)^{\beta} \tag{11}$$

where $\beta = \sqrt{1/n}$. Thus, if $\|Z^{(t)}\|_2 < \mathsf{E}[\|\bar{Z}\|_2] = (\frac{cn}{2-c})^{\frac{1}{2}}$ then the step size is decreased by a factor $\in (0, 1)$ whereas it is increased by a factor > 1 otherwise.

3.3 Discrete Mutations

Next, we intend to align the CSA rule given in (11) to the case with integer variables, discrete Laplace distributions, and ℓ_1-norm. Now each dimension in Z is i.i.d. with $Z_k \sim DLap(q)$. As a consequence, the above elaboration remains valid also in this case from Eqs. (4) to (10) without any change.

As we need the length of $\bar{Z}^{(t)}$ in ℓ_1-norm we have to alter our course of action. Note that

$$\mathsf{E}[\|\bar{Z}^{(t)}\|_1] = \mathsf{E}\left[\sum_{k=1}^{n} |\bar{Z}_k^{(t)}|\right] = \sum_{k=1}^{n} \mathsf{E}[|\bar{Z}_k^{(t)}|] = n\,\mathsf{E}[|\bar{Z}_1^{(t)}|] \tag{12}$$

where we exploited independence and identical distributions again. Thus, it suffices to consider the one-dimensional case. In virtue of (6) we get

$$\mathsf{E}[|\bar{Z}_1^{(t)}|] = \mathsf{E}\left[\left|(1-c)^t Z_1^{(0)} + c\sum_{i=0}^{t}(1-c)^i \cdot Z_1^{(t-1-i)}\right|\right]$$

$$\leq (1-c)^t\,\mathsf{E}[|Z_1^{(0)}|] + c\sum_{i=0}^{t}(1-c)^i \cdot \mathsf{E}[|Z_1^{(t-1-i)}|] \tag{13}$$

$$= (1-c)^t\,\mathsf{E}[|Z_1|] + c\cdot\mathsf{E}[|Z_1|]\cdot\frac{1-(1-c)^t}{1-(1-c)} \tag{14}$$

$$= \mathsf{E}[|Z_1|] \tag{15}$$

where we used the triangle inequality in (13) and the identity of distributions in (14). The bound obtained in (15) is hardly useful for our purposes.

Therefore we pursue an alternative approach: The i.i.d. random variables $Z^{(t)} \sim DLap(q)$ have $\mathsf{E}[Z_k^{(t)}] = 0$ and $\mathsf{V}[Z_k^{(t)}] = \frac{2(1-q)}{q^2}$ for all $t \geq 0$ and $k = 1, \ldots, n$. The central limit theorem is backing our assumption that the sum $\bar{Z}_k^{(t)}$ in (6) is approximately normally distributed with zero mean and variance as given in (10). Then it follows that $|\bar{Z}_k^{(t)}|$ is halfnormally distributed with

$$\mathsf{E}[|\bar{Z}_k^{(t)}|] = \sqrt{\frac{2}{\pi} \cdot \frac{c}{2-c} \cdot \frac{2(1-q)}{q^2}} = \sqrt{\frac{2}{\pi} \cdot \frac{c}{2-c} \cdot \frac{q}{2-q}} \cdot \mathsf{E}[|Z_k^{(t)}|]. \tag{16}$$

Notice that the value of q in (16) will be fixed since we need some kind of *standard* discrete Laplace distribution with variance or mean absolute deviation (MAD) set to 1 (similar to the *standard* normal distribution with variance equal to 1). When standardizing with the variance then $q = \sqrt{3} - 1$ and (16) reduces to $\sqrt{\frac{2}{\pi} \cdot \frac{c}{2-c}}$ and after insertion in (12) we finally arrive at the approximation

$$\mathsf{E}[\|\bar{Z}^{(t)}\|_1] = n\sqrt{\frac{2}{\pi} \cdot \frac{c}{2-c}}. \tag{17}$$

When standardizing with the MAD then $q = 2 - \sqrt{2}$ and we end up with the approximation

$$\mathsf{E}[\|\bar{Z}^{(t)}\|_1] = n\sqrt{\frac{2}{\pi} \cdot \frac{c}{2-c}} \cdot (\sqrt{2} - 1). \tag{18}$$

In the integer setting the generation of new offspring has a slightly different pattern than in the continuous case (3). The step size $s^{(t)}$ is hidden in the parameter $q^{(t)}$ for generating discrete Laplace random numbers. Therefore the extraction of the directional information from the accepted offspring requires more effort.

For each generated individual we know which value of q (or step size s) was used for its generation. After selection we know Y, i.e., the accepted offspring. Its realised mutation vector can be retrieved via $Z = Y - X$. This vector (or direction) can be normalised by division with the step length s yielding $Z^+ = Z/s$ leading to the path length update rule

$$\hat{Z}^{(t+1)} = c\,\hat{Z}^{(t)} + (1-c)\,Z^+. \tag{19}$$

The CSA method originally proposed in [16] was designed for a single-objective $(1,\lambda)$-EA in continuous space. Here, we apply it in the multi-objective case for ASEMO in integer space. Initially, the ASEMO behaves like the multiobjective $(1+1)$-strategy until it reaches the Pareto front. Then the ASEMO builds up a population of incomparable solutions (resp. individuals), where each individual is endowed with its own step size and path length vector. As a consequence, the ASEMO with CSA rule (termed ASEMO-CSA) presented in Algorithm 1 differs from the original proposal [16] considerably.

The explicit distinction of the four cases for selection in lines 13 to 20 of Algorithm 1 is close to the actual implementation and we regard it more comprehensible than the compact formulation that is common in pseudo-code formulations of SEMO-like algorithms.

4   Experiments

4.1   Test Problems

Let $f : \mathbb{Z}^n \to \mathbb{N}_0^2$, $u, v \in \mathbb{Z}^n$ with $u \neq v$. In [18] a class of biobjective optimization problems is given by

$$f(x) = \begin{pmatrix} \|x - u\|_1 \\ \|x - v\|_1 \end{pmatrix} \to \min! \tag{20}$$

where $\| \cdot \|_1$ denotes the ℓ_1-norm. The Pareto front is

$$F^* = \{h \in \mathbb{Z}^2 : h = (k, \|u-v\|_1 - k)^\top, k = 0, 1, \ldots, \|u-v\|_1\} \tag{21}$$

with $|F^*| = \|u-v\|_1 + 1$ and the Pareto set is

$$X^* = [u,v] \cap \mathbb{Z}^n \tag{22}$$

with $|X^*| = \prod_{i=1}^n (1 + |u_i - v_i|)$. Following [18], we set $n = 2$ and use the same choices for u, v and the same starting points (Table 1) leading to 16 test cases.

Algorithm 1: ASEMO-CSA: Evolutionary algorithm for a biobjective function $f: \mathbb{Z}^n \to \mathbb{R}^2$ with given starting point $x^{(0)} \in \mathbb{Z}^n$, mean step size $s^{(0)} \in \mathbb{R}_+$, mutation probability $p_m \in (0,1]$, hyperparameters c, β and $\eta = \mathsf{E}[\|\bar{Z}\|_1]$ as in (17) or (18).

---

1 choose initial individual $v = (v.x, v.s, v.p) \in \mathbb{Z}^n \times \mathbb{R}_+ \times \mathbb{R}^n$;
2 $P^{(0)} = \{v\}$;
3 $t = 0$;
4 **while** *termination criterion not met* **do**
5 $\quad$ choose v from $P^{(t)}$ uniformly at random;
6 $\quad$ **repeat**
7 $\quad\quad$ draw $Z \sim DLap(p_m, q(v.s))$;
8 $\quad$ **until** $Z \neq 0 \in \mathbb{Z}^n$;
9 $\quad$ $w.x = v.x + Z$;
10 $\quad$ $Z^+ = Z/v.s$;
11 $\quad$ $w.p = (1 - c)\, v.p + c\, Z^+$;
12 $\quad$ $w.s = v.s \cdot \exp(w.p/\eta - 1)^\beta$;
13 $\quad$ **if** $f(w.x)$ dominates any element in $P^{(t)}$ **then**
14 $\quad\quad$ $P^{(t+1)} = P^{(t)} \setminus \{u \in P^{(t)} : f(w.x) \prec f(u.x)\} \cup \{w\}$
15 $\quad$ **else if** $\exists u \in P^{(t)} : f(u.x) = f(w.x)$ and $u.x \neq w.x$ **then**
16 $\quad\quad$ $P^{(t+1)} = P^{(t)} \setminus \{u\} \cup \{w\}$
17 $\quad$ **else if** $f(w.x)$ is dominated by any element in $P^{(t)}$ **then**
18 $\quad\quad$ $P^{(t+1)} = P^{(t)}$
19 $\quad$ **else**
20 $\quad\quad$ $P^{(t+1)} = P^{(t)} \cup \{w\}$
21 $\quad$ $t = t + 1$;

4.2 Full Factorial Design

Since a reasonable parameterization for the new algorithm was unknown, we created a full factorial design (FFD) which is given in Table 2.

The FFD allowed us to investigate the impact of the configuration of our ASEMO-CSA. The results are shown in Fig. 1 (with initial step size $s^{(0)} = 1$) and Fig. 2 (with $s^{(0)} = 60\,000$). We focus on the results for the sub-dimensional mutation, as those with full-dimensional mutation were worse almost everywhere.

In terms of the overall runtime required, we note that the adaptation mechanism performed well, almost independently of the mechanism's configuration and regardless of the problem and starting point.

The configurations exhibiting the slowest performance were predominantly those with the smallest averaging factor ($c \leq 0.3$). We conjecture that this trend was influenced by the fact that the update of the path length in Line 11 of Algorithm 1 does not take into account the new directional information with sufficient strength. Regarding the β values, it appears that as β increased, the first solution on the front was found more quickly; this is shown by the green

Table 1. Problem parameters u and v for $f(\cdot)$ and starting points x in dimension $n = 2$.

id	0	1	2	3
u	$(-50, 0)$	$(-40, -10)$	$(-25, -25)$	$(0, -50)$
v	$(+50, 0)$	$(+40, +10)$	$(+25, +25)$	$(0, +50)$
x	$(0, 20000)$	$(10000, 10000)$	$(15000, 5000)$	$(20000, 0)$

Table 2. ASEMO-CSA: parameter ranges of FFD in dimension $n = 2$.

parameter	range of values
problem id (pid)	0, 1, 2, 3
starting point $x^{(0)}$ (xid)	0, 1, 2, 3
initial step size $s^{(0)}$	1, 60 000
mutation prob. p	$1/n$, 1
avg. factor c	0.1, 0.2, 0.3, 0.4, 0.5, 0.6, 0.7, 0.8, 0.9
amplifier β	0.5, 0.7, 1.0, 1.5, 2.0

bars typically becoming smaller (from left to right) within the groups of five. Let γ denote the argument in the exponential function in Line 12 of Algorithm 1. Since $\exp(\gamma)^\beta = \exp(\beta \cdot \gamma)$ large values of β lead to a stronger change of the step size. If $\gamma < 0$ we get a stronger decrease, otherwise a stronger increase.

4.3   Per-Instance Algorithm Configuration

Next, we compared ASEMO-CSA with ASEMO [18]. As both algorithms can be configured via hyperparameters, we employed so-called "automated algorithm configuration" (AAC) in order to evolve both to achieve their best performance.

In recent years, a number of AAC methods have been developed. General purpose approaches include SMAC [9], GGA [2]), and the iterated f-race procedure called irace [3]. For our experiments, we used irace 3.5 [14], giving it a budget of 10,000 algorithm runs. We measure the performance in the number of iterations[1] it takes to find the entire front, capped at 10^6 iterations per repetition. The used ranges (based on preliminary experiments) are listed in Table 3.

Figure 3 shows the resulting configurations in parallel coordinate plots. Because irace can return more than one configuration, we can sometimes see several configurations originating from the same pid-xid combination (shown in the left-most columns). Each axis stands for a parameter and each parameter configuration is described by a line that intersects each parallel axis in its corresponding value. We can see which parameter values have been most selected

---

[1] To be precise: in each run, we execute the algorithm 101 times and then report the median as the run's performance. We do this to mitigate noise and as our algorithm's implementation in C++ is *really* fast.

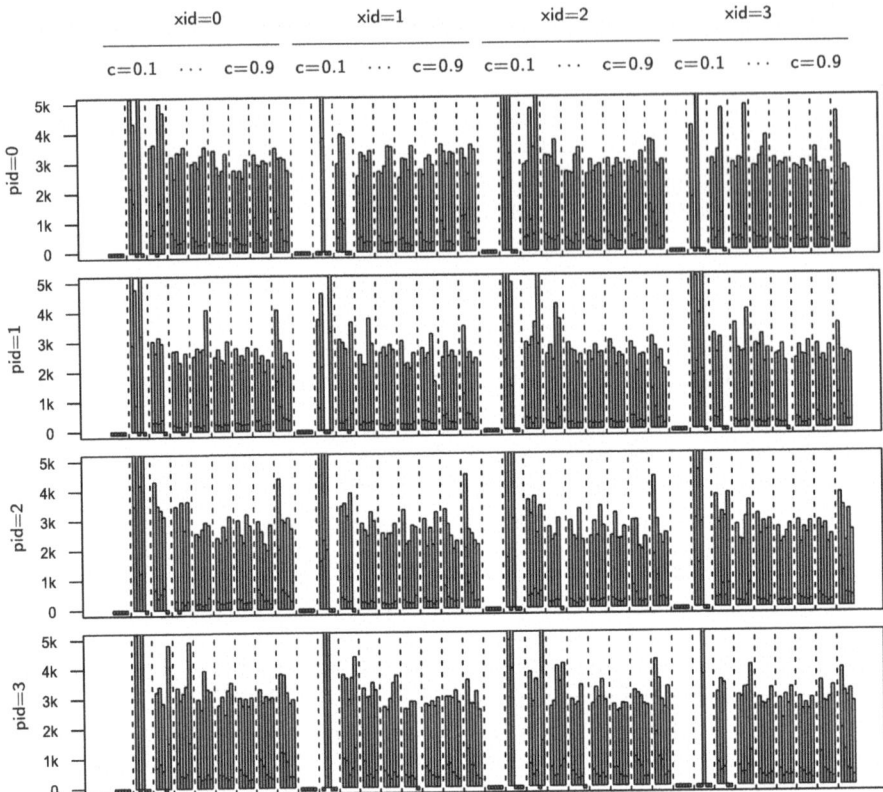

Fig. 1. Median runtime for 1st hitting of the Pareto front (green) and covering the entire Pareto front (gray) with sub-dimensional mutation and small initial step size $s^{(0)} = 1$ based on 15 runs per configuration. A small red box at the bottom indicates that not all of the 15 runs found the entire Pareto front within 10^6 function evaluations. The figures show the results for problems 0 to 3 from top to bottom. Each figure collects the results for starting points $xid = 0, 1, 2, 3$ in blocks consecutively, for each starting point there are 9 c-values, each c-value has 5 β values. (Color figure online)

among all tuning experiments by looking for "concentrations" of lines. We use different styles and colors to emphasize the results obtained for each individual group.[2]

We can make several observations. First, we notice that the choice of the initial step size has significant influence on the tuning outcome. For example, ASEMO requires much higher success rates (ps close to 1.0) when $s^{(0)} = 60000$, which makes sense as the goal is to quickly get to the front and to then perform (mostly) a local search to find all solutions on the front; similarly the averaging factor c for ASEMO-CSA is high then. Moreover, ASEMO-CSA's best configurations (per considered initial step size) are much more concentrated than

---

[2] All logfiles for these experiments will be published along with our code.

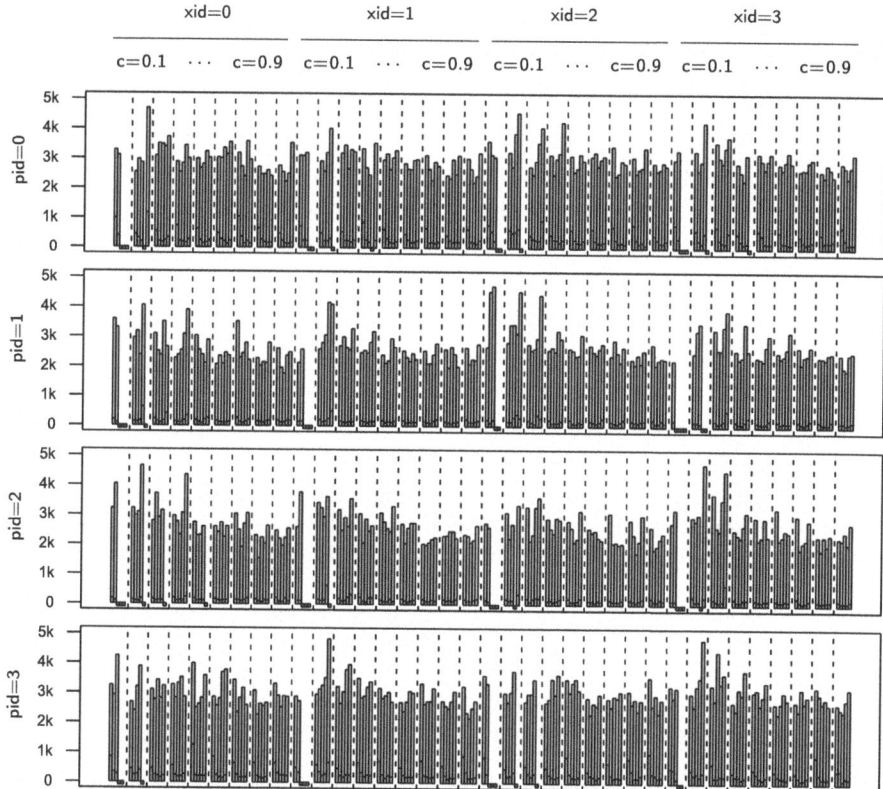

Fig. 2. Median runtime for 1st hitting of the Pareto front (green) and covering the entire Pareto front (gray) with sub-dimensional mutation and large initial step size $s^{(0)} = 60,000$ based on 15 runs per configuration. A small red box at the bottom indicates that not all of the 15 runs found the entire Pareto front within 10^6 function evaluations. The figures show the results for problems 0 to 3 from top to bottom. Each figure collects the results for starting points $xid = 0, 1, 2, 3$ in blocks consecutively, for each starting point there are 9 c-values, each c-value has 5 β values. (Color figure online)

ASEMO's best configurations, which appear to make use of almost the full ranges provided (except for the window size w).

Second, we notice across both algorithms, that problems the best configurations on problems 0 & 3 and the best configurations on problems 1 & 2 are similar, respectively: often, the dashed and solid lines are together, as are the dotted and short dotted lines. For example, for ASEMO-CSA the dotted and short dotted lines have smaller values of c and β than the other line styles, and for ASEMO, many concentrations of either (short) dotted lines are visible, as are concentrations of dashed and solid lines.

Table 3. Hyperparameter ranges used in tuning. We tune for each problem *pid*, each starting point *xid*, and each initial step size $s^{(0)}$ independently. "consider acceptances" refers to the use of either Eq. (9) (False) or Eq. (10) (True) of [18].

algorithm	parameter	range of values
ASEMO [18]	window size w	$[1, \ldots, 100]$
	success prob. p_s	$[0.0, \ldots, 1.0]$
	decrease factor c^-	$[0.0, \ldots, 1.0]$
	increase factor c^+	$[1.0, \ldots, 10.0]$
	consider acceptances (c.a.)	True/False
ASEMO-CSA	avg. factor c	$[0.0, \ldots, 1.0]$
	amplifier β	$[0.5, \ldots, 2.0]$
in common	mutation prob. p	$1/n$ (S), 1 (F)

Table 4. Median performance of the best performing configurations. The *average* and *standard deviation* are calculated over all problem (pid) and starting point (xid) combinations for the particular algorithm and the stated initial step size $s^{(0)}$.

pid	xid	$s^{(0)} = 1$		$s^{(0)} = 60000$	
		ASEMO	ASEMO-CSA	ASEMO	ASEMO-CSA
0	0	1924	2779.5	1897	2538
	1	1950.5	2769	1873	2553
	2	1913	2727.5	1876	2493
	3	1911.5	2731	1909	2588
1	0	1857	2397	1864	2261
	1	1881	2445	1796	2136
	2	1896	2354.5	1900	2174
	3	1937	2433	1806	2126.5
2	0	1917	2419	1910.5	2218
	1	1968.5	2390	1928.5	2201
	2	1956	2452	1886.5	2158
	3	1921	2374	1882.5	2162
3	0	1917	2767	1868	2566
	1	1931.5	2773	1875.5	2524
	2	1917	2827	1895	2579
	3	1938.5	2793	1895.5	2538
average		1921.0	2589.5	1878.9	2363.5
standard deviation		27.8	190.1	35.0	193.6

Third, while the choice of starting point (shown in different colours) appears to influence the best configurations (as different colours are differently concentrated), the overall patterns appears inconclusive, as different colours are concentrated depending on the situation.

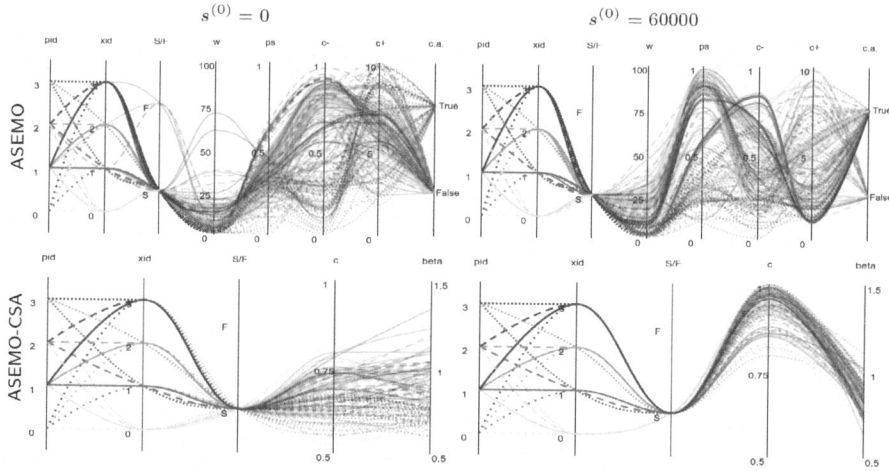

Fig. 3. irace results for ASEMO and ASEMO-CSA depending on the initial step size. Problems (pid) 0, 1, 2, and 3 are represented using line styles dotted, solid, dashed, and short dotted. Starting points (xid) 0, 1, 2, and 3 are represented using yellow, red, green, and blue. We show the pid xid aspects in every plot to facilitate readability: the reader can go from left to right, e.g. $pid = 1$ and $xid = 1$ results in a solid, red line. (Color figure online)

Fourth, across all experiments, almost all best performing configurations prefer the sub-dimensional mutations ($p = 1/n$, denoted by S) over the full-dimensional mutations ($p = 1$, denoted by F).

Table 4 complements Fig. 3 by showing for each combination of problem, starting point, and initial step size the median performance over all configurations that irace returned. First, we note that the tuned ASEMO-CSA configurations require 14% to 47% more evaluations to discover the entire fronts than the tuned ASEMO configurations; we attribute this to ASEMO having six hyperparameters (in addition to $s^{(0)}$), where as ASEMO-CSA has only three.

Second, we observe that the tuned configurations are at their fastest on problem 1 and at their slowest on problems 0 and 3, and this is independent of the starting point. This is not surprising as problems 0 and 3 have the smallest Pareto set, whereas the Pareto sets of problems 1 and 2 are considerably larger. Since the size of the Pareto front is equal for all problems (see Sect. 4.1) there is much "redundancy", i.e., many points in the decision space map to the same point on the Pareto front. As a consequence, the Pareto front is found faster, but the ASEMO-CSA fairly often replaces equivalent solutions (line 16) without progressing in enumerating the Pareto front. This conjecture needs deeper analysis and opens opportunities to think about improved replacement strategies.

5   Conclusions

In this work, we have replaced the population-level mutation adaptation of ASEMO by an individual-based adaptation. To achieve this, we have recast the cumulative step size adaptation method, which was originally formulated for single-objective optimization over continuous variables, for deployment in multi-objective optimization over unbounded integer spaces.

For this new ASEMO-CSA, we have studied the effects of its two hyperparameters by performing extensive tuning over different instances. This tuning showed that substantially different configurations are needed depending on the problem, the algorithm's starting point and the initial step size value.

We have made a few observations that warrant further research. First, given the performance advantages of the (more parameterized) ASEMO over the current ASEMO-CSA, it may be worthwhile to investigate hybridizations of the two, possible by balancing population-level and individual-level adaptations. Along similar lines, it may be necessary to make some of the hyperparameters self-adaptive, as we observed that the best configurations vary massively depending on the initial step sizes chosen; however, exploration and exploitation behaviours need to be carefully regulated. Lastly, further investigations are needed as to why the problems with the largest Pareto sets are the fastest to be solved for the tuned configurations; the results may yield new approaches for efficient handling of sets of non-dominated solutions.

Our data and code are available online [19].

References

1. Abbass, H.: The self-adaptive pareto differential evolution algorithm. In: Proceedings of the IEEE Congress on Evolutionary Computation (CEC), vol. 1, pp. 831–836 (2002). https://doi.org/10.1109/CEC.2002.1007033
2. Ansótegui, C., Sellmann, M., Tierney, K.: A gender-based genetic algorithm for the automatic configuration of algorithms. In: Proceedings of Constraint Programming (CP), pp. 142–157. Springer (2009). https://doi.org/10.1007/978-3-642-04244-7_14
3. Birattari, M., Stützle, T., Paquete, L., Varrentrapp, K.: A racing algorithm for configuring metaheuristics. In: Proceedings of the Genetic and Evolutionary Computation Conference (GECCO), pp. 11–18. ACM (2002)
4. Chand, S., Wagner, M.: Evolutionary many-objective optimization: a quick-start guide. Surv. Oper. Res. Manage. Sci. **20**(2), 35–42 (2015). https://doi.org/10.1016/j.sorms.2015.08.001
5. Doerr, B., Doerr, C., Kötzing, T.: Static and self-adjusting mutation strengths for multi-valued decision variables. Algorithmica **80**(5), 1732–1768 (2017). https://doi.org/10.1007/s00453-017-0341-1
6. Doerr, C., Wagner, M.: Sensitivity of parameter control mechanisms with respect to their initialization. In: Auger, A., Fonseca, C.M., Lourenço, N., Machado, P., Paquete, L., Whitley, D. (eds.) Proceedings of Parallel Problem Solving from Nature (PPSN XV), pp. 360–372. Springer (2018). https://doi.org/10.1007/978-3-319-99259-4_29

7. Doerr, C., Wagner, M.: Simple on-the-fly parameter selection mechanisms for two classical discrete black-box optimization benchmark problems. In: Proceedings of the Genetic and Evolutionary Computation Conference (GECCO), pp. 943–950. ACM (2018). https://doi.org/10.1145/3205455.3205560

8. Eiben, A., Hinterding, R., Michalewicz, Z.: Parameter control in evolutionary algorithms. IEEE Trans. Evol. Comput. **3**(2), 124–141 (1999). https://doi.org/10.1109/4235.771166

9. Hutter, F., Hoos, H.H., Leyton-Brown, K.: Sequential model-based optimization for general algorithm configuration. In: Proceedings of Learning and Intelligence Optimization (LION), pp. 507–523. Springer (2011). https://doi.org/10.1007/978-3-642-25566-3_40

10. Igel, C., Hansen, N., Roth, S.: Covariance matrix adaptation for multi-objective optimization. Evol. Comput. **15**(1), 1–28 (2007). https://doi.org/10.1162/evco.2007.15.1.1

11. Inusaha, S., Kozubowski, T.J.: A discrete analogue of the Laplace distribution. J. Stat. Plann. Infer. **136**(3), 1090–1102 (2006). https://doi.org/10.1016/j.jspi.2004.08.014

12. Laumanns, M., Thiele, L., Zitzler, E., Welzl, E., Deb, K.: Running time analysis of multi-objective evolutionary algorithms on a simple discrete optimization problem. In: Proceedings of Parallel Problem Solving from Nature (PPSN VII), pp. 44–53. Springer (2002). https://doi.org/10.1007/3-540-45712-7_5

13. Li, B., Li, J., Tang, K., Yao, X.: Many-objective evolutionary algorithms: a survey. ACM Comput. Surv. **48**(1) (2015). https://doi.org/10.1145/2792984

14. López-Ibáñez, M., Dubois-Lacoste, J., Pérez Cáceres, L., Birattari, M., Stützle, T.: The irace package: iterated racing for automatic algorithm configuration. Oper. Res. Perspect. **3**, 43–58 (2016). https://doi.org/10.1016/j.orp.2016.09.002, code at https://cran.r-project.org/web/packages/irace/. Accessed 1 Apr 2024

15. Meyer-Nieberg, S., Beyer, H.G.: Self-adaptation in evolutionary algorithms. In: Lobo, F.G., Lima, C.F., Michalewicz, Z. (eds.) Parameter Setting in Evolutionary Algorithms, pp. 47—75. Springer (2007). https://doi.org/10.1007/978-3-540-69432-8_3

16. Ostermeier, A., Gawelczyk, A., Hansen, N.: Step-size adaptation based on non-local use of selection information. In: Davidor, Y., et al. (eds.) Proceedings of 3rd Conference on Parallel Problem Solving from Nature (PPSN III), pp. 189–198. Springer (1994). https://doi.org/10.1007/3-540-58484-6_263

17. Rudolph, G.: An evolutionary algorithm for integer programming. In: Davidor, Y., Schwefel, H.P., Männer, R. (eds.) Parallel Problem Solving From Nature (PPSN III), pp. 139–148. Springer (1994). https://doi.org/10.1007/3-540-58484-6_258

18. Rudolph, G., Wagner, M.: Towards adaptation in multiobjective evolutionary algorithms for integer problems. In: Proceedings of the 2024 IEEE Congress on Evolutionary Computation (CEC), pp. 1–8. IEEE Press (2024). https://doi.org/10.1109/CEC60901.2024.10612114

19. Rudolph, G., Wagner, M.: Cumulative Step Size Adaptation for Adaptive SEMO in Integer Space (Code and Dataset) (2024). https://doi.org/10.5281/zenodo.14219908

Adaptive Normal-Boundary Intersection Directions for Evolutionary Many-Objective Optimization with Complex Pareto Fronts

Maha Elarbi[1]([✉])[iD], Slim Bechikh[1][iD], and Carlos A. Coello Coello[2][iD]

[1] SMART Lab, ISG, University of Tunis, Tunis, Tunisia
maha.elarbi@isg.rnu.tn, slim.bechikh@fsegn.rnu.tn
[2] Departamento de Computacion, CINVESTAV-IPN, Mexico City, Mexico
ccoello@cs.cinvestav.mx

Abstract. Decomposition-based Many-Objective Evolutionary Algorithms (MaOEAs) usually adopt a set of pre-defined distributed weight vectors to guide the solutions towards the Pareto optimal Front (PF). However, when solving Many-objective Optimization Problems (MaOPs) with complex PFs, the effectiveness of MaOEAs with a fixed set of weight vectors may deteriorate which will lead to an imbalance between convergence and diversity of the solution set. To address this issue, we propose here an Adaptive Normal-Boundary Intersection Directions Decomposition-based Evolutionary Algorithm (ANBID-DEA), which adaptively updates the Normal-Boundary Intersection (NBI) directions used in MP-DEA. In our work, we assist the selection mechanism by progressively adjusting the NBI directions according to the distribution of the population to uniformly cover all the parts of the complex PFs (i.e., those that are disconnected, strongly convex, degenerate, etc.). Our proposed ANBID-DEA is compared with respect to five state-of-the-art MaOEAs on a variety of unconstrained benchmark problems with up to 15 objectives. Our results indicate that ANBID-DEA has a competitive performance on most of the considered MaOPs.

Keywords: Many-objective optimization · Decomposition-based algorithms · Adaptive normal-boundary intersection directions

1 Introduction

Many real-world optimization problems normally have more than three (often conflicting) objectives. For example: Cloud task scheduling [31] and protein structure prediction [30], to mention just a few. These are the so-called Many-objective Optimization Problems (MaOPs). Researchers have shown that the conventional Multi-objective Evolutionary Algorithms (MOEAs) face some difficulties when the number of objectives increases mainly because the Pareto dominance relationship is not able to properly differentiate solutions [5]. Solutions

H. Singh et al. (Eds.): EMO 2025, LNCS 15512, pp. 132–147, 2025.
https://doi.org/10.1007/978-981-96-3506-1_10

quickly become non-dominated as we add more objectives and, consequently, the selection pressure dilutes, which prevents the algorithm from properly converging to the true Pareto optimal Front (PF). Several Many-Objective Evolutionary Algorithms (MaOEAs) have been proposed over the years. They can be roughly classified into the following four categories [9]: (1) Dominance relation-based MaOEAs, (2) indicator-based MaOEAs, (3) objective reduction-based MaOEAs, and (4) decomposition-based MaOEAs. The latter decompose the problem into a number of sub-problems that are then simultaneously optimized with the help of weight vectors (i.e., reference points). The work reported here will focus on this last category.

Decomposition-based algorithms have attracted a lot of interest and they are considered as one of the most promising options for handling MaOPs. MOEA/D [29] and NSGA-III [4] are the most representative decomposition-based algorithms and they are designed to perform well on high dimensional objective problems. However, they face several challenges in providing well-diversified solutions particularly when the problem complexity increases (i.e., in the presence of a large number of objectives and/or complicated PF shapes).

One interesting choice is to explore the merits of combining Pareto dominance and decomposition. A representative approach of such type is the Multi-objective Evolutionary Algorithm Based on Dominance and Decomposition (MOEA/DD) [13]. MOEA/DD favors the selection of non-dominated solutions over dominated ones and emphasizes the selection of solutions in isolated regions since these solutions are beneficial to maintain the population's diversity. The updating mechanism of MOEA/DD has shown its effectiveness in solving problems having regular PFs. Nevertheless, MOEA/DD does not provide a well-diversified set of solutions on some problems with irregular PF shapes (i.e., problems with degenerate, discontinuous, inverted, strongly convex, and/or strongly concave fronts). In fact, when we use pre-defined weight vectors, several weight search directions may miss several regions of the irregular PF. Since the performance of the decomposition-based algorithms that were originally proposed depends on the pre-defined set of reference points, they achieve promising performance on MaOPs with regular PFs, but the uniformity of the distribution of the solutions cannot be guaranteed with irregular PFs. To overcome this shortcoming, some authors have proposed to adapt the weight vectors during the evolutionary search process. Many adaptive weight vector-based algorithms have been proposed, such as MOEA/D-LTD [25] and ADEA [1]. VaEA eliminates the use of weight vectors and uses the solutions themselves as reference directions [26]. This approach uses a modified niche preservation operator that incorporates the worse-elimination and the maximum-vector-angle-first principles to balance between convergence and diversity. Nevertheless, VaEA emphasizes diversity and it is difficult for this algorithm to achieve good convergence in some MaOPs with regular PFs.

Motivated by the previously discussed issues of MOEA/DD and VaEA, we propose here a new Adaptive Normal Boundary Intersection Directions Decomposition-based Evolutionary Algorithm (ANBID-DEA) for MaOPs. ANBID-DEA adaptively updates the set of pre-defined Normal Boundary Intersection (NBI) directions employed in MP-DEA during the evolutionary process [6], favors the selection of isolated solutions as done in the update procedure of MOEA/DD, and integrates the mechanisms used in the worse-elimination principle of VaEA. The main contributions of this paper can be summarized as follows:

1. We propose ANBID-DEA that aims to enhance the update procedure of MOEA/DD and the worse-elimination mechanism of VaEA by ensuring the balance between the uniformity of the distribution of the solutions and the convergence when dealing with irregular PFs.
2. We investigate the importance of adaptively adjusting the NBI directions used in MP-DEA according to the distribution of the population to discover the missing parts of the PF and to detect misleading directions.
3. We show that ANBID-DEA is able to outperform several state-of-the-art approaches in terms of IGD and HV when applied to a variety of unconstrained benchmark problems.

The remainder of this paper is organized as follows. Section 2 introduces the previous related work and the main motivation for this research. In Sect. 3, we describe our proposed ANBID-DEA. Section 4 presents our experimental setup. In Sect. 5, we present the performance assessment of our proposed ANBID-DEA by comparing it to five MaOEAs. Section 6 provides our conclusions and some possible paths for future research.

2   Previous Related Work and Motivation

Most of the MaOEAs which belong to the first generation of decomposition-based algorithms follow the general assumption which states that evenly distributed weights result in an evenly distributed solution set [12]. Nevertheless, when facing problems with irregular PFs (i.e., disconnected, degenerated, strongly convex, etc.) it is hard to estimate the shape of the PF using a set of static distributed weights, since several weights may not intersect the PF. Therefore, researchers have proposed to dynamically adjust the weight directions during the search process to adapt the shape of the target PF according to the current population. In the literature, several attempts have been made in this direction. Recently, several works tended to consider the distribution of the current population during the evolutionary process when adjusting weights [18]. Some weight adaptation methods use the distribution of the solutions to guide the adaptation of weights, while other methods employ some solutions in the population to generate weights. Representative algorithms include A-NSGA-III [11], VaEA [26], MOEA/D-AM2M [15], and MaOEA-PDE [27]. Other existing approaches use an external solution set (i.e., an external archive) to preserve the best solutions from the population. These approaches utilize the preserved solutions in two manners: (1) using the archive to generate weights (such as in iRVEA [16], MOEA/D-AWA [19], and AdaW [14]) or (2) leveraging the solutions from the archive to estimate the shape of the PF and to guide the weight adaptation process (such as in RVEA-iGNG [17] and MOEA/D-SOM [8]). The main advantage of using an archive is that it is able to provide a robust representation of the PF shape by guiding the weight adaptation process. For more details on the proposed weight vector adaptation methods, refer to [18].

Although the aforementioned weight vector adaptation methods have shown good performance, three main issues remain. First, some of the previously mentioned methods adapt multiple weights at a single generation and at any time in the evolutionary process. However, as shown in [7], the frequent change of the weights may deteriorate the convergence of the solutions. Second, an unstable archive in which we perform changes on its solutions may harm the convergence of the weight adaptation algorithms [18]. Third, to the best of our knowledge all the existing adaptation methods adjust PBI directions (i.e., a line connecting the origin and a weight vector). Such directions are well-suited to solve MaOPs with regular PFs. However, when the shape of the PF is irregular, PBI-based adaptation methods struggle to provide a set of well-distributed solutions due to the inconsistencies between the shape of the PF and the distribution of the PBI directions [6,21].

The limitation of the existing weight adaptation methods motivated us to propose ANBID-DEA which replaces only one weight at a time. Moreover, we also propose an enhanced worse-elimination strategy that: (1) eliminates the worst solutions in terms of convergence and diversity and replaces them by better ones and (2) updates the NBI directions during the search process so that they uniformly intersect with the PF regardless of the complexity of its geometrical shape.

3   Our Proposed Approach: ANBID-DEA

3.1   General Framework

ANBID-DEA follows the same framework of MOEA/DD but it modifies its update mechanism. First, a population P of size N and a set of W well-spread reference points RP are generated. Then, a set of mirror points MP is generated so that each reference point in RP has its mirror point in MP. The RP and MP sets are used to create the NBI directions. After that, the loop iteration is executed until the termination criterion is met. A reproduction procedure is applied to generate offspring solutions by performing the mating selection and the variation operation. The mating selection is applied to choose the mating parents, while the variation operation generates new candidate solutions. The created offspring solutions are used to update the population P by considering an offspring solution x_c each time. Once the offspring solution x_c is added to P, we obtain a new population P' with size $N + 1$. Thereafter, we normalize the members of the P' population and we associate the solutions to their closest reference points by computing the acute angle between each solution and the reference points. After this, we apply non-dominated sorting to divide the population into different layers using Pareto dominance. Finally, we apply our enhanced worse-elimination mechanism to delete an inferior solution.

3.2   Construction of the NBI Directions

The generation of the reference points set RP is done using the two-layer generation method suggested in [13]. Using this method, an RP set with W well-distributed reference points is obtained and intermediate reference points within the simplex are guaranteed. Thereafter, the set of W mirror points MP is created using the same mirror points generation procedure employed in [6]. The latter constructs a set of mirror points by decreasing the coordinates of the reference points by 1. The obtained reference and mirror points are then used to create the NBI directions that connect each reference point with its corresponding mirror version.

3.3   Generation of the Offspring Solutions

The generation of offspring solutions takes place in two steps. First, mating selection is performed in which parents are chosen at random from the population. The second step is the variation operation. In this operation, genetic operators are applied on the mating parents. The operators used in our approach are the well-known Simulated Binary Crossover (SBX) and polynomial-based mutation. The SBX operator uses two parents to create two offspring solutions. This operator uses the distribution index parameter that is responsible for creating an offspring close or away from its parents.

3.4   Normalization and Association of the Solutions

After the creation of the P' population, we then normalize its members. This step is important specially when we deal with MaOPs having disparately scaled PFs. Thus, the objective value (i.e., $f_i, i = 1, \ldots, M$) of each solution x is normalized through the following equation:

$$f'_i(x) = \frac{f_i(x) - z_i^*}{z_i^{nad} - z_i^*} \tag{1}$$

where z_i^* and z_i^{nad} are the ideal and the nadir points of the population P', respectively. z_i^* corresponds to the minimum value of f_i, while z_i^{nad} is the ith objective value of the nadir point z^{nad}. For the estimation of z^{nad}, we use the same method employed in [28]. We first determine the extreme solution corresponding to each coordinate axis (i.e., f_j) by minimizing an Achievement Scalarizing Function (ASF). Then, we construct an M-dimensional hyperplane by connecting the extreme solutions. Next, the interception $a_i, i = 1, \ldots, M$ of the hyperplane with each objective axis is determined. Finally, the objective values of each solution are normalized using Eq. (1), where $z_i^{nad} - z_i^* = a_i$ is used and the value of z_i^{nad} is updated. For a degenerate PF, we may not be able to determine the extreme solutions that will serve to construct the hyperplane. In such a case, z_i^{nad} is assigned as the maximum value of each objective f_i for all solutions, where $i = 1, \ldots, M$.

After normalizing the solutions, each solution x is associated with a unique sub-region (i.e., reference direction) according to its acute angle value that is computed as follows:

$$angle(x, RP_j) \triangleq \arccos \left| \frac{F'(x) \bullet RP_j}{norm(x).norm(RP_j)} \right| \qquad (2)$$

where $F'(x) = (f'_1(x), f'_2(x), \dots, f'_M(x))^T$, $RP_j = (rp_{j,1}, rp_{j,2}, \dots, rp_{j,M})^T$, $norm(x) \triangleq \sqrt{\sum_{i=1}^{M} f'_i(x)^2}$, $F'(x) \bullet RP_j$ returns the inner product between $F'(x)$ and RP_j, and it is defined as follows:

$$F'(x) \bullet RP_j = \sum_{i=1}^{M} f'_i(x) \cdot rp_{j,i} \qquad (3)$$

A solution is associated to the reference point that has the smallest angle with it. In this manner, we can identify three types of reference directions: (1) reference directions that are not associated by any solution, (2) isolated reference directions with a single solution associated to them, and (3) crowded reference directions that are associated with more than one solution.

3.5 Enhanced Worse-Elimination Selection

Once the population members are associated to the reference directions, we apply non-dominated sorting to divide the population members into different levels using Pareto dominance. Next, we eliminate an inferior solution x from P' by following one of these two scenarios:

1. *Case 1: There is a single non-domination level (i.e., $l = 1$):* We start by identifying the non-isolated solution x having the minimum angle with its reference point:
   (a) If this angle is non-zero and less than σ, then the following steps are executed: (1) the solution x is eliminated, (2) the reference vector takes the direction of the solution y that has the maximum angle with it, (3) a new NBI direction is generated by creating the mirror point y' of the solution y, (4) and the solutions are re-associated using the new set of reference points. Figure 1 illustrates this case where the non-dominated solution x is deleted and the NBI direction of x is replaced by generating a new NBI direction (i.e., the line connecting the solution y and its new generated mirror point y').
   (b) Otherwise, if the angle is greater than σ, we identify the most crowded sub-region and we delete the solution x having the highest Euclidean distance to its corresponding mirror point.
2. *Case 2: There are multiple non-domination levels (i.e., $l > 1$):* We identify the last layer F_l:

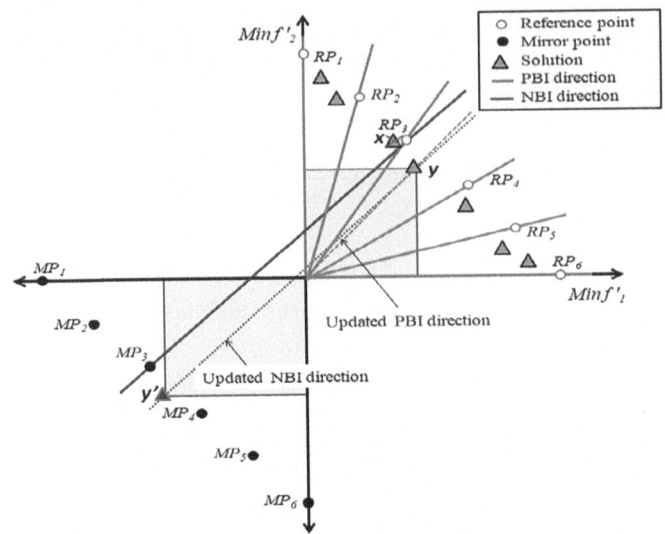

Fig. 1. Illustration of case 1(a) of the enhanced worse-elimination selection.

(a) If it contains only isolated solutions, we delete the solution x having the highest Euclidean distance to its corresponding mirror point in the most crowded sub-region.

(b) Otherwise, we look for the non-isolated solution x in F_l that has the minimum angle with its reference point and we perform the same steps of case 1.

In this work, $\sigma = \frac{\pi \div 2}{N+1}$ as set in [26]. It is important to note that the angle represents a metric of diversity and, in some cases, also of convergence, while the Euclidean distance measures uniformity and convergence. Moreover, our enhanced worse-elimination selection mechanism adaptively updates the NBI directions during the evolutionary process to uniformally cover the irregular PFs and eliminates the worst solutions in terms of convergence and diversity through the use of the PBI (acute angle) and NBI (Euclidean distance) metrics (cf. Figure 2).

4   Experimental Study

4.1   Benchmark Problems

In order to assess the performance of our proposed ANBID-DEA, we adopted the benchmarks used in the original papers of the algorithms from our comparative study: The three well-known test suites DTLZ, WFG, and MaF [6,13]. These test problems have several challenging features. In this paper, we have selected only the test problems DTLZ1-4, WFG2-3, WFG5, WFG9, MaF1, MaF3, and

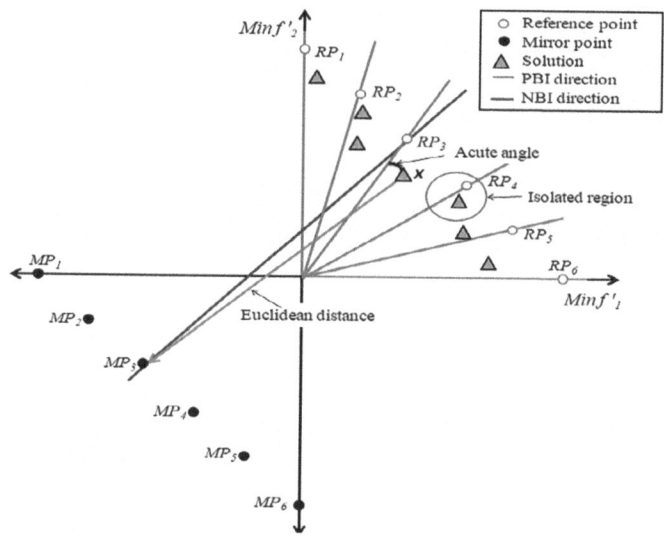

Fig. 2. Illustration of the acute angle and Euclidean distance metrics.

MaF6-7. The considered instances cover the following properties: linear, multi-modal, concave, convex, scaled, degenerate, deceptive, inverted, disconnected, mixed, and biased. In this paper, the number of objectives varies from 5 to 15, $M \in \{5, 10, 15\}$. The number of decision variables was set to $D = M + k - 1$, where k is set as 5 for DTLZ1 and 10 for DTLZ2-4. For the considered WFG test problems, the number of decision variables was set as $D = 2 \times (M - 1) + 20$. The MaF problems have the same number of decision variables as in DTLZ. For MaF1, MaF3, and MaF6, $k = 10$, while for MaF7, $k = 20$.

4.2 Baseline Approaches

We have compared the performance of our proposed ANBID-DEA with respect to that of two non-adaptive weight vector-based algorithms: MP-DEA (i.e., the fixed NBI direction-based algorithm version of ANBID-DEA) [6], and MOEA/DD [13]. Moreover, we have also conducted comparative experiments against three adaptive-based algorithms: VaEA [26] which uses the maximum-vector-angle-first rule to select individuals one by one as a reference direction, RVEA [3] that uses an adaptive strategy for reference vectors and an angle penalized distance to balance the convergence and diversity of the solutions in a high-dimensional objective space, and MOEA/D-AWA [19] that adds and deletes weights according to the sparsity degree of the solutions stored in the archive.

4.3 Performance Measures

To assess the performance of the six approaches adopted in our comparative study, we used the Inverted Generational Distance (IGD) [2] and the HyperVolume (HV) [32] performance measures since they are both commonly used in the specialized literature.

-   IGD calculates the distance between the set of non-dominated solutions obtained on the final population (S) and a reference set (normally, the true Pareto front of the problem). The lower the IGD value is, the better the quality of S. The reference set is generated using the open-source platform PlatEMO [24].
-   HV computes the volume covered by the set of non-dominated solutions obtained on the final population with respect to a specified reference point. It measures both convergence and maximum spread. As recommended in [26] the reference point was set to 1.1 times of the upper bounds of the true PFs. The larger the HV value is, the better the quality of S.

Table 1. Specific experimental parameters settings.

Algorithm	Parameter	Value
RVEA	Changing rate α of the penalty function	2
	Adaptive reference vector update frequency f_r	0.1
MOEA/D-AWA	Maximum capacity of the archive	$1.5N$
	Maximum number of adjusted sub-problems nus	$rate\_update\_weight \times N$
	$rate\_update\_weight$	0.05
	$rate\_evol$	0.8
MOEA/DD	Penalty parameter θ of PBI	5.0
	Number T of neighbors	20
	probability δ of selecting a neighbor	0.9

4.4 Parameters Settings and Statistical Testing

A parameter tuning process was conducted to find the best parameter values for each algorithm. In all the experiments, each algorithm was run 31 times on each test instance. The population sizes of MP-DEA, VaEA, and RVEA were set as 212, 276, and 136 for $M = 5$, $M = 10$, and $M = 15$, respectively. For ANBID-DEA, MOEA/DD, and MOEA/D-AWA the population size was set to 210 for $M = 5$, 275 for $M = 10$, and 135 for $M = 15$. The number of weight vectors was set the same as the population size of MOEA/DD. SBX and polynomial-based mutation were used to produce new offspring solutions. The crossover probability and the mutation probability were set to 1.0 and $1/D$, respectively. The distribution index of SBX was set to 30, while the distribution index of the polynomial-based mutation operator was set to 20. In this paper,

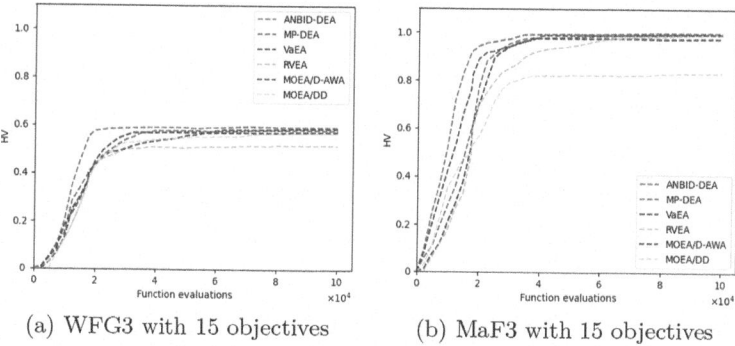

(a) WFG3 with 15 objectives   (b) MaF3 with 15 objectives

Fig. 3. Median HV variation curves of 31 independent runs performed by each algorithm on WFG3 and MaF3.

we used as a termination criterion a Maximum number of Function Evaluations (MFEs) for each algorithm. The MFEs were set as $MFEs = MaxGen \times N$, where MFE is equal 100.000 for $M = \{5, 10, 15\}$. Table 1 shows the settings of some specific parameters. In order to statistically compare the performance of the peer algorithms and to see whether there are statistical differences in their obtained results, we used the Friedman and Iman-Davenport statistical tests [23]. We have also applied the Wilcoxon test in a pairwise manner with a significance level of 0.05 [23]. The "+", "-", and "=" mean that the IGD or HV values of the considered algorithms are significantly better, significantly worse than, or without a significant difference to those of our proposed ANBID-DEA, respectively.

5   Results and Discussion

Table 2 shows the median IGD and HV results obtained on DTLZ1-4, WFG2-3, WFG5, WFG9, MaF1, MaF3, and MaF6-7. The statistical significance of the difference in results between our proposed ANBID-DEA and the peer algorithms is also shown by using the Wilcoxon test. We can see that ANBID-DEA had the best overall performance in almost all the considered test problems in terms of IGD and HV. MP-DEA had the second best performance and was very competitive with respect to ANBID-DEA, while VaEA ranked third and was able to obtain the second best performance on: (1) DTLZ2, MaF3, and MaF7 with 10, 5, and 10 objectives in terms of IGD, respectively and (2) the 5-objective version of MaF3 and the 10-objective version of MaF6 in terms of HV. MOEA/D-AWA, RVEA, and MOEA/DD had the worst position in the ranking. The performance of MOEA/D-AWA was promising on WFG3, MaF6, and MaF7 which have complex PF shapes (degenerate, disconnected, multi-modal, etc.). RVEA managed to obtain the best performance in the 5-objective version of MaF3 with respect to the IGD and HV indicators. Regarding MOEA/DD, it had a poor performance in almost all the considered test instances except for the 5- and 10-objective

Table 2. Median values of IGD and HV on DTLZ1-4, WFG2-3, WFG5, WFG9, MaF1, MaF3, and MaF6-7. The first line shows the IGD value, while the second line indicates the HV value. The best and the second best results for each test instance are shown in boldface and underlined, respectively.

Problem	M	ANBID-DEA	MP-DEA	VaEA	RVEA	MOEA/D-AWA	MOEA/DD
DTLZ1	5	**2.002E-1**	2.430E-1 (-)	2.089E-1 (-)	2.336E-1 (-)	3.382E-1 (-)	<u>2.005E-1</u> (-)
		1.00E+0	9.98E-1 (-)	9.88E-1 (-)	9.95E-1 (-)	9.83E-1 (-)	<u>9.99E-1</u> (-)
	10	**1.887E-1**	<u>1.893E-1</u> (-)	2.046E-1 (-)	1.915E-1 (-)	1.895E-1 (-)	2.864E-1 (-)
		1.09E+0	<u>1.07E+0</u> (-)	9.94E-1 (-)	1.00E+0 (-)	1.06E+0 (-)	9.23E-1 (-)
	15	**1.723E-1**	<u>1.752E-1</u> (-)	2.185E-1 (-)	2.085E-1(-)	1.761E-1 (-)	1.832E-1 (-)
		1.08E+0	<u>1.06E+0</u> (-)	9.97E-1 (-)	9.98E-1 (-)	1.03E+0 (-)	9.99E-1 (-)
DTLZ2	5	**2.123E-1**	<u>2.292E-1</u> (-)	2.389E-1 (-)	2.307E-1 (-)	2.302E-1 (-)	2.386E-1 (-)
		9.99E-1	<u>9.98E-1</u> (-)	9.89E-1 (-)	9.91E-1 (-)	9.96E-1 (-)	9.88E-1 (-)
	10	**4.616E-1**	4.811E-1 (-)	<u>4.712E-1</u> (-)	5.183E-1 (-)	5.712E-1 (-)	5.109E-1 (-)
		1.00E+0	9.99E-1 (=)	9.98E-1 (-)	9.73E-1 (-)	9.78E-1 (-)	9.86E-1 (-)
	15	**5.689E-1**	<u>5.807E-1</u> (-)	5.990E-1 (-)	6.199E-1 (-)	7.516E-1 (-)	6.123E-1 (-)
		9.89E-1	<u>9.73E-1</u> (-)	9.70E-1 (-)	9.53E-1 (-)	9.44E-1 (-)	9.65E-1(-)
DTLZ3	5	**1.695E-1**	<u>1.716E-1</u> (-)	1.983E-1 (-)	2.820E-1 (-)	1.816E-1 (-)	3.898E-1 (-)
		1.05E+0	<u>1.01E+0</u> (-)	9.96E-1 (-)	9.71E-1 (-)	9.97E-1 (-)	9.26E-1 (-)
	10	**4.598E-1**	<u>4.617E-1</u> (-)	4.788E-1 (-)	4.703E-1 (-)	4.726E-1 (-)	5.223E-1 (-)
		1.03E+0	<u>1.00E+0</u> (-)	9.92E-1 (-)	9.98E-1 (-)	9.94E-1 (-)	9.69E-1 (-)
	15	**5.993E-1**	6.126E-1 (-)	6.936E-1 (-)	6.882E-1 (-)	7.109E-1 (-)	6.233E-1 (-)
		9.97E-1	<u>9.94E-1</u> (-)	9.68E-1 (-)	9.29E-1 (-)	9.21E-1 (-)	9.86E-1 (-)
DTLZ4	5	**1.680E-1**	<u>1.692E-1</u> (=)	1.726E-1 (-)	1.795E-1 (-)	2.378E-1 (-)	2.531E-1 (-)
		1.09E+0	<u>1.07E+0</u> (-)	9.90E-1 (-)	9.84E-1 (-)	9.62E-1 (-)	9.63E-1 (-)
	10	**4.276E-1**	4.286E-1 (-)	4.622E-1 (-)	<u>4.283E-1</u> (+)	4.596E-1 (-)	5.690E-1 (-)
		9.99E-1	<u>9.97E-1</u> (-)	9.91E-1 (-)	9.95E-1 (-)	9.86E-1 (-)	9.75E-1 (-)
	15	**3.996E-1**	<u>4.223E-1</u> (-)	4.907E-1 (-)	4.386E-1 (-)	5.116E-1 (-)	5.396E-1 (-)
		1.08E+0	<u>1.06E+0</u> (-)	9.89E-1 (-)	1.00E+0 (-)	9.77E-1 (-)	9.70E-1 (-)
WFG2	5	**7.398E-1**	<u>7.413E-1</u> (-)	8.117E-1 (-)	3.209E+0 (-)	7.996E-1 (-)	8.345E-1 (-)
		9.97E-1	<u>9.94E-1</u> (-)	9.83E-1 (-)	9.69E-1 (-)	9.88E-1 (-)	9.84E-1(-)
	10	**1.279E-1**	<u>1.283E-1</u> (-)	1.316E-1 (-)	1.623E+0 (-)	1.356E-1 (-)	1.342E-1 (-)
		1.00E+0	<u>9.99E-1</u> (-)	9.92E-1 (-)	7.87E-1 (-)	9.77E-1 (-)	9.85E-1 (-)
	15	**1.189E-1**	<u>1.222E-1</u> (=)	1.324E-1 (-)	1.612E-1 (-)	1.637E+0 (-)	1.647E-1 (-)
		9.91E-1	<u>9.86E-1</u> (-)	9.74E-1 (-)	9.70E-1 (-)	9.38E-1 (-)	9.61E-1 (-)
WFG3	5	<u>4.896E-1</u>	5.101E-1 (-)	5.221E-1 (-)	5.117E-1 (-)	**4.870E-1** (+)	7.711E-1 (-)
		<u>7.47E-1</u>	7.41E-1 (=)	7.26E-1 (-)	7.34E-1 (-)	**7.48E-1** (+)	6.42E-1 (-)
	10	**1.115E-1**	<u>1.123E-1</u> (-)	1.126E-1 (-)	1.234E-1 (-)	1.174E-1 (-)	1.311E+0 (-)
		8.39E-1	<u>8.33E-1</u> (-)	8.27E-1 (-)	8.19E-1 (-)	8.20E-1 (-)	6.78E-1 (-)
	15	**3.196E+0**	3.226E+0 (-)	3.234E+0 (-)	4.101E+0 (-)	3.486E+0 (-)	3.839E+0 (-)
		5.91E-1	5.79E-1 (-)	5.71E-1 (-)	5.16E-1 (-)	<u>5.86E-1</u> (+)	5.67E-1 (-)
WFG5	5	**6.298E-1**	<u>6.464E-1</u> (-)	7.186E-1 (-)	9.912E-1 (-)	7.229E-1 (-)	7.236E-1 (-)
		8.73E-1	<u>8.61E-1</u> (-)	8.27E-1 (-)	7.49E-1 (-)	8.17E-1 (-)	8.16E-1 (-)
	10	**5.856E-1**	<u>5.937E-1</u> (-)	1.598E+0 (-)	1.221E+0 (-)	7.823E-1 (-)	3.909E+0 (-)
		1.08E+0	<u>1.07E+0</u> (-)	5.69E-1 (-)	5.18E-1 (-)	1.05E+0 (-)	4.76E-1 (-)

(continued)

Table 2. (*continued*)

Problem	M	ANBID-DEA	MP-DEA	VaEA	RVEA	MOEA/D-AWA	MOEA/DD
	15	**1.056E-1**	1.068E-1 (-)	2.221E+0 (-)	2.118E+0 (-)	4.685E+0 (-)	1.286E+0 (-)
		5.32E-1	**5.34E-1** (=)	4.68E-1 (-)	4.06E-1 (-)	2.31E-1 (-)	4.51E-1 (-)
WFG9	5	**3.254E-1**	3.385E-1 (-)	4.616E-1 (-)	4.128E-1 (-)	9.111E-1 (-)	3.487E-1 (-)
		9.91E-1	9.87E-1 (-)	9.53E-1 (-)	9.64E-1 (-)	7.46E-1 (-)	9.80E-1 (-)
	10	**6.163E-1**	6.213E-1 (-)	6.235E-1 (-)	6.594E-1 (-)	6.919E-1 (-)	6.783E-1 (-)
		9.33E-1	9.27E-1 (-)	9.11E-1 (-)	8.87E-1 (-)	8.93E-1 (-)	8.81E-1 (-)
	15	**7.992E+0**	8.129E+0 (-)	8.386E+0 (-)	8.207E+0 (-)	1.118E+1 (-)	1.382E+1 (-)
		3.69E-1	3.64E-1 (-)	3.51E-1 (-)	3.57E-1 (-)	2.67E-1 (-)	2.65E-1 (-)
MaF1	5	**1.146E-1**	1.211E-1 (-)	3.256E-1 (-)	3.036E-1 (-)	1.429E-1 (-)	1.252E-1 (-)
		9.27E-3	9.13E-3 (-)	2.00E-3 (-)	2.24E-3 (-)	7.91E-3 (-)	8.82E-3 (-)
	10	2.261E-1	**2.250E-1** (+)	5.352E-1 (-)	6.849E-1 (-)	6.972E-1 (-)	2.317E-1 (-)
		5.83E-7	5.80E-7 (-)	7.32E-9 (-)	5.86E-9 (-)	5.91E-9 (-)	5.81E-7 (-)
	15	**2.415E-1**	2.531E-1 (-)	6.934E-1 (-)	7.120E-1 (-)	5.928E-1 (-)	3.164E-1 (-)
		9.99E-11	9.97E-11 (-)	1.60E-13 (-)	2.90E-14 (-)	3.66E-14 (-)	8.00E-13 (-)
MaF3	5	9.623E-2	1.024E-1 (-)	9.463E-2 (-)	**9.358E-2** (+)	2.594E-1 (-)	2.599E-1 (-)
		9.53E-1	9.26E-1 (-)	9.60E-1 (-)	**9.80E-1** (+)	8.73E-1 (-)	8.87E-1 (-)
	10	**8.126E-2**	8.389E-2 (-)	1.288E-1 (-)	1.338E-1 (-)	1.088 E+0 (-)	9.821E-1 (-)
		9.99E-1	9.98E-1 (-)	9.87E-1 (-)	9.78E-1 (-)	1.11E-1 (-)	9.87E-1 (-)
	15	**8.194E-2**	8.337E-2 (-)	9.326E-2 (-)	9.984E-2 (-)	9.598E-1 (-)	2.883E-1 (-)
		9.99E-1	9.96E-1 (-)	9.76E-1 (-)	9.95E-1 (-)	9.94E-1 (-)	8.31E-1 (-)
MaF6	5	9.222E-3	9.394E-3 (-)	8.331E-2 (-)	9.505E-3 (-)	**9.191E-3** (-)	1.923E-1 (-)
		1.16E-1	1.12E-1(-)	1.08E-1 (-)	1.01E-1 (-)	**1.18E-1** (-)	1.07E-1 (-)
	10	**3.112E-3**	3.182E-3 (-)	3.341E-1 (-)	1.010E-1 (-)	4.154E-3 (-)	7.728E-1 (-)
		1.06E-1	1.00E-1 (-)	1.04E-1 (-)	7.91E-2 (-)	9.83E-2 (-)	4.35E-2 (-)
	15	9.635E-2	9.710E-2 (-)	9.992E-2 (-)	2.008E-1 (-)	9.915E-2 (-)	3.616E-1 (-)
		9.67E-2	9.63E-2 (-)	9.57E-2 (-)	8.73E-2 (-)	9.41E-2 (-)	8.66E-2 (-)
MaF7	5	3.213E-1	3.366E-1 (-)	4.508E-1 (-)	4.601E-1 (-)	**2.998E-1** (+)	5.468 E-1 (-)
		2.53E-1	2.51E-1 (-)	2.49E-1 (-)	2.43E-1 (-)	**2.56E-1** (+)	2.12E-1 (-)
	10	**8.218E-1**	8.686E-1 (-)	8.462E-1 (-)	2.122E+0 (-)	8.693E-1 (-)	1.889E+0 (-)
		1.86E-1	1.65E-1 (-)	1.84E-1 (=)	1.46E-1 (-)	**1.95E-1** (-)	1.51E-1 (-)
	15	**2.126E+0**	2.387E+0 (-)	2.661E+0 (-)	4.022E+0 (-)	6.659E+0 (-)	2.399E+0 (-)
		1.72E-1	1.57E-1 (-)	1.53E-1 (-)	6.13E-2 (-)	3.16E-2 (-)	1.55E-1 (-)
IGD: +/-/=	-		1/33/2	0/36/0	2/34/0	2/34/0	0/36/0
HV: +/-/=	-		0/33/3	0/35/1	1/35/0	3/33/0	0/36/0

instances of DTLZ1 and MaF1, respectively. Figure 3 shows the median HV values of each algorithm over the total number of function evaluations on WFG3 and MaF3 with 15 objectives. It can been seen from these figures that the median of ANBID-DEA converges faster than the other algorithms and remains stable at the maximum value. This can be explained by the fact that our approach is able to cover the different parts of the PF since the early stages of the search due to the application of its enhanced worse-elimination selection mechanism.

Table 3. Results of the Friedman and Iman-Davenport tests in terms of IGD and HV ($\alpha = 0.05$).

Test	Parameters			
	Crit. value	Value	Null hypothesis	p-value
IGD				
Friedman	11.07	**107.492**	Rejected	1.388E-21
Iman-Davenport	2.27	**51.887**	Rejected	1.110E-16
HV				
Friedman	11.07	**107.184**	Rejected	1.612E-21
Iman-Davenport	2.27	**51.419**	Rejected	1.110E-16

As can be seen from Table 2, our proposed ANBID-DEA shows a superior performance. ANBID-DEA significantly outperforms MP-DEA, VaEA, RVEA, MOEA/D-AWA, and MOEA/DD on 33, 36, 34, 34, and 36 problems from a total of 36 test instances in terms of IGD. Similar to the previous observation, ANBID-DEA significantly outperforms the other baseline approaches on 33, 35, 35, 33, and 36 problems from a total of 36 test instances in terms of the HV. Table 3 shows the obtained results of the Friedman and Iman-Davenport tests for the IGD and HV performance indicators. In fact, with a level of significance $\alpha = 0.05$, the obtained values by both statistical tests are clearly larger than their associated critical values. Therefore, there are significant differences among the obtained results and the null hypothesis is rejected. Thus, our proposed ANBID-DEA performs significantly better than all the other compared approaches.

This superior performance of our proposed ANBID-DEA is mainly due to the following aspects: (1) we use the NBI directions that uniformly intersect the PF regardless of its geometrical shape, (2) we adaptively update the NBI directions during the search process to cover the non-discovered parts of the PF with some solutions, and (3) we ensure a balance between convergence and diversity by considering the importance of preserving isolated solutions and adopting the Euclidean and acute angle mechanisms in our proposed worse-elimination selection mechanism. For all these reasons, our proposed ANBID-DEA is able to outperform the other algorithms with respect to which it was compared when dealing with high dimensional problems with complex PFs.

6   Conclusions and Future Work

This paper introduced ANBID-DEA, a new decomposition-based algorithm that adaptively updates the NBI directions used in MP-DEA when applying its enhanced worse-elimination selection mechanism. An empirical study was carried out to evaluate the performance of ANBID-DEA on a set of selected many-objective unconstrained benchmark problems with irregular PFs and with a number of objectives that goes from 5 to 15. The obtained results showed that our proposed approach is competitive when compared against five state-of-the-art algorithms on the majority of the test instances adopted. As part of our future work, we are interested in designing an efficient constraint-handling technique and integrate it into ANBID-DEA [22]. We are also interested in the development of a surrogate-assisted evolutionary algorithm to solve expensive MaOPs where a small number of real-objective function evaluations are allowed [10]. Finally, we are also interested in applying machine learning methods to solve MaOPs [20].

References

1. Bao, C., Gao, D., Gu, W., Xu, L., Goodman, E.D.: A new adaptive decomposition-based evolutionary algorithm for multi- and many-objective optimization. Expert Syst. Appl. **213**, 119080 (2023)
2. Bosman, P.A., Thierens, D.: The balance between proximity and diversity in multi-objective evolutionary algorithms. IEEE Trans. Evol. Comput. **7**(2), 174–188 (2003)
3. Cheng, R., Jin, Y., Olhofer, M., Sendhoff, B.: A reference vector guided evolutionary algorithm for many-objective optimization. IEEE Trans. Evol. Comput. **20**(5), 773–791 (2016)
4. Deb, K., Jain, H.: An evolutionary many-objective optimization algorithm using reference-point-based nondominated sorting approach, part I: solving problems with box constraints. IEEE Trans. Evol. Comput. **18**(4), 577–601 (2014)
5. Elarbi, M., Bechikh, S., Ben Said, L., Datta, R.: Multi-objective optimization: Classical and evolutionary approaches. Recent advances in evolutionary multi-objective optimization pp. 1–30 (2017)
6. Elarbi, M., Bechikh, S., Coello, C.A.C., Makhlouf, M., Said, L.B.: Approximating complex Pareto fronts with predefined normal-boundary intersection directions. IEEE Trans. Evol. Comput. **24**(5), 809–823 (2019)
7. Giagkiozis, I., Purshouse, R.C., Fleming, P.J.: Towards understanding the cost of adaptation in decomposition-based optimization algorithms. In: 2013 IEEE International Conference on Systems, Man, and Cybernetics, pp. 615–620. IEEE (2013)
8. Gu, F., Cheung, Y.M.: Self-organizing map-based weight design for decomposition-based many-objective evolutionary algorithm. IEEE Trans. Evol. Comput. **22**(2), 211–225 (2017)
9. Guo, X.: A survey of decomposition based evolutionary algorithms for many-objective optimization problems. IEEE Access **10**, 72825–72838 (2022)
10. He, C., Cheng, R., Jin, Y., Yao, X.: Surrogate-assisted expensive many-objective optimization by model fusion. In: 2019 IEEE congress on evolutionary computation (CEC), pp. 1672–1679. IEEE (2019)
11. Jain, H., Deb, K.: An evolutionary many-objective optimization algorithm using reference-point based nondominated sorting approach, part II: handling constraints and extending to an adaptive approach. IEEE Trans. Evol. Comput. **18**(4), 602–622 (2013)
12. Li, K.: A survey of multi-objective evolutionary algorithm based on decomposition: past and future. IEEE Trans. Evol. Comput. (2024). https://doi.org/10.1109/TEVC.2024.3496507

13. Li, K., Deb, K., Zhang, Q., Kwong, S.: An evolutionary many-objective optimization algorithm based on dominance and decomposition. IEEE Trans. Evol. Comput. **19**(5), 694–716 (2015)

14. Li, M., Yao, X.: What weights work for you? Adapting weights for any Pareto front shape in decomposition-based evolutionary multi-objective optimisation. Evol. Comput. **28**(2), 227–253 (2020)

15. Liu, H.L., Chen, L., Zhang, Q., Deb, K.: Adaptively allocating search effort in challenging many-objective optimization problems. IEEE Trans. Evol. Comput. **22**(3), 433–448 (2017)

16. Liu, Q., Jin, Y., Heiderich, M., Rodemann, T.: Adaptation of reference vectors for evolutionary many-objective optimization of problems with irregular Pareto fronts. In: 2019 IEEE Congress on Evolutionary Computation (CEC), pp. 1726–1733. IEEE (2019)

17. Liu, Q., Jin, Y., Heiderich, M., Rodemann, T., Yu, G.: An adaptive reference vector-guided evolutionary algorithm using growing neural gas for many-objective optimization of irregular problems. IEEE Trans. Cybern. **52**(5), 2698–2711 (2020)

18. Ma, X., Yu, Y., Li, X., Qi, Y., Zhu, Z.: A survey of weight vector adjustment methods for decomposition-based multiobjective evolutionary algorithms. IEEE Trans. Evol. Comput. **24**(4), 634–649 (2020)

19. Qi, Y., Ma, X., Liu, F., Jiao, L., Sun, J., Wu, J.: MOEA/D with adaptive weight adjustment. Evol. Comput. **22**(2), 231–264 (2014)

20. Qu, Q., Ma, Z., Clausen, A., Jørgensen, B.N.: A comprehensive review of machine learning in multi-objective optimization. In: 2021 IEEE International Conference on Big Data and Artificial Intelligence (BDAI), pp. 7–14. IEEE (2021)

21. Sato, H.: Analysis of inverted PBI and comparison with other scalarizing functions in decomposition based MOEAs. J. Heuristics **21**(6), 819–849 (2015)

22. Sharma, A.K., Datta, R., Elarbi, M., Bhattacharya, B., Bechikh, S.: Practical applications in constrained evolutionary multi-objective optimization. In: Bechikh, S., Datta, R., Gupta, A. (eds.) Recent Advances in Evolutionary Multi-objective Optimization, pp. 159–179 (2017)

23. Sheskin, D.J.: Handbook of Parametric and Nonparametric Statistical Procedures. Chapman and Hall/CRC (2003)

24. Tian, Y., Cheng, R., Zhang, X., Jin, Y.: PlatEMO: a MATLAB platform for evolutionary multi-objective optimization [educational forum]. IEEE Comput. Intell. Mag. **12**(4), 73–87 (2017)

25. Wu, M., Li, K., Kwong, S., Zhang, Q., Zhang, J.: Learning to decompose: a paradigm for decomposition-based multiobjective optimization. IEEE Trans. Evol. Comput. **23**(3), 376–390 (2018)

26. Xiang, Y., Zhou, Y., Li, M., Chen, Z.: A vector angle-based evolutionary algorithm for unconstrained many-objective optimization. IEEE Trans. Evol. Comput. **21**(1), 131–152 (2016)

27. Xu, Y., Li, F., Zhang, H., Li, W.: An adaptive reference vector guided many-objective optimization algorithm based on the Pareto front density estimation. Swarm Evol. Comput. **88**, 101601 (2024)

28. Yuan, Y., Xu, H., Wang, B., Yao, X.: A new dominance relation-based evolutionary algorithm for many-objective optimization. IEEE Trans. Evol. Comput. **20**(1), 16–37 (2015)

29. Zhang, Q., Li, H.: MOEA/D: a multiobjective evolutionary algorithm based on decomposition. IEEE Trans. Evol. Comput. **11**(6), 712–731 (2007)

30. Zhang, Z., Gao, S., Lei, Z., Xiong, R., Cheng, J.: Pareto dominance archive and coordinated selection strategy-based many-objective optimizer for protein structure prediction. IEEE/ACM Trans. Comput. Biol. Bioinf. **20**(3), 2328–2340 (2023)
31. Zhang, Z., Zhao, M., Wang, H., Cui, Z., Zhang, W.: An efficient interval many-objective evolutionary algorithm for cloud task scheduling problem under uncertainty. Inf. Sci. **583**, 56–72 (2022)
32. Zitzler, E., Thiele, L.: Multiobjective evolutionary algorithms: a comparative case study and the strength Pareto approach. IEEE Trans. Evol. Comput. **3**(4), 257–271 (1999)

Encodings for Multi-objective Free-Form Coverage Path Planning

Lukas Bostelmann-Arp[1]([✉]) [iD], Christoph Steup[1] [iD], and Sanaz Mostaghim[1,2] [iD]

[1] Otto von Guericke University Magdeburg, Magdeburg, Germany
{lukas.bostelmann-arp,christoph.steup,sanaz.mostaghim}@ovgu.de
[2] Fraunhofer Institute for Transportation and Infrastructure Systems IVI,
Dresden, Germany

Abstract. Coverage path planning (CPP) is the problem of determining a path that covers any given area and is mainly applied in the field of robotics. To ensure efficient coverage, objectives like path length, overlaps, and traversal time are considered. However, in certain scenarios, a simplistic total coverage approach may not be optimal, necessitating a trade-off strategy. This paper addresses a novel challenge in CPP: the multi-objective weighted coverage path planning problem, where total coverage is not strictly required but balanced against other objectives and constraints. We present an approach to solve this problem using evolutionary multi-objective algorithms with free-form path representations. The focus lies on comparing different path representations, ranging from polygonal chains to Bézier curves and B-splines, to Non-Uniform Rational B-splines (NURBs). Additionally, we incorporate an overlaid rectangular grid for comparison with a graph-based approach.

Keywords: Multi-Objective Optimization · Coverage Path Planning · Free-Form · Path Representation

1 Introduction

Nowadays, mobile robots are utilized in various domains: underwater [1,10], on land, for example in fields [15], and in the air as unmanned aerial vehicles (UAVs). In the latter case, they fulfill various tasks, including videography, remote sensing [25], agricultural monitoring [23], and aiding in disaster scenarios such as earthquake [6]. Despite their diverse applications, they share a common challenge: coverage path planning (CPP). These paths must cover the area of interest while considering metrics such as path length, overlaps, curvature, and traversal time, as well as application-specific constraints like no-fly zones (NFZs) and obstacles. However, in some scenarios, a simple total coverage approach is not sufficient. Instead, a trade-off is necessary. This happens in search and rescue scenarios, for example, when searching for a missing person in a large field with limited time and energy resources. In these cases, a value function can be employed to prioritize certain parts of the area. For instance, in UAV search

H. Singh et al. (Eds.): EMO 2025, LNCS 15512, pp. 148–163, 2025.
https://doi.org/10.1007/978-981-96-3506-1_11

and rescue missions, this function could represent the probability distribution of the missing person's location. Additionally, there is a need for adaptable, free-form paths that can adjust to any situation. Thus, arises a novel challenge: the multi-objective weighted coverage path planning problem.

Multi-objective evolutionary algorithms (EAs) have been widely applied to solve coverage path planning (CPP) problems. In most of these works, the area is discretized into subregions or a set of waypoints, and the EA is used to optimize the order of traversal. In addition, the majority of papers either focus on a single objective problem or combine multiple objectives into one. For instance, in [13], an agricultural field is clustered into blocks, and the sequence of traversal of these blocks, along with the respective entry and exit points, is optimized. Further, waypoints can be generated by employing domain knowledge [8] or by overlaying a grid and assigning a waypoint to each cell [22]. Only a few papers have used true multi-objective evolutionary algorithms to solve the CPP problem. One such study optimized the traversal of waypoints to minimize energy usage and maximize coverage for an autonomous underwater vehicle inspecting complex structures [10]. In another paper, the energy usage and coverage for an underwater robot are optimized [1]. Moreover, evolutionary algorithms are used for continuous path optimization using a single objective. Use cases include path planning for UAVs [12,18,21] and general mobile robots [11,14,20]. Although these methods employ a continuous space for the waypoints that form a path, the waypoints are typically connected by straight lines. Some studies use smoothing techniques to convert these polylines into free-form paths afterward. Only two works [7,19] utilized actual free-form path representations, specifically B-splines and Bézier curves. There is also a multi-objective approach [24], but it still uses only line segments between waypoints as the path representation. Lastly, two notable papers integrate multi-objective evolutionary algorithms with free-form path planning [4,5]. These studies focus on generating a coverage path for an agricultural field, both with and without prior decomposition. However, only one seed curve is optimized in these approaches, which is then offset to cover the entire field, rather than optimizing the entire path.

The goal of this paper is to employ EAs to address a multi-objective weighted CPP problem using free-form curves. Our major focus is to study the impact of the path representations in the evolutionary multi-objective optimization context. This aspect is fundamental, as the operators and the evaluation functions highly depend on the selected representation. For this paper, we propose abstract path representations at a mathematical level. Such representations offer scalability and can map nearly any path. We explore various options, ranging from simple polygonal chains to more complex Bézier curves, B-splines, and NURBs. Additionally, we implement an overlaid rectangular grid to facilitate comparisons with a discrete graph-based approach. We examine the proposed representations based on their ability to generate a well spread and converged Pareto front. While cardinal B-splines are not as fast as polygonal chains or as divers as the graph-based approach, they provide the best trade-off between runtime and convergence, making them the most promising approach.

2   Problem Statement

An area for the weighted coverage path planning problem consists of three components: a value function, no-fly zones, and an outer border. The value function is discrete and defined over a high-resolution grid, resulting in the matrix
$A \in \mathbb{R}^{m \times n}$. Each NFZ is defined by a polygon describing its outer shape. All
generated paths within this area must lie within the outer border of the area and
cover as much of the value function as possible, while optimizing both path length
and smoothness. The selected scenarios are illustrated in Fig. 3 and explained in
more detail in Sect. 4.

2.1   Path Representations

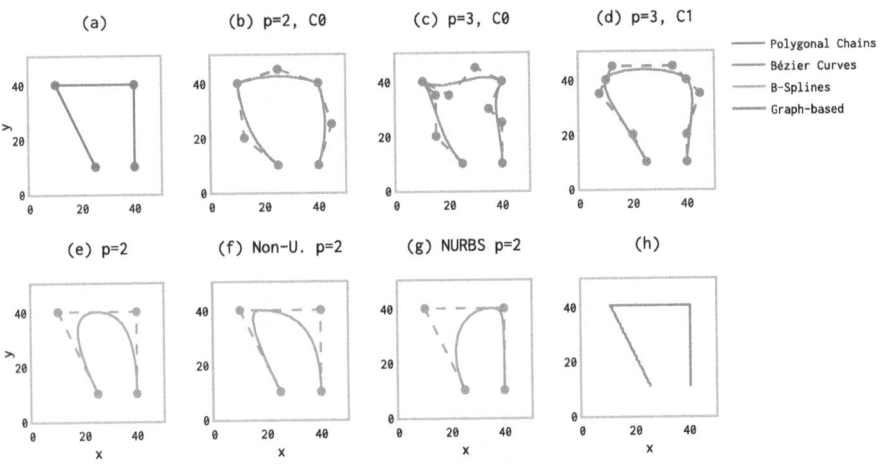

Fig. 1. Visualizations of selected path representations: Polygonal Chains (a), Composite Bézier Curves (b-d), B-Splines (e-g), and Graph-based (h). The additional markers
connected by dashed lines indicate the control nodes of the Bézier curves and nodes of
the B-Splines, respectively.

Polygonal Chains are the simplest path representation. They consist of N control points $[P_0, \dots, P_{N-1}]$, connected by linear segments, as visualized in Fig. 1
(a). While this representation does not feature any additional degree of freedom,
its simplicity results in a very low computational complexity. The polygonal
chain, and all following path representations, are defined over the parameter
$u \in [0, 1]$. For this representation, each linear segment gets a unit interval of
u assigned corresponding to the index of the first vertex. This results in the
following mathematical formulation:

$$P_{Polygonal}(u) = P_i + \hat{u}\frac{P_{i+1} - P_i}{\|P_{i+1} - P_i\|} \tag{1}$$

with $\qquad i = \lfloor u(N-1) \rfloor \qquad (2) \qquad$ and

$\hat{u} = u(N-1) \bmod 1 \qquad (3)$

Composite Bézier Curves consist of individual Bézier curves, each of degree p, with a C^0 continuity constraint. This constraint requires that the last point of one Bézier curve coincides with the starting point of the subsequent curve. Each segment is defined by $p+1$ control points as seen in Fig. 1: (b-d) $[P_0^i, \ldots, P_p^i]$, where i is the index of the segment within the whole path. These segments can be expressed as

$$B^i(\hat{u}) = \sum_{j=0}^{p} \binom{p}{j}(1 - \hat{u})^{p-j}\hat{u}^j P_j^i \quad (4) \quad \text{and} \quad P_{B\acute{e}zier}(u) = B^i(\hat{u}), \quad (5)$$

where i and $\hat{u}$ are based on the same parameterization method used for the polygonal chains and can be computed according to Eqs. 2 and 3. Additional continuity constraints can be established, but in this work, they are restricted to C^1 (velocity continuity). Its effect on the connections of the individual Bézier curves is clearly visible in Fig. 1 (c) and (d). Stricter continuity constraints lead to a cascading loss of control over subsequent control points. Equations 6 and 7 for C^0 and C^1 continuity show how these constraints already affect the degree of freedom.

$$P_1^{i+1} = 2P_p^i - P_{p-1}^i \tag{7}$$

$$P_0^{i+1} = P_p^i \tag{6}$$

B-Spline paths are a type of spline represented as a linear combination of basis functions, each of order n and degree $p = n - 1$. The path is parameterized over u and the values $[u_0, u_1, \ldots, u_m]$ at which the polynomials meet are called knots. These knots are sorted in non-decreasing order. Given that $u \in [0, 1]$, a unique spline representation can be constructed as

$$P_{B-spline}(u) = \sum_j P_j B_{j,n}(u), \tag{8}$$

where P_j are the control points. The individual B-splines $B_{j,n}(u)$ can be constructed recursively, starting from order one

$$WB_{j,0}(u) := \begin{cases} 1 & if\ u_j \le u \le u_{j+1} \\ 0 & otherwise \end{cases} \tag{9}$$

$$B_{j,k+1}(u) := w_{j,k}(u)B_{j,k}(u) + [1 - w_{j+1,k}(u)]B_{j+1,k}(u) \tag{10}$$

with

$$w_{j,k} := \begin{cases} \frac{u-u_i}{u_{j+k}-u_i}, & u_{j+k} \neq u_j \\ 0 & \text{otherwise.} \end{cases} \tag{11}$$

In this paper, a B-spline has equidistant knots and is uniquely defined by the control points. If this restriction is not enforced, they are called non-uniform (N-U) B-splines and feature an additional degree of freedom. Further, they can also be rational (R). In this case, they are called NURBS for non-uniform rational B-splines. In addition to the control points and the knot vector, they feature a weight w for each control point. A higher weight pulls the curve towards the respective control point, as showcased in Fig. 1 (h). In the case of the weights being all 1, NURBS generalize to non-uniform B-splines. A NURBS of order n or degree $p = n - 1$ can be defined by

$$P_{NURBS}(u) = \sum_j P_j R_{j,n}(u) \quad (12) \qquad R_{j,n}(u) = \frac{B_{j,n}(u)w_j}{\sum_k B_{k,n}(u)w_k} \tag{13}$$

where P_j are the control points, $R_{j,n}$ the rational basis functions, and $B_{j,n}$ the B-splines defined above.

Graph-based paths are implemented to serve as a comparison to traditional coverage path planning. They work on a regular grid with a von Neumann neighborhood topology. A path is encoded by a sequence of cell indices. The resulting path can be interpreted as a polygonal chain, with the center points of the visited cells being the control points.

2.2 Objectives

As motivated in the introduction, the main goal is to optimize paths that aggregate as much as possible of the value function. However, to be usable in the real world, the paths need to be efficient. This includes minimizing the length and ensuring smoothness, as fewer turns and sharp corners lead to more efficient traversal. These three objectives are formalized below.

Length is a crucial property of every path. The operational time of robots is often limited by their respective battery capacity, especially for UAVs. Therefore, the optimized paths should be short while achieving high coverage. The length of a path is defined as

$$f_1 = \int_0^1 |P'(u)|\,du, \tag{14}$$

but it is solved via numerical integration or by summing the lengths of the linear segments in the case of polygonal chains and the graph-based approach.

Smoothness of a path determines how well a robot can traverse it. While UAVs can maneuver quite well, quick directional changes still cost time and increase energy consumption. For differentiable paths, the smoothness objective is based on the squared arc length derivative of the curvature. It is a physics-motivated measure to reduce jerk [17], which has been applied for optimizing smooth paths before [2]. The computation is shown in Eq. 15 with $K(u)$ being the curvature for a given path $P(u)$. For paths that are not differentiable because they consist of $n + 1$ linear segments, the smoothness is computed as the average absolute turning angles α_i between segment i and $i + 1$ as shown in Eq. 16.

$$f_2 = \int_0^1 \frac{K'(u)^2}{\sqrt{1 + P'(u)^2}} \quad (15) \qquad f_2 = \frac{\sum_{i=1}^n \alpha_i}{n} \quad (16)$$

Weighted Coverage is determined by the area visible while traversing a path, combined with the values of the value-function A. At each sampled position along the path, a square portion of the area can be seen, resulting in the matrix $V \in \mathbb{R}^{m \times n}$, as described in Eq. 17. The proportion of the area covered by the evaluated path is calculated by dividing the element-wise multiplication of A and V by the total sum of A. To formulate this as a minimization problem, the fraction of the area that has not been covered is used as the objective, as shown in Eq. 18.

$$V_{i,j} = \begin{cases} 1 & \text{if } (i,j)^T \text{ is seen} \\ 0 & \text{else.} \end{cases} \quad (17) \qquad f_3 = 1 - \frac{\sum_{i=1}^m \sum_{j=1}^n A_{i,j} V_{i,j}}{\sum_{i=1}^m \sum_{j=1}^n A_{i,j}} \quad (18)$$

2.3   No-Fly Zone Constraint

Compliance with NFZs is enforced by a single inequality constraint $g \leq 0$, where g represents the total length of the path sections that run within at least one NFZ. This results in the following equation:

$$g = \sum_i \int_0^1 |f(u, NFZ_i)| du \quad (19)$$

$$f(u, NFZ) = \begin{cases} P'(u) & \text{if } P(u) \in NFZ \\ 0 & \text{else} \end{cases} \quad (20)$$

3   Algorithm

The goal is to minimize the three objectives described in Subsect. 2.2 by optimizing the coverage paths. The NSGA-II algorithm [9] is employed, as it is a simple-to-use algorithm capable of generating solutions for three objectives. A binary tournament selector chooses the parents from the current population P, which are used to create the children C with $|P| = |C| = n_{pop}$. The encoding, custom initialization, crossover, and mutation operators are explained in the following sections. The optimization was implemented using pymoo [3].

3.1 Encodings

All representations, except for the graph-based one, are encoded as one-dimensional arrays of floating-point values. However, the number of decision variables differs among them. Therefore, the representations must be compared in terms of the dimension of the search space, given the number of waypoints N and the degree p or order n of the curves used. The resulting formulas are derived below and summarized in Table 1.

Polygonal chains require storing only a control point per waypoint. As the experiments are limited to two dimensions, the total number of decision variables is $2N$. A Bézier curve requires $p + 1$ control points. When having $N - 1$ curves, the number of decision variables totals to $2(N - 1)(p + 1)$. However, additional constraints make some of this information redundant. Due to the C^0 constraint, the first control point of all but the first curve are duplicates, reducing the number of variables to $2(N - 1)p + 2$. Similarly, the C^1 constraint makes the second control point of each Bézier curve redundant, as it must be symmetric to the second-to-last control point of the previous segment. Consequently, the number of values required to represent the path is $2(N - 1)(p - 1) + 4$. For a cardinal B-spline, the curve is defined solely by its control points. Therefore, the number of decision variables is the same as for polygonal chains, namely $2N$. For non-cardinal B-splines, the knot vector also needs to be stored. It has $N + p + 1$ knots, but the first and last $p + 1$ knots are zero or one, respectively, to ensure the path starts and ends at the first and last waypoint. Therefore, the total number of decision variables is $3N - p - 1$. NURBS extend B-splines by adding a weight vector, contributing N additional values, resulting in a total of $4N - p - 1$. For graph-based paths, no simple equation can be provided, as it depends on the grid size and the length of the path.

Table 1. Comparison of the required decision variables. N is the number of waypoints and n and p are the order and degree, respectively.

Representation	Parameters	Constraints	Decision Variables
Polygonal Chain	N		$2N$
Bézier curves	N, p	C^0	$2(N - 1)p + 2$
		C^1	$2(N - 1)(p - 1) + 4$
B-spline	N, p		$2N$
Non-Uniform B-spline	N, p		$3N - p - 1$
NURBS	N, p		$N - p - 1$

3.2   Initialization

All paths start from the same predetermined position. Additional points are sampled uniformly within the area. From the start point, these points are connected using a greedy approach, selecting the closest neighbor that has not yet been included in the path. While polygonal chains can be directly instantiated from these ordered waypoints, representations with higher degrees of freedom are not uniquely defined. For Bézier curves, the additional control nodes are placed evenly along the lines connecting the waypoints. For B-splines, the waypoints are used directly as control nodes, with a uniform knot vector and equal weights of one. Lastly, for the graph representation, the Bresenham line algorithm is used to connect the waypoints on the grid.

3.3   Crossover

The crossover operator is implemented as a one-point crossover. A random waypoint index is selected from the shorter path, at which both paths are crossed. This is a simple implementation, as the focus lies on the representations. However, a more sophisticated version is possible and has already been used in other works. Instead of selecting a random waypoint to cross, an intersection between the two parent paths could be used. This results in more realistic offspring, as no new connections need to be made at the crossover point. The drawback, however, is that computing the intersection point can be computationally expensive, especially for B-spline-based representations.

3.4   Mutation

In the case of mutation, one of three independent operators is applied, each depicted schematically in Fig. 2 and explained below. The first operator modifies either a waypoint or any other value of the respective representation. The other two operators add or delete a waypoint, allowing for the creation of shorter or longer paths. Since this paper aims to compare the representations themselves, the individual operators are implemented as consistently as possible across the representations. Though, different representations may benefit from individually tailored variation operators. However, such a comparison is not possible within the scope of this work.

The modification operator randomly selects a waypoint and translates it based on a randomly sampled vector d, with the magnitude sampled from a normal distribution with mean μ and standard deviation σ and the angle from a uniform distribution. In the case of composite Bézier paths, this also applies to the additional control nodes. For representations based on B-splines, instead of modifying a control node, the additional values can be modified with equal chances: either a knot vector is replaced with a new value sampled from $\mathcal{U}_{(0.0,1.0)}$, or a weight is replaced with a new one sampled from $\mathcal{U}_{(0.0,2.0)}$. Implementing the same behavior for the graph-based representation is challenging, as the notion of a global waypoint is missing due to the underlying grid. Therefore, the two neighboring global waypoints are those with a distance on the path of approximately $\|\boldsymbol{d}\|$ to the selected point. For the mutation that adds a new waypoint, two subsequent waypoints are first selected. A new point is uniformly sampled from a circular area, with the center being the middle of the connecting line of the two selected waypoints and the diameter being the distance between them. Again, the graph-based representation requires an exception for the same reason as before: there is no notion of two neighboring global waypoints. As a result, the addition boils down to the modification mutation. Lastly, the delete mutation removes a randomly selected waypoint, except the starting point. For the graph-based approach, the same strategy as for the modify mutation is used: the two points between which the path is replaced with the shortest path are found by traversing on the path by a distance $\|\boldsymbol{d}\|$ in each direction from the selected point.

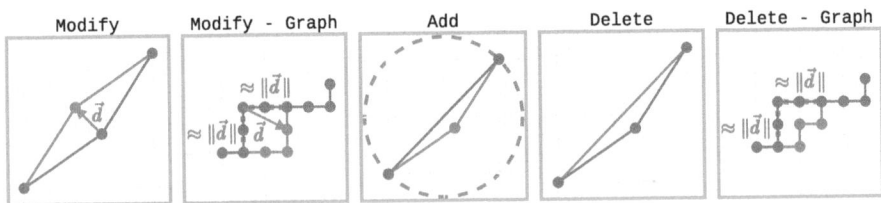

Fig. 2. Examples for the mutation operators, with the original path in blue and the mutated version in red. (Color figure online)

4   Experiments

A total of 14 different representations are tested: polygonal chains, quadratic composite Bézier curves with C^0 continuity, cubic composite Bézier curves with C^0 or C^1 continuity, quadratic or cubic B-splines, non-uniform B-splines or NURBS, and lastly the graph-based approach with cell sizes of 1.0, 2.0, 4.0, or 5.0. Larger cell sizes are not tested, as the view size is set to 5.0. These representations are tested on six different scenarios depicted in Fig. 3. The scenarios vary in the complexity of the value function, ranging from a uniform distribution and sine and cosine functions, to a realistic example in scenario six, where a road-like structure is highlighted in the middle along with regions of special interest. Each scenario can be tested with and without the NFZs, resulting in 12 different test cases.

For initialization, all paths start in the lower-left corner of the area, and 49 additional points are sampled for each individual in the starting population. A population size of 100 is used, with a crossover probability of 0.9 and a mutation probability of 0.75. The parameters μ and σ, which determine the magnitude of the shift for the modify mutation, are set to 10 and 2.5, respectively. These values are based on preliminary experiments that are outside the scope of this paper but should be examined regarding their impact across the different path representations in more detail in future research through ablation studies. Each optimization terminates after 100,000 function evaluations. Finally, 31 runs are computed for each combination, resulting in 5,208 total runs. Moreover, since comparing all 14 different path representations at once is challenging, the best parameter configuration of each variant is determined first before comparing them against each other.

A visual data analysis based on the optimized fronts, HV, GD+, and IGD+ is used to determine the best parameters. Since no true Pareto front is known for this problem, nor can it be computed easily, it is approximated by combining all runs for each scenario and identifying the non-dominated front. However, there is no guarantee that it is well distributed, which is a requirement for IGD and its variants. As a result, the findings based on those metrics need to be interpreted with caution.

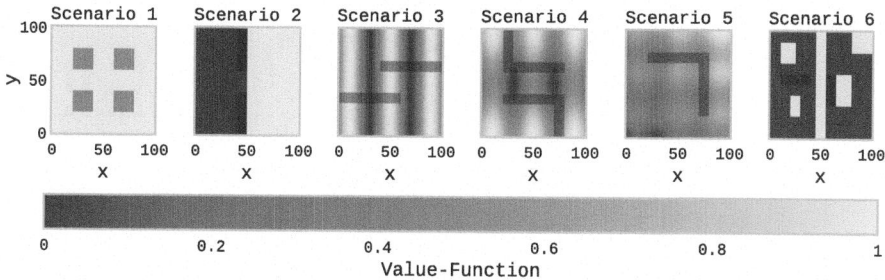

Fig. 3. The six used scenarios with their respective value functions. The shaded areas mark no-fly zones.

5   Evaluations

Parameter Comparison: The first row of Fig. 4 shows two plots of the HV over the generations for the third scenario, with and without NFZs, comparing the different composite Bézier curve representations. Notably, the representation based on cubic Bézier curves with the C^1 constraint appears to perform the best. This observation holds for most other scenarios as well. The likely reason is that it features smooth curves between segments and a higher degree of freedom, resulting in higher coverage with the same number of segments.

When inspecting the GD+ and IGD+ metrics in subplot (c) and (d), no clear favorite emerges among the different B-spline variants. However, when looking at the HV over the generations, normal B-splines perform best in all 12 tested scenarios. An example is shown in subplot (e) of Fig. 4. Out of the 12 scenarios, quadratic B-splines perform best in seven, while the remaining five are draws. This difference is due to quadratic B-splines generating longer paths with good

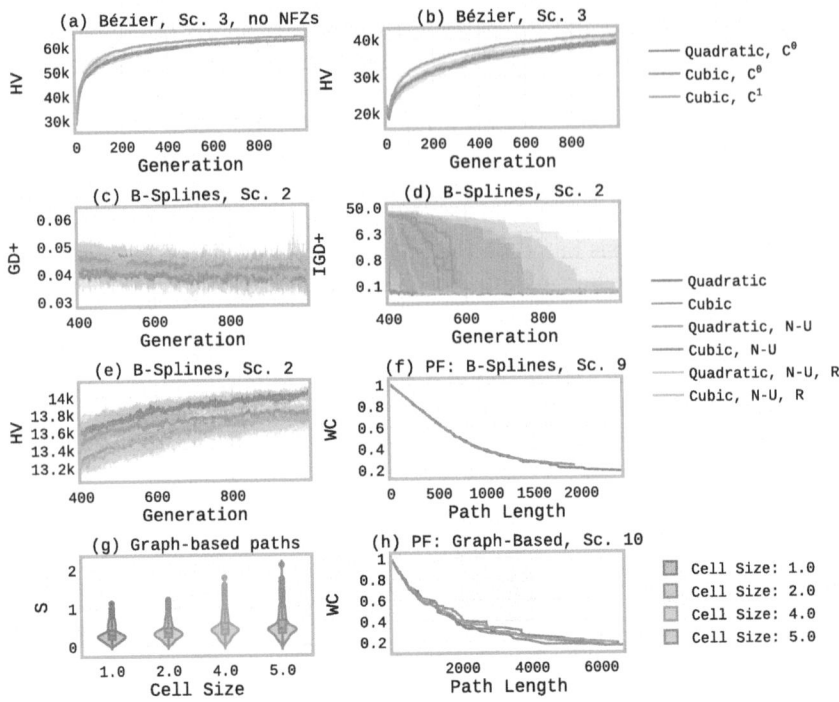

Fig. 4. Selected plots for the parameter comparison of the different path representations, with the shaded area marking values between the 25th and 75th percentile. (HV: Hypervolume, WC: Weighted Coverage, S: Smoothness, Sc.: Scenario, PF: Combined and connected Pareto Front)

coverage. A corresponding 2D Pareto front, that shows this difference, is visualized in plot (f) of Fig. 4.

Lastly, the graph-based paths show similar performance across the HV, GD+, and IGD+ metrics. For this reason and due to space constraints, these illustrations are not included. A slight trend is visible in the distribution of the resulting fitness values. A smaller cell size leads, as expected, to a smoother path, while a larger cell size results in better coverage per path length. This effect is especially noticeable for solutions with higher coverage. The respective plots are illustrated in Fig. 4 (g) and (h). Since the main goal of the optimization is to achieve good coverage, the largest cell size is selected for further comparisons with the other path representations. Overall, polygonal chains, composite cubic Bézier curves with a C^1 constraint, quadratic B-splines, and the graph-based approach with a cell size of 5.0 are selected for comparison in the next section.

Representation Comparison: Since the smoothness has been calculated differently, the remaining two objectives are used to compute a comparable HV. Additionally, only solutions that pass a certain smoothness threshold are considered. Firstly, polygonal chains and composite Bézier curves perform similarly. However, in most scenarios, the Bézier curves tend to perform slightly better. The IGD+ metric shows this difference, for example in the fourth scenario, depicted in plot (d) of Fig. 6. Additionally, polygonal chains are inherently less smooth compared to composite Bézier curves with a C^1 continuity, as seen in the direct comparison between plots (e) and (f) of the same figure. Yet, polygonal chains have a substantial advantage in computational effort, as shown in Fig. 5. When judging B-splines solely based on the HV, it is the worst representation. Not only the HV increases slowly, but also it does not always reach the same level as the other representations. The reason becomes clear when looking at the Pareto front itself in Fig. 6 (b): B-splines actually find a better set of solutions for the most part but do not cover the entire front. Their advantage, however, is seen in the GD+ and IGD+ metrics in plots (c) and (d), respectively. Runtime-wise, B-splines outperform Bézier curves but lose against the graph-based and polygonal chain representations. The graph-based approach has its distinct advantages and disadvantages: As visible in plot (a) of Fig. 6, the HV initially increases the fastest but then flattens out or even decreases. Plot (b) of the same figure shows the reasons: the approach is excellent in diversity, covering the whole front and generating solutions not found by other representations, but the convergence is comparatively poor, which is strongly reflected in the GD+ metric. The bottom row of Fig. 6 depicts one path per representation that has the best coverage while being between 950 and 1050 units long. All representations can prioritize the yellow, more important areas. Notably, the polygonal chains and B-splines require fewer crossing paths in the less important areas. Apart from the inherently better smoothness of the Bézier and B-spline representations, graph-based paths are the only representations that sometimes resemble how a human would plan a path.

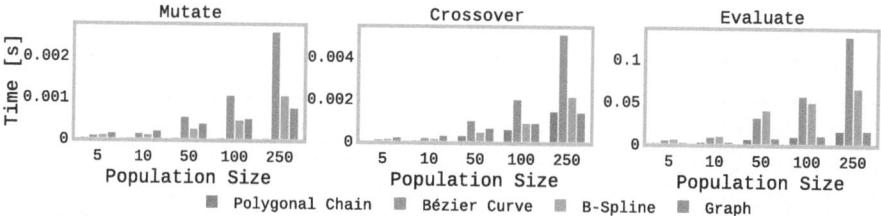

Fig. 5. Average runtime in seconds for the evaluate function and the mutation and crossover operator over the population size (Computed as single tasks with 31 CPU cores per task and 2 GB of RAM per core on a single node of a Slurm cluster [16] running an AMD Epyc 7543 with no additional workload on the same node).

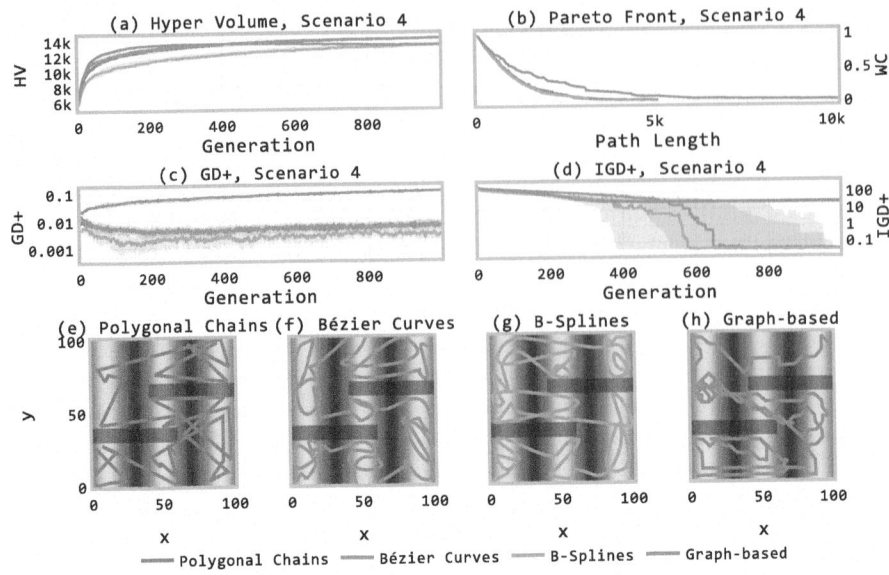

Fig. 6. The three metrics HV, GD+, and IGD+ in (a), (c), and (d), respectively, plus the combined Pareto front for each representation of the fourth scenario in (b) with WC being the weighted coverage. The shaded area marks values between the 25th and 75th percentile. (e)-(h) in the last row show solutions with a length between 950 and 1050 with the best respective coverage.

6 Conclusion and Future Work

This paper proposed and compared four different mathematical representations for free-form paths used to optimize a weighted coverage path planning problem using a multi-objective algorithm. The representations evaluated were polygonal chains, composite Bézier curves, B-splines, and a graph-based approach. In the first step, the best parameters for each representation were determined: composite cubic Bézier curves with a C^1 continuity, quadratic cardinal B-splines, and a cell size equal to the visible area of a UAV for the graph-based approach. All representations were able to optimize solutions even for complex scenarios and find suitable trade-offs. Nonetheless, differences were observed that make some approaches more or less suitable for certain scenarios: **Polygonal chains** are substantially fast and feature good performance but are inherently not smooth. **Composite cubic Bézier curves with C^1 continuity** often slightly outperform polygonal chains and are inherently smooth, but at a notable increase in computational cost. **Cardinal B-splines** show good convergence but lack diversity, providing the best solutions for most of the Pareto front while missing the extreme parts. Runtime-wise, they are between polygonal chains and Bézier curves. The **Graph-Based approach** behaves contrary to B-splines, featuring good diversity but poor convergence. This leads to an initially fast increase in the HV that flattens out quickly, resulting in final values lower than those of the other representations. However, the mathematical representation is only one part of the optimization. Mutation and crossover operators can also significantly impact the performance of the individual representations, which need to be evaluated in future research. Additionally, in this study, exclusively NSGA-II was employed; other algorithms, such as indicator-based or decomposition-based approaches, should also be investigated for their applicability.

Acknowledgments. This research was partially funded by the German Research Foundation (DFG) under project number 502167710.

Disclosure of Interests. The authors have no competing interests to declare that are relevant to the content of this article.

References

1. Batista, V.R., Zampirolli, F.A.: Optimising robotic pool-cleaning with a genetic algorithm. J. Intell. Rob. Syst. **95**(2), 443–458 (2018). https://doi.org/10.1007/s10846-018-0953-y

2. Berglund, T., Brodnik, A., Jonsson, H., Staffanson, M., Soderkvist, I.: planning smooth and obstacle-avoiding B-spline paths for autonomous mining vehicles. IEEE Trans. Autom. Sci. Eng. **7**(1), 167–172 (2010). https://doi.org/10.1109/TASE.2009.2015886

3. Blank, J., Deb, K.: Pymoo: multi-objective optimization in python. IEEE Access **8**, 89497–89509 (2020). https://doi.org/10.1109/ACCESS.2020.2990567

4. Bostelmann-Arp, L., Steup, C., Mostaghim, S.: Linking field decomposition and coverage path planning: a coevolution approach. In: 2023 IEEE Conference on Artificial Intelligence (CAI), pp. 294–295. IEEE, Santa Clara, CA, USA (2023). https://doi.org/10.1109/CAI54212.2023.00131

5. Bostelmann-Arp, L., Steup, C., Mostaghim, S.: Multi-objective seed curve optimization for coverage path planning in precision farming. In: Proceedings of the Genetic and Evolutionary Computation Conference, pp. 1312–1320. ACM, Lisbon Portugal (2023). https://doi.org/10.1145/3583131.3590490

6. Calamoneri, T., Coro, F., Mancini, S.: A realistic model to support rescue operations after an earthquake via UAVs. IEEE Access **10**, 6109–6125 (2022). https://doi.org/10.1109/ACCESS.2022.3141216

7. Chen, H., Xie, H., Sun, L., Shang, T.: Research on tractor optimal obstacle avoidance path planning for improving navigation accuracy and avoiding land waste. Agriculture **13**(5), 934 (2023). https://doi.org/10.3390/agriculture13050934

8. Dai, R., Fotedar, S., Radmanesh, M., Kumar, M.: Quality-aware UAV coverage and path planning in geometrically complex environments. Ad Hoc Netw. **73**, 95–105 (2018). https://doi.org/10.1016/j.adhoc.2018.02.008

9. Deb, K., Pratap, A., Agarwal, S., Meyarivan, T.: A fast and elitist multiobjective genetic algorithm: NSGA-II. IEEE Trans. Evol. Comput. **6**(2), 182–197 (2002). https://doi.org/10.1109/4235.996017

10. Ellefsen, K., Lepikson, H., Albiez, J.: Multiobjective coverage path planning: enabling automated inspection of complex, real-world structures. Appl. Soft Comput. **61**, 264–282 (2017). https://doi.org/10.1016/j.asoc.2017.07.051

11. Elshamli, A., Abdullah, H., Areibi, S.: Genetic algorithm for dynamic path planning. In: Canadian Conference on Electrical and Computer Engineering 2004 (IEEE Cat. No.04CH37513), pp. 677–680. IEEE, Niagara Falls, Ont., Canada (2004). https://doi.org/10.1109/CCECE.2004.1345203

12. Flores-Caballero, G., Rodriguez-Molina, A., Aldape-Perez, M., Villarreal-Cervantes, M.G.: Optimized Path-planning in continuous spaces for unmanned aerial vehicles using meta-heuristics. IEEE Access **8**, 176774–176788 (2020). https://doi.org/10.1109/ACCESS.2020.3026666

13. Hameed, I.A., Bochtis, D., Sørensen, C.A.: An optimized field coverage planning approach for navigation of agricultural robots in fields involving obstacle Areas. Int. J. Adv. Rob. Syst. **10**(5), 231 (2013). https://doi.org/10.5772/56248

14. Hu, C., Jin, Y.: Path planning for autonomous systems design: a focus genetic algorithm for complex environments. J. Auton. Veh. Syst. **2**(4), 041001 (2022). https://doi.org/10.1115/1.4063013

15. Hameed, I.A., Bochtis, D.D., Sorensen, C.G.: Driving angle and track sequence optimization for operational path planning using genetic algorithms. Appl. Eng. Agric. **27**(6), 1077–1086 (2011). https://doi.org/10.13031/2013.40615

16. Jette, M.A., Wickberg, T.: Architecture of the slurm workload manager. In: Klusáček, D., Corbalán, J., Rodrigo, G.P. (eds.) Job Scheduling Strategies for Parallel Processing, vol. 14283, pp. 3–23. Springer Nature Switzerland, Cham (2023). https://doi.org/10.1007/978-3-031-43943-8_1, series Title: Lecture Notes in Computer Science

17. Kanayama, Y., Hartman, B.: Smooth local path planning for autonomous vehicles. In: Proceedings, 1989 International Conference on Robotics and Automation, pp. 1265–1270. IEEE Comput. Soc. Press, Scottsdale, AZ, USA (1989). https://doi.org/10.1109/ROBOT.1989.100154

18. Leng, S., Sun, H.: UAV path planning in 3D complex environments using genetic algorithms. In: 2021 33rd Chinese Control and Decision Conference (CCDC), pp. 1324–1330. IEEE, Kunming, China (2021). https://doi.org/10.1109/CCDC52312.2021.9601765

19. Mahamat Pierre, D., Zakaria, N.: Genetic algorithm approach to path planning for intelligent camera control for scientific visualization. In: Zain, J.M., Wan Mohd, W.M.B., El-Qawasmeh, E. (eds.) Software Engineering and Computer Systems, vol. 180, pp. 205–213. Springer Berlin Heidelberg, Berlin, Heidelberg (2011). https://doi.org/10.1007/978-3-642-22191-0_18, series Title: Communications in Computer and Information Science

20. Ou, J., Hong, S.H., Ziehl, P., Wang, Y.: GPU-based global path planning using genetic algorithm with near corner initialization. J. Intell. Rob. Syst. **104**(2), 34 (2022). https://doi.org/10.1007/s10846-022-01576-6

21. Roberge, V., Tarbouchi, M., Labonte, G.: Comparison of parallel genetic algorithm and particle swarm optimization for real-time UAV path planning. IEEE Trans. Industr. Inf. **9**(1), 132–141 (2013). https://doi.org/10.1109/TII.2012.2198665

22. Sadek, M.G., Mohamed, A.E., El-Garhy, A.M.: Augmenting multi-objective genetic algorithm and dynamic programming for online coverage path planning. In: 2018 13th International Conference on Computer Engineering and Systems (ICCES), pp. 475–480. IEEE, Cairo, Egypt (2018). https://doi.org/10.1109/ICCES.2018.8639412

23. Tsouros, D.C., Bibi, S., Sarigiannidis, P.G.: A review on UAV-based applications for precision agriculture. Information **10**(11), 349 (2019). https://doi.org/10.3390/info10110349

24. Xue, Y.: Mobile robot path planning with a non-dominated sorting genetic algorithm. Appl. Sci. **8**(11), 2253 (2018). https://doi.org/10.3390/app8112253
25. Yao, H., Qin, R., Chen, X.: Unmanned aerial vehicle for remote sensing applications: a review. Remote Sens. **11**(12), 1443 (2019). https://doi.org/10.3390/rs11121443

VBEA: Voting-Based Evolutionary Algorithm for Multi-objective Planning

Daniel Merino[1] and Raj Korpan[1,2]([✉]) (iD)

[1] Hunter College, City University of New York, New York, NY 10065, USA
`daniel.merino86@myhunter.cuny.edu`
[2] The Graduate Center, City University of New York, New York, NY 10016, USA
`raj.korpan@hunter.cuny.edu`

Abstract. This paper presents VBEA, the Voting-Based Evolutionary Algorithm, that efficiently solves multi-objective path planning problems with voting and iterative evolutionary improvement. VBEA uses problem decomposition to create an initial population of candidate solutions that are each optimal in a single objective or randomly generated. VBEA then applies social choice theory through voting as a fitness function for the evolutionary algorithm. Each objective is a voter that evaluates the candidate solutions and assigns each of them a score or ranking depending on the voting method used. Voting identifies the top candidates and they are used to create the next generation of solutions. VBEA's novel hybrid approach combines the ability of voting mechanisms to balance multiple perspectives and priorities with the ability of evolutionary algorithms to iteratively improve solutions to form a dense and diverse Pareto-front approximation. Extensive evaluation in difficult and complex environments demonstrates VBEA's efficiency and performance.

Keywords: multi-objective · path planning · evolutionary algorithms

1 Introduction

Real-world multiple-objective path planning problems arise when a plan needs to consider multiple factors simultaneously [24]. For example, when planning the route of a truck carrying hazardous material, one must balance the travel distance, the amount of traffic, and the potential risk of harm in highly populated areas. Multi-objective path planning problems often do not have a single "optimal" solution, instead, there are many solutions that are equally "optimal" because they trade-off among the objectives (e.g., the shortest path may go through the most populated areas) [24]. Two major challenges in multi-objective settings are to identify a set of possible optimal solutions and then selecting one of them to execute [24]. The *Voting-Based Evolutionary Algorithm* (VBEA) is a

Supplementary Information The online version contains supplementary material available at https://doi.org/10.1007/978-981-96-3506-1_12.

novel multi-objective path planning method that addresses these two challenges by combining the principles of decomposition and evolutionary optimization with social choice theory.

VBEA begins by generating an initial population of plans, which includes solutions optimized for individual objectives and additional plans derived from random weighted combinations of objectives. This population serves as a diverse starting point. Through iterative evolutionary processes, VBEA enhances both the diversity and optimality of the solution set. A key innovation of the algorithm is its voting mechanism, which evaluates and ranks candidate solutions based on their ability to balance multiple objectives, like a social choice process. This hybrid approach merges the strengths of decomposing complex multi-objective problems into simpler single-objective tasks and leveraging evolutionary algorithms to refine solutions. VBEA's design not only efficiently explores the solution space but also ensures a well-distributed Pareto frontier. The empirical evaluation compares VBEA against a naive approach and A*pex [33] on benchmark environments with multiple objectives. The thesis of this work is that integrating social choice theory through a voting mechanism into an evolutionary algorithm framework provides an efficient and effective approach to solving multi-objective path planning problems by improving both the diversity and optimality of solutions while balancing competing objectives.

The next sections of the paper summarize the background and related work in multi-objective path planning, evolutionary algorithms, and social choice theory. Subsequent sections describe the relevant background and VBEA. Experiments demonstrate the efficacy of voting-based multi-objective planning. The final section discusses the results and directions for future work.

2   Background and Problem Definition

An optimal graph-search algorithm finds the least cost path from a start vertex to a target vertex. Typically, the algorithm exploits a weighted graph that represents a real-world problem, such as a navigable two-dimensional space. Such a graph $G = (V, E)$ represents unobstructed locations there as vertices V. Edges E in G each connect two vertices, normally only if one can move directly between them. Each edge is associated with a label for the cost to traverse it. For example, if the objective β were to minimize path length, edge labels could record the Euclidean distance between pairs of vertices. A single-objective path planner seeks a plan P, a sequence of connected vertices from v_{start} to v_{goal} in G, that minimizes objective β. A plan P is *optimal* with respect to β only if no other plan P' has a lower total cost $\beta(P)$ for that objective, that is, for every other plan $P', \beta(P) \leq \beta(P')$. In this work, without loss of generality, all objectives are represented as a cost that should be minimized.

A *multi-objective* path planner seeks a plan P that performs well with respect to a set $B = \{\beta_1, \beta_2, \ldots, \beta_J\}$ of J planning objectives. In the multi-objective setting, each edge in the graph is labeled with a vector that contains the cost for each objective instead of a single cost. Figure 1 shows an example of the edge

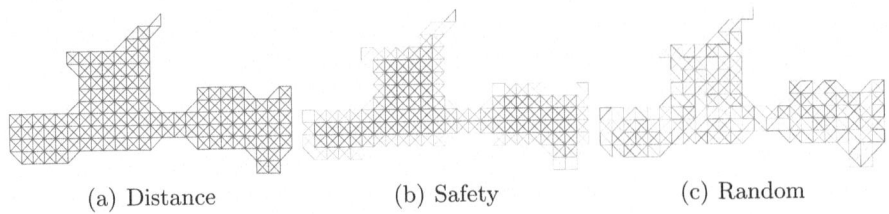

|(a) Distance|(b) Safety|(c) Random|

Fig. 1. Benchmark map [27] with edge costs (green: low, red: high): (a) Euclidean distance (b) Safety (average degree of vertices) (c) Random uniform costs.

costs for $B = \{\beta_1, \beta_2, \beta_3\}$, where β_1 is travel distance, β_2 is proximity to obstacles, and β_3 is random uniform costs. Because planning objectives often conflict, no single plan can simultaneously optimize all objectives in B, as improvements in one objective often lead to increased costs in others unless the objectives are perfectly correlated [12]. A *Pareto-optimal* solution is one where improving any objective results in at least one other becoming worse [12]. The *Pareto frontier* is the set of Pareto-optimal solutions [15]. Given a graph G, start and goal vertices, and a set of objectives B, the multi-objective path planning problem is to identify solutions on this frontier, while often leaving the final selection of a plan to an external decision maker. However, enumerating the entire Pareto frontier is infeasible because it exponentially grows with the number of objectives [12], so most methods identify a subset of the frontier.

There are several ways to compare plans for multi-objective path planners. If the costs for plan P on J objectives is $\{\beta_1(P), \beta_2(P), \ldots, \beta_J(P)\}$, a plan P_1 *dominates* another plan P_2 ($P_1 \ll P_2$) when $\beta(P_1) \leq \beta(P_2)$ for every $\beta \in B$ and $\beta_j(P_1) < \beta_j(P_2)$ for at least one objective $\beta_j \in B$. Dominance is transitive, that is, if $P_1 \ll P_2$ and $P_2 \ll P_3$, then $P_1 \ll P_3$ [18]. Some metrics treat the Pareto frontier as a multi-dimensional space where each axis represents the cost for an objective. A plan P is represented in this space as a point located at $\{\beta_1(P), \beta_2(P), \ldots, \beta_J(P)\}$. The origin of this multi-dimensional space represents a plan that optimally minimizes all objectives. The Euclidean distance d of a plan's costs to the origin represents how close a solution is to this hypothetical optimal solution. Sets of plans, $\mathcal{P}$, can also be evaluated in this multi-dimensional space. *Sparsity* measures how well a set of plans $\mathcal{P}$ covers this space by calculating the average proximity of the points [22]. *Hypervolume*, or the measurement of the area the points of $\mathcal{P}$ casts, is a measurement of how optimal a solution set is [36]. An ideal set of plans is one with low sparsity and low hypervolume, representing a dense set of solutions close to the true Pareto frontier.

3 Related Work

Previous work in multi-objective planning has used weights to balance the objectives, modified the graph search algorithms to account for dominance, or used evolutionary approaches to find non-dominated solutions. For example, the multi-objective problem can be reduced to a single objective by using a simple weighted sum of the objectives [32] and then applying any efficient single-objective planning algorithm. The challenge is weight selection–either a human expert has to tune the weights to reflect their priorities [17] or an algorithm can select them. In either case, small weight adjustments can produce very different outcomes. Best-first search is a class of graph search algorithms that prioritizes the exploration of vertices in the graph that are most likely to move the search area toward the target [19]. All discovered, but not explored vertices are held in an *open* set and assigned an f-score, a number representing how promising it is. Typically, this f-score is given by some heuristic function h. A* is a single-objective best-first graph search algorithm that requires an admissible heuristic (one that underestimates the f-score to the true cost) to be optimal [10].

Many multi-objective path planning algorithms incorporate a best-first approach, choosing a heuristic function that compares multiple objectives [8,11,26,29,33]. Multi-objective A* (MOA*) maintains an *open* set that prioritizes exploring non-dominated vertices [26]. NAMOA* extends MOA* with an open set that prioritizes partial solution paths instead of vertices, but it is inefficient and does not scale well with the number of objectives [16]. Recent work has sought to identify informative admissible heuristics for an improved version of NAMOA* and create an improved dominance check method, which has been a computational bottleneck for algorithms that require non-dominated sorting or filtering [7,11,20]. NAMOA*dr seeks to improve upon NAMOA* by improving its dominance check process but has the limitation of only two objectives [20].

Other work has addressed the inefficiency of multi-objective planners, but only for two objectives [9,29]. Also in the bi-objective context, others have focused on finding the extreme supported non-dominated plans on the Pareto frontier [25] or approximate Pareto-optimal solutions [33]. PP-A* is a best-first bi-criteria algorithm that represents elements in the open set as a pair of paths whose g-scores are within a human-defined bound ϵ [11]. A*pex generalized this idea to allow each element to represent any number of paths with a single representative path and a single cost vector [33]. However, A*pex has only been tested on a few objectives and environments. In contrast, VBEA produces non-dominated plans on the Pareto frontier for multiple objectives without modifying how elements are represented in the open set.

An evolutionary algorithm (EA) creates a population of solutions and utilizes a heuristic "fitness" function to evaluate individual solutions and determine members of future populations [1]. EAs have solved various multi-objective optimization problems, typically with a method to find non-dominated solutions as its fitness function [5]. EAs usually do not guarantee optimality [3], often require tuning many hyperparameters, and are computationally expensive [28,35]. NSGA-II incorporates "elitism" to ensure that only the best solutions are carried over to the next generation [5]. Its fitness function uses a non-dominated sorting method to order solutions along with a crowding metric to iteratively create more optimal solutions. Several approaches have attempted to improve the non-dominated sorting method by adding to or changing the internal functions because they are a computational bottleneck [2,4,21]. MOEA/D uses problem decomposition by creating a set of scalar optimization sub-problems from the objective functions [34]. Unlike NSGA-II and MOEA/D, VBEA uses efficient voting mechanisms to filter solutions instead of slowly sorting them and decomposes the problem without any prior knowledge.

Social choice theory studies how voting can be utilized to fairly make decisions and order choices. Given a set of voters that vote on a set of *candidates* (i.e., choices), a *voting method* which incorporate mechanisms like ranking, approval, and scoring [23] to selects the winning candidate [30]. In the *Condorcet Method*, voters express a preference in every pair of candidates, and, in each pairing, the candidate with more voters gets a point. The candidate with the most points is the winner. A voter can *rank* candidates according to their preferences [6]. *Borda* voting assigns values to the c candidates based on the voters' rankings: a voter's first choice receives a value of $c - 1$, its second choice a value of $c - 2$, and so on. The candidate with the largest total value is the winner. In other voting methods, voters can approve or disapprove each candidate or indicate their level of approval with a score. In *range voting* each voter gives a score within a given range (e.g., 0 to 10) to each candidate and in *combined approval voting* (CAV) voters assign a score of -1, 0, or +1 to indicate disapproval, apathy, or approval, respectively. In both methods, the candidate with the highest sum of scores wins.

Voting methods are efficient. Given n candidates and j voters, Borda voting has a time efficiency of $O(n * log(n) * j)$ and requires linear space $O(n)$. Range voting and CAV both have a time efficiency of $O(n * j)$. The Condorcet Method has a time efficiency of $O(n^2 * j)$. Range, CAV, and Condorcet all require constant space $O(1)$. Compared to methods like non-dominated sorting, voting can done in a similar or quicker time and constant or linear space.

VBEA is a novel approach to the multi-objective path planning problem that combines problem decomposition, voting methods to evaluate solutions, and evolutionary methods to refine and improve solutions. VBEA extends the Voting-Based Multi-Objective (VBMO) path planning algorithm [13,14], an algorithm that only used voting to select among a set of plans without any iterative evolutionary refinement. The next section describes VBEA. Subsequent sections describe the evaluation methodology and the results.

4   Voting-Based Evolutionary Algorithm

This section presents the Voting-Based Evolutionary Algorithm (VBEA) for multi-objective path planning. VBEA iteratively improves and diversifies the solutions so that it increases coverage of the Pareto frontier. The algorithm has two main parameters, T for the number of generations and k for the size of the child population for each generation. The initial population $\mathcal{P}_0$ consists of plans optimized for single objectives. To increase the diversity of the population, VBEA also adds several plans created by using random weighted sums of the objectives until the population size reaches k. Graph search is done with a modified version of A* to perform the weighted sum during search. VBEA uses

---

Algorithm 1. VBEA: Voting-Based Evolutionary Algorithm

Require: objectives B, graph G, voting method, child size k, no. of generations T

1: $\mathcal{P}_0 \leftarrow \{\}$ ▷ Initialize empty population of solutions
2: **for** each objective $\beta_j \in B$ **do**
3:      Use A* search to find plan P_j in G that minimizes β_j
4:      $\mathcal{P}_0 \leftarrow \mathcal{P}_0 \cup P_j$ ▷ Add single-objective solutions to population
5: **while** $|\mathcal{P}_0| < k$ **do**
6:      Generate random weight vector W for objectives in B
7:      Use A* search with weighted sum $\beta_W = \sum_j W[j] \cdot \beta_j$ to generate plan P
8:      $\mathcal{P}_0 \leftarrow \mathcal{P}_0 \cup P$ ▷ Add random weight solutions to population
9: Remove dominated plans and duplicates from $\mathcal{P}_0$ ▷ Eliminate poor solutions
10: Normalize costs of plans in $\mathcal{P}_0$ as $norm_0$
11: Score plans in $\mathcal{P}_0$ using voting method and $norm_0$ ▷ Evaluate fitness
12: Rank plans in $\mathcal{P}_0$ based on scores to obtain $rank_0$
13: **for** $t = 1$ to T **do**
14:      $Children \leftarrow \{\}$ ▷ Initialize child population
15:      **for** $i = 1$ to $min(k, |\mathcal{P}_{t-1}|)$ **do**   ▷ Generate children with mutation
16:          Select parent plan P_i ranked i in $rank_{t-1}$
17:          Create Combined or Conscious weight vector W_i to address P_i's deficiencies
18:          Use A* search with weighted sum $\beta_{Wi} = \sum_j W_i[j] \cdot \beta_j$ to generate plan P_{Wi}
19:          $Children \leftarrow Children \cup P_{Wi}$ ▷ Add child solution to child population
20:      **while** $|Children| < k$ **do**   ▷ Maintain diversity with random plans
21:          Generate random weight vector W for objectives in B
22:          Use A* search with β_W to generate plan P
23:          $Children \leftarrow Children \cup P$ ▷ Add random solution to child population
24:      $\mathcal{P}_t \leftarrow Children \cup$ top $min(k, |\mathcal{P}_{t-1}|)$ plans from $\mathcal{P}_{t-1}$ ▷ Form population
25:      Remove dominated plans and duplicates from $\mathcal{P}_t$ ▷ Eliminate poor solutions
26:      Normalize costs of plans in $\mathcal{P}_t$ as $norm_t$
27:      Score plans in $\mathcal{P}_t$ using voting mechanism and $norm_t$ ▷ Evaluate fitness
28:      Rank plans in $\mathcal{P}_t$ based on scores to obtain $rank_t$
29: $P_{best} \leftarrow$ plan in $\mathcal{P}_T$ that is ranked 1 in $rank_T$ ▷ Select the top-ranked plan
30: **return** P_{best}

---

voting as a fitness function, either to select the plan that maximally satisfies the most objectives or return a set of Pareto-optimal solutions. After creating the initial population, subsequent generations are created using mutation, where deficiencies in a parent plan are used to inform the weights used to generate a child plan. Pseudocode for VBEA appears in Algorithm 1.

To evaluate plan $P_i = \langle v_1, v_2, \ldots, v_m \rangle$ from the perspective of objective β_j, VBEA sums β_j's edge costs from the sequence of vertices in P_i. In this way, each objective β_j calculates a *cost* C_{ij} for each stored plan P_i. VBEA then removes from $\mathcal{P}_0$ any dominated plans and those that have duplicate costs with another plan. To avoid any biases in the voting introduced by the magnitude of an objective's values, all costs from any β_j are normalized in $[0, 1]$. Because VBEA seeks to minimize its objectives, a cost C_{ij} near 0 indicates that plan P_i closely conforms to objective β_j, while a cost near 1 indicates that P_i strongly violates

β_j. Once every objective evaluates every plan, VBEA uses a voting mechanism as a fitness function to score the plans.

VBEA has four voting mechanisms available to it. *Range voting* scores each plan P_i based on its total cost from all J objectives: $\sum_{j=1}^{J} C_{ij}$. *Borda Count* first assigns a rank r_{ij} to each plan's cost C_{ij} for each objective β_j and then assigns points to each plan as $(J+1) - r_{ij}$. It scores each plan P_i based on its total points: $\sum_{j=1}^{J} (J+1) - r_{ij}$. *Combined approval voting* assigns values v_{ij} as -1 if $C_{ij} = 1$, 1 if $C_{ij} = 0$, and 0 otherwise. It scores each plan P_i based on its total value: $\sum_{j=1}^{J} v_{ij}$. The *Condorcet Method* compares every pair of plans for each objective β_j. Each comparison gives a point to the plan with a smaller objective cost and no points if it is a tie. It scores each plan P_i based on its total points. Table 1 shows an example with all four voting methods. It demonstrates that VBEA's voting methods balance the objectives differently and score plans differently. In that example, plan P_3 dominates plan P_4 so plan P_4 would have been removed from the initial population. Once the plans have been scored with a voting method, they are ranked based on those scores.

Table 1. An example with six plans P_i from six objectives β_j that shows how the four voting methods score the plans differently.

Range	β_1	β_2	β_3	β_4	β_5	β_6	Score	Borda	β_1	β_2	β_3	β_4	β_5	β_6	Score
P_1	0	0	0.5	0.6	0	0.7	1.8	P_1	6	6	2	2	6	2	24
P_2	0.1	0	0.2	0.1	1	0.3	1.7	P_2	5	6	5	4	2	4	26
P_3	0.2	0.7	0	0	0.7	0.2	1.8	P_3	4	4	6	6	4	5	29
P_4	1	0.8	1	0	0.8	1	4.6	P_4	1	3	1	6	3	1	15
P_5	0.5	1	0.2	1	0	0.6	3.3	P_5	3	2	5	1	6	3	20
P_6	0.5	1	0.2	0.1	1	0	2.8	P_6	3	2	5	4	2	6	22

CAV	β_1	β_2	β_3	β_4	β_5	β_6	Score	Condorcet	β_1	β_2	β_3	β_4	β_5	β_6	Score
P_1	1	1	0	0	1	0	3	P_1	5	4	1	1	4	1	16
P_2	0	1	0	0	-1	0	0	P_2	4	4	2	2	0	3	15
P_3	0	0	1	1	0	0	2	P_3	3	3	5	4	3	4	22
P_4	-1	0	-1	1	0	-1	-2	P_4	0	2	0	4	2	0	8
P_5	0	-1	0	-1	1	0	-1	P_5	1	0	2	0	4	2	9
P_6	0	-1	0	0	-1	1	-1	P_6	1	0	2	2	0	5	10

VBMO, VBEA's precursor, only generated single-objective plans and used a voting mechanism to select a winner. That approach, however, assumes that plans that are optimal for a single objective will also perform somewhat well on the other objectives. If the objectives perfectly trade off, however, then VBMO's approach fails. For example, if the shortest path is the most crowded and the least crowded path is the longest. Instead, VBEA seeks a compromise that better balances the objectives, even if the solution is not optimal in any one objective.

VBEA supplements the initial single-objective plans with plans based on randomly generated weights to increase the diversity of solutions. It then uses the initial parent population of plans $\mathcal{P}_0$ to generate a set of (child) plans using weights that attempt to improve upon the parent plans coverage of the Pareto frontier. VBEA repeats this process for T generations and uses one of its voting methods in the last generation to select a winner P_{best}.

On each iteration (in its primary evolutionary loop), VBEA first selects the fittest plans for reproduction. It uses the rankings from the voting mechanism to select the top plans k in the population to be parents. If the population size is smaller than k, then it uses all the plans in the population as parents. This means that every generation after the initial one will have at most $2k$ plans. VBEA generates a set of child plans based on weights from those parent plans. If $k = 3$, then plans P_2, P_1, and P_3 are the top 3 plans by their range voting scores in Table 1. For each parent plan P_i, VBEA identifies a weight set $W_i = \{w_{i1}, w_{i2}, \ldots, w_{iJ}\}$ where J is the number of objectives. The weights are calculated as $w_{ij} = 1 - C_{ij}$, where C_{ij} are the normalized scores from each β_j. For example, plan P_1 in Table 1 has normalized scores $C_{1j=1\ldots6} = \{0, 0, 0.5, 0.6, 0, 0.7\}$ so its weight set would be $W_1 = \{1, 1, 0.5, 0.4, 1, 0.3\}$. Recall that a score C_{ij} near 0 indicates that plan P_i closely conforms to objective β_j, while a score near 1 indicates that P_i strongly violates β_j. By taking the complement of the score, the weights lower the cost of the objectives on which the plan performed worse.

VBEA implicitly applies the weights at run time in two ways to generate the child plans. The first approach, Combined generation, uses a weight set W_i to create a new objective β_{Wi} to evaluate each edge $e \in E$ with a weighted sum of the objectives. This sum is calculated as $\beta_{Wi}(e) = \Sigma_{j=1}^{J} w_{ij} * \beta_j(e)$. For example, an edge e's costs could be $\{2, 41, 3, 1, 10, 11\}$. With weights $W_1 = \{1, 1, 0.5, 0.4, 1, 0.3\}$, the new objective cost for that edge would be $\beta_{W1}(e) = 58.2$. Weights W_2 and W_3 from plans P_2 and P_3 in Table 1, would result in different costs for the same edge: $\beta_{W2}(e) = 53.8$ and $\beta_{W3}(e) = 29.7$. This example demonstrates how the weights force the objectives that the parent plan performed poorly on to have a lower cost relative to the other objectives. As the path planning algorithm seeks the minimum cost path with β_{Wi} it will seek edges that have a lower total cost because the objectives that it performed worse on will have been discounted.

The second approach, Conscious generation, also uses the weight set W_i to create a new objective β_{Wi}. The only difference with Combined generation is that it selects the objective β_j with the maximum score to focus on to create a child. It modifies W_i so that the focus has weight $w_{ij} = 1$. For example, if the focus is $j = 6$ then the weight set $W_1 = \{1, 1, 0.5, 0.4, 1, 0.3\}$ would be modified to $W_1 = \{1, 1, 0.5, 0.4, 1, 1\}$. This modified weight set would result in $\beta_{W1}(e) = 65.9$, compared to 58.2 from Combined. The A* algorithm would then be less likely to select edges with a higher cost due to the focused objective.

In summary, VBEA uses A* search on each new weighted-sum objective (from Combined or Conscious) to create a new child plan. If there are fewer than k child plans created, additional plans are generated using random weights. The created plans are combined with the parent plans to form a new population $\mathcal{P}_t$. Any dominated solutions and duplicates are removed from $\mathcal{P}_t$, the scores for the remaining plans are normalized, and a voting mechanism evaluates, scores, and ranks the plans for the next generation. VBEA repeats this process for T generations and uses the voting mechanism at the end to pick a winner P_{best}.

5   Experimental Design

To evaluate VBEA's quality and efficiency, we compare its performance to A*pex, a recent state-of-the-art algorithm. For A*pex, we tested different approximation factors (ϵ) and merge methods (random R and greedy G). For VBEA, we tested all combinations of the voting method (Range, Borda, CAV, Condorcet) and the child generation mechanism (Combined or Conscious). The number of generations T was set to 6. The metrics for evaluation are run time, sparsity, hypervolume, front size, and failure rate (percentage of instances solved within a time limit). All the algorithms were implemented in C++[1] and evaluated on 156 Dragon Age: Origins (DAO) benchmark grid environments [27] and the Colorado (COL) and Bay Area (BAY) road networks from the 9th DIMACS Implementation Challenge: Shortest Path[2]. We use Euclidean distance for A*'s heuristic in the DAO environments and Haversine distance for the DIMACS road networks. VBEA's child size k was set depending on the environment type ($k = 20$ for road networks and $k = 50$ for the DAO environments). The failure time limit is 5 min for the road networks and 3 min for the DAO environments. Performance is averaged over 25 randomly selected start and target vertices for each road network environment and 5 randomly selected start and target vertices for each DAO environment. All significant differences ($p < 0.05$) were first evaluated with an ANOVA followed by Tukey post-hoc tests.

The objectives for the DAO environments are: β_1 is Euclidean distance, β_2 is a uniform cost of 1, β_3 is chosen uniformly between 1 and 20, β_4 is a safety metric, and β_5 is a danger metric. For each edge $e = (u, v)$, the safety metric is defined as $\beta_4(e) = (10 - |u| + 10 - |v|)/2$. For the danger metric, 10% of the vertices were randomly selected to be "dangerous" by making the incoming edges have a cost of 10, and the remaining edges have a uniform cost of 1.5. The objectives for the DIMACS road networks are: β_1 is distance, β_2 is time, β_3 is an artificially generated objective calculated as $\beta_3(e) = g(e) * (\beta_1(e) + \beta_2(e))$, where $g(e) \in [0.3, 0.4]$ and is uniformly distributed, and β_4 is a delay metric [31].

6   Results

Table 2 summarizes the results[3]. As very few differences were observed between the A*pex's merge methods, the results for A*pex were averaged across them.

---

[1] Code available at https://github.com/RajKorpan/VBMO.
[2] http://www.diag.uniroma1.it/~challenge9/download.shtml.
[3] See supplementary material for complete details.

Similarly, for VBEA, results were combined across the six generations tested, to capture the general trends and overall performance of the algorithms. The difference between VBEA's generations, voting methods, and child generation mechanisms is examined separately.

Table 2. Summary of the results across the two environments.

	Road Networks				DAO Environments				
	Time	Failure	Hypervolume	Sparsity	Front Size	Time	Failure	Hypervolume	Sparsity	Front Size
VBEA-Combined-Borda	1.02	0.0%	2.52E+22	1.46E+13	14.0	0.38	1.7%	6.26E+15	4.67E+03	54.7
VBEA-Combined-Cav	1.22	0.0%	1.96E+22	1.55E+13	13.2	0.42	2.1%	5.75E+15	4.88E+03	66.4
VBEA-Combined-Condorcet	1.22	0.0%	3.71E+22	1.32E+13	15.2	0.42	2.0%	5.82E+15	1.27E+04	48.8
VBEA-Combined-Range	1.22	0.0%	1.06E+23	1.28E+13	15.6	0.42	2.0%	6.12E+15	4.46E+03	69.2
VBEA-Conscious-Borda	1.18	0.0%	2.31E+22	1.76E+13	13.1	0.42	2.1%	6.04E+15	4.41E+03	54.3
VBEA-Conscious-Cav	1.21	0.0%	1.74E+22	1.91E+13	12.3	0.42	2.0%	5.81E+15	4.64E+03	65.9
VBEA-Conscious-Condorcet	1.25	0.0%	3.44E+22	1.58E+13	14.5	0.40	1.7%	5.67E+15	1.32E+04	47.8
VBEA-Conscious-Range	3.10	4.7%	3.22E+22	1.46E+13	14.8	0.44	2.2%	5.98E+15	4.51E+03	68.7
A*pex-1	0.03	0.0%	3.37E+22	1.36E+12	1.1	0.02	0.1%	1.45E+16	9.36E+03	1.2
A*pex-0.5	0.09	0.0%	4.54E+22	3.67E+12	1.8	0.21	3.2%	1.04E+16	4.59E+03	5.9
A*pex-0.1	1.25	16.0%	4.63E+22	1.09E+11	27.9	1.20	31.3%	4.27E+15	1.06E+02	103.0
A*pex-0.01	2.77	45.0%	3.10E+22	1.33E+10	175.1					
A*pex-0.001	3.68	63.0%	2.91E+22	1.13E+09	579.8					
A*pex-0.0001	3.95	76.0%	3.08E+22	2.73E+08	929.8					

6.1 Road Networks

In the road network environments, VBEA demonstrated significantly faster in run time for smaller approximation factors of A*pex ($\epsilon = 0.0001$ and 0.001), with 62.5% and 49% of VBEA configurations significantly faster, respectively. This advantage diminished as ϵ increased, with VBEA showing no significant difference in 92.71% of cases for $\epsilon = 0.01$, and only minor performance degradation at $\epsilon \geq 0.1$ (10.4% worse for $\epsilon = 0.5$ and 1). Notably, VBEA never performed worse than A*pex for $\epsilon \leq 0.01$. In terms of failure rate, VBEA consistently outperformed A*pex at smaller ϵ values, achieving a 100% lower failure rate for $\epsilon \leq 0.01$. For $\epsilon = 0.1$, VBEA still outperformed A*pex in 93.75% of cases. At higher ϵ values ($\epsilon \geq 0.5$), there was no significant difference between the two methods. For sparsity and hypervolume, there were no significant differences between VBEA and A*pex across any configurations. However, A*pex consistently outperformed VBEA on front size for $\epsilon \leq 0.01$, with 100% of VBEA configurations yielding smaller fronts. At higher ϵ values, front sizes were comparable.

6.2 DAO Grid Environments

In the DAO environments, VBEA exhibited a significant run time advantage over A*pex for $\epsilon = 0.1$, outperforming A*pex across all configurations (see Fig. 2 for details). However, as ϵ increased, A*pex demonstrated faster run times, with 57.3% and 83.3% of VBEA configurations performing worse for $\epsilon = 0.5$ and 1, respectively. Failure rates followed a similar trend. VBEA consistently outperformed A*pex for $\epsilon = 0.1$ with a 100% lower failure rate. For $\epsilon = 0.5$, VBEA was better in 36.5% of cases but worse in 16.7%. At $\epsilon = 1$, VBEA had a higher failure rate in 33.3% of cases. For sparsity and hypervolume, no significant differences were observed across all configurations. In contrast, VBEA produced larger front sizes for $\epsilon \geq 0.5$, with all configurations outperforming A*pex. At $\epsilon = 0.1$, A*pex outperformed VBEA in all configurations.

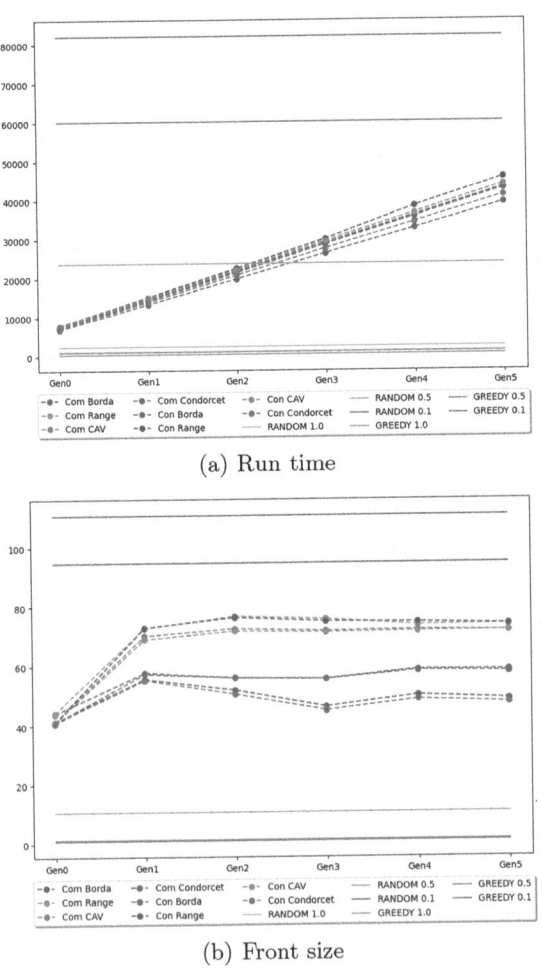

(a) Run time

(b) Front size

Fig. 2. Run time and front size for VBEA and A*pex on the DAO dataset.

6.3 Analysis of Generations, Voting Methods and Child Methods

The performance of VBEA is strongly influenced by the choice of child mechanism, voting method, and number of generations. The Conscious child generation method consistently produced smaller front sizes compared to the Combined method in both the road networks and DAO grid environments. In the road networks, Conscious was also slower, exhibited worse sparsity, achieved lower hypervolume, and had a higher failure rate compared to Combined. These results suggest that while Conscious may perform better on hypervolume, it does so at the cost of efficiency and robustness in road network environments.

The voting method also had an impact on VBEA's performance. While range voting method was slower than other methods and had worse hypervolume and failure rates in the road network environments, it produced larger fronts. The Condorcet voting method had worse sparsity in the DAO environments. The generation had a large effect in the DAO environments–run time, failure rate, and front size consistently increased across generations while sparsity improved.

6.4 Summary

VBEA consistently showed lower failure rates and achieved faster run times when compared to A*pex with smaller ϵ values in both the road networks and DAO environments. Its performance diminished when compared to A*pex with higher ϵ values, particularly in the DAO grids, where A*pex excelled in speed. Despite both algorithms not having any statistically significant difference in terms of sparsity and hypervolume, A*pex takes more time to produce larger front sizes at low ϵ values. This trade-off suggests VBEA produces a just as diverse solution set as A*pex with a smaller front size in faster time. Analysis of VBEA's hyperparameters suggests that the Combined child generation method along with the Borda and CAV voting methods achieve better performance while increase in generations can improve sparsity.

7 Discussion

This paper presents VBEA, an efficient and scalable approach for multi-objective path planning that combines voting mechanisms with evolutionary algorithms to generate solutions on the Pareto frontier. By leveraging social choice theory, VBEA uses voting methods, such as Range, Borda, CAV, and Condorcet, to rank and select candidate solutions. VBEA's flexibility allows it to either return a final non-dominated plan or provide a Pareto-approximation, leaving the decision to an external decision maker. Our empirical results demonstrate that VBEA is both efficient and effective across a range of complex environments, outperforming another state-of-the-art algorithm in terms of solution quality and run time. While this approach offers several advantages, there are also limitations and opportunities for future improvement.

One of the key innovations in VBEA is the use of a voting mechanism as a fitness function for the evolutionary process, which is novel and computationally efficient. VBEA's range voting has been proven to always select a non-dominated plan [13]. Similar proofs can trivially show that Borda, CAV, and the Condorcet method always select a non-dominated plan as well. A potential drawback of this approach, however, is the introduction of bias through these mechanisms during reproduction, as described in the results. Future work will investigate the impact of these voting mechanisms on solution quality in other multi-objective environments. Additionally, there is an opportunity to examine the performance of multiple voting mechanisms within a single framework and to explore the potential of other voting strategies. Future work will also consider the adaptability of parent, child, or combined population sizes, as well as introducing a stopping metric, which could also help minimize the number of hyperparameters, making the algorithm more efficient.

An important challenge is that many voting and non-dominated sorting systems do not provide a strict total ordering. This can lead to situations where multiple candidates are considered equally optimal. To address this, future research could investigate voting methods that enforce a strict total ordering or develop tie-breaking mechanisms that maintain efficiency while ensuring a clear order of preferences. Another challenge of voting is that alone it does not guarantee that solutions will closely approximate the Pareto frontier. Non-dominated filtering can resolve this issue without increasing the algorithm's time complexity, though it would add to the computational overhead of the algorithm.

Another area for improvement is VBEA's child population generation method, which could benefit from strategies to prevent populations from being trapped in local extremes. Furthermore, the current methods of child population generation are proportional, where child populations are based on the size of the parent population. This can be inefficient in scenarios with small parent populations. Future research could investigate random weight sets or other strategies to ensure more efficient child population generation. Although the voting process and non-dominated filtering are asymptotically similar in complexity, like other evolutionary algorithms, voting can be a computational bottleneck for VBEA. Instead, future work could integrate parallel computing, which is rarely used in multi-objective path planning [24]. VBEA is well suited for parallelization, especially in its voting and child generation methods.

8   Conclusion

In conclusion, VBEA advances multi-objective path planning by offering a flexible, scalable, and efficient solution for complex, real-world problems. Its hybrid approach uses voting mechanisms with evolutionary methods to evaluate and improve solutions. Empirical results show that it efficiently produces a diverse set of Pareto optimal solutions.

References

1. Back, T.: Evolutionary algorithms in theory and practice: evolution strategies, evolutionary programming, genetic algorithms. Oxford University Press, USA (1996)
2. Bao, C., Xu, L., Goodman, E.D., Cao, L.: A novel non-dominated sorting algorithm for evolutionary multi-objective optimization. J. Comput. Sci.**23**, 31–43 (2017). https://doi.org/10.1016/j.jocs.2017.09.015, https://www.sciencedirect.com/science/article/pii/S1877750317310530
3. Blum, C., Roli, A.: Metaheuristics in combinatorial optimization: overview and conceptual comparison. ACM Comput. Surv. **35**(3), 268–308 (2003). https://doi.org/10.1145/937503.937505
4. Cong, R., Qi, J., Wu, C., Wang, M., Guo, J.: Multi-UAVs cooperative detection based on improved NSGA-II algorithm. In: 2020 39th Chinese Control Conference (CCC), pp. 1524–1529 (2020). https://doi.org/10.23919/CCC50068.2020.9188354
5. Deb, K., Pratap, A., Agarwal, S., Meyarivan, T.: A fast and elitist multiobjective genetic algorithm: NSGA-II. IEEE Trans. Evol. Comput. **6**(2), 182–197 (2002)
6. Flach, P.: Machine learning: the art and science of algorithms that make sense of data. Cambridge University Press (2012)
7. Geißer, F., Haslum, P., Thiébaux, S., Trevizan, F.: Admissible heuristics for multi-objective planning. In: Proceedings of the International Conference on Automated Planning and Scheduling, vol. 32, pp. 100–109 (2022)
8. Goldin, B., Salzman, O.: Approximate bi-criteria search by efficient representation of subsets of the pareto-optimal frontier. In: Proceedings of the International Conference on Automated Planning and Scheduling **31**(1), 149–158 (2021). https://doi.org/10.1609/icaps.v31i1.15957, https://ojs.aaai.org/index.php/ICAPS/article/view/15957
9. Goldin, B., Salzman, O.: Approximate bi-criteria search by efficient representation of subsets of the pareto-optimal frontier. In: Proceedings of the International Conference on Automated Planning and Scheduling, vol. 31, pp. 149–158 (2021)
10. Hart, P.E., Nilsson, N.J., Raphael, B.: A formal basis for the heuristic determination of minimum cost paths. IEEE Trans. Syst. Sci. Cybern. **4**(2), 100–107 (1968)
11. Hernández Ulloa, C., Yeoh, W., Baier, J.A., Zhang, H., Suazo, L., Koenig, S.: A simple and fast bi-objective search algorithm. In: Proceedings of the International Conference on Automated Planning and Scheduling , vol. 30, no. 1, pp. 143–151 (2020). https://doi.org/10.1609/icaps.v30i1.6655, https://ojs.aaai.org/index.php/ICAPS/article/view/6655
12. Jaimes, A.L., Coello, C.A.C.: Many-objective problems: challenges and methods. In: Springer Handbook of Computational Intelligence, pp. 1033–1046. Springer (2015)
13. Korpan, R.: VBMO: Voting-based multi-objective path planning. In: IJCAI 2023 First International Workshop on Search and Planning with Complex Objectives (2023)
14. Korpan, R., Epstein, S.: Contrastive natural language explanations for multi-objective path planning. In: ICAPS 2021 Workshop on Explainable AI Planning (2021)
15. LaValle, S.M.: Planning algorithms. Cambridge University Press (2006)
16. Mandow, L., De La Cruz, J.L.P.: Multiobjective A* search with consistent heuristics. J. ACM (JACM) **57**(5), 1–25 (2008)
17. Marler, R.T., Arora, J.S.: The weighted sum method for multi-objective optimization: new insights. Struct. Multidiscip. Optim. **41**(6), 853–862 (2010)

18. Pardalos, P.M., Migdalas, A., Pitsoulis, L.: Pareto optimality, game theory and equilibria, vol. 17. Springer Science and Business Media (2008)
19. Pearl, J.: Heuristics: Intelligent Search Strategies for Computer Problem Solving. Addison-Wesley Pub. Co., Inc, Reading, MA (1984)
20. Pulido, F.J., Mandow, L., de-la Cruz, J.L.P.: Dimensionality reduction in multi-objective shortest path search. Comput. Oper. Res. **64**, 60–70 (2015). https://api.semanticscholar.org/CorpusID:22259230
21. Qiao, S., Dai, X., Liu, Z., Huang, J., Zhu, G.: Improving the optimization performance of NSGA-II algorithm by experiment design methods. In: 2012 IEEE International Conference on Computational Intelligence for Measurement Systems and Applications (CIMSA) Proceedings, pp. 82–85 (2012). https://doi.org/10.1109/CIMSA.2012.6269589
22. Riquelme, N., Von Lücken, C., Baran, B.: Performance metrics in multi-objective optimization. In: 2015 Latin American Computing Conference (CLEI), pp. 1–11. IEEE (2015)
23. Rossi, F., Venable, K.B., Walsh, T.: A short introduction to preferences: between artificial intelligence and social choice. Synth. Lect. Artif. Intell. Mach. Learn. **5**(4), 1–102 (2011)
24. Salzman, O., Felner, A., Hernández, C., Zhang, H., Chan, S.H., Koenig, S.: Heuristic-search approaches for the multi-objective shortest-path problem: progress and research opportunities. In: Elkind, E. (ed.) Proceedings of the Thirty-Second International Joint Conference on Artificial Intelligence, IJCAI-23, pp. 6759–6768. International Joint Conferences on Artificial Intelligence Organization (2023). https://doi.org/10.24963/ijcai.2023/757, survey Track
25. Sedeno-Noda, A., Raith, A.: A Dijkstra-like method computing all extreme supported non-dominated solutions of the biobjective shortest path problem. Comput. Oper. Res. **57**, 83–94 (2015)
26. Stewart, B.S., White, C.C., III.: Multiobjective A*. J. ACM (JACM) **38**(4), 775–814 (1991)
27. Sturtevant, N.: Benchmarks for grid-based pathfinding. Trans. Comput. Intell. AI Games **4**(2), 144 –148 (2012). http://web.cs.du.edu/~sturtevant/papers/benchmarks.pdf
28. Talbi, E.G., Basseur, M., Nebro, A.J., Alba, E.: Multi-objective optimization using metaheuristics: non-standard algorithms. Int. Trans. Oper. Res. **19**(1–2), 283–305 (2012)
29. Ulloa, C.H., Yeoh, W., Baier, J.A., Zhang, H., Suazo, L., Koenig, S.: A simple and fast bi-objective search algorithm. In: Proceedings of the International Conference on Automated Planning and Scheduling, vol. 30, pp. 143–151 (2020)
30. Van Erp, M., Vuurpijl, L., Schomaker, L.: An overview and comparison of voting methods for pattern recognition. In: Proceedings of the Eighth International Workshop on Frontiers in Handwriting Recognition, pp. 195–200. IEEE (2002)
31. Weise, J., Mostaghim, S.: A scalable many-objective pathfinding benchmark suite. IEEE Trans. Evol. Comput. **26**(1), 188–194 (2022). https://doi.org/10.1109/tevc.2021.3089050
32. Zadeh, L.: Optimality and non-scalar-valued performance criteria. IEEE Trans. Autom. Control **8**(1), 59–60 (1963)
33. Zhang, H., Salzman, O., Kumar, T.S., Felner, A., Ulloa, C.H., Koenig, S.: A* pex: efficient approximate multi-objective search on graphs. In: Proceedings of the International Conference on Automated Planning and Scheduling, vol. 32, pp. 394–403 (2022)

34. Zhang, Q., Li, H.: MOEA/D: a multiobjective evolutionary algorithm based on decomposition. IEEE Trans. Evol. Comput. **11**(6), 712–731 (2007). https://doi.org/10.1109/TEVC.2007.892759

35. Zhao, F., Huan, L., Zhang, Y., Ma, W., Zhang, C.: A novel multi-objective optimization algorithm based on differential evolution and NSGA-II. In: 2018 IEEE 22nd International Conference on Computer Supported Cooperative Work in Design (CSCWD), pp. 570–575 (2018). https://doi.org/10.1109/CSCWD.2018.8465326

36. Zitzler, E., Thiele, L.: Multiobjective optimization using evolutionary algorithms–a comparative case study. In: International Conference on Parallel Problem Solving from Nature, pp. 292–301. Springer (1998)

Enhancing NSGA-II with a Knee Point for Constrained Multi-objective Optimization

Lie Meng Pang, Hisao Ishibuchi[✉], and Yang Nan

Guangdong Provincial Key Laboratory of Brain-inspired Intelligent Computation, Department of Computer Science and Engineering, Southern University of Science and Technology, Shenzhen 518055, China
{panglm,hisao}@sustech.edu.cn, 12132350@mail.sustech.edu.cn

Abstract. To handle constrained multi-objective optimization problems (CMOPs), many constrained multi-objective evolutionary algorithms (CMOEAs) have been proposed. However, a recent study has shown that many of these CMOEAs do not perform well on real-world CMOPs. In contrast, NSGA-II, proposed over 20 years ago with a simple constrained dominance principle, has demonstrated better performance than recent CMOEAs on many real-world CMOPs. Motivated by NSGA-II's promising results, this paper aims to further enhance its performance. We explore the idea of enhancing NSGA-II with a knee point for solving CMOPs. Specifically, a knee point is identified using the minimum distance from the estimated ideal point, and always included in the next population of NSGA-II. Experimental results show that this simple idea improves the performance of NSGA-II on real-world CMOPs.

Keywords: Constrained multi-objective optimization · Evolutionary multi-objective optimization · Knee point · NSGA-II

1 Introduction

Real-world applications often involve problems with multiple objectives and constraints that must be addressed simultaneously. Such problems are known as constrained multi-objective optimization problems (CMOPs). In recent years, an increasing number of evolutionary algorithms have been developed specifically for solving CMOPs [10], giving rise to a class of algorithms known as constrained multi-objective evolutionary algorithms (CMOEAs). To handle CMOPs, various constraint-handling techniques (CHTs), such as the constrained dominance principle, coevolutionary strategies, and two-stage strategies, have been utilized in CMOEAs. Many of the recently-proposed CMOEAs have demonstrated strong performance on artificial benchmark test problems.

However, a recent study has shown that many of these CMOEAs do not perform well on real-world CMOPs [13]. In contrast, NSGA-II [4], proposed

H. Singh et al. (Eds.): EMO 2025, LNCS 15512, pp. 180–192, 2025.
https://doi.org/10.1007/978-981-96-3506-1_13

over 20 years ago with a simple constrained dominance principle, has demonstrated better performance on many real-world CMOPs than recently-proposed CMOEAs. Motivated by the reported promising results of NSGA-II on real-world CMOPs, this paper aims to further enhance its performance. A simple and straightforward approach is to keep a knee point in the evolutionary process of NSGA-II. It is expected that a knee point can help improve the convergence quality of the final solution set obtained by NSGA-II. In fact, the use of knee points in the evolutionary process is not a new idea. For example, knee points have been employed to improve the performance of evolutionary multi-objective optimization (EMO) algorithms in many-objective optimization [16], multi-modal multi-objective optimization [11], and dynamic multi-objective optimization [7]. However, to the best of our knowledge, the usefulness of incorporating a knee point to enhance the performance of NSGA-II on CMOPs has not been examined.

In this paper, we explore the idea of incorporating a knee point into NSGA-II to improve its performance on CMOPs. Specifically, a knee point is identified using the minimum distance from the estimated ideal point, and always included in the next population of NSGA-II. Our experimental results show that incorporating a knee point into NSGA-II generally has a positive effect on its performance in real-world CMOPs.

This paper is organized as follows: Sect. 2 provides the background knowledge. Section 3 details our proposed idea and its implementation in NSGA-II. Section 4 reports experimental results. Finally, Sect. 5 concludes the paper.

2   Background

2.1   Constrained Multi-objective Optimization

In this paper, a CMOP is defined as follows:

$$\text{Minimize } (f_1(\mathbf{x}), f_2(\mathbf{x}), ..., f_m(\mathbf{x})),$$

$$\text{s.t. } \begin{cases} \mathbf{x} \in \mathbf{X} \subseteq \mathbb{R}^d, \\ g_j(\mathbf{x}) \leq 0, & j = 1, ..., l, \\ h_j(\mathbf{x}) = 0, & j = l+1, ..., l+k. \end{cases} \tag{1}$$

where $f_i(\mathbf{x})$ is the i-th objective to be minimized ($i = 1, 2, ..., m$), m is the number of objectives, $\mathbf{x} = (x_1, x_2, ..., x_d)$ is a vector with d decision variables, and $\mathbf{X}$ is the search space of $\mathbf{x}$. $g_j(\mathbf{x})$ and $h_j(\mathbf{x})$ are the jth inequality and equality constraints, respectively, where l and k are the number of inequality constraints and equality constraints, respectively.

The feasibility of a solution $\mathbf{x}$ can be identified based on the constraint violation (CV) value. For each constraint j, its CV value (denoted as $\psi_j(\mathbf{x})$) can be calculated as follows:

$$\psi_j(\mathbf{x}) = \begin{cases} \max(0, \ g_j(\mathbf{x})), & j = 1, ..., l, \\ \max(0, \ |h_j(\mathbf{x})| - \delta), & j = l+1, ..., l+k, \end{cases} \tag{2}$$

where δ is a small threshold value (which is specified as 10^{-4} in this study) used for relaxing the equality constraints.

The overall CV value (denoted as ϕ) for each solution $\mathbf{x}$ is calculated as

$$\phi(\mathbf{x}) = \sum_{j=1}^{l+k} \psi_j(\mathbf{x}). \tag{3}$$

A solution $\mathbf{x}$ is handled as a feasible solution if it satisfies all the constraints, i.e., $\phi(\mathbf{x}) = 0$. Otherwise, it is handled as an infeasible solution.

When two feasible solutions $\mathbf{x}^a$ and $\mathbf{x}^b$ are given, $\mathbf{x}^a$ is said to be constrained Pareto dominating $\mathbf{x}^b$ if and only if $f_i(\mathbf{x}^a) \leq f_i(\mathbf{x}^b)$, $\forall i \in \{1, 2, ..., m\}$, and $f_j(\mathbf{x}^a) < f_j(\mathbf{x}^b)$, $\exists j \in \{1, 2, ..., m\}$. If there are no other feasible solutions in the search space dominating $\mathbf{x}^a$, then $\mathbf{x}^a$ is known as a constrained Pareto optimal solution. The set of all constrained Pareto optimal solutions is known as the constrained Pareto set, and it forms the constrained Pareto front (CPF) in the objective space.

2.2   Knee Point

In evolutionary multi-objective optimization, knee points refer to a subset of solutions on the Pareto front where a small improvement in one objective value leads to a large deterioration in some other objective values [1]. In Fig. 1, Solution A (represented by the red point) is a knee point for the Pareto front represented by the blue line. It can be seen that a slight improvement in one objective value of Solution A results in a severe deterioration of the other objective value. When no user preferences are available, knee points are often considered interesting or preferred solutions by decision makers, as they usually represent the best trade-off among the objectives [3]. Knee points are not always obtained by standard diversification mechanisms as shown in Fig. 1.

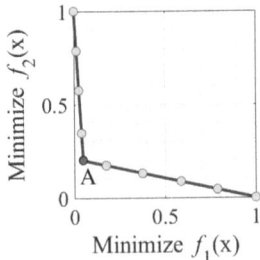

Fig. 1. Illustration of a knee point A (red circle) and uniformly distributed nine solutions (yellow circles) on the Pareto front. (Color figure online)

2.3 NSGA-II

NSGA-II has been one of the most widely-used EMO algorithms. It uses Pareto dominance as the primary criterion to guide the population towards the Pareto front, while crowding distance is used as a secondary criterion for diversity maintenance (i.e., to find well-distributed solutions as shown in Fig. 1 by yellow circles). For solving CMOPs, NSGA-II uses the constrained dominance principle as its constraint handling method. According to the constrained dominance principle, a solution $\mathbf{x}^a$ is said to constrained-dominate a solution $\mathbf{x}^b$ if any of the following conditions holds [4]:

1. $\mathbf{x}^a$ is feasible and $\mathbf{x}^b$ is infeasible.
2. Both $\mathbf{x}^a$ and $\mathbf{x}^b$ are infeasible, and $\mathbf{x}^a$ has a smaller overall CV than $\mathbf{x}^b$.
3. Both $\mathbf{x}^a$ and $\mathbf{x}^b$ are feasible, and $\mathbf{x}^a$ dominates $\mathbf{x}^b$.

3 Proposed Idea

As shown in a recent study [13], NSGA-II performs well on many real-world CMOPs and even outperforms several recently-proposed CMOEAs. To further enhance NSGA-II's performance on real-world CMOPs, we propose a simple modification: identify a single knee solution from the merged population and ensure its survival to the next population. This modification is applied only when the number of non-dominated solutions in the merged population exceeds the population size. With this simple modification, it is expected that the knee point will be obtained (which is not always obtained by NSGA-II as shown in Fig. 1).

An important issue is how to identify a knee point from the merged population. A simple approach is to use the distance from each solution to the ideal point in the normalized objective space [2]. If a solution has the minimum distance to the ideal point, it is selected as a knee point. In our implementations, we examine the following two definitions:

– Solution with the minimum Euclidean distance to the estimated ideal point,
– Solution with the minimum Manhattan distance to the estimated ideal point.

The ideal point $\mathbf{Z}^*$ is estimated based on the historically minimum value of each objective among feasible solutions. If no feasible solutions are found during the evolutionary process, $\mathbf{Z}^*$ is estimated based on the historically minimum value of each objective among infeasible solutions. To normalize the objective space, a nadir point $\mathbf{Z}^{nad}$ is also required. It is estimated using the maximum value of each objective among feasible solutions of the merged population. If no feasible solutions are available, $\mathbf{Z}^{nad}$ is estimated based on the maximum value of each objective among infeasible solutions in the merged population. It should be noted that the distance of each solution to the estimated ideal point is calculated in the normalized objective space. The solution with the minimum distance to the estimated ideal point is selected and survived to the next population.

4 Experiments

4.1 Experimental Settings

In order to examine the usefulness of incorporating a knee point in NSGA-II, we first compare the proposed modified NSGA-II with the original NSGA-II on a real-world problem suite, i.e., RCM [8]. We denote the modified NSGA-II with a knee point based on the Euclidean distance as KNSGA-II-E, and the modified NSGA-II with a knee point based on the Manhattan distance as KNSGA-II-M. After examining the usefulness of our idea, we compare the proposed modified NSGA-II with four CMOEAs that were proposed between 2014 and 2024.

The population size is set to 100, 105, and 126 for two-, three-, and five-objective problems, respectively, with the termination condition of 1,000 generations. These population size settings are based on commonly-used settings for decomposition-based EMO algorithms (since C-MOEA/D is used in Sect. 4.3 and its population size cannot be set arbitrarily), ensuring that all algorithms use the same population size for a fair performance comparison. Each algorithm is run independently 101 times on each problem. Since the true CPF of each real-world problem is unknown, we collect all feasible solutions from the final populations of the 101 runs of each algorithm on each problem. Non-dominated solutions are selected from all feasible solutions to approximate the CPF for each RCM problem. We use the hypervolume (HV) indicator to evaluate the performance of each algorithm. The reference point for calculating the HV value is specified as $1 + 1/H$ [5] in the normalized objective space, where H is specified as 99, 13 and 4 for two-, three-, and five-objective problems, respectively. All experiments are performed on the PlatEMO platform [14].

The RCM problem suite consists of 50 CMOPs (i.e., RCM1 to RCM50). Among them, it should be noted that RCM36 to RCM49 contain many equality constraints, which are very difficult for all the compared algorithms. Actually, no algorithm is able to find feasible solutions for these 14 problems in our experiments. Therefore, in this paper, we present results only for RCM1 to RCM35 and RCM50 (i.e., a total of 36 real-world problems).

4.2 Comparison with the Original NSGA-II

Table 1 presents the average HV values over 101 runs by NSGA-II, KNSGA-II-E, and KNSGA-II-M. The standard deviation values are shown in parentheses. The Wilcoxon rank-sum test at the 5% significance level is used for statistical comparison. The symbols '+', '-', and '=' indicate that the modified NSGA-II with a knee point is statistically better than, worse than, or equivalent to the original NSGA-II, respectively. The best average HV value for each problem is highlighted in gray. Overall, it can be seen that the incorporation of a single knee point improves the performance of NSGA-II on many real-world CMOPs. The performance of KNSGA-II-E and KNSGA-II-M are statistically better than the original NSGA-II on 3 and 4 problems, respectively. While KNSGA-II-E and KNSGA-II-M are statistically similar to the original NSGA-II on 33 and

Table 1. Average HV values over 101 runs by NSGA-II, KNSGA-II-E and KNSGA-II-M on each real-world CMOP.

Problem	m	d	NSGA-II	KNSGA-II-E	KNSGA-II-M
RCM1	2	4	0.5429 (0.0007)	0.5429 (0.0006) ($\approx$)	0.5430 (0.0006) ($\approx$)
RCM2	2	5	0.5982 (0.3830)	0.6004 (0.3728) ($\approx$)	0.6297 (0.3657) ($\approx$)
RCM3	2	3	0.9607 (0.0002)	0.9607 (0.0002) ($\approx$)	0.9607 (0.0002) ($\approx$)
RCM4	2	4	0.9266 (0.0006)	0.9266 (0.0005) ($\approx$)	0.9266 (0.0005) ($\approx$)
RCM5	2	4	0.8164 (0.0004)	0.8164 (0.0004) ($\approx$)	0.8163 (0.0005) ($\approx$)
RCM6	2	7	0.9896 (0.0001)	0.9896 (0.0001) ($\approx$)	0.9896 (0.0001) ($+$)
RCM7	2	4	0.5810 (0.0004)	0.5811 (0.0003) ($\approx$)	0.5810 (0.0004) ($\approx$)
RCM8	3	7	0.9633 (0.0078)	0.9666 (0.0047) ($+$)	0.9695 (0.0028) ($+$)
RCM9	2	4	0.6912 (0.0004)	0.6913 (0.0003) ($\approx$)	0.6913 (0.0004) ($\approx$)
RCM10	2	2	1.0081 (0.0003)	1.0081 (0.0001) ($\approx$)	1.0081 (0.0002) ($\approx$)
RCM11	5	3	1.7789 (0.0154)	1.7840 (0.0143) ($+$)	1.7861 (0.0145) ($+$)
RCM12	2	4	0.9232 (0.0003)	0.9232 (0.0003) ($\approx$)	0.9232 (0.0003) ($\approx$)
RCM13	3	7	1.1729 (0.0049)	1.1775 (0.0014) ($+$)	1.1778 (0.0012) ($+$)
RCM14	2	5	0.8683 (0.0009)	0.8684 (0.0009) ($\approx$)	0.8683 (0.0011) ($\approx$)
RCM15	2	3	0.7909 (0.0002)	0.7909 (0.0002) ($\approx$)	0.7909 (0.0002) ($\approx$)
RCM16	2	2	0.8911 (0.0002)	0.8910 (0.0002) ($\approx$)	0.8910 (0.0002) ($\approx$)
RCM17	3	6	0.0639 (0.0002)	0.0639 (0.0002) ($\approx$)	0.0639 (0.0002) ($\approx$)
RCM18	2	3	0.6366 (0.0004)	0.6366 (0.0003) ($\approx$)	0.6366 (0.0003) ($\approx$)
RCM19	3	10	0.8740 (0.0255)	0.8730 (0.0246) ($\approx$)	0.8735 (0.0255) ($\approx$)
RCM20	2	4	0.6031 (0.0632)	0.6066 (0.0589) ($\approx$)	0.6043 (0.0590) ($\approx$)
RCM21	2	6	0.5944 (0.0005)	0.5944 (0.0005) ($\approx$)	0.5944 (0.0005) ($\approx$)
RCM22	2	9	0.0000 (0.0000)	0.0000 (0.0000) ($\approx$)	0.0000 (0.0000) ($\approx$)
RCM23	2	6	0.1093 (0.0855)	0.1124 (0.0851) ($\approx$)	0.1093 (0.0855) ($\approx$)
RCM24	3	9	0.0000 (0.0000)	0.0000 (0.0000) ($\approx$)	0.0000 (0.0000) ($\approx$)
RCM25	2	2	0.4047 (0.0003)	0.4048 (0.0003) ($\approx$)	0.4048 (0.0003) ($\approx$)
RCM26	2	3	0.3184 (0.0733)	0.3155 (0.0791) ($\approx$)	0.3218 (0.0781) ($\approx$)
RCM27	2	3	0.6807 (0.0003)	0.6807 (0.0002) ($\approx$)	0.6807 (0.0003) ($\approx$)
RCM28	2	7	0.0000 (0.0000)	0.0000 (0.0000) ($\approx$)	0.0000 (0.0000) ($\approx$)
RCM29	2	7	0.5823 (0.0533)	0.5823 (0.0533) ($\approx$)	0.5823 (0.0533) ($\approx$)
RCM30	2	25	0.5716 (0.4384)	0.5651 (0.4423) ($\approx$)	0.5732 (0.4404) ($\approx$)
RCM31	2	25	0.1617 (0.2477)	0.1686 (0.2516) ($\approx$)	0.1695 (0.2527) ($\approx$)
RCM32	2	25	0.3249 (0.2962)	0.3130 (0.3018) ($\approx$)	0.3209 (0.2993) ($\approx$)
RCM33	2	30	0.1771 (0.2691)	0.1683 (0.2630) ($\approx$)	0.1610 (0.2557) ($\approx$)
RCM34	2	30	0.1779 (0.2812)	0.1751 (0.2821) ($\approx$)	0.1891 (0.2900) ($\approx$)
RCM35	2	30	0.0634 (0.1184)	0.0671 (0.1260) ($\approx$)	0.0662 (0.1220) ($\approx$)
RCM50	2	6	0.2336 (0.0909)	0.2336 (0.0909) ($\approx$)	0.2336 (0.0909) ($\approx$)
($+$/-/$\approx$)				(3/0/33)	(4/0/32)

32 problems, respectively, their average HV values are generally better than the original NSGA-II on many problems.

In Table 1, many real-world CMOPs in the RCM suite are two-objective problems. Since the population size used in our experimental studies is 100 for two-objective problems, this is usually sufficient for the original NSGA-II to fully cover the entire Pareto front with 100 solutions. Thus, it is generally easy for NSGA-II to obtain a knee solution or a solution very close to the knee region. An example is shown in Fig. 2, which illustrates the feasible solutions in the final populations obtained by NSGA-II, KNSGA-II-E, and KNSGA-II-M. It is clear that 100 solutions are enough to fully cover the entire Pareto front, so the solution distributions from the three algorithms are very similar. Therefore, in Table 1, we observe only a very minor improvement in HV values by KNSGA-II-E and KNSGA-II-M on many RCM problems.

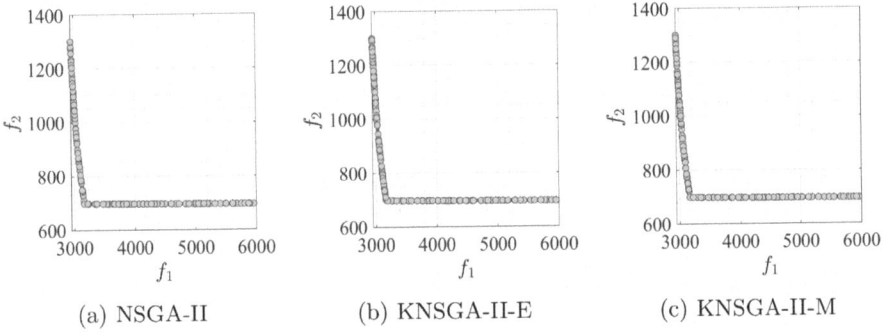

Fig. 2. Feasible solutions in the final populations obtained by NSGA-II, KNSGA-II-E and KNSGA-II-M on RCM6. A single run with the median HV value is selected from 101 runs of each algorithm. The blue points are feasible solutions and the red curve is the approximated CPF. (Color figure online)

For the three- and five-objective CMOPs in Table 1 (i.e., RCM8, RCM11, and RCM13), it can be observed that KNSGA-II-E and KNSGA-II-M obtain statistically better HV values compared to the original NSGA-II. This is because the solution distribution obtained by EMO algorithms is usually sparse in the objective space (since only 105 solutions are used for the three-objective problems and 126 solutions are used for the five-objective problem), and thus the Pareto front is not densely covered. In this scenario, the original NSGA-II usually cannot obtain a knee solution in its final population. Figure 3 shows the feasible solutions in the final populations obtained by the three algorithms on the RCM8 problem. The solutions obtained by KNSGA-II-E and KNSGA-II-M contain knee solutions. Figure 4 shows the feasible solutions in the final populations obtained by the three algorithms on the RCM13 problem. It is clear that KNSGA-II-E and KNSGA-II-M obtain a clear knee solution, whereas the original NSGA-II cannot find it.

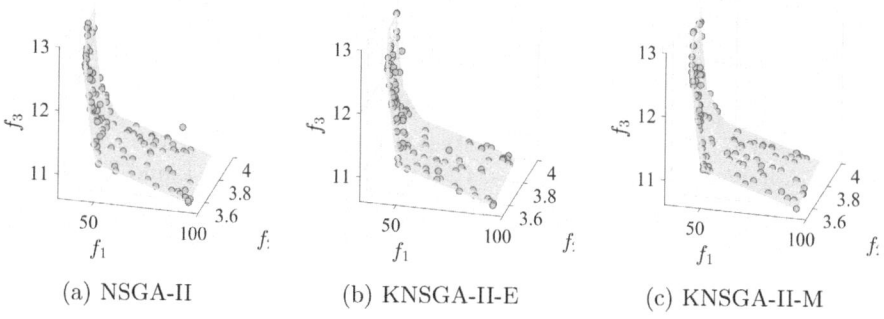

(a) NSGA-II   (b) KNSGA-II-E   (c) KNSGA-II-M

Fig. 3. Feasible solutions in the final populations obtained by NSGA-II, KNSGA-II-E and KNSGA-II-M on RCM8. A single run with the median HV value is selected from 101 runs of each algorithm. The blue points are feasible solutions and the pink surface is the approximated CPF. (Color figure online)

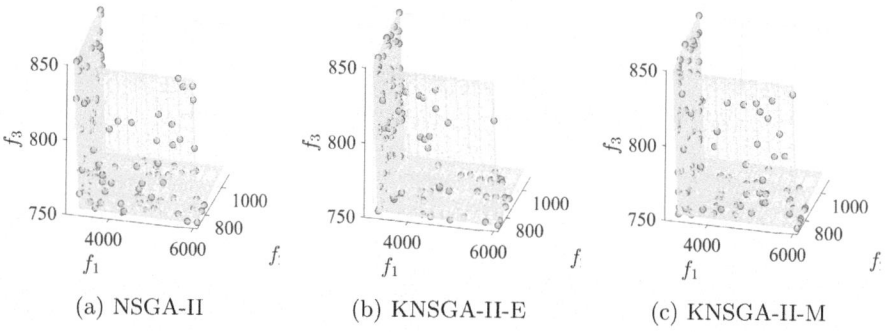

(a) NSGA-II   (b) KNSGA-II-E   (c) KNSGA-II-M

Fig. 4. Feasible solutions in the final populations obtained by NSGA-II, KNSGA-II-E and KNSGA-II-M on RCM13. A single run with the median HV value is selected from 101 runs of each algorithm. The blue points are feasible solutions and the pink surface is the approximated CPF. (Color figure online)

In addition, we also observe that the performance of KNSGA-II-E and KNSGA-II-M is very similar on many RCM problems. When problems have more than two objectives (that is, RCM8, RCM11, RCM13, and RCM19), KNSGA-II-M with the Manhattan distance shows better performance than KNSGA-II-E with the Euclidean distance. This suggests that the use of the Manhattan distance in identifying a knee solution is more effective, especially in higher-dimensional objective spaces.

4.3   Comparison with Other CMOEAs

In the previous subsection, the proposed KNSGA-II-E and KNSGA-II-M were compared with the original NSGA-II. The modified NSGA-II showed better performance than NSGA-II on many real-world CMOPs. In this subsection, we further compare KNSGA-II-M (as it achieves statistically better results than

KNSGA-II-E when compared to the original NSGA-II) with four state-of-the-art CMOEAs: C-MOEA/D [6], C-TAEA [9], CMOEA-MS [15], and CMOEMT [12]. These four algorithms, proposed in 2014, 2019, 2022, and 2024, respectively, can be viewed as representative CMOEAs for different CHTs, as shown in Table 2. As explained in Sect. 1, most CMOEAs are based on the first three CHTs in Table 2. Among the four algorithms, CMOEMT uses multitask and knowledge transfer framework that considers three tasks collaboratively: the first task uses the constrained dominance principle, the second task ignores constraints, and the third task applies constraint relaxation techniques, which can be viewed as a hybrid of different CHTs.

Table 2. Compared CMOEAs

Algorithm	CHT	Proposed Year
C-MOEA/D	Constrained dominance principle	2014
C-TAEA	Two-archive framework	2019
CMOEA-MS	Two-stage strategy	2022
CMOEMT	Multitask and knowledge transfer	2024

Table 3 presents the average HV over 101 runs of each algorithm. The symbols '+', '-', and '=' indicate that the compared CMOEAs is statistically better than, worse than, or equivalent to KNSGA-II-M, respectively. The best HV value for each problem is highlighted in gray. Overall, KNSGA-II-M outperforms C-MOEA/D, C-TAEA, and CMOEA-MS on 21, 25, and 24 problems, respectively, and demonstrates competitive performance with CMOEMT.

Figure 5 shows the feasible solutions in the final population of each algorithm on RCM3. For comparison, the feasible solutions obtained by the original NSGA-II are also presented in Fig. 5. The solutions obtained by both KNSGA-II-M and the original NSGA-II are very similar and well distributed over the approximated CPF. In contrast, all the other four CMOEAs fail to obtain well-distributed solutions over the entire approximated CPF.

Figure 6 presents the feasible solutions in the final populations obtained by KNSGA-II-M, C-MOEA/D, and C-TAEA on RCM13, as these are the top three performing algorithms for this problem. A single run with the median HV value is selected. KNSGA-II-M finds more uniformly distributed solutions along with a knee solution over the entire Pareto front, whereas the solution distributions of C-MOEA/D and C-TAEA are less well distributed. However, we observe that both C-MOEA/D and C-TAEA also obtain a knee point, which explains why their HV values are not worse, even though their solution distributions are not good. This suggests the importance of including a knee point in the solution set to improve the HV value for problems with this type of Pareto front shape.

Table 3. Average HV value over 101 runs of each algorithm on the 36 real-world problems.

Problem	m	d	KNSGA-II-M	C-MOEA/D	C-TAEA	CMOEA-MS	CMOEMT
RCM1	2	4	0.5430	0.0293 (-)	0.5461 (+)	0.3219 (-)	0.5448 (+)
RCM2	2	5	0.6297	0.0196 (-)	0.4065 (-)	0.6127 (-)	0.8459 (≈)
RCM3	2	3	0.9607	0.0286 (-)	0.9444 (-)	0.9126 (-)	0.9557 (-)
RCM4	2	4	0.9266	0.0005 (-)	0.9151 (-)	0.8395 (-)	0.9191 (-)
RCM5	2	4	0.8163	0.7962 (-)	0.8130 (-)	0.7956 (-)	0.8164 (≈)
RCM6	2	7	0.9896	0.9869 (-)	0.7721 (-)	0.9900 (+)	0.9855 (-)
RCM7	2	4	0.5810	0.5715 (-)	0.5812 (+)	0.5823 (+)	0.5842 (+)
RCM8	3	7	0.9695	0.0503 (-)	0.9810 (+)	0.9773 (+)	0.9665 (-)
RCM9	2	4	0.6913	0.0105 (-)	0.6921 (+)	0.6903 (-)	0.6924 (+)
RCM10	2	2	1.0081	0.0119 (-)	1.0016 (-)	0.9954 (-)	1.0000 (-)
RCM11	5	3	1.7861	1.1715 (-)	1.7898 (≈)	1.6250 (-)	1.7381 (-)
RCM12	2	4	0.9232	0.0139 (-)	0.9155 (-)	0.7129 (-)	0.9202 (-)
RCM13	3	7	1.1778	1.1707 (-)	1.1598 (-)	1.0618 (-)	1.1491 (-)
RCM14	2	5	0.8683	0.0608 (-)	0.8678 (-)	0.5128 (-)	0.8659 (-)
RCM15	2	3	0.7909	0.0102 (-)	0.7796 (-)	0.7909 (≈)	0.7909 (≈)
RCM16	2	2	0.8910	0.0102 (-)	0.8900 (-)	0.8788 (-)	0.8890 (-)
RCM17	3	6	0.0639	0.0340 (-)	0.0611 (-)	0.0601 (-)	0.1360 (+)
RCM18	2	3	0.6366	0.6374 (+)	0.6378 (+)	0.6384 (+)	0.6386 (+)
RCM19	3	10	0.8735	0.3336 (-)	0.2182 (-)	0.8588 (-)	0.9985 (+)
RCM20	2	4	0.6043	0.0000 (-)	0.0148 (-)	0.1641 (-)	0.4757 (-)
RCM21	2	6	0.5944	0.0238 (-)	0.5876 (-)	0.5967 (+)	0.5968 (+)
RCM22	2	9	0.0000	0.0055 (≈)	0.0000 (≈)	0.0000 (≈)	0.2402 (+)
RCM23	2	6	0.1093	0.1008 (≈)	0.0000 (-)	0.1276 (≈)	0.1586 (+)
RCM24	3	9	0.0000	0.0017 (≈)	0.0629 (+)	0.0822 (+)	0.1060 (+)
RCM25	2	2	0.4048	0.3950 (-)	0.4055 (+)	0.3919 (-)	0.4063 (+)
RCM26	2	3	0.3218	0.3153 (≈)	0.2054 (-)	0.1974 (-)	0.4531 (+)
RCM27	2	3	0.6807	0.6818 (+)	0.6811 (+)	0.6822 (+)	0.6820 (+)
RCM28	2	7	0.0000	0.0258 (+)	0.0000 (≈)	0.1448 (+)	0.0850 (+)
RCM29	2	7	0.5823	0.6010 (≈)	0.3329 (-)	0.6001 (+)	0.6069 (+)
RCM30	2	25	0.5732	0.6102 (≈)	0.1818 (-)	0.0367 (-)	0.3989 (-)
RCM31	2	25	0.1695	0.1509 (≈)	0.0032 (-)	0.0040 (-)	0.0529 (-)
RCM32	2	25	0.3209	0.3839 (≈)	0.0000 (-)	0.0000 (-)	0.0638 (-)
RCM33	2	30	0.1610	0.1570 (≈)	0.0000 (-)	0.0000 (-)	0.0638 (-)
RCM34	2	30	0.1891	0.1850 (≈)	0.0000 (-)	0.0000 (-)	0.0555 (-)
RCM35	2	30	0.0662	0.0780 (≈)	0.0000 (-)	0.0000 (-)	0.0051 (-)
RCM50	2	6	0.2336	0.2594 (+)	0.0000 (-)	0.0375 (-)	0.3636 (+)
(+/-/≈)				(4/21/11)	(8/25/3)	(9/24/3)	(16/17/3)

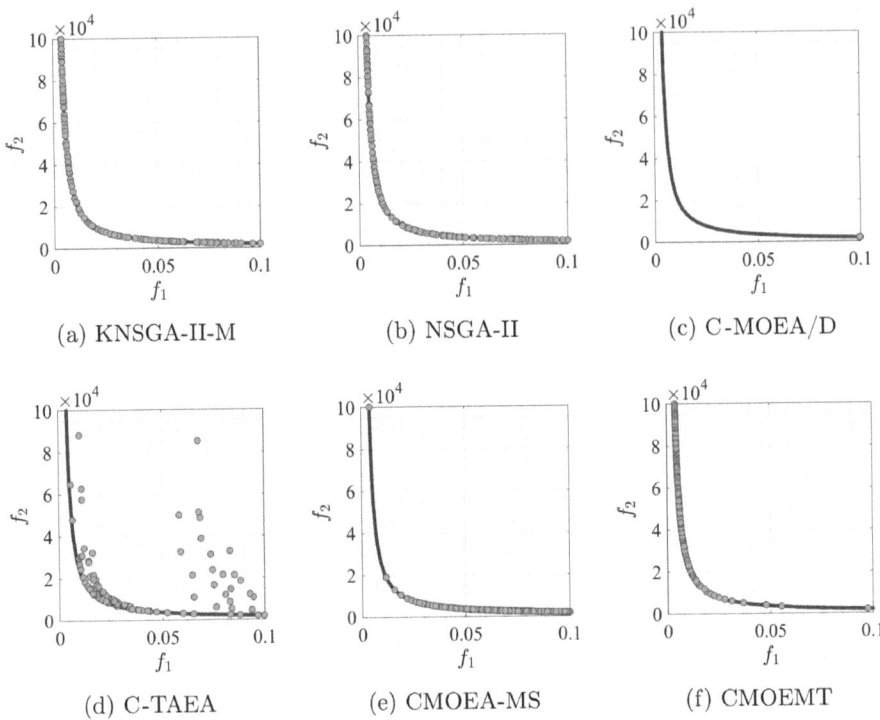

Fig. 5. Feasible solutions in the final population of each algorithm on RCM3. A single run with the median HV value is selected. The blue points are feasible solutions and the red curve is the approximated CPF. (Color figure online)

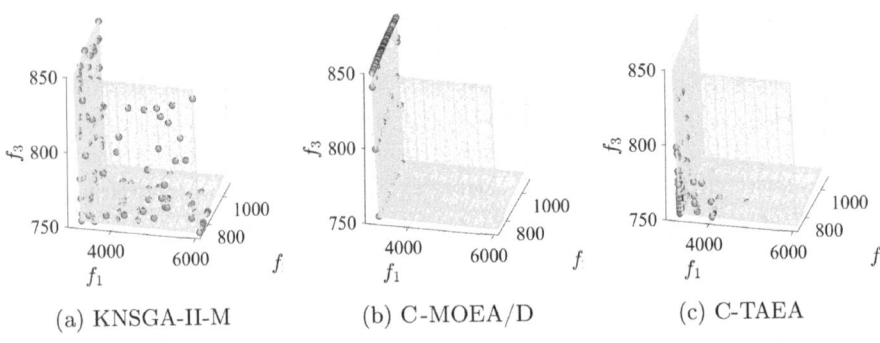

Fig. 6. Feasible solutions in the final populations obtained by KNSGA-II-M, C-MOEA/D and C-TAEA on RCM13. A single run with the median HV value is selected. The blue points are feasible solutions and the pink surface is the approximated CPF. (Color figure online)

5   Conclusions

In this paper, we proposed a simple modification of NSGA-II to further improve its performance on real-world CMOPs. In our modification, a knee point is always ensured to survive to the next population. The knee point is identified based on the minimum distance to the estimated ideal point. We examined two different distance metrics: Euclidean distance and Manhattan distance. Our experimental results clearly demonstrated the usefulness of including a knee point in improving the performance of NSGA-II on real-world CMOPs. We also compared the proposed KNSGA-II with Manhattan distance to four state-of-the-art CMOEAs: C-MOEA/D, C-TAEA, CMOEA-MS and CMOEMT. Our experimental results showed that our proposed method outperformed C-MOEA/D, C-TAEA, and CMOEA-MS on many real-world CMOPs, and performed competitively with the most recently proposed CMOEMT.

One future research topic is to further examine the effectiveness of alternative knee point selection methods, such as using the highest trade-off points, which could avoid the reliance on an ideal point in the identification of a knee point in the evolutionary process.

Acknowledgements. This work was supported by National Natural Science Foundation of China (Grant No. 62376115), Guangdong Provincial Key Laboratory (Grant No. 2020B121201001).

Disclosure of Interests. The authors have no competing interests to declare that are relevant to the content of this article.

References

1. Branke, J., Deb, K., Dierolf, H., Osswald, M.: Finding knees in multi-objective optimization, pp. 722–731. Springer Berlin Heidelberg (2004). https://doi.org/10.1007/978-3-540-30217-9_73
2. Chiu, W.Y., Yen, G.G., Juan, T.K.: Minimum Manhattan distance approach to multiple criteria decision making in multiobjective optimization problems. IEEE Trans. Evol. Comput. **20**(6), 972–985 (2016). https://doi.org/10.1109/tevc.2016.2564158
3. Cuate, O., Schütze, O.: Pareto explorer for finding the knee for many objective optimization problems. Mathematics **8**(10), 1651 (2020). https://doi.org/10.3390/math8101651
4. Deb, K., Pratap, A., Agarwal, S., Meyarivan, T.: A fast and elitist multiobjective genetic algorithm: NSGA-II. IEEE Trans. Evol. Comput. **6**(2), 182–197 (2002). https://doi.org/10.1109/4235.996017
5. Ishibuchi, H., Imada, R., Setoguchi, Y., Nojima, Y.: How to specify a reference point in hypervolume calculation for fair performance comparison. Evol. Comput. **26**(3), 411–440 (2018). https://doi.org/10.1162/evco_a_00226
6. Jain, H., Deb, K.: An evolutionary many-objective optimization algorithm using reference-point based nondominated sorting approach, part ii: handling constraints and extending to an adaptive approach. IEEE Trans. Evol. Comput. **18**(4), 602–622 (2014). https://doi.org/10.1109/tevc.2013.2281534

7. Jiang, M., Wang, Z., Hong, H., Yen, G.G.: Knee point-based imbalanced transfer learning for dynamic multiobjective optimization. IEEE Trans. Evol. Comput. **25**(1), 117–129 (2021). https://doi.org/10.1109/tevc.2020.3004027

8. Kumar, A., et al.: A benchmark-suite of real-world constrained multi-objective optimization problems and some baseline results. Swarm Evol. Comput. **67**, 100961 (2021). https://doi.org/10.1016/j.swevo.2021.100961

9. Li, K., Chen, R., Fu, G., Yao, X.: Two-archive evolutionary algorithm for constrained multiobjective optimization. IEEE Trans. Evol. Comput. **23**(2), 303–315 (2019). https://doi.org/10.1109/tevc.2018.2855411

10. Liang, J., et al.: A survey on evolutionary constrained multiobjective optimization. IEEE Trans. Evol. Comput. **27**(2), 201–221 (2023). https://doi.org/10.1109/tevc.2022.3155533

11. Liang, J., Li, Z., Qu, B., Yu, K., Qiao, K., Ge, S.: A knee point based NSGA-II multi-objective evolutionary algorithm, pp. 454–467. Springer Singapore (2020). https://doi.org/10.1007/978-981-15-3425-6_35

12. Ming, F., Gong, W., Wang, L., Gao, L.: Constrained multiobjective optimization via multitasking and knowledge transfer. IEEE Trans. Evol. Comput. **28**(1), 77–89 (2024). https://doi.org/10.1109/tevc.2022.3230822

13. Nan, Y., Ishibuchi, H., Shu, T., Shang, K.: Analysis of real-world constrained multi-objective problems and performance comparison of multi-objective algorithms. In: Proceedings of the Genetic and Evolutionary Computation Conference, pp. 576–584. GECCO'24, ACM (2024). https://doi.org/10.1145/3638529.3653994

14. Tian, Y., Cheng, R., Zhang, X., Jin, Y.: PlatEMO: a MATLAB platform for evolutionary multi-objective optimization [educational forum]. IEEE Comput. Intell. Mag. **12**(4), 73–87 (2017). https://doi.org/10.1109/mci.2017.2742868

15. Tian, Y., Zhang, Y., Su, Y., Zhang, X., Tan, K.C., Jin, Y.: Balancing objective optimization and constraint satisfaction in constrained evolutionary multiobjective optimization. IEEE Trans. Cybern. **52**(9), 9559–9572 (2022). https://doi.org/10.1109/tcyb.2020.3021138

16. Zhang, X., Tian, Y., Jin, Y.: A knee point-driven evolutionary algorithm for many-objective optimization. IEEE Trans. Evol. Comput. **19**(6), 761–776 (2015). https://doi.org/10.1109/tevc.2014.2378512

Benchmarking

Single and Multi-objective Optimization Benchmark Problems Focusing on Human-Powered Aircraft Design

Nobuo Namura[✉][iD]

Fujitsu Limited, Kawasaki 211-8588, Japan
namura.nobuo@fujitsu.com

Abstract. The landscapes of real-world optimization problems can vary strongly depending on the application. In engineering design optimization, objective functions and constraints are often derived from governing equations, resulting in moderate multimodality. However, benchmark problems with such moderate multimodality are typically confined to low-dimensional cases, making it challenging to conduct meaningful comparisons. To address this, we present a benchmark test suite focused on the design of human-powered aircraft for single and multi-objective optimization. This test suite incorporates governing equations from aerodynamics and material mechanics, providing a realistic testing environment. It includes 60 problems across three difficulty levels, with a wing segmentation parameter to scale complexity and dimensionality. Both constrained and unconstrained versions are provided, with penalty methods applied to the unconstrained version. The test suite is computationally inexpensive while retaining key characteristics of engineering problems. Numerical experiments indicate the presence of moderate multimodality, and multi-objective problems exhibit diverse Pareto front shapes.

Keywords: benchmark · multi-objective optimization · aircraft design

1 Introduction

Various methods for black-box optimization, such as evolutionary algorithms (EAs) and Bayesian optimization (BO), have been widely applied across fields, including engineering design, facility operation, material development, drug discovery, and machine learning. The landscapes of objective functions in these applications have become increasingly diverse. In engineering design optimization, objective functions often exhibit moderate multimodality due to governing equations, such as partial differential equations, which typically result in smooth landscapes [6,8,23,24]. The successful use of BO with Gaussian process (GP) surrogate models in this field can be attributed to these characteristics [30,40].

Conversely, the development and evaluation of algorithms for black-box optimization commonly rely on synthetic benchmark problems, which are defined by mathematical equations. These benchmarks significantly influence the research

© The Author(s), under exclusive license to Springer Nature Singapore Pte Ltd. 2025
H. Singh et al. (Eds.): EMO 2025, LNCS 15512, pp. 195–210, 2025.
https://doi.org/10.1007/978-981-96-3506-1_14

direction of optimization algorithms. In single-objective optimization, fundamental functions like the sphere and Rastrigin function, as well as composite functions formed from these, are frequently used [26]. In multi-objective optimization, benchmark problems often rely on similar fundamental functions [11, 39], as they impact convergence toward the Pareto front (PF). These fundamental functions can generally be classified into two categories: those with simple unimodal landscapes (e.g., sphere, ellipsoid) and those with complex landscapes that exhibit an exponential increase in local optima as the dimensionality grows (e.g., Rastrigin, Styblinski-Tang). Benchmark problems with moderate multimodality (e.g., Branin, Hartmann), are typically available only in lower dimensions. Recent studies [31, 36] have proposed adjustable benchmark problems which create multimodality by combining multiple simple basis functions like ellipsoid functions. However, their landscape can be oversimplified due to the small number of basis functions to achieve moderate multimodality.

In multi-objective cases, benchmark problems possess characteristics that differ from real-world problems, raising concerns about overfitting algorithms to these benchmarks [21]. Ishibuchi et al. [19] noted that many synthetic benchmark problems lack unique optimal solutions for each objective, and in three-objective problems, the PF often forms a triangle. To address this, benchmark problems like Minus-DTLZ and Minus-WFG [21], which generate PFs resembling the inverted triangles frequently observed in real problems, have gained popularity.

In recent years, practical benchmark problems based on real-world problems [33, 35, 37] have been used instead of synthetic benchmark problems. While these problems exhibit complex PF shapes, making it challenging to obtain diverse Pareto-optimal solutions, they are typically available only in low-dimensional spaces up to 10 dimensions. This has raised concerns that convergence to the PF may be too easy [28]. Additionally, they often require computationally expensive numerical simulations [9, 17, 34], which can limit the number of function evaluations. Therefore, benchmark problems with moderate multimodality that mimic engineering design optimization and allow dimensionality changes while keeping evaluation costs low are scarce. Setting up appropriate benchmark problems under these conditions can be challenging.

In this paper, we propose single and multi-objective benchmark problems related to the aerostructural design of human-powered aircraft (HPA), which emulate engineering design optimization tasks. The objective functions and constraints are derived from integral equations in aerodynamics and differential equations in material mechanics. These benchmark problems are designed to reflect the characteristics of real-world engineering design optimization, while ensuring short evaluation times. Additionally, by adjusting the definition of design variables, we introduce three levels of difficulty and enable changes in dimensionality through parameter modifications, making these problems scalable. While the original benchmark problems include constraints, we also provide unconstrained versions using penalty methods. Python source code for these benchmark problems is available on GitHub[1].

---

[1] https://github.com/Nobuo-Namura/hpa.

Fig. 1. Human-powered aircraft.

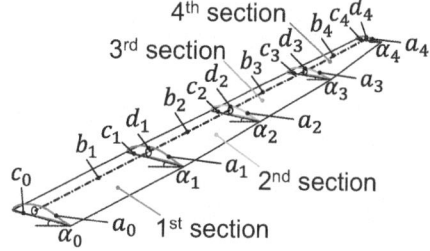

Fig. 2. Wing shape definition.

2   Benchmark Problem Definition

2.1   Definition of Variables for HPA Design

An HPA gains propulsion by the pilot pedaling like a bicycle to rotate a propeller, as depicted in Fig. 1. Wings of HPA are typically made of foam and balsa wood, covered with heat-shrinkable film, and supported by carbon fiber reinforced plastic (CFRP) pipe frameworks. In this paper, we assume this structural configuration for defining the design optimization problem.

The variables defining the main wing shape are based on dividing the right wing into n segments, defined by $(n + 1)$ cross-sections, as shown in Fig. 2 for the case where $n = 4$. The variables include a_i for airfoil (cross-sectional shape) choice from DAE series [13], b_i for the length of each segment, c_i for the chord length (wing segment length in fore-aft direction), α_i for the angle of attack (incidence angle of airflow), and d_i for the diameter of the CFRP pipe forming the main beam. These variables are real-valued.

Variables related to the stacking sequence of the CFRP pipe forming the main beam for segment i are shown in Fig. 3. The CFRP pipe is manufactured by laminating sheets of material called prepregs, which consist of carbon fibers aligned in a specific direction, at angles (orientation angles) that match the expected loads. The CFRP pipe with a diameter d_i for segment i consists of a fixed set of four full-circumference laminates and m variable flange laminates, which primarily support the lift force. m varies depending on the optimization problem while Fig. 3 shows an example configuration for $m = 4$. In the cross-sectional view, the black area represents the full-circumference laminates, while the red, green, orange, and blue areas represent the flange laminates. The variables related to the stacking sequence include the starting and ending points $s_{i,j}$ and $e_{i,j}$, and the width $w_{i,j}$ for each of the $j \in 1, \cdots, m$ flange laminates. $s_{i,j}$ and $e_{i,j}$ are non-dimensional position on the spanwise coordinate where the $(i - 1)$ and i-th cross-sections are defined as 0 and 1, respectively. Note that for manufacturing reasons, $s_{i,j} \leq s_{i,j+1}$, $e_{i,j} \geq e_{i,j+1}$, and $w_{i,j} < w_{i,j+1}$. These constraints are automatically satisfied based on the definition of the design variables.

Other variables include the dihedral angle at the wing root γ_0, the tension force T of the flying wires, and the payload W_p. Figure 4 illustrates the deflection curve of the main wing when viewed from the front at both parked and flight

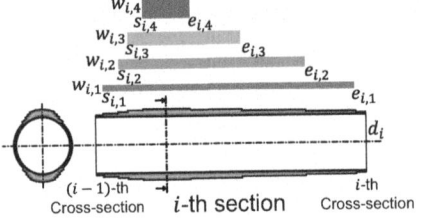

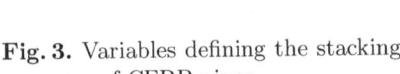

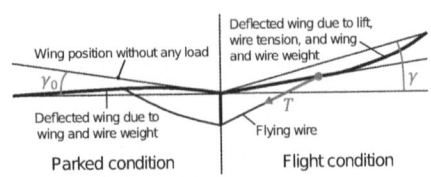

Fig. 3. Variables defining the stacking sequence of CFRP pipes.

Fig. 4. Relationship between wing deflection at parked and flight conditions, dihedral angle, and tension force of the flying wires.

conditions. By varying γ_0, it is possible to adjust the dihedral angle at the wingtip γ during flight, considering the need to provide clearance between the wing and the ground at the parked condition. The flying wires are introduced to relieve some of the bending moment due to lift during flight, thus reducing the weight of the inner CFRP pipes compared to when no flying wire is used. Payload W_p represents the mass of cargo or passengers carried by the HPA. These three variables are included as variables in some problems.

2.2 Design Variables

The design variables **x** for the benchmark problem change with the difficulty level in the problem. Therefore, we denote the design variables at three difficulty levels as $\mathbf{x}_l$ for $l \in 0, 1, 2$. Depending on the optimization problem and its difficulty level, a subset of variables used to define the wing is selected as design variables. However, some of the variables for defining the wing are calculated from different design variables for each difficulty level through variable transformations tailored to the difficulty. In the definition of design variables, the higher-level design space includes the lower-level design space, allowing lower-level design variables to be transformed into higher-level design variables. All design variables are normalized to the range [0,1] in the implementation, as designers can arbitrarily define the upper and lower bounds, which are predetermined parameters even in real-world problems.

Difficulty Level $l = 0$. In this case, the design variables include segment lengths b_i, chord lengths c_i, an angle of attack at wing root α_0, washout angles $\tilde{\alpha}_i$, a dihedral angle at wing root γ_0, wire tension T, payload W_p, and the reduction coefficients for reference strains at flight and parked conditions, r_0 and $r_1 \in (0, 1]$. Note that depending on the problem, γ_0, T, and W_p may be treated as constants. For $l = 0$, airfoil a_i is considered a constant, and the diameter of the CFRP pipe d_i is defined as $d_i = \min_{\tilde{y}_i} t(\tilde{y}_i)c(\tilde{y}_i)$, where $t(\tilde{y}_i)$ and $c(\tilde{y}_i)$ are functions that linearly interpolate wing thickness and chord length in the wing span direction within the i-th segment using $\tilde{y}_i \in [0, 1]$ as the non-dimensional spanwise coordinate. The angle of attack α_i at each cross-section is transformed from α_0 and $\dot{\alpha}_i$ as follows:

$$\alpha_i = \alpha_0 + \sum_{i'=1}^{i} \dot{\alpha}_{i'}. \tag{1}$$

The variables $s_{i,j}$, $e_{i,j}$, and $w_{i,j}$ for each segment are greedily optimized to satisfy constraint $g'_{1,i}(\tilde{y}_i, \mathbf{x}_l) \le 0$ with the use of r_0 and r_1:

$$g'_{1,i}(\tilde{y}_i, \mathbf{x}_l) = \frac{n_m n_s}{\epsilon_u} \max\left[\frac{\epsilon_0(\tilde{y}_i, \mathbf{x}_l)}{r_0}, \frac{\epsilon_1(\tilde{y}_i, \mathbf{x}_l)}{r_1}\right] - 1, \tag{2}$$

where, $n_m = 1.5$, $n_s = 2$, and $\epsilon_u = 0.0027$ are constants representing load factor, safety factor, and reference strain. $\epsilon_0(\tilde{y}_i, \mathbf{x}_l)$ and $\epsilon_1(\tilde{y}_i, \mathbf{x}_l)$ are absolute values of compressive strains on the outer surface of CFRP pipe at $\tilde{y}_i$ at flight and parked conditions, respectively.

Difficulty Level $l = 1$. In addition to the design variables from level $l = 0$, airfoil a_i and the diameter reduction factor $\tilde{d}_i \in (0, 1]$ for the CFRP pipe are included as design variables for level $l = 1$. The diameter of the CFRP pipe is defined as $d_i = \tilde{d}_i \min_{\tilde{y}_i} t(\tilde{y}_i) c(\tilde{y}_i)$. The flange laminates $s_{i,j}$, $e_{i,j}$, and $w_{i,j}$ are optimized in the same way as for level $l = 0$. However, the reduction factors $r_{0,i}$ and $r_{1,i}$ for each segment vary, and they are used as design variables instead of r_0 and r_1.

Difficulty Level $l = 2$. In level $l = 2$, flange laminates $s_{i,j}$, $e_{i,j}$, and $w_{i,j}$ are determined differently from level $l = 1$. The design variables consist of the change in length and width between each layer of flange laminate $\dot{l}_{i,j}$ and $\dot{w}_{i,j}$, and the spanwise reference position $\xi_i \in [0, 1]$. The flange laminate is defined using the following equations:

$$l_{i,j} = \max\left(0, 1 - \sum_{j'=1}^{j} \dot{l}_{i,j'}\right), \quad \tilde{\xi}_i = \text{round}\left(\frac{1}{1 + \exp(-50(\xi_i - 0.5))}, 4\right), \tag{3}$$

$$s_{i,j} = \tilde{\xi}_i(1 - l_{i,j}), \quad e_{i,j} = \tilde{\xi}_i + l_{i,j}(1 - \tilde{\xi}_i), \quad w_{i,j} = \frac{\pi d_i}{12} - \Delta w + \sum_{j'=1}^{j} \dot{w}_{i,j'}, \tag{4}$$

where $\Delta w = 0.002$ [m] represents the minimum increment of the laminate width. Equation 3 uses a sigmoid function and rounding to convert ξ_i to $\tilde{\xi}_i$, where the rounding (round) operation truncates the value to four decimal places. These improve the probability that each laminate connects to one end of the CFRP pipe and leads to a reasonable design.

Table 1. Fundamental functions and penalty weights for unconstrained problems.

Function	Unit	Weight	Function	Unit	Weight
$f_1 = P(\mathbf{x}_l) = D(\mathbf{x}_l)V(\mathbf{x}_l)/\eta$	W	$v_1 = 10$	$f_9 = \alpha_0$	deg	$v_9 = 1$
$f_2 = D(\mathbf{x}_l)$	N	$v_2 = 1$	$f_{10} = T$	N	$v_{10} = 200$
$f_3 = -V(\mathbf{x}_l)$	m/s	$v_3 = 1$	$f_{11} = -W_p$	kg	$v_{11} = 10$
$f_4 = \max(|\delta(\mathbf{x}_l)|, |\delta_{\text{park}}(\mathbf{x}_l)|)$	m	$v_4 = 0.5$	$g_1 = n_m n_s \epsilon_{\max}(\mathbf{x}_l)/\epsilon_u - 1$	–	$w_1 = 10$
$f_5 = \Phi(\mathbf{x}_l)$	deg	$v_5 = 0.1$	$g_2 = B(\sin\gamma(\mathbf{x}_l) - \sin\gamma_u)/2$	m	$w_2 = 2$
$f_6 = -E(\mathbf{x}_l)$	–	$v_6 = 0.1$	$g_3 = -\delta_{\text{park}}(\mathbf{x}_l)$	m	$w_3 = 2$
$f_7 = W_0(\mathbf{x}_l)$	kg	$v_7 = 1$	$g_4 = P(\mathbf{x}_l) - P_{\max}$	W	$w_4 = 0.1$
$f_8 = B = 2\sum_{i=1}^{n} b_i$	m	$v_8 = 1$	$g_5 = 1 - (V(\mathbf{x}_l)/V_{\min})^3$	–	$w_5 = 10$

2.3   Objective Functions and Constraints

Each benchmark problem is constructed by selecting a subset of the fundamental 11 objective functions to be minimized, f_i, and 5 constraint conditions, $g_i \leq 0$, as shown in Table 1. The functions P, D, V, Φ, E, W_0, and B represent the required power, drag, cruise speed, twist angle at wingtip, wing efficiency, empty weight, and wing span, respectively. The variables δ and δ_{park} denote the wingtip displacement (positive upwards) at flight and parked conditions, relative to the wing root height. $\epsilon_{\max}$ represents the maximum strain in CFRP pipes at both parked and flight conditions, and γ represents the dihedral angle at wingtip at the flight condition. Additionally, $\eta = 0.85 \times 0.95$ is the product of propeller and drivetrain efficiency, $\gamma_u = 8°$ is maximum dihedral angle, $P_{\max} = 400$ [W] is maximum required power, and $V_{\min} = 7.3$ [m/s] is the minimum cruise speed. Since V, E, and W_p are functions to be maximized, a negative sign is applied to f_3, f_6, and f_{11} to convert them into minimization problems.

Many of the objective functions and constraints are functions of most elements in $\mathbf{x}_l$. However, the wing efficiency E for f_6 depends only on the variables related to the wing shape: airfoil a_i, section length b_i, chord length c_i, and angle of attack α_i. f_8 is the sum of b_i, while f_9 through f_{11} are specific design variables themselves. Additionally, functions that have the dihedral angle at wing root γ_0 as a variable are limited to f_4, g_2, and g_3, and only functions f_4 and g_2 have all elements in $\mathbf{x}_l$ as variables.

The objective functions and constraints are evaluated by solving integral equations based on lifting line theory and differential equations for deflection based on beam-column theory. Computational grids with 50 and 301 points are used for solving these equations, respectively.

2.4   Definition of Each Problem

By selecting a subset of functions from Table 1, we define 3 single-objective problems and 17 multi-objective problems. Each problem has three difficulty levels, resulting in a total of 60 benchmark problems. The benchmark problems proposed in this paper are denoted as HPAMNL-l, where M is the number of objective functions, N is the number of inequality constraints (excluding box constraints), L is the problem ID, and l is the difficulty level, which may be omitted if irrelevant. The wing segmentation number n is a parameter that increases or decreases the problem dimension, and in this paper, we set $n = 4$. n should be an even number to obtain a realistic design.

Table 2. Benchmark problem definitions and dimensionality when $n = 4$.

Problem	f_1	f_2	f_3	f_4	f_5	f_6	f_7	f_8	f_9	f_{10}	f_{11}	g_1	g_2	g_3	g_4	g_5	γ_0	T	W_p	m	$|\mathbf{x}_0|$	$|\mathbf{x}_1|$	$|\mathbf{x}_2|$
HPA131, HPA101	✓											✓	✓	✓			✓			10	17	32	108
HPA142, HPA102	✓											✓	✓	✓	✓		✓			20	17	32	188
HPA143, HPA103			✓									✓	✓	✓	✓		✓			20	17	32	188
HPA241, HPA201	✓	✓										✓	✓	✓	✓		✓	✓		10	18	33	109
HPA222, HPA202	✓		✓									✓					✓			20	16	31	187
HPA233, HPA203			✓						✓			✓	✓	✓			✓	✓	✓	20	19	34	190
HPA244, HPA204				✓	✓							✓	✓	✓	✓		✓	✓		20	18	33	189
HPA245, HPA205			✓					✓				✓	✓	✓	✓		✓	✓		20	18	33	189
HPA341, HPA301	✓	✓		✓								✓	✓	✓	✓		✓	✓		10	18	33	109
HPA322, HPA302	✓			✓	✓							✓					✓			20	16	31	187
HPA333, HPA303			✓				✓		✓			✓	✓	✓			✓	✓	✓	20	19	34	190
HPA344, HPA304	✓	✓		✓								✓	✓	✓	✓		✓	✓		20	18	33	189
HPA345, HPA305	✓							✓				✓	✓	✓	✓		✓	✓		20	18	33	189
HPA441, HPA401	✓	✓		✓		✓						✓	✓	✓	✓		✓	✓		20	18	33	189
HPA422, HPA402	✓			✓	✓		✓					✓					✓			20	16	31	187
HPA443, HPA403			✓			✓	✓		✓			✓	✓	✓	✓		✓	✓		20	18	33	189
HPA541, HPA501	✓	✓		✓	✓	✓						✓	✓	✓	✓		✓	✓		20	18	33	189
HPA542, HPA502	✓		✓						✓	✓	✓	✓	✓	✓	✓		✓	✓	✓	20	19	34	190
HPA641, HPA601	✓		✓		✓	✓	✓					✓	✓	✓	✓		✓	✓		20	18	33	189
HPA941, HPA901	✓		✓		✓	✓	✓	✓	✓	✓		✓	✓	✓	✓		✓	✓	✓	20	19	34	190

In Table 2, we present the objective functions, constraints, and the design variables used for each problem, as well as the maximum number of layers in CFRP flange laminates, m, and the dimension of design variables $|\mathbf{x}_l|$ when $n = 4$ for each difficulty level. The dimension of the design variables varies with n, m, and k as follows: $|\mathbf{x}_0| = 3n + 4 + k$, $|\mathbf{x}_1| = 7n + 3 + k$, and $|\mathbf{x}_2| = (2m + 6)n + 3 + k$, where k is the number of variables used among γ_0, T, and W_p listed in Table 2. Each problem is defined based on the intended use and configuration of the aircraft. For example, HPA101 and HPA102 are both designed for long-distance flights, but they differ in whether flying wires are included. In contrast, HPA103 is tailored for high-speed flight.

In unconstrained problems with $N = 0$, we modify the objective functions f_i as f_i' using the penalty weights v_i and w_j from Table 1 as:

$$f_i' = f_i + v_i \sum_{j \in \mathcal{G}} w_j \max(0, g_j) \tag{5}$$

where, $\mathcal{G} \subset \{1, 2, 3, 4, 5\}$ is a set composed of constraint indices used in each problem from Table 2.

3 Numerical Experiment

3.1 Setups

We conducted experiments on 60 unconstained HPA problems with Eq. 5 as objective functions because most widely available EAs and BO methods lack sufficient support for handling constraints.

Single-Objective Problems. In the single-objective problem, we verify whether the primary objective functions exhibit smooth landscapes and moderate multimodality. We employed algorithms from the black-box optimization libraries pymoo [5], BoTorch [2], and Optuna™[1]. From pymoo, we utilized four EAs, namely covariance matrix adaptation evolution strategy (CMA-ES) [15], particle swarm optimization (PSO), differential evolution (DE), and genetic algorithm (GA), with default settings for parameters except for the population size. From BoTorch, we utilized BO methods, namely GP model with a Matérn-5/2 kernel and expected improvement (GP-EI), and trust region BO (TuRBO) [14]. Optuna™ provided the tree-structured Parzen estimator (TPE) [3].

In all algorithms, the population size and the number of initial sample points were set to 20, the function evaluation budget was set to 1,000, the number of independent runs was set to 11. The batch size (number of additional sample points at each iteration) of GP-EI, TuRBO, and TPE was set to 1. Other parameters were set to the default values in each library.

Multi-objective Problems. In the multi-objective HPA problem, we reveal the PF shapes, the characteristics of non-dominated solutions (NDSs) achievable by existing algorithms, and the differences from conventional benchmark problems. We employed six algorithms from pymoo: non-dominated sorting genetic algorithm II (NSGA-II) [12] and III (NSGA-III) [10], multi-objective EA based on decomposition (MOEA/D) [38], S-metric selection evolutionary multi-objective optimisation algorithm (SMS-EMOA) [4], reference vector guided EA (RVEA) [7], and adaptive geometry estimation based many-objective EA II (AGE-MOEA-II) [29]. In all algorithms, the population size was set to $40M$, where M is the number of objective functions, and the function evaluation budget was set to 72,000 for problems with $l = 0, 1$, and 216,000 for problems with $l = 2$. Reference vectors for NSGA-III, MOEA/D, and RVEA are generated by the Riesz s-Energy method [16], and the number of vectors is the same as the population size. As pointed out by He et al. [18], objective function normalization was employed for MOEA/D, SMS-EMOA, and RVEA to improve their performance. Other parameters were set to the default values in pymoo.

We conducted 11 independent runs and calculated the inverted generational distance plus (IGD$^+$) [20] for the normalized objective functions. The reference points for IGD$^+$ were selected from NDSs obtained by hot-started runs of the six algorithms under the same settings as the cold-started runs, except for the initialization, where the initial population consisted of NDSs extracted from the external archive of solutions obtained across all cold-started runs, encompassing all problems, difficulty levels, and algorithms. The normalization also used the utopia and nadir points derived from the reference points.

As conventional benchmark problems, we use the RE [33] problems, and 30-dimensional DTLZ1-7 [11] and Minus-DTLZ1-7 [21] problems ($M = 2, 3, 6$). The experimental settings are identical to those for the HPA problems. For the RE problems, DTLZ5, 6 ($M = 6$), and Minus-DTLZ5-7, we used a subset of NDSs from all cold-started runs of six algorithms as reference points for IGD$^+$.

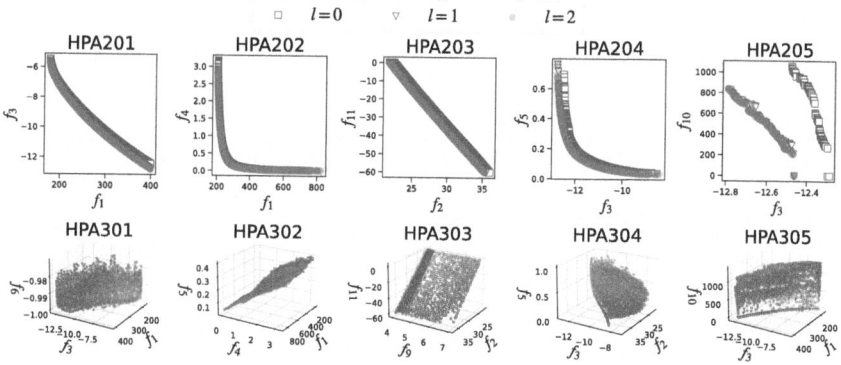

Fig. 5. Pareto front shapes with reference points for IGD$^+$ in each difficulty level.

3.2 Pareto Front Shapes

The IGD$^+$ reference points for two-objective and three-objective problems are shown in Fig. 5. While many problems have convex PF, HPA203 and 303 have linear PF and HPA205 and 305 have concave PF in particular cross-sections. When HPA305 is sliced parallel to the f_{10} axis, a PF shape similar to HPA205 appears. HPA304 forms an inverted triangular PF. In HPA302, there is a strong positive correlation between f_4 and f_5, causing a partially degenerated PF near the minimum values of these objectives. In HPA problems, the PFs of higher-difficulty level dominate those of lower-difficulty level since the design space of higher-difficulty level includes that of lower-difficulty levels.

3.3 Results

Single-Objective Problems. Figure 6 presents the averaged results over 11 runs of the best objective function values and their standard errors at each point up to 1,000 function evaluations. In HPA101-0,1 and HPA102-0,1, algorithms such as TuRBO, GP-EI, and PSO demonstrated consistently high performance across a broad range. These algorithms are widely utilized in computationally expensive problems [27,32]. The effective application of algorithms incorporating GP models indicates that HPA problems likely exhibit smooth landscapes, as intended. Conversely, PSO, CMA-ES, and DE achieved favorable outcomes in HPA103-0,1, while GP-EI and TuRBO showed only moderate success. This suggests that these problems might pose challenges for surrogate model approximation. For problems at difficulty level $l = 2$, TuRBO, specifically designed for high-dimensional problems, generally outperformed others, with DE following.

To validate the moderate multimodality of the HPA problems, we generated fitness-distance scatter plots [22] for each problem, as shown in Fig. 7, using all solutions. The vertical axis represents the difference between the normalized objective function value of each solution and that of the best solution, while the horizontal axis shows the normalized distance between each solution and the best

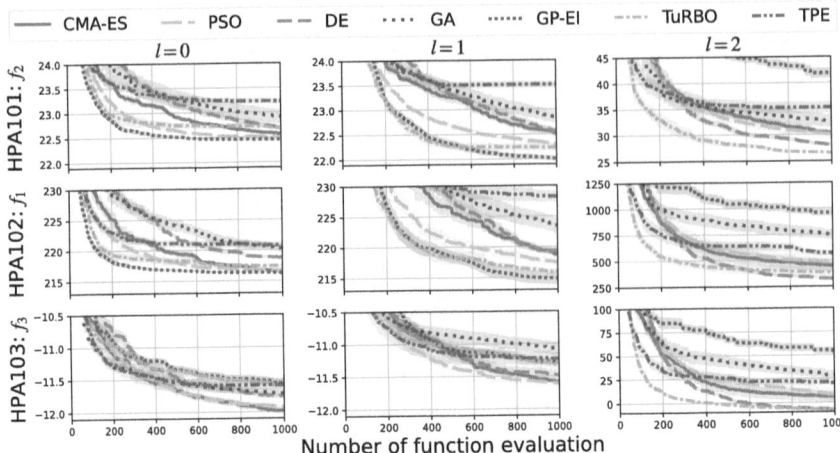

Fig. 6. Histories of mean objective function values and standard errors in the single-objective HPA problems.

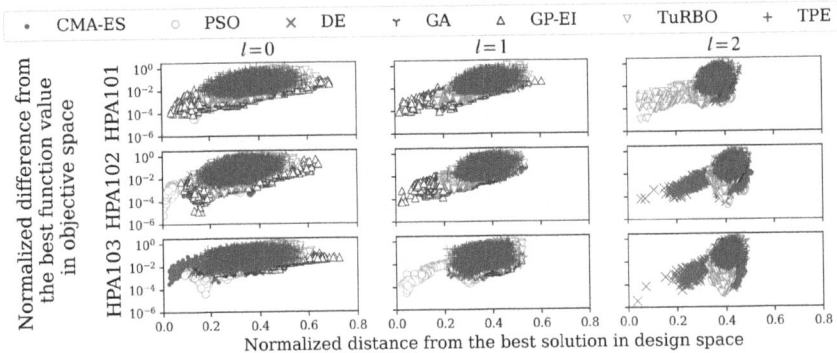

Fig. 7. Fitness-distance scatter plots for the single-objective HPA problems.

solution. The results reveal that each HPA problem exhibits a large global valley but also contains multiple local optima. Specifically, HPA101-0,1, HPA102-0,1, and HPA103-0 present relatively simple structures, whereas the problems with $l = 2$ and HPA103-1 have many local optima or deceptive structures.

Multi-objective Problems. Table 3 presents the comparison results of the mean IGD$^+$ for each benchmark problem. For HPA problems, Table 4 also shows the geometric mean of mean IGD$^+$ across problems categorized by their M and l. AGE-MOEA-II achieves the smallest IGD$^+$ across 17 HPA problems, including 14 many-objective problems. It also shows comparable performance with no significant difference from the best across 18 problems. NSGA-II (smallest IGD$^+$ across 13 problems) and SMS-EMOA (smallest IGD$^+$ across 11 prob-

Table 3. Comparison of mean IGD$^+$ across 11 runs. Values separated by '/' indicate: the number of problems with the best mean IGD$^+$, those with no significant difference (Wilcoxon rank-sum test, $p = 0.05$) from the best, and the total number of problems. The best algorithm (sum of a and b in '$a/b/c$') for each problem set is in bold.

Problem	M	NSGA-II	NSGA-III	MOEA/D	SMS-EMOA	RVEA	AGE-MOEA-II
HPA	2	**8/6/15**	1/2/15	0/1/15	2/6/15	3/2/15	1/12/15
HPA	3	3/5/15	1/3/15	0/0/15	**9/4/15**	0/1/15	2/3/15
HPA	4-9	2/3/21	3/6/21	0/0/21	0/1/21	2/0/21	**14/3/21**
HPA	Total	13/14/51	5/11/51	0/1/51	11/11/51	5/3/51	**17/18/51**
RE	2	2/0/5	0/0/5	0/0/5	**3/0/5**	0/0/5	0/0/5
RE	3	2/0/7	**2/2/7**	0/0/7	2/0/7	0/0/7	1/0/7
RE	4-9	0/0/4	0/0/4	0/0/4	**2/0/4**	0/0/4	2/0/4
RE	Total	4/0/16	2/2/16	0/0/16	**7/0/16**	0/0/16	3/0/16
DTLZ	2	**3/1/7**	0/3/7	2/0/7	1/1/7	1/0/7	0/3/7
DTLZ	3	2/0/7	**3/0/7**	0/1/7	1/1/7	0/2/7	1/1/7
DTLZ	6	0/0/7	1/0/7	2/1/7	0/0/7	**3/1/7**	1/0/7
DTLZ	Total	5/1/21	**4/3/21**	4/2/21	2/2/21	**4/3/21**	2/4/21
Minus-DTLZ	2	**4/0/7**	0/0/7	0/0/7	2/0/7	0/0/7	1/1/7
Minus-DTLZ	3	**4/0/7**	1/1/7	0/0/7	1/0/7	0/0/7	1/1/7
Minus-DTLZ	6	**4/1/7**	0/0/7	1/0/7	0/0/7	1/1/7	1/1/7
Minus-DTLZ	Total	**12/1/21**	1/1/21	1/0/21	3/0/21	1/1/21	3/3/21

Table 4. Geometric mean of mean IGD$^+$ and mean evaluation time per solution in HPA problems. The smallest IGD$^+$ in each problem set is highlighted in bold.

M	l	NSGA-II	NSGA-III	MOEA/D	SMS-EMOA	RVEA	AGE-MOEA-II	Time [s]
2	0	**0.01863**	0.02785	0.05085	0.02201	0.03101	0.02108	0.12108
2	1	**0.02957**	0.04429	0.11759	0.03294	0.04911	0.03351	0.12228
2	2	**0.21735**	0.25177	0.31389	0.23509	0.27890	0.22171	0.03230
3	0	0.01400	0.01471	0.03950	**0.01019**	0.02526	0.01464	0.12073
3	1	0.02031	0.01949	0.08164	**0.01234**	0.03362	0.01888	0.12191
3	2	**0.09508**	0.10224	0.21946	0.09585	0.17314	0.10319	0.03200
4-9	0	0.03078	0.02168	0.05425	0.02649	0.03630	**0.01947**	0.12860
4-9	1	0.04746	0.03094	0.10488	0.03458	0.04864	**0.02765**	0.13146
4-9	2	0.11569	0.12582	0.32590	0.16379	0.20113	**0.10993**	0.03356

lems) exhibit superior performance in two and three-objective problems, respectively. On the other hand, MOEA/D exhibits the largest IGD$^+$ in most HPA problems although objective function normalization was employed. RVEA also shows modest performance while it achieves the smallest IGD$^+$ across 5 HPA problems.

In real-world-inspired RE problems, SMS-EMOA, NSGA-II, and AGE-MOEA-II achieve favorable results as observed in the HPA problems, suggesting certain similarities between the two test suites. However, noticeable differences exist in the algorithm rankings within each problem set. Since RE problems tend to converge more easily to the PF, algorithms emphasizing diversity preservation over convergence demonstrate better performance. These algorithms also exhibit

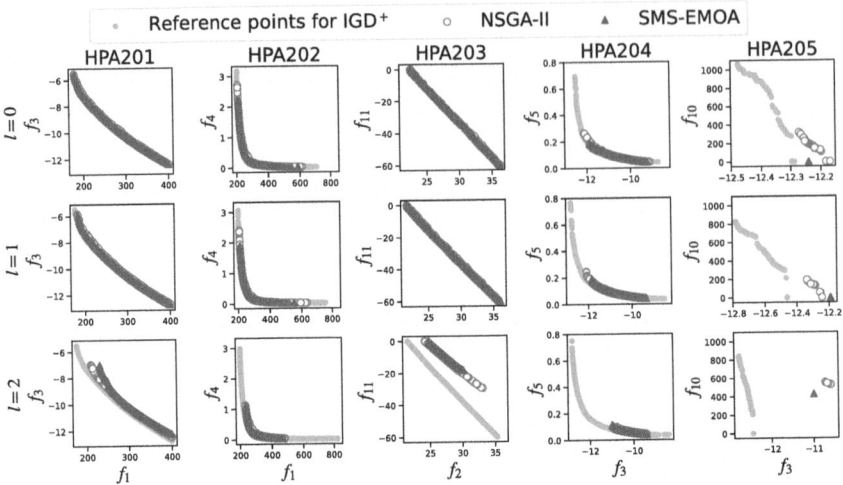

Fig. 8. NDSs at the median IGD$^+$ runs in the two-objective HPA problems.

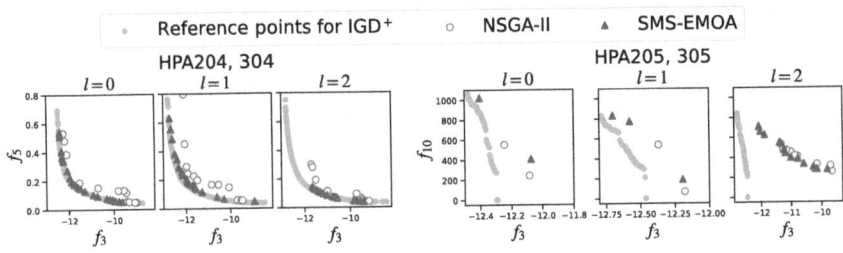

Fig. 9. NDSs at the median IGD$^+$ runs in HPA304 and 305, projected into corresponding two-objective problems.

superior performance in Minus-DTLZ problems. However, unlike the HPA and RE problems, NSGA-II consistently outperforms the other algorithms regardless of the number of objectives. DTLZ problems, on the other hand, show trends distinct from those observed in the HPA, RE, and Minus-DTLZ problems. In the DTLZ problems, NSGA-III, RVEA, and MOEA/D, which perform moderately in the other test suites, achieve strong performance. Conversely, AGE-MOEA-II and SMS-EMOA, which excel in the HPA problems, do not demonstrate superior performance in the DTLZ problems. This highlights the unique characteristics of the HPA problems compared to conventional benchmark problems.

In HPA problems, the IGD$^+$ values for $l = 2$ are significantly higher than for $l = 1$. Despite both $l = 1$ and $l = 2$ problems having nearly identical PFs, as shown in Fig. 5, it suggests that the six algorithms did not obtain well-converged and diverse NDSs for the $l = 2$ problems due to their high dimensionality. Figure 8 shows NDSs obtained by NSGA-II and SMS-EMOA at the median IGD$^+$ runs in the two-objective problems for each difficulty level. Both convergence and diversity are not sufficient for the $l = 2$ problems.

Additionally, HPA204 and 205 are hard to optimize even for $l = 0, 1$ especially near the extreme solution for f_3 because solutions around the f_3 minimum have different features in design variables from those mapping to other regions of the PF. Such solutions were easily obtained by extending the number of objective functions from HPA204 to HPA304 and from HPA205 to HPA305. Figure 9 shows NDSs for HPA204 and 205 obtained by NSGA-II and SMS-EMOA at the median IGD^+ runs in HPA304 and 305, respectively. Solving two-objective problems as if they were three-objective problems, similar to the approach of transforming a single-objective problem into a multi-objective one as discussed in [25], improves the diversity of NDSs as compared to the case shown in Fig. 8.

Table 4 also includes the mean evaluation time of objective functions when generating 1,000 random solutions for each problem. The CPU used for calculations was an AMD Ryzen 5 3400G 3.70GHz. In all problems, the evaluation time per solution is within 0.15 s, and 10,000 solutions can be evaluated within 25 min. For problems with $l = 0, 1$, where multiple strength evaluations are performed during the flange laminate optimization, the evaluation time is approximately four times longer than that of $l = 2$ problems.

4   Conclusion

We proposed a set of single and multi-objective optimization benchmark problems focusing on the design of human-powered aircraft. Each problem can be adjusted across three difficulty levels by modifying the definition of the design variables, and the problem dimensionality can be further increased or decreased through a wing segmentation parameter. While the original benchmark problems include constraints, we also defined unconstrained versions using penalty methods. In the multi-objective problems, the Pareto fronts display diverse shapes, including the inverted triangle commonly observed in real-world problems. By applying representative evolutionary algorithms and Bayesian optimization methods to these benchmark problems, we confirmed that they likely exhibit moderate multimodality, a typical feature of engineering design problems. Moreover, existing algorithms rarely produce well-converged and diverse non-dominated solutions at the highest difficulty level. Regarding evaluation time, each solution can be evaluated in under 0.15 s, making the suite suitable for benchmarking multiple algorithms over tens of thousands of function evaluations.

Disclosure of Interests. The authors have no competing interests to declare that are relevant to the content of this article.

References

1. Akiba, T., Sano, S., Yanase, T., Ohta, T., Koyama, M.: Optuna: a next-generation hyperparameter optimization framework. In: ACM SIGKDD International Conference on Knowledge Discovery and Data Mining, pp. 2623–2631 (2019)
2. Balandat, M., et al.: BoTorch: a framework for efficient Monte-Carlo Bayesian optimization. In: Advances in Neural Information Processing Systems, vol. 33, pp. 21524–21538 (2020)
3. Bergstra, J., Bardenet, R., Bengio, Y., Kégl, B.: Algorithms for hyper-parameter optimization. In: Advances in Neural Information Processing Systems, vol. 24 (2011)
4. Beume, N., Naujoks, B., Emmerich, M.: SMS-EMOA: multiobjective selection based on dominated hypervolume. Eur. J. Oper. Res. **181**(3), 1653–1669 (2007)
5. Blank, J., Deb, K.: Pymoo: multi-objective optimization in python. IEEE Access **8**, 89497–89509 (2020)
6. Bons, N.P., He, X., Mader, C.A., Martins, J.R.: Multimodality in aerodynamic wing design optimization. AIAA J. **57**(3), 1004–1018 (2019)
7. Cheng, R., Jin, Y., Olhofer, M., Sendhoff, B.: A reference vector guided evolutionary algorithm for many-objective optimization. IEEE Trans. Evol. Comput. **20**(5), 773–791 (2016)
8. Chernukhin, O., Zingg, D.W.: Multimodality and global optimization in aerodynamic design. AIAA J. **51**(6), 1342–1354 (2013)
9. Daniels, S.J., Rahat, A.A.M., Everson, R.M., Tabor, G.R., Fieldsend, J.E.: A suite of computationally expensive shape optimisation problems using computational fluid dynamics. In: Auger, A., Fonseca, C.M., Lourenço, N., Machado, P., Paquete, L., Whitley, D. (eds.) PPSN 2018. LNCS, vol. 11102, pp. 296–307. Springer, Cham (2018). https://doi.org/10.1007/978-3-319-99259-4_24
10. Deb, K., Jain, H.: An evolutionary many-objective optimization algorithm using reference-point-based nondominated sorting approach, part I: solving problems with box constraint. IEEE Trans. Evol. Comput. **18**(4), 577–601 (2014)
11. Deb, K., Thiele, L., Laumanns, M., Zitzler, E.: Scalable multi-objective optimization test problems. In: IEEE Congress on Evolutionary Computation, vol. 1, pp. 825–830 vol. 1 (2002)
12. Deb, K., Pratap, A., Agarwal, S., Meyarivan, T.: A fast and elitist multiobjective genetic algorithm: NSGA-II. IEEE Trans. Evol. Comput. **6**(2), 182–197 (2002)
13. Drela, M.: XFOIL: an analysis and design system for low Reynolds number airfoils. In: Mueller, T.J. (ed.) Low Reynolds Number Aerodynamics, pp. 1–12. Springer, Berlin, Heidelberg (1989)
14. Eriksson, D., Pearce, M., Gardner, J., Turner, R.D., Poloczek, M.: Scalable global optimization via local Bayesian optimization. In: Advances in Neural Information Processing Systems, vol. 32 (2019)
15. Hansen, N., Ostermeier, A.: Completely derandomized self-adaptation in evolution strategies. Evol. Comput. **9**(2), 159–195 (2001)
16. Hardin, D.P., Saff, E.B.: Minimal Riesz energy point configurations for rectifiable D-dimensional manifolds. Adv. Math. **193**(1), 174–204 (2005)
17. He, C., Tian, Y., Wang, H., Jin, Y.: A repository of real-world datasets for data-driven evolutionary multiobjective optimization. Complex Intell. Syst. **6**(1), 189–197 (2020)

18. He, L., Nan, Y., Ishibuchi, H., Srinivasan, D.: Effects of objective space normalization in multi-objective evolutionary algorithms on real-world problems. In: Genetic and Evolutionary Computation Conference, pp. 670–678 (2023)
19. Ishibuchi, H., He, L., Shang, K.: Regular Pareto front shape is not realistic. In: IEEE Congress on Evolutionary Computation, pp. 2034–2041 (2019)
20. Ishibuchi, H., Masuda, H., Tanigaki, Y., Nojima, Y.: Modified distance calculation in generational distance and inverted generational distance. In: Gaspar-Cunha, A., Henggeler Antunes, C., Coello, C.C. (eds.) EMO 2015. LNCS, vol. 9019, pp. 110–125. Springer, Cham (2015). https://doi.org/10.1007/978-3-319-15892-1_8
21. Ishibuchi, H., Setoguchi, Y., Masuda, H., Nojima, Y.: Performance of decomposition-based many-objective algorithms strongly depends on Pareto front shapes. IEEE Trans. Evol. Comput. 21(2), 169–190 (2016)
22. Jones, T., Forrest, S., et al.: Fitness distance correlation as a measure of problem difficulty for genetic algorithms. In: International Conference on Genetic Algorithms, vol. 95, pp. 184–192 (1995)
23. Kanazaki, M., Matsuno, T., Maeda, K., Kawazoe, H.: Wind tunnel evaluation-based optimization for improvement of flow control by plasma actuator using Kriging model-based genetic algorithm. In: IEEE Congress on Evolutionary Computation, pp. 2564–2571. IEEE (2013)
24. Khurana, M., Winarto, H., Sinha, A.: Airfoil optimisation by swarm algorithm with mutation and artificial neural networks. In: AIAA Aerospace Sciences Meeting, p. 1278 (2009)
25. Knowles, J.D., Watson, R.A., Corne, D.W.: Reducing local optima in single-objective problems by multi-objectivization. In: Zitzler, E., Thiele, L., Deb, K., Coello Coello, C.A., Corne, D. (eds.) EMO 2001. LNCS, vol. 1993, pp. 269–283. Springer, Heidelberg (2001). https://doi.org/10.1007/3-540-44719-9_19
26. Li, X., Tang, K., Omidvar, M.N., Yang, Z., Qin, K., China, H.: Benchmark functions for the CEC 2013 special session and competition on large-scale global optimization. Gene 7(33), 8 (2013)
27. Namura, N., Shimoyama, K., Obayashi, S., Ito, Y., Koike, S., Nakakita, K.: Multipoint design optimization of vortex generators on transonic swept wings. J. Aircr. 56(4), 1291–1302 (2019)
28. Pang, L.M., Ishibuchi, H., Shang, K.: Analysis of algorithm comparison results on real-world multi-objective problems. In: IEEE Congress on Evolutionary Computation, pp. 1–9 (2024)
29. Panichella, A.: An improved Pareto front modeling algorithm for large-scale many-objective optimization. In: Genetic and Evolutionary Computation Conference, pp. 565–573 (2022)
30. Sakata, S., Ashida, F., Zako, M.: Structural optimization using Kriging approximation. Comput. Methods Appl. Mech. Eng. 192(7–8), 923–939 (2003)
31. Schäpermeier, L., Kerschke, P., Grimme, C., Trautmann, H.: Peak-a-boo! generating multi-objective multiple peaks benchmark problems with precise Pareto sets. In: Emmerich, M., et al. (eds.) EMO 2023, pp. 291–304. Springer, Cham (2023)
32. Sun, C., Jin, Y., Cheng, R., Ding, J., Zeng, J.: Surrogate-assisted cooperative swarm optimization of high-dimensional expensive problems. IEEE Trans. Evol. Comput. 21(4), 644–660 (2017)
33. Tanabe, R., Ishibuchi, H.: An easy-to-use real-world multi-objective optimization problem suite. Appl. Soft Comput. 89, 106078 (2020)
34. Volz, V., Naujoks, B., Kerschke, P., Tušar, T.: Single-and multi-objective game-benchmark for evolutionary algorithms. In: Genetic and Evolutionary Computation Conference, pp. 647–655 (2019)

35. Wang, Z., Gehring, C., Kohli, P., Jegelka, S.: Batched large-scale Bayesian optimization in high-dimensional spaces. In: International Conference on Artificial Intelligence and Statistics, pp. 745–754. PMLR (2018)
36. Yazdani, D., Omidvar, M.N., Yazdani, D., Deb, K., Gandomi, A.H.: GNBG: a generalized and configurable benchmark generator for continuous numerical optimization. arXiv preprint arXiv:2312.07083 (2023)
37. Zapotecas-Martínez, S., García-Nájera, A., Menchaca-Méndez, A.: Engineering applications of multi-objective evolutionary algorithms: a test suite of box-constrained real-world problems. Eng. Appl. Artif. Intell. **123**, 106192 (2023)
38. Zhang, Q., Li, H.: MOEA/D: a multiobjective evolutionary algorithm based on decomposition. IEEE Trans. Evol. Comput. **11**(6), 712–731 (2007)
39. Zitzler, E., Deb, K., Thiele, L.: Comparison of multiobjective evolutionary algorithms: empirical results. Evol. Comput. **8**(2), 173–195 (2000)
40. Zuhal, L.R., Palar, P.S., Shimoyama, K.: A comparative study of multi-objective expected improvement for aerodynamic design. Aerosp. Sci. Technol. **91**, 548–560 (2019)

An Extension of the Welded Beam Problem that Includes Multiple Interacting Design Concepts

Angus Kenny$^{(\boxtimes)}$ ⓘ, Tapabrata Ray ⓘ, and Hemant Kumar Singh ⓘ

University of New South Wales, Canberra, Australia
{angus.kenny,t.ray,hemant.singh}@unsw.edu.au

Abstract. Multi-objective multi-concept (MOMC) problems address the simultaneous optimization of diverse design concepts to identify solutions that are optimal for the objectives across all concepts. This paper presents a MOMC formulation of the classic welded beam problem, updated with contemporary cost estimates and metric units. Unlike the original model, which assumes a fixed cross-section, the proposed formulation incorporates multiple design concepts, each featuring distinct cross-sectional geometries and corresponding design variables. The formulation is validated through comparison with existing welded beam problem formulations, and an in-depth analysis of the objective space is conducted for both individual concepts and the combined multi-concept case. Baseline results are presented using two evolutionary algorithms—NSGA-II and IDEA—applied to each design concept separately. Their effectiveness on the multi-concept problem was also evaluated by merging the results from each individual concept. Both algorithms successfully identified near-optimal solutions for the individual concepts; however, their performance declined for the multi-concept case, especially under limited computational budgets. These findings highlight the unique complexities inherent in MOMC problems and emphasize the need for more dedicated optimization approaches to address this class of problems.

Keywords: Multi-objective optimization · multi-concept optimization · evolutionary algorithms

1 Introduction and Related Work

Engineering design processes can be decomposed into several critical stages: problem definition, conceptual design, preliminary design, and detailed design [7]. During the conceptual design phase, engineers develop multiple solutions that address the defined requirements. These concepts often vary significantly in form or function (or both), applying different scientific principles

Supplementary Information The online version contains supplementary material available at https://doi.org/10.1007/978-981-96-3506-1_15.

to achieve the same desired outcomes. Decisions made during this stage can significantly influence the final product's configuration and performance [10]. Therefore, effective exploration of multiple competing concepts is essential, as early commitment to a single concept can lead to long-term compromises and increased lifecycle costs, potentially accounting for up to 70% of the total expenditure [5]. Numerous case studies demonstrate the practical importance of evaluating diverse concepts across various engineering domains, such as naval architecture [11], powertrain design [10], structural engineering [16], and acoustics [9].

However, optimizing across multiple concepts simultaneously presents substantial challenges [12]. Each concept may involve a different number and type of design variables, complicating the comparison and combination of solutions across these decision spaces. Additionally, the necessity to evaluate solutions using a uniform set of criteria, irrespective of their originating concept, adds another layer of complexity. This uniform evaluation becomes particularly difficult when Pareto fronts of various concepts overlap, resulting in scenarios where a solution which is Pareto optimal within its own concept is dominated by solutions from other concepts in the overall objective space. The limited computational budget of many engineering design optimization problems exacerbates these challenges, making exhaustive exploration of each concept's design space impractical due to the high costs associated with numerical simulations and/or physical experiments [21,23].

Despite the potential utility of methods to solve multi-objective multi-concept (MOMC) problems in engineering and design contexts, the topic has received relatively scarce attention. Existing optimization approaches are typically built for a fixed model, rendering them more suitable for later design stages and neglecting the potential benefits of early multi-concept exploration. Recent studies have begun to address MOMC problems, highlighting the need for advanced evolutionary algorithms capable of efficiently and concurrently navigating the search landscapes of multiple concepts. There may be various scenarios in terms of relative positions of the Pareto fronts for individual concepts [1,2,15,21]. Except for the unlikely case where each individual Pareto front is entirely non-dominated to all others, we refer to the scenario as 'interacting' Pareto fronts for brevity. Earlier studies [16] introduced a concept selection framework for multi-objective problems by applying the idea of s-Pareto frontiers combined with normal constraint methods. Subsequent studies have focused on developing additional case studies [15,21] and evaluating the effectiveness of various evolutionary optimization techniques specifically designed for MOMC problems [1,19–21].

Due to the relatively nascent stage of this field of research, there are not many explicitly formulated practical problems in the literature which comprise multiple design concepts with interacting Pareto fronts, to aid in the development of algorithms to tackle this class of problems. Towards addressing this gap, this paper presents a multi-concept adaptation of the well-studied practical problem of welded beam design [22]. In the traditional formulation of this constrained, multi-objective problem, a beam with a rectangular cross-section is affixed to a wall using two 45° fillet welds, subjected to a load at its free end. The objective is to minimize the deflection and the cost of producing the beam.

While the original formulation of the problem assumes the beam to have a solid, rectangular cross section, this paper proposes a MOMC variant, called the multi-concept welded beam (MCWB) problem, which allows for multiple cross-section geometries. The new formulation is validated against existing implementations, and a detailed analysis of the objective space for each design concept is provided to demonstrate their individual behaviours, along with a description of how their Pareto fronts interact with each other when combined. Recognizing that the original formulation dates back to 1976, with constant factors (including material/labor costs) based on estimates from over half a century ago, this extension also updates the problem for modern times by adopting metric units and more contemporary cost estimates.

To provide baseline results for the newly formulated MCWB problem, two algorithms are applied: the non-dominated sorting algorithm (NSGA-II) [6]; and, the infeasibility driven evolutionary algorithm (IDEA) [24], which employs enhanced constraint handling. These are applied to each new beam design concept formulation, with a variety of population sizes and generation settings to explore their performance across different computational budgets. The experimental results demonstrate that while each design concept exhibits an objective landscape similar in shape to the original problem, their behaviours are sufficiently distinct to warrant their use as standalone test problems—expanding the repertoire of problems available for testing and developing multi-objective optimization algorithms based on real-world scenarios. Finally, the best solutions obtained for the individual design concepts are combined to produce naive solutions to the MOMC formulation. This demonstrates the complexities that emerge when multiple design concepts are considered simultaneously, highlighting the need for more nuanced, and dedicated, approaches to solve this class of problem.

2   Multi-concept Welded Beam Problem (MCWB)

First formulated by Ragsdell [22] in 1976, the welded beam problem is a well-studied test case in constrained, single and multi-objective design optimization. Several formulations of this problem have been widely used in the literature and are implemented in optimization toolboxes such as Pymoo [3] and PlatEMO [25]. However, these implementations assume that the beam has a fixed rectangular cross-section. In contrast, the multi-concept welded beam (MCWB) problem presented in this paper[1] does not make this assumption. Instead, it allows for five different beam design concepts, with a variety of geometries. This provides both a test problem for multi-concept algorithms, and a new set of variations on the

---

[1] Python source code—using the Pymoo optimization framework—provided in the supplementary materials for this paper, or available at: https://www.mdolab.net/Ray/Research-Data/mcwb_problem.zip.

welded beam problem—with differently shaped objective spaces—for standard multi-objective search algorithms.

2.1   Multi-concept Problem Formulation

Figure 1 illustrates the problem as originally formulated by Ragsdell [22]. In this problem, a beam with width b, height h, and length L is secured to a vertical wall by two 45° fillet welds located at the top and bottom of the beam. These welds have a height a and a length l. The weld length l is a variable in the optimization, while the section of the beam under consideration has a fixed length L measured from the end of the weld, resulting in a total beam length of $l + L$. The beam is considered to be cantilevered from the end of the weld, so its effective length for deflection and stress calculations is L.

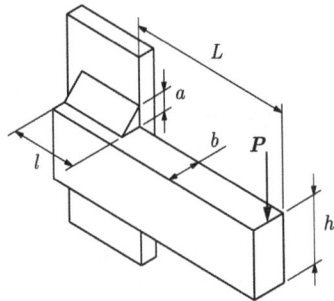

Fig. 1. Original Ragsdell formulation [22] of the welded beam problem.

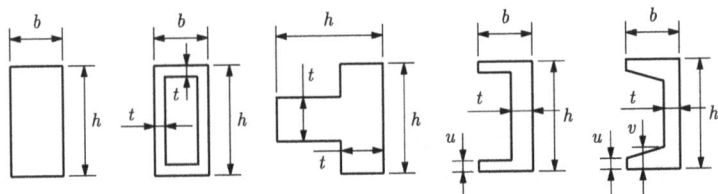

Fig. 2. Additional welded beam design concepts (left to right) SolidRectangular, HollowRectangular, EquilateralTBeam, SquareChannel, TaperedChannel.

The problem has two primary objectives: minimizing the total cost of the beam-including both the material cost of the beam and the welding costs, and minimizing the deflection of the beam under an applied point load P acting at the end of the beam. In the original formulation, the load is placed at the center of the beam's cross-section. However, in this multi-concept variant, some design concepts involve more complex and asymmetrical cross-sectional geometries. Therefore, it is assumed that the load passes through the shear center of the beam to avoid twisting of the cross-section.

Complementary to the solid rectangular beam cross-section defined in the original problem formulation, four additional design concepts are included in this multi-concept adaptation. These design concepts, illustrated in Fig. 2 (from left to right), are: SolidRectangular, HollowRectangular, EquilateralTBeam, SquareChannel, and TaperedChannel. The SolidRectangular design concept is analogous to the original formulation. The additional concepts introduce varying levels of complexity to the problem and are defined using 2–5 design variables. Each design concept has its own formula for calculating the cross-sectional area A_s and the second moment of area I_{xx}. They also require different calculations for the constraints g_4 to g_7, which are specific to the geometry of each design concept. Detailed formulations for each design concept, including the specific equations and constraints, are provided in Appendix C of the supplementary materials.

Generalized Formulation: In its general form, the problem can be formulated as a multi-objective optimization problem with two objectives, f_1 and f_2, to be minimized, subject to a set of constraints $g_i \leq 0$ for $i = 1, \ldots, 7$:

$$\text{minimize} \quad f_1, f_2,$$
$$\text{subject to} \quad g_i \leq 0, \quad i = 1, \ldots, 7. \tag{1}$$

Since the different design concepts are defined by their respective beam cross-sections, it is necessary to reformulate the original problem in terms of the beam cross-sectional properties. The objectives can be expressed in terms of the cross-sectional area of the beam A_s and the second moment of area I_{xx} along the bending (neutral) axis. The first objective, f_1, is the total cost of the beam, including both the cost of welding and the material cost of the beam itself:

$$f_1 = C_w \cdot a^2 \cdot l + C_b \cdot A_s \cdot (l + L), \tag{2}$$

where C_w and C_b are constants representing the cost factors of the weld and the beam, respectively, and L is the fixed length of the beam. The second objective, f_2, is the deflection of the cantilevered beam under the applied load P:

$$f_2 = \frac{PL^3}{3EI_{xx}}, \tag{3}$$

where E is the Young's modulus of the beam material.

Constraints g_1, g_2, and g_3 represent the shear stress constraint of the weld, the axial stress constraint of the weld, and the buckling stress constraint of the beam, respectively. These constraints are analogous to constraints ϕ_1, ϕ_2, and ϕ_6 in Ragsdell's original formulation [22]. Constraint g_4 is a geometric constraint for the weld, ensuring that the height of the weld does not exceed the dimensions of the beam at the weld point. In the original formulation, this corresponds to constraint ϕ_3. However, since different design concepts may have varying geometries, this is left as a general constraint, and defined specifically for each design concept. Constraints g_5, g_6, and g_7 are geometric constraints for the beam cross-sections in the different design concepts. These constraints ensure that the design variables define a feasible beam cross-section for the more complex design concepts. The full formulation of the problem, including all specific equations and constraints for each design concept, is provided in Appendices B and C of the supplementary materials. In cases where a constraint is not applicable to a given design concept, a "dummy" constraint is used, with a value of zero (i.e., always satisfied).

Updated Problem Constant Factors and Bounds: The original welded beam problem uses estimates of material and labor costs from nearly half a century ago. Reformulating it as a multi-concept optimization problem presents an opportunity to update these estimates to reflect current values and to convert the units from imperial to metric. It is important to note that the updated values are not simply direct conversions from the original constants into metric units; the original problem used rounded values to simplify its formulation, and a similar philosophy has been adopted here. The original constants and their updated values are listed in Table 1 of Appendix A of the supplementary materials.

2.2   Validating the Formulation

This new MOMC formulation of the welded beam problem was validated by performing a comparative analysis of it against existing formulations—available in the Pymoo [3] and PlatEMO [25] optimization toolboxes—using the original bounds and constants. Due to space constraints, the details of this comparison are presented in Appendix E of the supplementary materials.

2.3   Objective Space Analysis

Figure 3 illustrates the objective space for each individual design concept in the multi-concept welded beam (MCWB) problem. These plots were generated by evaluating 10^7 solutions randomly sampled using Latin hypercube sampling [17]. Feasible solutions are plotted in blue, while infeasible solutions are plotted in red. The approximated Pareto front is represented by a dashed black line (Appendix D of the supplementary material details how the fronts were approximated). The figure is organized into three rows for each design concept. The top row demonstrates the shape of the entire objective space, providing a broad overview of the solution landscape. The axis limits for the middle row are chosen to clearly illustrate the entire feasible region, and the bottom row zooms in further to highlight the region of interest around the approximated Pareto front.

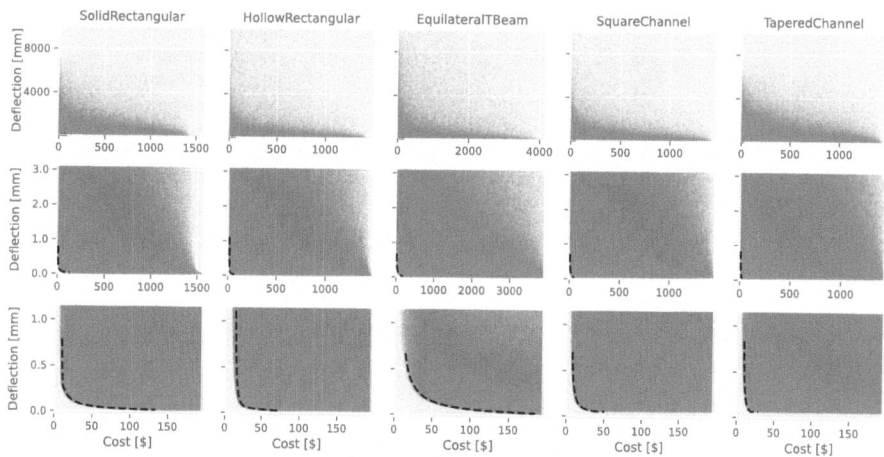

Fig. 3. Objective space visualization for individual concepts (left to right). Black dashed line indicates the approximated Pareto front, blue and red points denote feasible and infeasible solutions, respectively. Y-axis limits for the top row are illustrative of the full objective space, middle row limits show the feasible regions, bottom row limits show the region of interest around the approximated Pareto front. (Color figure online)

The plots reveal that the objective spaces for all design concepts have similar shapes, with the exception of the EquilateralTBeam. This deviation can be explained by its slightly wider variable bounds, which allow for a broader range of possible designs. The plots also show that the variable bounds can generate solutions that are very far from the feasible region, indicating that a significant portion of the decision space maps to infeasible solutions. Examining the feasible regions, all concepts exhibit similar shapes—again, with the exception of the EquilateralTBeam. For this design concept, while the range of deflection values is similar to the others, there is a much longer tail for the cost objective. This extended tail results from the wider variable bounds.

In most cases, the approximated Pareto fronts for the beam design concepts exhibit a distinctive 'L' shape, characterized by a sharp bend and a long tail extending in the direction of at least one objective. The distribution of feasible solutions is very sparse around the approximated Pareto front for all concepts, suggesting that it is difficult to randomly sample high-quality solutions, particularly in the direction of the cost objective. Furthermore, the tails of the approximated fronts appear truncated in the cost objective direction, implying that this objective likely contains many dominance-resistant solutions.

The overlapping nature of the feasible and infeasible regions for the plots in Fig. 3 support the findings in [18]. In their paper, Nan et al. demonstrated that multi-objective optimization problems found in real-world scenarios often have complex interactions between feasible and infeasible regions in the objective space. Typically, this is due to the lack of a one-to-one mapping between the

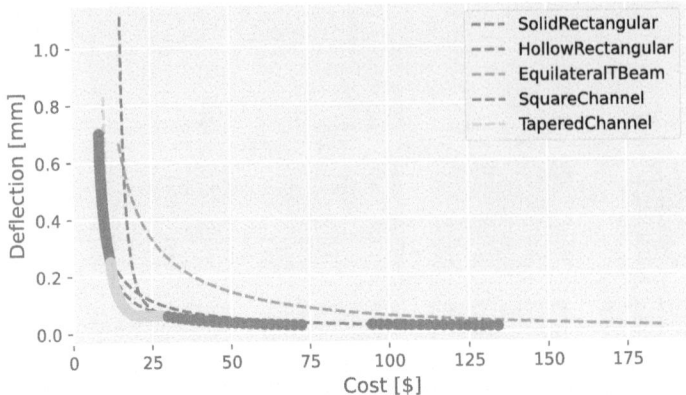

Fig. 4. Approximated Pareto front of all design concepts in the MCWB problem.

decision and objective spaces and results in an overlap between the feasible and infeasible regions. This is in contrast to artificially constructed multi-objective constrained test problems, which often have infeasible and feasible regions in discrete blocks with no overlap between them [8,13]. While such an approach simplifies the construction and analysis of test problems, it is less representative of real-world situations and could result in a bias towards algorithms better suited to these types of problems.

The plots in Fig. 3 suggest that the formulated design concepts in the MCWB do not suffer from this oversimplification. Instead, they demonstrate behaviour more aligned with real-world problems, featuring overlapping feasible and infeasible regions and complex mappings between design variables and objectives. This makes the design concept formulations in MCWB a more realistic test case for multi-objective optimization algorithms.

Combining the Concepts: One of the main aspects that sets MOMC problem instances apart from typical multi-objective problem instances, is the interaction between different design concepts within the objective space. When multiple design concepts are combined, regions of the Pareto front associated with one design concept may dominate regions of the Pareto front associated with another. This means that a solution which is Pareto-optimal within its own design concept may not remain Pareto-optimal when all design concepts are considered together. As a result, the combined Pareto front can become more complex and composite, with different design concepts dominating different regions of the front, often leading to discontinuities.Figure 4 illustrates the combined approximated Pareto front for all design concepts in the MCWB problem (see Appendix D for details). In the plot, the approximated Pareto front for each design concept is represented with dashed lines, while the points on the combined front are plotted using colours corresponding to their respective design concepts. The plot shows that the SquareChannel design concept forms the left vertical region of the front, offering the lowest cost but with relatively high deflection. The TaperedChannel design concept provides solutions closest to the ideal point, balancing both objectives effectively, but in a relatively small region of the total front. The HollowRectangular concept offers slightly better deflection properties but at a higher cost compared to the TaperedChannel. The SolidRectangular design concept contributes solutions with the least deflection but at a significantly higher cost, occupying the extreme right of the front.

Notably, the approximated Pareto front for the combined MOMC formulation does not contain any solutions from the EquilateralTBeam design concept. This design concept was intentionally constructed with wider variable bounds and less competitive performance to discourage naive optimization approaches that allocate equal resources to all design concepts independently. In such cases, evaluating solutions from the EquilateralTBeam concept would be an inefficient use of the computational budget, as these solutions are dominated in the combined objective space. This approach promotes more sophisticated optimization strategies that consider all design concepts simultaneously, efficiently allocating resources to explore the most promising regions of the combined objective space.

3   Preliminary Numerical Experiments

To establish some baseline results to aid in the future development of more dedicated approaches, numerical experiments were conducted using two existing evolutionary algorithms (EAs): NSGA-II [6] and IDEA [24]. These are applied to each design concept under varying budget constraints, specified by adjusting the population size and the number of generations—both of which were a function of the number of design variables for each concept. The resulting non-dominated (ND) front obtained for each concept, in each experiment, was also combined to produce a single ND front for the MOMC formulation. This provides an initial evaluation of the algorithms' performance on the overall MCWB problem.

All experiments were implemented using the Pymoo Python framework [3], with default parameter settings for NSGA-II. The IDEA algorithm parameters were configured to NSGA-II; however, it introduces a distinctive mechanism during the survival stage, to better handle constrained problems. Specifically, IDEA allows a subset of infeasible solutions—in this case up to 15% of the total population size—to advance to the next generation as top-ranked candidates. This encourages the algorithm to explore promising areas of the search space around the boundaries between the feasible and infeasible regions.

Both algorithms were applied to each concept, with a population/generation combination of $5D/5D, 10D/5D, 10D/10D$, where D is the number of design variables for a given concept. To account for the stochastic nature of EAs, each experiment was replicated across 21 independent runs, with different random seeds. The performance of the algorithms were assessed using the hypervolume [26] (HV) and inverted generational distance (IGD) [4] indicators, reporting the mean and standard deviation over all runs. The indicators are computed in normalized objective space, using reference sets generated with the method described in Appendix D, shown in Fig. 4. The reference point for the HV indicator was set as (1.1,1.1). As the same set of random seeds were used for each experiment, the data is paired; therefore, the Mann-Whitney-Wilcoxon test [14] was used to assess the statistical significance of the observed differences, with a p-value threshold of less than 0.05 being indicative of significant results.

4   Results and Discussion

Tables 1 and 2 present a comparative analysis of the performance of NSGA-II and IDEA, detailing the mean and standard deviation for both HV and IGD. The data indicate that IDEA marginally outperforms NSGA-II—likely attributable to its constraint-handling mechanisms—however, the difference is not statistically significant in most cases. Furthermore, while both methods identify solutions along the approximated Pareto front for individual concepts, their effectiveness diminishes when the non-dominated (ND) fronts for each concept

Table 1. HV results for NSGA-II [6] and IDEA [24] with different parameter settings. Given are the mean and standard deviation obtained over 21 runs, along with the p-value for the MWW statistical test. Bold indicates winner of the pair, with underlined p-value denoting a statistically significant result ($p < 0.05$).

	NSGA-II	IDEA	p-value
Pop.: 5D, Gen.: 5D			
SolidRectangular	9.8890e-01 (±1.06e-01)	**1.0614e+00** (±7.20e-02)	0.005
HollowRectangular	1.0195e+00 (±6.40e-02)	**1.0339e+00** (±6.11e-02)	0.189
EquilateralTBeam	8.8772e-01 (±8.83e-02)	**9.2507e-01** (±7.07e-02)	0.036
SquareChannel	**1.0364e+00** (±4.57e-02)	1.0331e+00 (±6.02e-02)	0.869
TaperedChannel	8.9137e-01 (±1.83e-01)	**9.7336e-01** (±8.09e-02)	0.261
Combined concepts	1.1382e+00 (±1.08e-02)	**1.1440e+00** (±7.42e-03)	0.114
Pop.: 10D, Gen.: 5D			
SolidRectangular	**1.0837e+00** (±5.75e-02)	1.1064e+00 (±3.28e-02)	0.189
HollowRectangular	**1.0932e+00** (±2.93e-02)	1.0888e+00 (±2.84e-02)	0.596
EquilateralTBeam	9.9059e-01 (±6.15e-02)	**1.0134e+00** (±2.92e-02)	0.216
SquareChannel	1.0787e+00 (±2.29e-02)	**1.0893e+00** (±1.42e-02)	0.133
TaperedChannel	1.0368e+00 (±6.97e-02)	**1.0709e+00** (±2.82e-02)	0.245
Combined concepts	1.1509e+00 (±6.75e-03)	**1.1553e+00** (±3.30e-03)	0.090
Pop.: 10D, Gen.: 10D			
SolidRectangular	1.1198e+00 (±3.01e-02)	**1.1337e+00** (±1.58e-02)	0.165
HollowRectangular	**1.1252e+00** (±1.97e-02)	1.1144e+00 (±2.17e-02)	0.058
EquilateralTBeam	1.0309e+00 (±3.32e-02)	**1.0456e+00** (±1.86e-02)	0.123
SquareChannel	1.1077e+00 (±1.07e-02)	**1.1092e+00** (±6.94e-03)	0.812
TaperedChannel	1.1012e+00 (±3.74e-02)	**1.1086e+00** (±1.77e-02)	0.956
Combined concepts	1.1622e+00 (±2.73e-03)	**1.1630e+00** (±1.78e-03)	0.388

Table 2. IGD results for NSGA-II [6] and IDEA [24] with different parameter settings. Given are the mean and standard deviation obtained over 21 runs, along with the p-value for the MWW statistical test. Bold indicates winner of the pair, with underlined p-value denoting a statistically significant result ($p < 0.05$).

	NSGA-II	IDEA	p-value
Pop.: 5D, Gen.: 5D			
SolidRectangular	1.6025e-01 ($\pm$5.95e-02)	**1.3941e-01** ($\pm$3.96e-02)	0.177
HollowRectangular	1.9965e-01 ($\pm$6.38e-02)	**1.8047e-01** ($\pm$5.36e-02)	0.231
EquilateralTBeam	1.5114e-01 ($\pm$7.67e-02)	**1.2258e-01** ($\pm$5.65e-02)	0.143
SquareChannel	1.2672e-01 ($\pm$5.41e-02)	**1.1927e-01** ($\pm$5.92e-02)	0.648
TaperedChannel	2.1572e-01 ($\pm$1.38e-01)	**1.8141e-01** ($\pm$7.27e-02)	0.388
Combined concepts	7.2810e-02 ($\pm$4.55e-02)	**6.9019e-02** ($\pm$3.90e-02)	0.756
Pop.: 10D, Gen.: 5D			
SolidRectangular	1.3545e-01 ($\pm$4.77e-02)	**1.2856e-01** ($\pm$4.09e-02)	0.985
HollowRectangular	**1.2223e-01** ($\pm$5.04e-02)	1.4910e-01 ($\pm$6.72e-02)	0.114
EquilateralTBeam	9.0408e-02 ($\pm$5.06e-02)	**7.0004e-02** ($\pm$3.09e-02)	0.105
SquareChannel	7.5841e-02 ($\pm$4.57e-02)	**4.6163e-02** ($\pm$2.52e-02)	0.058
TaperedChannel	9.7095e-02 ($\pm$6.14e-02)	**7.9922e-02** ($\pm$4.16e-02)	0.475
Combined concepts	4.6435e-02 ($\pm$3.18e-02)	**3.3169e-02** ($\pm$2.08e-02)	0.202
Pop.: 10D, Gen.: 10D			
SolidRectangular	1.2573e-01 ($\pm$4.45e-02)	**1.0944e-01** ($\pm$4.13e-02)	0.189
HollowRectangular	**1.0784e-01** ($\pm$5.50e-02)	1.2378e-01 ($\pm$6.96e-02)	0.498
EquilateralTBeam	6.3812e-02 ($\pm$3.74e-02)	**4.0848e-02** ($\pm$2.81e-02)	0.070
SquareChannel	3.2672e-02 ($\pm$2.82e-02)	**1.9567e-02** ($\pm$1.16e-02)	0.097
TaperedChannel	5.0930e-02 ($\pm$3.94e-02)	**4.9515e-02** ($\pm$3.05e-02)	0.927
Combined concepts	2.1671e-02 ($\pm$1.58e-02)	**1.2975e-02** ($\pm$6.40e-03)	0.053

are aggregated into a single front. This decline in performance is particularly pronounced when the computational budget is limited.

These findings are supported by the plots in Fig. 5, which display the ND fronts for the median runs of HV and IGD for each algorithm. The plots have been scaled using the extremes of the approximated Pareto front for the full multi-concept welded beam (MCWB) problem, and offset to facilitate easier visual comparison. Across all parameter settings, the behaviour of NSGA-II and IDEA appears similar. In cases where the computational budget is highly restricted ($5D/5D$), the combined ND fronts exhibit a patchy distribution with substantial gaps, with solutions from different concepts intermingling within the same regions of the Pareto front. As the computational budget increases ($10D/5D$), the combined ND fronts begin to cover the approximated Pareto front more comprehensively, with more distinctly defined regions. When the budget is large ($10D/10D$), the combined ND fronts closely resemble the approximated Pareto front depicted in Fig. 4, indicating the budget is nearly sufficient to find the complete Pareto front for each concept individually, obviating the need for a sophisticated multi-concept optimization approach to achieve this in lower computational cost.

A key observation can be made by considering the distribution of smaller points within these plots, representing solutions within the ND fronts of each individual concept that do not contribute the to overall ND front, across concepts. In all cases, a significant portion of the search budget is consumed evaluating solutions that, despite being ND within their respective concepts, fail to feature in the final combined front. This is especially evident with the EquilateralTBeam concept, which has been designed so as to not contribute any solutions to the approximated Pareto front for the MCWB problem. Such observations highlight the complexity of this class of problems, and the need for more sophisticated approaches. Specifically, there is a need for methods which consider solutions across all concepts, filtering out those that may be high quality within the context of their own concepts, but not in the broader multi-concept landscape.

Additionally, the L-shaped nature of the Pareto front—characterized by a sharp bend and long tails—means that solutions towards the extremes are more likely to be dominated. This is apparent even in the $10D/10D$ case, and occurs because a very small change in the direction of one objective can represent a very large change in the other direction. This limitation demonstrates the need

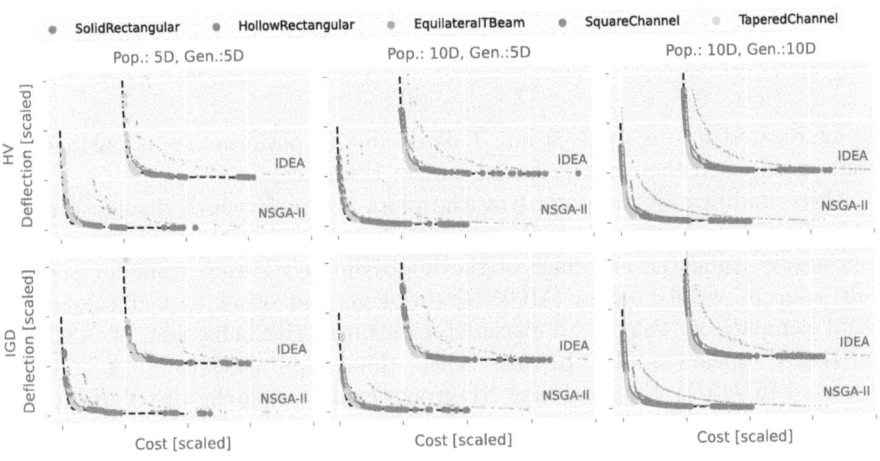

Fig. 5. Comparison of the resulting non-dominated (ND) fronts for median HV (top) and IGD (bottom) runs for NSGA-II and IDEA, with different parameter settings. Small points indicate the ND fronts obtained by solving each concept separately, with larger points denoting solutions which are ND over all concepts. The dashed line represents the approximated Pareto front of the full MCWB problem.

for improved strategies to manage solutions near the extremes, both in a single- and multi-concept context. This could be potentially be achieved through mechanisms such as scaling during dominance determination in the survival stage. Such approaches would allow marginally dominated solutions to progress to subsequent generations of the search.

5   Conclusion and Future Work

This paper introduced a multi-objective multi-concept (MOMC) formulation for the well-established welded beam problem, updating it to incorporate contemporary cost estimates and metric units. Unlike the original formulation, which assumes a fixed cross-section geometry for the beam, the proposed formulation accommodates multiple design concepts, each featuring distinct cross-sectional geometries and varying design variables.

The formulation was validated against existing formulations of the welded beam problem, and an analysis of the objective landscapes for each individual concept and the combined multi-concept case was conducted. Baseline performance was established for two EAs—NSGA-II and IDEA—to each design concept separately. Their performance on the full multi-concept problem was evaluated by naively combining the results from each individual concept. The comparative analysis indicated that both algorithms demonstrated reasonable success in identifying solutions along the Pareto front for individual concepts. However, their effectiveness diminished when the ND fronts of each concept were merged, particularly under limited computational budgets, as evidenced by the patchy distribution and overlapping solutions in the combined Pareto front.

These observations highlight the characteristic complexities of this class of problems. They also demonstrate the need for future work developing more sophisticated approaches which consider solutions from multiple concepts simultaneously during the search, and a method for managing solutions at the extremes of L-shaped Pareto fronts.

References

1. Avigad, G., Moshaiov, A.: Interactive evolutionary multiobjective search and optimization of set-based concepts. IEEE Trans. Syst. Man Cybern. Part B **39**(4), 1013–1027 (2009)
2. Avigad, G., Moshaiov, A.: Simultaneous concept-based evolutionary multiobjective optimization. Appl. Soft Comput. **11**(1), 193–207 (2011)
3. Blank, J., Deb, K.: pymoo: Multi-objective optimization in python. IEEE Access **8**, 89497–89509 (2020)
4. Coello Coello, C.A., Reyes Sierra, M.: A study of the parallelization of a coevolutionary multi-objective evolutionary algorithm. In: Monroy, R., Arroyo-Figueroa, G., Sucar, L.E., Sossa, H. (eds.) MICAI 2004. LNCS (LNAI), vol. 2972, pp. 688–697. Springer, Heidelberg (2004). https://doi.org/10.1007/978-3-540-24694-7_71

5. Corbett, J., Crookall, J.: Design for economic manufacture. CIRP Ann. **35**(1), 93–97 (1986)
6. Deb, K., Pratap, A., Agarwal, S., Meyarivan, T.: A fast and elitist multiobjective genetic algorithm: NSGA-II. IEEE Trans. Evol. Comput. **6**(2), 182–197 (2002)
7. Dym, C.L., Little, P., Orwin, E.: Engineering Design: A Project-Based Introduction. Wiley, New York (2013)
8. Fan, Z., et al.: An improved epsilon constraint-handling method in MOEA/D for CMOPs with large infeasible regions. Soft. Comput. **23**, 12491–12510 (2019)
9. Franklin, J.: Design and Testing of Lattice Structures for Noise Reduction. Ph.D. thesis, Worcester Polytechnic Institute (2022)
10. Georgiou, A., Haritos, G., Fowler, M., Imani, Y.: Advanced phase powertrain design attribute and technology value mapping. J. Eng. Des. Technol. **14**(1), 115–133 (2016)
11. Grubišić, I., Munić, I.: Multiple models in the multi-attribute concept design of fast ferries. In: International Design Conference (2006)
12. Kenny, A., Ray, T., Singh, H.: A framework for design optimization across multiple concepts. Sci. Rep. **14**(1), 7858 (2024)
13. Ma, Z., Wang, Y.: Evolutionary constrained multiobjective optimization: test suite construction and performance comparisons. IEEE Trans. Evol. Comput. **23**(6), 972–986 (2019)
14. Mann, H.B., Whitney, D.R.: On a test of whether one of two random variables is stochastically larger than the other. Ann. Math. Stat. 50–60 (1947)
15. Mattson, C., Mullur, A., Messac, A.: Case studies in concept exploration and selection with s-Pareto frontiers. Int. J. Prod. Dev. **9**(1–3), 32–59 (2009)
16. Mattson, C.A., Messac, A.: Concept selection using s-Pareto frontiers. AIAA J. **41**(6), 1190–1198 (2003)
17. McKay, M.D., Beckman, R.J., Conover, W.J.: A comparison of three methods for selecting values of input variables in the analysis of output from a computer code. Technometrics **42**(1), 55–61 (2000)
18. Nan, Y., Ishibuchi, H., Shu, T., Shang, K.: Analysis of real-world constrained multi-objective problems and performance comparison of multi-objective algorithms. In: Proceedings of the Genetic and Evolutionary Computation Conference, pp. 576-584. GECCO '24, Association for Computing Machinery, New York, NY, USA (2024)
19. Niloy, R.S., Singh, H.K., Ray, T.: A brief review of multi-concept multi-objective optimization problems. In: 2023 IEEE Symposium Series on Computational Intelligence (SSCI), pp. 1511–1517 (2023)
20. Niloy, R.S., Singh, H.K., Ray, T.: A benchmark test suite for evolutionary multi-objective multi-concept optimization. Swarm Evol. Comput. **84**, 101429 (2024)
21. Parker, B., Singh, H.K., Ray, T.: Multi-objective optimization across multiple concepts: a case study on lattice structure design. In: ACM Genetic and Evolutionary Computation Conference, pp. 1035–1042 (2021)
22. Ragsdell, K.M., Phillips, D.T.: Optimal design of a class of welded structures using geometric programming. J. Eng. Ind. **98**(3), 1021–1025 (1976)
23. Rahi, K.H., Singh, H.K., Ray, T.: A steady-state algorithm for solving expensive multi-objective optimization problems with non-parallelizable evaluations. IEEE Trans. Evol. Comput. **27**(5), 1544–1558 (2023). https://doi.org/10.1109/TEVC. 2022.3219062
24. Singh, H.K., Ray, T., Sarker, R.: Optimum oil production planning using infeasibility driven evolutionary algorithm. Evol. Comput. **21**(1), 65–82 (2013)

25. Tian, Y., Cheng, R., Zhang, X., Jin, Y.: PlatEMO: a MATLAB platform for evolutionary multi-objective optimization. IEEE Comput. Intell. Mag. **12**(4), 73–87 (2017)

26. Zitzler, E., Thiele, L.: Multiobjective optimization using evolutionary algorithms-a comparative case study. In: International Conference on Parallel Problem Solving from Nature, pp. 292–301. Springer (1998)

Extended Results on Analytical Hypervolume Indicator Calculation of Linear and Quadratic Pareto Fronts

Hemant Kumar Singh$^{(\boxtimes)}$ [ID]

The University of New South Wales, Canberra ACT 2600, Australia
h.singh@unsw.edu.au

Abstract. In evolutionary multi-objective optimization (EMO), the quality of Pareto front (PF) approximations obtained using various algorithms are benchmarked using set-based unary indicators. Hypervolume (HV) is an indicator that has attracted widespread attention as it attempts to capture both convergence and diversity, is scalable in terms of objectives, and is Pareto-compliant. Even so, HV is not without its limitations, ignoring which may lead to erroneous judgments about algorithm performance, especially for problems with more than three objectives, where visualization of the objective space is not straightforward. Various theoretical studies have therefore been conducted to improve understanding of HV behavior and its implications in EMO benchmarking, including a recent one that focuses on computing HV for some common PF shapes analytically. This paper aims to extend these theoretical results and discussions, by analyzing continuous subsets (symmetric *patches*) on some common shapes of PFs (linear and quadratic). Towards this end, a simple parametrization scheme is proposed to represent the symmetric patches on linear and quadratic PFs, and their HV is analytically derived. The resulting expressions are used to observe some HV trends with respect to the patch size, reference point specification and number of objectives, to provide related insights for benchmarking.

Keywords: Hypervolume · Multi-objective optimization · Benchmarking

1 Introduction

Practical optimization problems often involve consideration of multiple conflicting criteria. The optimum of such multi-objective optimization problems (MOPs) comprises a set of trade-off solutions in the objective space, referred to as the Pareto-optimal front (POF), or Pareto front (PF) for short. The underlying computations for objective/constraint functions may be highly non-linear or black-box, making it infeasible to use exact methods that require certain mathematical properties (such as linearity, differentiability). The development and analysis of metaheuristics such as Multi-objective Evolutionary Algorithms (MOEAs) has therefore been of significant interest to solve such problems in lieu of exact methods. Given that MOEAs typically do not provide theoretical guarantees on the obtained results, quantitative indicators have been developed

© The Author(s), under exclusive license to Springer Nature Singapore Pte Ltd. 2025
H. Singh et al. (Eds.): EMO 2025, LNCS 15512, pp. 226–241, 2025.
https://doi.org/10.1007/978-981-96-3506-1_16

to measure the quality of the obtained solution sets obtained using MOEAs. The development and analysis of new MOEAs commonly involves benchmarking them against other algorithms of similar class on a range of problems using these indicators. Various performance indicators have been developed in the field of evolutionary multi-objective optimization (EMO) towards this end, which measure convergence, diversity, or both, for the solution sets. Some of the commonly used performance indicators include generational distance (GD), inverted generational distance (IGD), hypervolume (HV), and R2 indicator [21]. For an extensive review of the indicators used for evaluating EMO algorithms, the interested readers may refer to [1,21].

Among the above-mentioned indicators, HV has attracted particular attention due to a confluence of reasons. Foremost, it is *Pareto-compliant*, which entails that any solution (set) that dominates another solution (set) will have a better HV value (with respect to a fixed reference point dominated by both of them). Secondly, it attempts to characterize a combination of convergence and diversity, the two key desirable attributes of the PF approximation. IGD also attempts the same, but it requires a set of reference solutions for calculation. HV, on the other, requires only a single reference point for calculation, which is easier in practice. HV also has a number of interesting theoretical properties, which has prompted significant research in understanding its behavior. These advantages of HV also come with some downsides, such as high computational complexity and significant variations in the optimum HV subset depending on the shape of the PF and the specification of reference point. A recent survey on HV [26] discusses the key research topics related to HV. These include methods to expedite the computation of HV or HV contributions [8,9,20,27,29], HV optimal distribution of μ points [3,11,15,25], HV-based subset selection [10,14,22], integration of HV in multi-objective optimization methods [4–6,12,23,24,31], and variants/extensions of HV [30,32].

Most of the research works that study theoretical aspects of HV have dealt with low dimensional (typically two objectives) and/or discrete point sets. Moreover, the empirical studies that attempt to study the impact of reference point specification on the distribution of points, especially for higher objective problems, also used discrete point sets to make inferences. In a recent work [28], an attempt was made to address this research gap by analytically deriving HV for certain common shapes of PF. These shapes included linear and quadratic, "regular" and "inverted" PFs. Together, these represent majority of the two scalable problem sets commonly used in the EMO field, i.e., DTLZ suite [13] and WFG suite [17]. The developments in [28] were intended to provide analytically calculated HV that could be used as upper bounds to normalize the HV obtained from algorithms during benchmarking. They also enable parametric studies to understand the impact of the number of points and reference point specification on HV, and the contribution of various components like corners and edges of the PF to the overall HV.

In this paper, the study from [28] is extended by developing analytical calculations of HV for symmetric *patches* on these linear/quadratic PF shapes. The motivation of the work is broadly similar to [28], i.e., to provide closed form expressions that could be useful for parametric studies to understand the behavior of HV. Towards this end, this study contributes the following.

- A simple parametrization scheme is proposed to represent a symmetric patch on linear (triangular/inverted triangular) and quadratic (orthant/inverted orthant) PFs.
- HV calculation is derived for symmetric linear and quadratic patches on these PFs.
- Parametric studies are conducted to observe the effect of patch size on HV with reference point location and number of objectives.

The analytical derivations of HV for symmetric patches on linear and quadratic PFs are given in Sect. 2, followed by some trends analysis and related discussions in Sect. 3. Conclusions and potential for further work are discussed in Sect. 4.

2 Derivation of HV for Symmetric Patches

In this section, expressions to calculate HV for patches are derived using geometric analysis of the PF shapes. All objective values comprising the PF are assumed to be in the linearly normalized range of [0,1] for the analysis. In this way, the problems with unequal ranges of objectives can be mapped to $[0, 1]^M$ space for analysis, with $(0, 0, \ldots, 0)$ and $(1, 1, \ldots, 1)$ representing the theoretical ideal point and nadir point, respectively.

2.1 Linear Regular Pareto Fronts

A typical linear *regular* PF, scaled by its ideal and nadir points, is visualized in Fig. 1(a) for $M = 3$ objectives. It is contained within the unit hyperbox $\mathcal{C}_1$, the vertices of which are labeled as $P_1 = (0, 0, 0), P_2 = (1, 0, 0), P_3 = (1, 1, 0), P_4 = (0, 1, 0), P_5 = (0, 0, 1), P_6 = (1, 0, 1), P_7 = (1, 1, 1), P_8 = (0, 1, 1)$. A larger hyperbox, $\mathcal{C}_k$, is formed by the reference point $R = (k, k, k)$. As discussed in [28], the surface of the PF divides the volume contained within $\mathcal{C}_k$ into two regions: one dominated by the PF (which is equal to its HV), and other that dominates it. The dominated volume in this case can be calculated by subtracting volume of the pyramid ($\mathcal{P}_1$) enclosed by the points P_1, P_2, P_4, P_5 from the volume of $\mathcal{C}_k$. Since $\mathcal{P}_1$ is a pyramid with M orthogonal sides of unit length, the enclosed volumes (Vol) and the hypervolume ($\mathcal{H}$) can be calculated as shown in Eq. (1).

$$\mathcal{H}(PF) = Vol(\mathcal{C}_k) - Vol(\mathcal{P}_1) = k^M - \frac{1}{M!} \tag{1}$$

Following from this, the HV calculation is extended here for a symmetric patch, shown as the inside triangle on the PF in Fig. 1(b). To control its coverage relative to the full PF, a parameter η is introduced. The parameter η simply corresponds to the f_M of the corner point (vertex) closest to the f_M axis, without loss of generality. The reason for this choice of parametrization is that it allows coordinates of all vertices to be conveniently calculated through symmetry. The cube enclosing the scaled front is referred to as $\mathcal{C}_\eta$, which lies wholly inside $\mathcal{C}_1$. With above quantities, the other coordinates of the corner point, and the length l_η of each side of $\mathcal{C}_\eta$, can then be calculated as shown in Eq. (2).

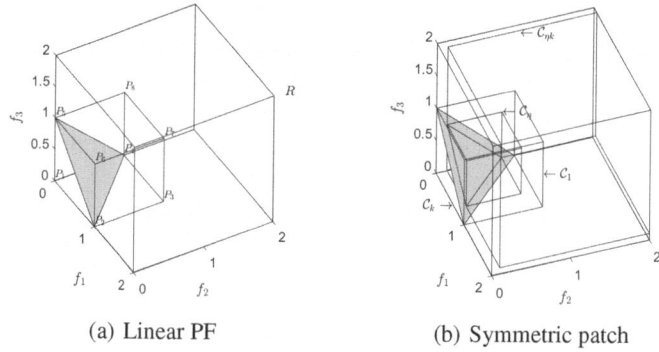

(a) Linear PF   (b) Symmetric patch

Fig. 1. Example of a linear regular PF.

Given $\sum_{i=1}^{M} f_i = 1$ for linear PF; $f_M = \eta$

$$\Rightarrow f_1 = f_2 = f_3 = \ldots = f_{M-1} = \frac{1 - f_M}{M - 1} = \frac{1 - \eta}{M - 1} \Rightarrow l_\eta = \eta - \frac{1 - \eta}{M - 1} = \frac{\eta M - 1}{M - 1} \tag{2}$$

Based on the calculations in Eq. (2), the ideal point for the patch can thus be constructed as $z_\eta^I = (\frac{1-\eta}{M-1}, \frac{1-\eta}{M-1}, \ldots, \frac{1-\eta}{M-1})$. Now, denoting the cube enclosed between z_η^I and R as $\mathcal{C}_{\eta k}$, and the pyramid enclosed between z_η^I and the patch as $\mathcal{P}_\eta$, the dominated volume by the patch can be calculated as shown in Eq. (3).

$$l_{\eta k} = k - \frac{1 - \eta}{M - 1} (\text{ side length of } \mathcal{C}_{\eta k}); \quad Vol(\mathcal{C}_{\eta k}) = l_{\eta k}^M; \quad Vol(\mathcal{P}_\eta) = \frac{1}{M!} l_\eta^M$$

$$\Rightarrow \mathcal{H}(PF_\eta) = Vol(\mathcal{C}_{\eta k}) - Vol(\mathcal{P}_\eta) = \left(k - \frac{1 - \eta}{M - 1} \right)^M - \frac{1}{M!} \left(\frac{\eta M - 1}{M - 1} \right)^M \tag{3}$$

2.2   Linear Inverted Pareto Fronts

A number of recent works, e.g. [2,7,16,18,19], have studied "inverted" linear PFs, with an aim to avoid over-fitting decomposition-based algorithms to regular PF shapes. A normalized version of such a PF is shown in Fig. 2(a). Each of the vertices in this case lies on a plane rather than one of the objective axes; resulting in one of the coordinates being 0 (e.g., P_3 lies on the plane $f_3 = 0$). The PF is formed by the objective values that satisfy $\sum_{i=1}^{M} f_i = M - 1$.

The calculations for the volume dominated by the full PF in this case were detailed in [28] and summarized here. In this case, unlike the regular PF, the volume enclosed between the ideal and reference points is not divided into dominated and non-dominated regions solely by the plane containing the PF. There are regions outside the unit cube

C_1 that are not dominated by the PF. These are prism-like volumes with constant cross-sections translated along the objective axes [28], denoted here as T_{1k}. The have a cross-section area A_{1k} and height h_{1k}. Note that the subscript 1 here is used to denote that the calculations are done for the full PF; this will change to η when considering patches later. In Fig. 2(a), the cross-section is the enclosed shape (triangle) formed by the points $\{P_5, P_6, P_8\}$, which is translated along f_3 axis (from $f_3 = 1$ to $f_3 = k$) to form the prism T_{1k}. There are M such regions, one along each objective. Additionally, the volume inside C_1 below the PF is also not-dominated by PF. This could be calculated by taking away the volume of pyramid P_1, enclosed between the PF and nadir point z_1^N, from the volume of C_1. The HV of the PF is calculated by taking away all these non-dominated volumes from C_k, as shown in Eq. (4).

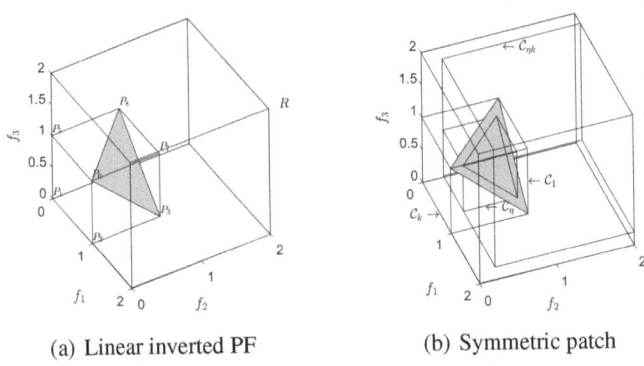

(a) Linear inverted PF   (b) Symmetric patch

Fig. 2. Example of an inverted linear PF.

$$Vol(T_{1k}) = A_{1k} \times h_{1k} = \left(1 - \frac{1}{(M-1)!}\right) \times (k-1)$$

$$\Rightarrow \mathcal{H}(PF) = Vol(C_k) - M \times Vol(T_{1k}) - (Vol(C_1) - Vol(P_1)) \qquad (4)$$

$$\Rightarrow \mathcal{H}(PF) = k^M - M \times Vol(T_{1k}) - 1 + \frac{1}{M!}$$

Next, the extension to a symmetric patch is considered, shown as the inside triangle on the PF in Fig. 2(b). In this case, the parameter η to control the coverage of the patch corresponds to the f_M of the corner point closest to the f_M plane (unlike the one closest to the f_M axis in the case of the regular PF). For example, in Fig. 2(b), η is the f_3 coordinate of the bottom point, the one closest to the f_3 plane. Following the same notation as earlier, the cube enclosing the patch is referred to as C_η. The other coordinates of this corner point, as well as the length l_η of each side of C_η can then be calculated as shown in Eq. (5).

Given $\sum_{i=1}^{M} f_i = M - 1$ for linear inverted PF; $f_M = \eta$

$$\Rightarrow f_1 = f_2 = f_3 = \ldots = f_{M-1} = \frac{M-1-\eta}{M-1} \Rightarrow l_\eta = \frac{M-1-\eta}{M-1} - \eta = \frac{M - \eta M - 1}{M - 1} \tag{5}$$

From the coordinates calculated above, the nadir point for the patch can be constructed as $z_\eta^N = \left(\frac{M-1-\eta}{M-1}, \frac{M-1-\eta}{M-1}, \ldots, \frac{M-1-\eta}{M-1} \right)$. The pyramid enclosed between z_η^N and the PF is denoted as $\mathcal{P}_\eta$. It can be seen from Fig. 5(b) that the patch assumes the same relative position to $\mathcal{C}_{\eta k}$ as the full PF does with respect to $\mathcal{C}_k$. Thus, similar to the process followed in Eq. (4), the calculations for the patch are done as shown in Eq. (6).

$$l_{\eta k} = k - \eta \quad \text{(side length of } \mathcal{C}_{\eta k}); \quad Vol(\mathcal{C}_{\eta k}) = l_{\eta k}^M$$

$$Vol(\mathcal{T}_{\eta k}) = A_{\eta k} \times h_{\eta k} = \left(1 - \frac{1}{(M-1)!} \right) l_\eta^{M-1} \times \left(k - \frac{M-1-\eta}{M-1} \right)$$

$$\Rightarrow \mathcal{H}(PF_\eta) = Vol(\mathcal{C}_{\eta k}) - M \times Vol(\mathcal{T}_{\eta k}) - (Vol(\mathcal{C}_\eta) - Vol(\mathcal{P}_\eta)) \tag{6}$$

$$\Rightarrow \mathcal{H}(PF_\eta) = l_{\eta k}^M - M \times Vol(\mathcal{T}_{\eta k}) - l_\eta^M + \frac{l_\eta^M}{M!}; \quad \text{where } l_\eta = \frac{M - \eta M - 1}{M - 1}$$

2.3 Quadratic Pareto Fronts

Having discussed linear PFs in the previous two subsections, the quadratic PFs are analyzed next. These include spherical/elliptical PFs in the normalized objective space, shown in Fig. 3(a). A number of test functions exhibit this type of PF, such as DTLZ2-DTLZ3 [13] and WFG4-WFG9 [17]. The PF is a positive orthant with its corners (vertices) on the objective axes and satisfies the relationship $\sum_{i=1}^{M} f_i^2 = 1$; where $f_i \geq 0 \forall i$ and M is the number of objectives. For a 3-objective problem, the PF is shown in Fig. 3.

The volume dominated by the quadratic PF can be calculated in the similar way as that for the linear PF, i.e., Eq. (1). The difference in this case is that the volume of the ball of unit radius in the positive orthant (denoted here as $\mathcal{B}_1$) needs to be computed in lieu of a pyramid ($\mathcal{P}_1$).

The volume of the ball $\mathcal{B}$ as a function of its radius r and number of objectives M, i.e., $V_{\mathcal{B}}(r, M)$, can be calculated using the Euler's gamma function [28]. Since the volume contained within each orthant is equal (by symmetry) and there are 2^M orthants, the volume contained in the positive orthant $V_{\mathcal{O}+}(r, M)$ will be $1/2^M$ times the volume of the ball. Using these results, the HV can thus be calculated as shown in Eq. (7).

$$Vol(\mathcal{C}_k) = k^M; \quad Vol(\mathcal{B}_1) = V_{\mathcal{O}+}(1, M) = V_{\mathcal{B}}(1, M)/2^M;$$

$$\Rightarrow \mathcal{H}(PF) = k^M - V_{\mathcal{O}+}(1, M) \tag{7}$$

Next, the analysis is extended to a symmetric patch which is fully contained within the PF, shown in Fig. 3(b). Similar to the parametrization in the linear case, a parameter

η is assumed which represents the f_M coordinate of the corner closest to the f_M axis. A cube enclosing this scaled PF can be formed as shown in Fig. 3(b). The remaining coordinates of the corner point are calculated as shown in Eq. (8). The coordinates of the other corner points can be constructed through symmetry. With these limits, one can construct the cube $\mathcal{C}_\eta$ that encloses this patch.

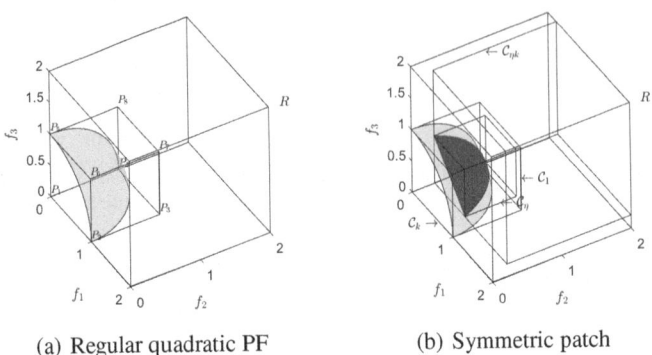

(a) Regular quadratic PF   (b) Symmetric patch

Fig. 3. Example of a regular quadratic PF.

Given $\sum_{i=1}^{M} f_i^2 = 1$ for quadratic PF; $f_M = \eta$

$$\Rightarrow f_1 = f_2 = f_3 = \ldots = f_{M-1} = \sqrt{\frac{1 - f_M^2}{M - 1}} = \sqrt{\frac{1 - \eta^2}{M - 1}} \Rightarrow l_\eta = \eta - \sqrt{\frac{1 - \eta^2}{M - 1}}$$

(8)

The ideal point for the patch can be constructed in this case as $z_\eta^I = (\eta, \eta, \ldots, \eta)$. An important point to note here is that the volume enclosed between z_η^I and the scaled PF *cannot* be calculated using the same formula as for the full PF (Eq. (7)). The reason is that since the patch is a subset of the full PF, its radius is 1 (and not l_η). Therefore, the volume enclosed by the patch and its ideal point z_η^I does not constitute a standard orthant of a ball; rendering the standard volume formula inapplicable. An approximation is considered for this volume instead - it is calculated for the positive orthant $\mathcal{B}_\eta$ of a ball with radius $r = l_\eta$, centered at the ideal point z_η^I. With this assumption, the (approximate) HV calculations can proceed as shown in Eq. (9).

$$l_{\eta k} = k - \sqrt{\frac{1 - \eta^2}{M - 1}} \quad \text{(side length of } \mathcal{C}_{\eta k})$$

$$\Rightarrow Vol(\mathcal{C}_{\eta k}) = l_{\eta k}^M = \left(k - \sqrt{\frac{1 - \eta^2}{M - 1}} \right)^M$$

(9)

$$\Rightarrow \mathcal{H}(PF_\eta) = Vol(\mathcal{C}_{\eta k}) - Vol(\mathcal{B}_\eta) = \left(k - \sqrt{\frac{1 - \eta^2}{M - 1}} \right)^M - V_{O+}(l_\eta, M)$$

Since the curvature of this assumed patch surface is higher, it can be inferred that the dominated volume will end up to be an under-estimate of the exact HV. The errors introduced in the HV computation of patches through this assumption can be quantified and is generally small. The errors are shown in Fig. 4 and are computed as follows. The center point of the true patch surface (with radius 1) and that of the approximated patch surface (with radius l_η) is determined using their geometric symmetry. The distance between these points, say δr, represents the maximum discrepancy between the two surfaces. Thus, the upper bound of the volume enclosed between the two surfaces can calculated as difference of the volumes of two orthants - one with radius l_η, and another with radius $l_\eta - \delta r$. This difference, $\Delta V_{max} = V_{O+}(l_\eta, M) - V_{O+}(l_\eta - \delta r, M)$ is the maximum error introduced in the computed hypervolume. The variation of δr and % error of ΔV_{max} relative to $\mathcal{H}(PF_\eta)$ is non-linear with η, with maxima occuring at different values for different objectives. At its worse, the error is close to 30% for $M = 3$ at the lowest value of $k(= 1)$. For the commonly used setting of $k = 1.1$, the error drops down to 16% for the $M = 3$, while for $k = 2$, the maximum error is 1.5% even for $M = 3$. The errors also reduce significantly for higher values of M, e.g., maximum errors for $M = 4$ are nearly half compared of those for $M = 3$.

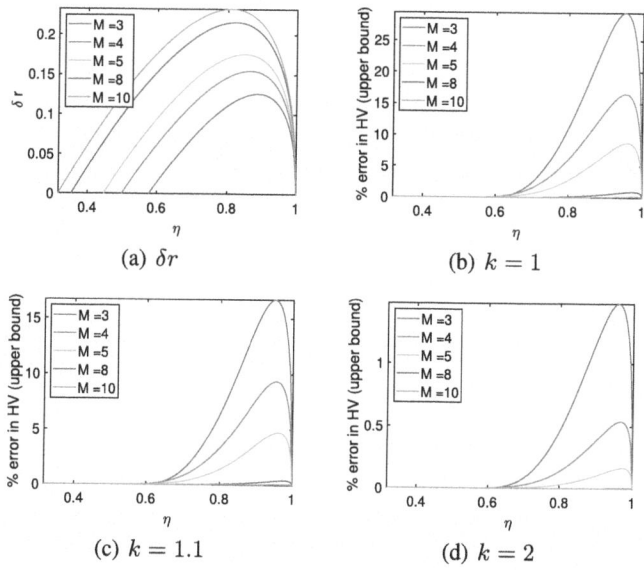

Fig. 4. δr and upper bound error in HV calculations of patches on quadratic PFs

2.4   Quadratic Inverted Pareto Fronts

Quadratic inverted PFs correspond to, e.g., problems introduced in [18] by simply negating each of the objectives for a problem that originally had a regular quadratic

PF. In its normalized form, the PF is visualized in Fig. 5. Akin to the linear inverted case, each of the corners in this case lies on an objective plane instead of an objective axis. Consequently, one of the coordinates is equal to 0 (e.g., P_3 lies on the plane $f_3 = 0$). The PF satisfies the equation of sphere with a unit radius centered at $(1,1,\ldots,1)$, i.e., $\sum_{i=1}^{M}(f_i - 1)^2 = 1$.

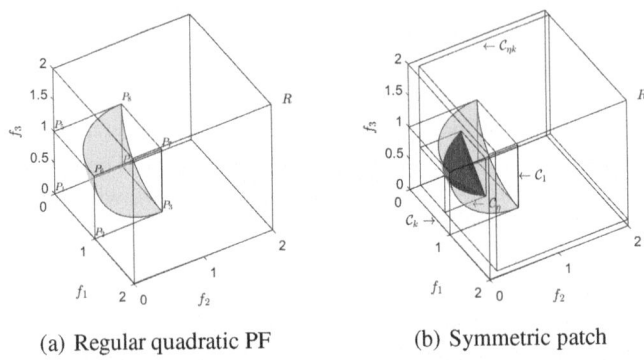

(a) Regular quadratic PF   (b) Symmetric patch

Fig. 5. Example of an inverted quadratic PF.

The calculation of HV for the inverted quadratic PF follows the same steps as that for inverted linear PF. The difference is that the base of the non-dominated prismatic region $\mathcal{T}_{1k}$ has a curved surface. Its area $\mathcal{A}_{1k}$ is calculated by deducting orthant of a lower dimensional hypersphere (circle in case of $M = 3$) from the lower-dimensional hypercube (square in case of $M = 3$) [28]. The non-dominated volume inside $\mathcal{C}_1$ is computed by deducting the volume of the orthant $\mathcal{B}_1$ (enclosed by the nadir point and the PF) from the volume of $\mathcal{C}_1$. Thus, the HV is computed as shown in Eq. (10).

$$Vol(\mathcal{T}_{1k}) = \mathcal{A}_{1k} \times h_{1k} = \left(1 - V_{\mathcal{O}+}(1, M-1)\right) \times (k-1)$$
$$\Rightarrow \mathcal{H}(PF) = Vol(\mathcal{C}_k) - M \times Vol(\mathcal{T}_{1k}) - (Vol(\mathcal{C}_1) - Vol(\mathcal{B}_1)) \tag{10}$$
$$\Rightarrow \mathcal{H}(PF) = k^M - M \times Vol(\mathcal{T}_{1k}) + V_{\mathcal{O}+}(1, M) - 1$$

Lastly, the extension of the analysis to a symmetric patch on the inverted quadratic PF is considered, shown in Fig. 5(b). The parameter η in this case corresponds to f_M of the corner point closes to the f_M plane. Following the same notation as for the linear case, the other coordinates of the corner point, as well as the length l_η of each side of $\mathcal{C}_\eta$ can then be calculated as shown in Eq. (11).

Given $\sum_{i=1}^{M}(f_i - 1)^2 = 1$ for quadratic inverted PF; $f_M = \eta$

$$\Rightarrow f_1 = f_2 = f_3 = \ldots = f_{M-1} = 1 - \sqrt{\frac{1 - (\eta - 1)^2}{M - 1}}; \Rightarrow l_\eta = 1 - \sqrt{\frac{1 - (\eta - 1)^2}{M - 1}} - \eta \tag{11}$$

It can be observed from Fig. 5(b) that the patch assumes the same relative position to $\mathcal{C}_{\eta k}$ as the full PF does with respect to $\mathcal{C}_k$. Thus, similar to Eq. (10), the calculations for the patch can be done as shown in Eq. (12). Once again, the approximation similar to the case of patches on regular quadratic PF is used, i.e., the radius of the patch is assumed to be l_η instead of 1. The resulting errors are same as those in Fig. 4, but will result in an *over-estimation* of the HV, unlike under-estimation in the regular case.

$$l_{\eta k} = k - \eta \quad \text{(side length of } \mathcal{C}_{\eta k}\text{)}; Vol(\mathcal{C}_{\eta k}) = l_{\eta k}^M$$

$$Vol(\mathcal{T}_{\eta k}) = \mathcal{A}_{\eta k} \times h_{\eta k} = \left(l_\eta^{M-1} - V_{\mathcal{O}+}(l_\eta, M-1) \right) \times \left(k - \left(1 - \sqrt{\frac{1 - (\eta - 1)^2}{M - 1}} \right) \right)$$

$$\mathcal{H}(PF_\eta) = Vol(\mathcal{C}_{\eta k}) - M \times Vol(\mathcal{T}_{\eta k}) - (Vol(\mathcal{C}_\eta) - Vol(\mathcal{B}_\eta))$$

$$\mathcal{H}(PF_\eta) = l_{\eta k}^M - M \times Vol(\mathcal{T}_{\eta k}) - l_\eta^M + V_{\mathcal{O}+}(l_\eta, M)$$

$$(12)$$

3   Numerical Studies and Discussion

The expressions derived in for HV of symmetric patches in linear and quadratic PFs, in conjunction with those derived in [28] can be used for conducting parametric studies. Such studies can help extend the understanding of the HV behavior for, e.g., different numbers of objectives, reference points, and patch sizes. Moreover, this approach does not require large sampling to compute the HV values, avoiding the corresponding computational expense. Some examples of such parametric studies are presented here.

3.1   Regular Pareto Fronts

For the regular PFs, the variation of HV of the patches is tracked as a ratio with respect to the HV of the full PF. For the patches, the value of η is uniformly sampled between its upper and lower bounds. From the extremities, the bounds can be deduced as $\eta \in [1/M, 1]$ for linear PF and $\eta \in [1/\sqrt{M}, 1]$ for quadratic PF. The lower bound of η corresponds to the patch that degenerates to a symmetrically located single point on the PF: $(1/M, 1/M \ldots, 1/M)$ for the linear PF and $(1/\sqrt{M}, 1/\sqrt{M} \ldots, 1/\sqrt{M})$ for the quadratic PF. The upper bound, i.e., $\eta = 1$ corresponds to the patch being identical to the full PF. The trends visualized in Fig. 6 for different values of reference point location k and the number of objectives M. Note that in Figs. 6, 7 and 8, 'HV (Corner/Full)' is used for brevity to denote the ratio of the theoretical HV of the corners (vertices) alone and that of the full PF. Likewise, 'HV (Edge/Full)' denotes the ratio of the theoretical HV of the edges (line segments joining the adjacent corner points) and that of the full PF. Finally, 'HV (Patch/Full)' denotes the ratio of the theoretical HV of the patches computed herein and that of the full PF. Some key observations are as follows.

For the linear PFs, it can be seen in Fig. 6(a)–(c) that the HV ratio increases gradually with the increase of η, from bottom (black) line to the top. This is understandable as higher η value corresponds to a larger coverage of the PF in this case. Interestingly, when these values are compared to the HV ratio of the corners (blue line) and edges (red line), certain geometric biases emerge. The HV of edges alone is higher than that for all η values considered (except $\eta = 1$). The HV ratio of the patches increases as the reference point location moves farther (as k increases), however, it approaches 1 much slower than the HV of edges. The HV of the corner points alone is 0 when $k = 1$, i.e., nadir point is the same as reference point. However, as k is increased, this number approaches 1 rapidly, overtaking most of the η values considered before $k = 2$ for $M = 3$. This rise is even steeper for $M > 3$. In effect, both these observations suggest that obtaining the solutions that cover corners and edges of the PF have disproportionately higher impact on the HV compared to the solutions inside the PF, even though the latter covers much larger area of the PF surface (manifold). Thus, somewhat counterintuitively, a PF approximation that is well-spread and only marginally smaller than the full PF may be judged to be worse than the corners or edges alone using HV.

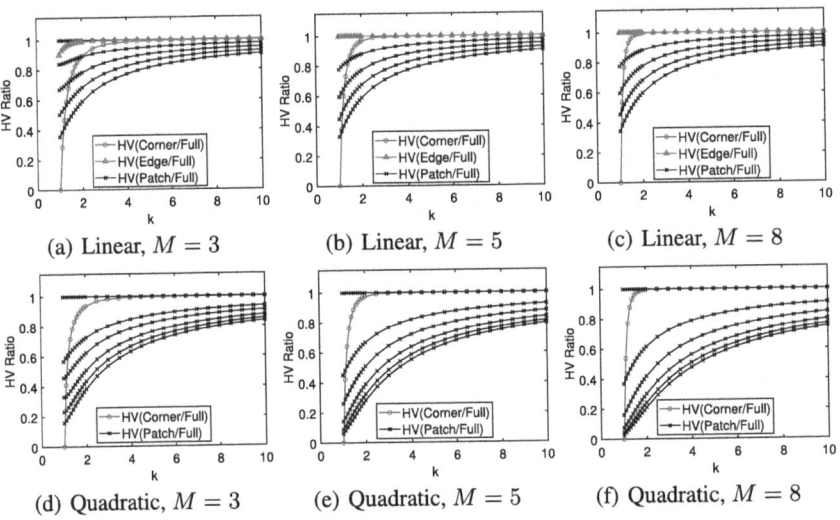

Fig. 6. HV ration trends for regular PFs. For the HV ratio of patches, each (black) line is for a different value of η, which increases uniformly between its lower and upper bounds from bottom to top line.

The above observations also hold for regular quadratic PFs, shown in Fig. 6(d)–(f). The notable difference from the linear case, however, is that the relative HV covered becomes even smaller for similar values of η. For example, $\eta = 0.9$ would result in a much higher HV for the linear case compared to the quadratic case. This can be explained based on the concavity of the surface. For the same given height of the f_3 coordinate (parameter η), the surface covered by the linear patch relative to the full linear PF is much higher than the surface covered by the quadratic patch relative to the full quadratic PF. The behavior of the HV ratio for corner points for quadratic and linear cases are identical (as corners are the same for both types of PF). It can be seen that except for cases with k on or very close to the nadir point (≈ 1), the HV of corner points will be significantly higher than that obtained from the internal patches (more so than the linear PF case). The latter aspect becomes clearer when the plots of HV ratio for different values of k are observed in Fig. 7. It can be seen that for both linear and quadratic cases, HV of the internal patches is comparable to that of the corners only when $k = 1.1$; and the HV of edges is higher even for this case. For all other cases, the HV of corners (and edges) is higher than that of all η (< 1) values considered.

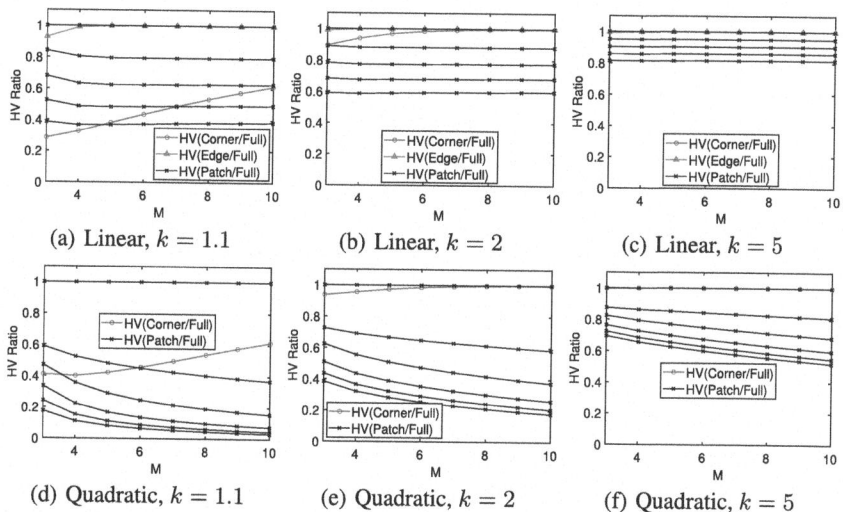

Fig. 7. HV ratio trends for different values of k for regular PFs.

3.2 Inverted Pareto Fronts

For the inverted PFs, a limited set of observations are presented. More specifically, only 3-objective PFs are considered for this study. This is because the expressions could be numerically verified (via large sampling) to be exact only for $M = 3$ in the previous work [28].

For the inverted PFs, the bounds can be deduced as $\eta \in [0, (M - 1)/M]$ for linear and $\eta \in [0, 1 - 1/\sqrt{M}]$ for quadratic PFs. In these cases, contrary to the regular PFs, the *upper* bound of η corresponds to the patch that degenerates to a symmetrically located single point on the PF, while $\eta = 0$ corresponds to the patch being the full PF.

For the linear inverted PFs, the trends look different from the case of linear regular PFs, especially when k is close to 1. In particular, the HV ratio does not monotonically increase with k in this region, but rather it dips first before settling into an increasing trend. The reason for this is that when $k = 1$, the edges of the PF have no contribution to the overall HV. However, the edges of the patch have a contribution, as can be interpreted from Fig. 2(b). When k increases slightly, the volume dominated by the edges of the full PF comes into picture. Given the edge length of the PF is larger than that of the patch, the volume dominated by it grows faster than that of the patch, resulting in lowering of the ratio. However, after a certain point, the volume dominated beyond the unit hyperbox (the volume between the nadir point and the reference point), which is identical for the patch and the full PF, becomes a much larger contributor to the HV, hence the ratio starts to increase again. Intuitively, one can visualize that when the reference point is far away, HV of the patch will approach HV of the full PF.

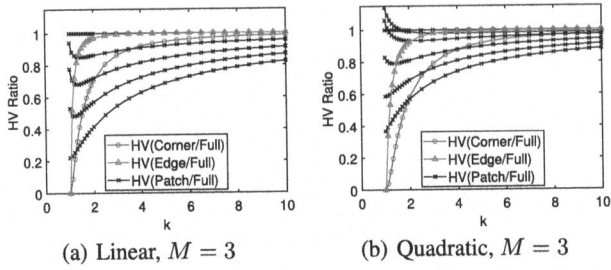

(a) Linear, $M = 3$ (b) Quadratic, $M = 3$

Fig. 8. HV ratio trends for $M = 3$ for inverted PFs. For the HV ratio of patches, each (black) line is for a different value of η, which increases uniformly between its lower and upper bounds from top to bottom line.

For the inverted quadratic PF, one can observe an anomaly for the two lowest values of η. This is because of the approximations discussed in Fig. 4. The assumed curvature of the quadratic patch is higher than actual, which results in overestimation of its HV. As indicated in Fig. 4, for low values of k and M, this error can be up to 30%, making the HV ratio go beyond 1. The errors reduce rapidly with increase in k, hence the HV ratio comes down below 1 and trends revert to the expected ones afterwards.

An interesting takeaway from the trends for the inverted PFs is that the HV of the edges start from 0, unlike for the regular case. Therefore, for certain k values close to 1, the volume dominated by the internal patches, especially for low η values, is higher than the edges. Further, if the corner points are considered, the increase in HV ratio towards 1 is significantly slower than that for the regular case. In effect, it means that for k values up to ≈ 3, the solution sets that are internally located will be evaluated as better (have a higher HV) than the corner points.

4   Conclusions and Future Work

In this study, closed-form analytical expressions are derived for calculating HV of symmetric patches on linear and quadratic PFs. This study extends the previous work that derived HV for edges, corners and full PFs for these shapes. The presented developments provide a means to conduct parametric studies to draw further insights while benchmarking EMO algorithms, and improve the understanding and interpretation of results while using HV as an indicator. Some scenarios were discussed where performance evaluation based on HV might favor solutions obtained on patches vs edges/corners for the regular PFs and vice-versa for inverted PFs.

The scope of the current work is limited to continuous subsets of the PFs. While this is helpful for deducing some representative trends, MOEAs typically approximate the PF as discrete sets. Thus, to improve the practical relevance of the work, empirical experiments can be conducted with different distributions of discrete sets on the patches. It would be interesting to observe how they correlate with the HV trends presented. Additionally, the error bounds for the quadratic PFs could be further improved. Lastly, the analysis could be extended to more diverse irregular shapes compared to the limited geometries considered in this work.

Acknowledgement. The author acknowledges Discovery Project DP220101649 from the Australian Research Council. He also thanks Professor Tapabrata Ray for some discussions related to this work.

References

1. Afsar, B., Fieldsend, J.E., Guerreiro, A.P., Miettinen, K., Rojas Gonzalez, S., Sato, H.: Many-objective quality measures. In: Brockhoff, D., Emmerich, M., Naujoks, B., Purshouse, R. (eds.) Many-Criteria Optimization and Decision Analysis: State-of-the-Art, Present Challenges, and Future Perspectives, pp. 113–148. Springer International Publishing, Cham (2023). https://doi.org/10.1007/978-3-031-25263-1_5
2. Asafuddoula, M., Singh, H.K., Ray, T.: An enhanced decomposition-based evolutionary algorithm with adaptive reference vectors. IEEE Trans. Cybern. **48**(8), 2321–2334 (2018)
3. Auger, A., Bader, J., Brockhoff, D.: Theoretically investigating optimal μ-distributions for the hypervolume indicator: first results for three objectives. In: Schaefer, R., Cotta, C., Kołodziej, J., Rudolph, G. (eds.) Parallel Problem Solving from Nature, PPSN XI: 11th International Conference, Kraków, Poland, September 11-15, 2010, Proceedings, Part I, pp. 586–596. Springer Berlin Heidelberg, Berlin, Heidelberg (2010). https://doi.org/10.1007/978-3-642-15844-5_59
4. Auger, A., Bader, J., Brockhoff, D., Zitzler, E.: Hypervolume-based multiobjective optimization: theoretical foundations and practical implications. Theoret. Comput. Sci. **425**, 75–103 (2012)
5. Bader, J., Zitzler, E.: Hype: an algorithm for fast hypervolume-based many-objective optimization. Evol. Comput. **19**(1), 45–76 (2011)
6. Beume, N., Naujoks, B., Emmerich, M.: Sms-emoa: multiobjective selection based on dominated hypervolume. Eur. J. Oper. Res. **181**(3), 1653–1669 (2007)
7. Bhattacharjee, K.S., Singh, H.K., Ray, T., Zhang, Q.: Decomposition based evolutionary algorithm with a dual set of reference vectors. In: IEEE Congress on Evolutionary Computation (CEC), pp. 105–112 (2017)
8. Bringmann, K., Friedrich, T.: An efficient algorithm for computing hypervolume contributions. Evol. Comput. **18**(3), 383–402 (2010)
9. Bringmann, K., Friedrich, T.: Approximating the least hypervolume contributor: Np-hard in general, but fast in practice. Theoret. Comput. Sci. **425**, 104–116 (2012)
10. Bringmann, K., Friedrich, T., Klitzke, P.: Two-dimensional subset selection for hypervolume and epsilon-indicator. In: ACM Genetic and Evolutionary Computation Conference (GECCO), pp. 589–596 (2014)

11. Brockhoff, D.: Optimal μ-distributions for the hypervolume indicator for problems with linear bi-objective fronts: Exact and exhaustive results. In: Asia-Pacific Conference on Simulated Evolution and Learning (SEAL), pp. 24–34 (2010)

12. Brockhoff, D., Friedrich, T., Neumann, F.: Analyzing hypervolume indicator based algorithms. In: Rudolph, G., Jansen, T., Beume, N., Lucas, S., Poloni, C. (eds.) Parallel Problem Solving from Nature – PPSN X, pp. 651–660. Springer Berlin Heidelberg, Berlin, Heidelberg (2008). https://doi.org/10.1007/978-3-540-87700-4_65

13. Deb, K., Thiele, L., Laumanns, M., Zitzler, E.: Scalable multi-objective optimization test problems. In: IEEE Congress on Evolutionary Computation (CEC), vol. 1, pp. 825–830 (2002)

14. Deng, J., Sun, J., Zhang, Q., Li, H.: Efficient greedy decremental hypervolume subset selection using space partition tree. IEEE Transactions on Evolutionary Computation (2024)

15. Friedrich, T., Neumann, F., Thyssen, C.: Multiplicative approximations, optimal hypervolume distributions, and the choice of the reference point. Evol. Comput. **23**(1), 131–159 (2015)

16. Habib, A., Singh, H.K., Chugh, T., Ray, T., Miettinen, K.: A multiple surrogate assisted decomposition-based evolutionary algorithm for expensive multi/many-objective optimization. IEEE Trans. Evol. Comput. **23**(6), 1000–1014 (2019)

17. Huband, S., Hingston, P., Barone, L., While, L.: A review of multiobjective test problems and a scalable test problem toolkit. IEEE Trans. Evol. Comput. **10**(5), 477–506 (2006)

18. Ishibuchi, H., Setoguchi, Y., Masuda, H., Nojima, Y.: Performance of decomposition-based many-objective algorithms strongly depends on pareto front shapes. IEEE Trans. Evol. Comput. **21**(2), 169–190 (2017)

19. Jain, H., Deb, K.: An evolutionary many-objective optimization algorithm using reference-point based nondominated sorting approach, Part II: Handling constraints and extending to an adaptive approach. IEEE Trans. Evol. Comput. **18**(4), 602–622 (2014)

20. Jaszkiewicz, A.: Improved quick hypervolume algorithm. Comput. Oper. Res. **90**, 72–83 (2018)

21. Li, M., Yao, X.: Quality evaluation of solution sets in multiobjective optimisation: a survey. ACM Comput. Surv. **52**(2) (2019)

22. Nan, Y., Shang, K., Ishibuchi, H., He, L.: An improved local search method for large-scale hypervolume subset selection. IEEE Trans. Evol. Comput. **27**(6), 1690–1704 (2022)

23. Nguyen, A.Q., Sutton, A.M., Neumann, F.: Population size matters: rigorous runtime results for maximizing the hypervolume indicator. In: ACM Genetic and Evolutionary Computation Conference (GECCO), pp. 1613–1620 (2013)

24. Shang, K., Ishibuchi, H.: A new hypervolume-based evolutionary algorithm for many-objective optimization. IEEE Trans. Evol. Comput. **24**(5), 839–852 (2020)

25. Shang, K., Ishibuchi, H., Chen, W., Nan, Y., Liao, W.: Hypervolume-optimal μ-distributions on line/plane-based pareto fronts in three dimensions. IEEE Trans. Evol. Comput. **26**(2), 349–363 (2021)SD

26. Shang, K., Ishibuchi, H., He, L., Pang, L.M.: A survey on the hypervolume indicator in evolutionary multiobjective optimization. IEEE Trans. Evol. Comput. **25**(1), 1–20 (2020)

27. Shang, K., Ishibuchi, H., Ni, X.: R2-based hypervolume contribution approximation. IEEE Trans. Evol. Comput. **24**(1), 185–192 (2019)

28. Singh, H.K.: Understanding hypervolume behavior theoretically for benchmarking in evolutionary multi/many-objective optimization. IEEE Trans. Evol. Comput. **24**(3), 603–610 (2020)

29. While, L., Bradstreet, L., Barone, L.: A fast way of calculating exact hypervolumes. IEEE Trans. Evol. Comput. **16**(1), 86–95 (2012)

30. Yang, K., Emmerich, M., Deutz, A., Bäck, T.: Efficient computation of expected hypervolume improvement using box decomposition algorithms. J. Global Optim. **75**(1), 3–34 (2019). https://doi.org/10.1007/s10898-019-00798-7
31. Zhao, L., Zhang, Q.: Hypervolume-guided decomposition for parallel expensive multiobjective optimization. IEEE Trans. Evol. Comput. **28**(2), 432–444 (2023)
32. Zitzler, E., Brockhoff, D., Thiele, L.: The hypervolume indicator revisited: on the design of pareto-compliant indicators via weighted integration. In: Obayashi, S., Deb, K., Poloni, C., Hiroyasu, T., Murata, T. (eds.) Evolutionary Multi-Criterion Optimization, pp. 862–876. Springer Berlin Heidelberg, Berlin, Heidelberg (2007). https://doi.org/10.1007/978-3-540-70928-2_64

MO-IOHinspector: Anytime Benchmarking of Multi-objective Algorithms Using IOHprofiler

Diederick Vermetten[1]([✉]), Jeroen Rook[2], Oliver L. Preuß[3], Jacob de Nobel[1], Carola Doerr[4], Manuel López-Ibañez[5], Heike Trautmann[2,3], and Thomas Bäck[1]

[1] LIACS Leiden University, Leiden, The Netherlands
d.l.vermetten@liacs.leidenuniv.nl
[2] University of Twente, Enschede, The Netherlands
[3] Paderborn University, Paderborn, Germany
[4] LIP6 CNRS Sorbonne Université, Paris, France
[5] Alliance Manchester Business School, University of Manchester, Manchester, UK

Abstract. Benchmarking is one of the key ways in which we can gain insight into the strengths and weaknesses of optimization algorithms. In sampling-based optimization, considering the anytime behavior of an algorithm can provide valuable insights for further developments. In the context of multi-objective optimization, this anytime perspective is not as widely adopted as in the single-objective context. In this paper, we propose a new software tool which uses principles from unbounded archiving as a logging structure. This leads to a clearer separation between experimental design and subsequent analysis decisions. We integrate this approach as a new Python module into the IOHprofiler framework and demonstrate the benefits of this approach by showcasing the ability to change indicators, aggregations, and ranking procedures during the analysis pipeline.

Keywords: Benchmarking Framework · Multi-Objective Optimization · Anytime Performance · Robust Ranking · Visualization

1 Introduction

Benchmarking is a core aspect of the process of developing new optimization algorithms [2] as it serves as a way to provide comparisons of a new algorithm to the state of the art, providing insight into its relative strengths and weaknesses. In this spirit, benchmarking is more than a competitive race for more performance but serves our *understanding* of algorithm behavior. Robust benchmarking of existing algorithms has the potential to provide a wealth of knowledge about the status of algorithmic development for specific types of problems and drive new development of algorithmic ideas to fill the gaps.

To extract as much information from a given benchmark setup as possible, we should not be limited to looking only at the final solution(s) returned by an

H. Singh et al. (Eds.): EMO 2025, LNCS 15512, pp. 242–256, 2025.
https://doi.org/10.1007/978-981-96-3506-1_17

algorithm [18]. By looking at the full trajectory of an algorithm, we can identify regions of complementarity not just on different problems but at different stages of the optimization process. Looking at the *anytime performance* of an algorithm can thus showcase the potential, e.g., for dynamically switching between algorithms [25], or provide a more detailed understanding of the relation between the evaluation budget and the relative rankings of different algorithms [18].

While this view on anytime performance has been widely adopted in single-objective optimization (SOO) [19], it faces several challenging design decisions to translate to the multi-objective optimization (MOO) setting. This is mainly due to the additional degree of freedom imposed by having not a single objective value but a set of optimal trade-off solutions, leading to differences, e.g., between which performance indicator is favored for a particular study. While for a given indicator value an anytime performance can be logged (e.g. the hypervolume indicator in bi-objective BBOB [6]), this approach imposes an analysis decision on the experimental setup.

However, there is a great variety of unary set-based performance indicators [1], ranging from Pareto-compliant indicators such as hypervolume [41] and R2 (under the condition of a continuous, uniform distribution of (Tchebycheff) utility functions [33]) to indicators which focus on decision space diversity [17,31]. Pareto compliance of an indicator means that the indicator respects the Pareto dominance relation. Specifically, if one solution dominates another, the indicator assigns a strictly better value to the dominating solution. Indicators focusing on decision space diversity are more targeted towards multi-modal problems than the former. As such, some indicators might be more suited for specific research questions than others, and any imposed indicator choice limits how the resulting data can be re-used for new types of comparison.

In this paper, we argue that the **later choice of analysis methodology need not influence design decisions** related to experimental setup, or vice versa. Instead, we show the benefits of using a data-logging approach based on the idea of unbounded archives [16]. This not only supports the ability to easily consider anytime performance but also provides the freedom to decide about the indicator independently from the experiment design. While this requires a tradeoff regarding the amount of data stored, this data can subsequently be shared and re-used for various other analyses by the same or different groups of researchers.

To simplify this type of logging, subsequent data analysis, and visualization, we introduce **MO-IOHinspector**, which builds upon the IOHprofiler framework [30,37]. While initially developed as an extension of the COCO platform [19] for SOO, we now present an extension of the modular benchmarking toolkit to the multi-objective domain. With this new module, we provide an integration with the popular PyMOO library [5], which we use to showcase the available analysis methods by running a benchmark study on several well-known multi-objective evolutionary optimization algorithms (MOEAs). Among the included analysis methods, we also incorporate the recently proposed robust ranking methodology [32], aimed at creating a reliable and meaningful ranking that takes into account the variability in performance across different problem instances and simultaneously checks for statistical significance of performance differences. This usually results in groups of algorithms that are internally tied regarding performance but have different ranks across groups.

2   Background and Related Work

2.1   Anytime Performance and Archiving

When faced with an optimization problem, the amount of evaluation budget available is one of the critical aspects determining what algorithm or algorithm configuration would be most appropriate. As such, clearly understanding the relation between the number of function evaluations and the relative ranking of a set of algorithms is often an essential goal of benchmarking studies. Rather than looking only at the performance at the end of a fixed budget, looking at the full search trajectory provides some insights into this budget-dependence [18]. This is often viewed as *anytime performance analysis* and has been widely used in benchmarking frameworks such as COCO [19] and IOHprofiler [14].

In SOO, the common practice is to look at the evolution of the best-so-far objective value over time, which ensures a monotonic performance measure. This anytime analysis has led to the creation of powerful algorithm selection wizards, which are budget-dependent [29]. Additionally, comparing areas of the search trajectories where different algorithms perform well has led to studies into the potential of dynamically switching between optimizers [25].

The anytime analysis of multi-objective optimizers is more challenging [23, 24], not only because of the lack of consensus on how to measure the quality of a population of solutions but also due to the difficulty of ensuring a monotonic increment of quality over time unless the population update (or archiving strategy) satisfies certain prerequisites, which is not the case for many multi-objective optimizers [26,34]. As a result, the population of many multi-objective optimizers does not have the anytime property for any Pareto-compliant quality indicator, and only some optimizers are anytime for some quality indicators, such as hypervolume, but not for others [26]. The only indicator-independent way to capture the anytime behavior of a multi-objective optimizer is to store all evaluated solutions in an external unbounded archive (or all solutions which are non-dominated at the time of evaluation, if the indicator is Pareto-compliant).

Detailed surveys on archiving in MOO are available in [26,34]. These include bounded archivers, which maintain archives within a fixed size limit, often using adaptive grid selections or hypervolume approximations of the Pareto front. Other strategies use ϵ-dominance to create respective finite-size approximations. However, our approach of using an unbounded external archive [16,22,35] allows for maximum flexibility for parsing solutions during the analysis step for further performance analysis in an anytime fashion: The value of any Pareto-compliant quality indicator applied to this archive after each solution evaluation is monotonic. Thus, we can employ the same techniques for anytime analysis as in the single-objective case.

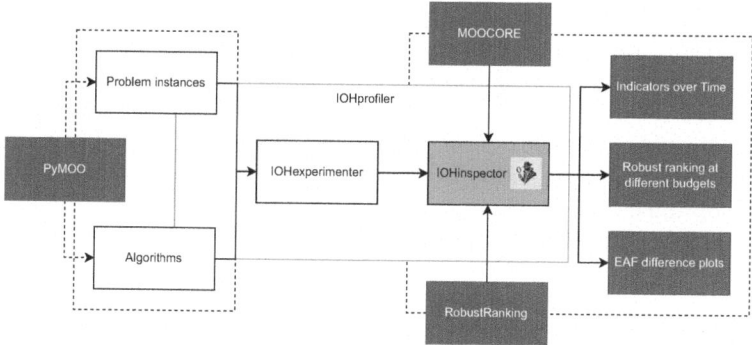

Fig. 1. Schematic Overview of our benchmarking pipeline.

2.2 Algorithm Comparisons/Rankings

When comparing algorithm performance, we are typically interested in how algorithms perform across a set of problem instances, multiple independent runs, or a combination of both [28]. Two common approaches are ranking algorithms based on their performance (indicators) on individual instances or by examining the aggregated/mean performance. Instance-level ranking provides insights into the relative performance differences but does not account for absolute counterparts. This approach is also used to test for statistical difference, e.g., the Friedman test, and is commonly visualized using Critical Difference plots [12]. Mean performance, on the other hand, does account for these absolute performance differences; however, it is susceptible to permutations in the underlying instance distribution. Furthermore, obtaining statistical insights is difficult without making further assumptions about the underlying distributions.

A recently introduced, more robust alternative to comparing algorithms is to take a bootstrapping approach [15]. Here, many resamples of the problem instance set are created, after which algorithms are ranked based on their overall performance in each resample. Statistical guarantees can be obtained with the resulting ranks while focusing on overall performance. In another work, this method was extended to obtain robust rankings when multiple performance objectives are considered [32].

3 IOHprofiler for Multi-objective Optimization

This work proposes a new module for benchmarking multi-objective optimization algorithms that fits into the existing IOHprofiler framework. IOHprofiler is a modular set of tools that comprises different parts of the benchmarking pipeline: IOHexperimenter [30] is mainly used for performing experiments and ensuring consistent data logging. In contrast, IOHanalyzer [37] can use those logs to perform various analyses and create corresponding visualizations. This separation between experimentation and analysis allows data to be re-used between experiments, even when the analysis has different goals.

Our proposed extension to IOHprofiler consists of two parts: a preliminary logging methodology (using IOHexperimenter [30]), which we link with the existing PyMOO library [5] to showcase its functionality, and a Python package for analyzing the resulting performance logs, called 'IOHinspector'. Note that this does not integrate with the existing IOHanalyzer website; instead, it serves as a purely local package that supports a subset of visualization methods for single-objective optimization. In the remainder of this section, we will outline the key functionalities and design decisions underlying the multi-objective components of IOHinspector.

To preserve the separation between experimental design and analysis methods, simply logging the value of a chosen indicator would not be sufficient. Instead, we log all (or optionally all non-dominated [13]) points evaluated during the search, from which we can then re-compute any indicator value during analysis. This way, we essentially use an unbounded archive strategy (see Sect. 2.1) for data logging. Since this archive only needs to observe the calls from the algorithm to the problem, the logging can remain independent from the algorithm's implementation, simplifying its use for arbitrary benchmarking setups. Figure 1 outlines the way in which these tools can integrate with a standard benchmarking setup, as we will show in more detail in Sect. 4.

Since a benchmarking study can have a wide variety of goals, the flexibility of the analysis pipeline is key. To achieve this, we start from the most informative set of logged data and reduce this to the required indicators or measures depending on the specific analysis or visualization method. In particular, we provide interfaces to various performance indicators, each of which can be calculated at any point in the search. However, since some indicators can be computationally expensive, we perform the calculation lazily, i.e., only at the points used in the resulting visualization (which is user-adjustable). Additionally, all indicators that rely on some problem-specific input, such as reference points or sets, can be modified during the analysis.

Our current version of 'IOHInspector' contains the following indicators: hypervolume [39], IGD+ [21], R2 [7], Epsilon [41] (additive and multiplicative versions). The majority of these indicators are computed by the `moocore` package[1], which provides efficient implementations for their calculation.

4   Experiments

To illustrate the benefits of the anytime approach to benchmarking MOO algorithms and showcase the proposed framework's functionalities, we perform a benchmarking study on a set of well-known problems and MOEAs. To ensure full reproducibility and showcase how to use our proposed toolbox, we provide a full set of reproducibility documents on our Zenodo repository [36]. This repository contains several notebooks that outline the steps taken to produce the included results, as well as some additional analyses and visualizations that could not be

---

[1] https://multi-objective.github.io/moocore/python/.

included in this paper. The IOHinspector package can also be found on GitHub (https://github.com/IOHprofiler/IOHinspector).

4.1 Experimental Setup

Since we focus on integration with existing tools for MOO, we select two of the most well-known problem suites as our benchmark set: ZDT [40] and DTLZ [11]. For both sets, we utilize the default settings from PyMOO. This means that the problems from ZDT have $d = 2$ and those from DTLZ have $d = 3$ as their objective space dimensionality, respectively.

As algorithms we use NSGA-2 [10], SMS-EMOA [3], NSGA-3 [9], MOEA/D [38], RVEA [8] and random search as baseline. For each of these algorithms (except random search), we vary the population size[2] to be in $\{10, 25, 50, 100, 250, 500\}$. When reference vectors need to be provided, such as in MOEA/D, they are generated based on Riesz's-Energy [4] method integrated into PyMOO.

Each algorithm configuration is run 25 times on each problem, with a budget of 50 000 function evaluations. To enable more straightforward normalization in our analysis, we translate each function so its single-objective minima are 0 (for each objective in the objective space).

Throughout the remainder of this paper, we will use normalization of the objective values to allow for convenient aggregation across problems. While many normalization approaches exist, we opt to use min-max normalization based on the ideal and worst attained point across all runs. We note that the proposed software is fully flexible in this aspect, and other normalization approaches can be used without impacting any other design decisions.

4.2 Hypervolume over Time

We focus on the hypervolume indicator for our first set of results. Since we normalized our objective values, we take $[1.1]^d$ as our reference point, following the methodology from [20]. Using this setup, we can compute the hypervolume at any point in the search (every evaluation, not just every generation, as the specific order of evaluation is determined within the algorithm). We visualize this in Fig. 2, where we show hypervolume on four selected problems. We can see, e.g., from the results on ZDT2, that relative rankings between algorithms can vary significantly throughout the search, with MOEA/D starting out very effectively but being overtaken by most other algorithms after 10^4 evaluations. On ZDT6, we see MOEA/D as the best overall algorithm, while the performance of RVEA flattens out, and NSGA-3 surpasses it towards the end. In contrast, on DTLZ1, we can see poor performance of MOEA/D being worse than RandomSearch and only after 10^3 evaluations catching up with other algorithms and surpassing RandomSearch. On ZDT5, we can see NSGA-2 consistently being the best algorithm and MOEA/D being the worst solver while the other algorithms

---

[2] Or number of reference vectors. Algorithms where both population size and number of reference vectors can be set always have these parameters equal to each other.

have similar performance. From these examples, we see that while, in many cases, multiple algorithms reach similar performance at the end of the search, there are significant differences in the number of evaluations they need to reach this value. Simultaneously, changing rankings for different numbers of evaluations can be observed.

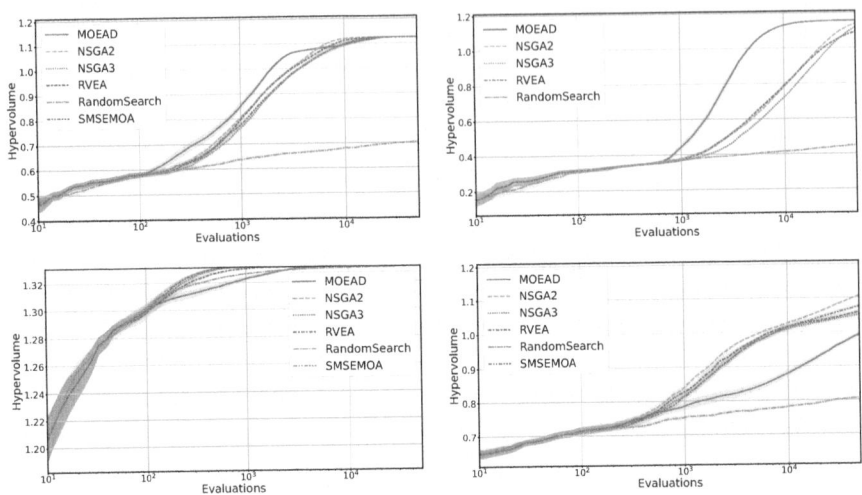

Fig. 2. Evolution of hypervolume over time for the selected algorithms on selected problems. Within each subplot, algorithms have been set to a common population size/number of reference vectors. From left to right, top to bottom, the function (population size) of each figure is as follows: ZDT2 (100), ZDT6 (500), DTLZ1 (50), and ZDT5 (100). The reference point is always set to $[1.1]^d$ after normalizing the objectives ($d = 2$ for ZDT, $d = 3$ for DTLZ). Shaded areas show the 95% confidence intervals, lines show the mean.

In addition to the common comparison of different algorithms, we can also compare the performance of different settings of the same algorithm. Here, we focus on population size, as this is usually a parameter that prevents fair comparisons when only the final solution set returned by the algorithm is considered. To illustrate this type of comparison, we show different settings of MOEA/D on ZDT4 on the left side of Fig. 3. This figure shows that the hypervolume of the initial random sample is the same until the desired population size is reached. This shows that every population size has the same starting point, and the specific behavior of different population sizes can be analyzed. Most interesting here are the low and high population sizes. Population size 10 has the worst performance with few evaluations but achieves the best performance around 10^3 evaluations. Population sizes of 250 and 500 have the worst performances but converge after 10^4 evaluations like the other population sizes.

4.3   Changing Indicators

Since we track all individual objectives rather than a single indicator, we can use the same data for multiple comparisons based on different indicators. This is a clear example of the separation between analysis and experimental setup, which also enables data to be reused for different purposes. In this section, we change the focus to the IGD+ indicator.

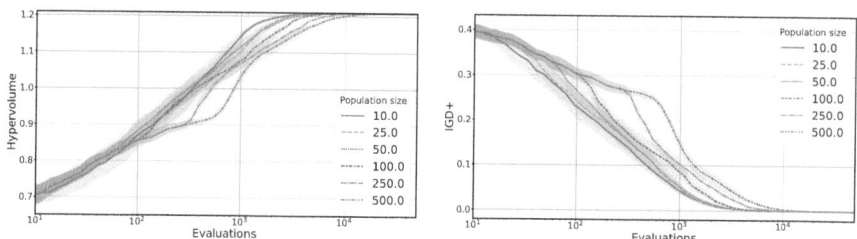

Fig. 3. Evolution of hypervolume (left) and IGD+ (right) over time for the selected parameterizations for the MOEA/D algorithm on ZDT4. The used reference set for IGD+ is taken from PyMOO, while the reference point for the hypervolume is set to $[1.1]^2$ after normalizing the objectives. Shaded areas show the 95% confidence intervals.

To calculate the IGD+, we need to define a reference set for each problem. In our case, we can either take the provided set from PyMOO or extract a reference set from the existing data. We opt for the former in this paper but provide access in our toolbox to the latter as well (using filtering of data from many runs). The resulting performance over time is plotted on the right side of Fig. 3, from which we can see that it shows the same characteristics as the hypervolume plot on the left, e.g., the curves for population sizes 250 and 500 have distinctive bends at the same position. These bends visualize the transition from the 1st (randomly initialised) to the 2nd (selected by selection) generation. This visual change is also present for the other population sizes, but to a lesser exend. Population sizes 25, 50, and 100 show a slightly wider spread but converge simultaneously. Noteworthy is the consistently good performance of population size 10.

4.4   Aggregations: ECDF

In addition to the per-function evolution of indicator values, we can also take a more aggregated view of our performance data. By normalizing performance to $[0, 1]$, we can aggregate, e.g., hypervolume over time for all functions in our benchmark. Note that this normalization is done in addition to the objective-normalization, to allow for aggregating objective spaces of different dimensionality. In our case, this normalization is done by using the maximum hypervolume based only on the reference and ideal points ($[0]^d$ and $[1.1]^d$ respectively), but this could also be done, e.g., using the reference front information. These normalized performance values can then be aggregated to provide an overview of the general behavior of the algorithm over the full set of benchmark problems we consider. Using this aggregation of normalized performance is equivalent to the commonly used Empirical Cumulative Distribution Functions, where we don't need to define an a priori set of quality targets[3].

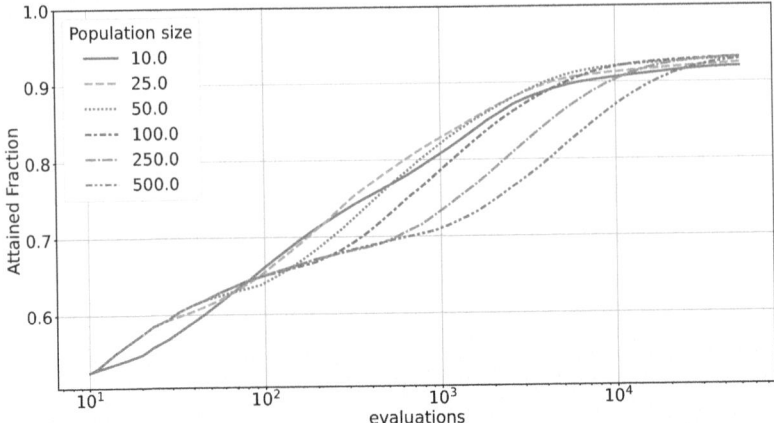

Fig. 4. Example plot for ECDF of hypervolume (where the reference point is $[1.1]^d$ and then hypervolume is scaled to $[0, 1]$). This plot aggregates the hypervolume over time behavior on all considered benchmark problems for the selected algorithm (NSGA-2) with different population sizes.

Figure 4 shows this aggregated EAF-based ECDF [27] for the hypervolume indicator on NSGA-2. Somewhat surprisingly, we see that, for every population size, the first iteration after initialization generally leads to a worse hypervolume fraction compared to having a larger initial population. We also notice that the algorithm with the highest hypervolume fraction changes over time, with larger population sizes overtaking the smaller ones near the end of the budget.

4.5   Comparing Attainment Surfaces

In addition to the anytime performance, we can also compare the differences in solution sets returned by the algorithm relative to all points it has visited during the search. Corresponding Empirical Attainment Surface (EAF) plots considering the final solution and all points can be seen in Fig. 5. Based on these plots, we can create an EAF-difference plot between the returned and full set of solutions (i.e., the whole external archive) to show the regions of the objective space that get 'lost' when only looking at the final population. Such an EAF-difference plot for NSGA-2 with population size 10 on ZDT5 is shown in the bottom part of Fig. 5. Here, we can see that the final solution of NSGA-2 is able

---

[3] Instead of targets, we use the normalized performance values directly [27].

to mostly cover the outer parts of the possible attainable Pareto front compared to all visited solutions but falls short of consistently covering the middle part.

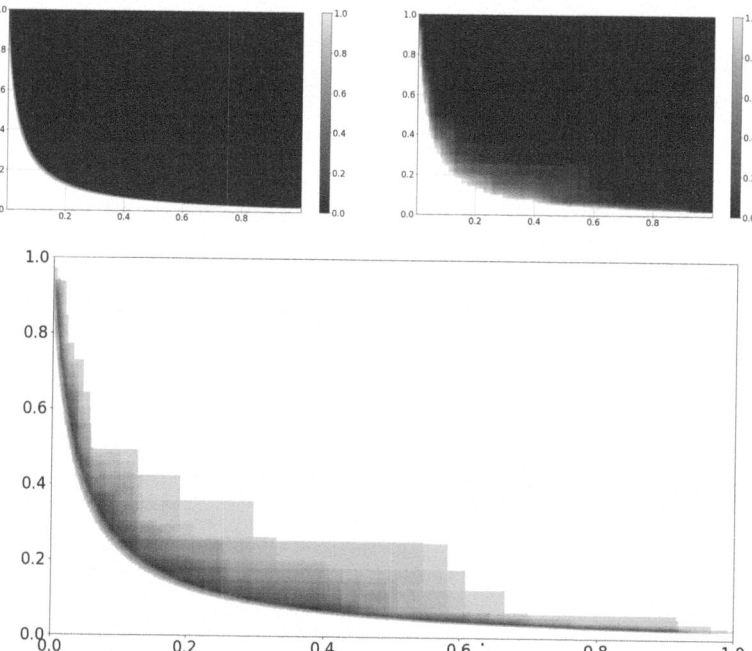

Fig. 5. EAF plots of the full set of solutions evaluated by NSGA-2 with population size 10 (top left) and the final set of solutions returned by the algorithm (top right) on ZDT5. The colors indicate the fraction of runs in which a solution dominating the point was attained. The bottom plot shows the EAF-difference between these two plots, where colors correspond to the fraction of runs where a dominating solution was found in the archive, but not in the final population.

4.6   Robust Ranking over Time

We can also look at other types of comparison at different points during the search. One example is robust ranking [15], which makes rankings based on a single indicator at different budgets or even extends to multiple indicators [32]. IOHinspector interfaces with the `robustranking` package of [32] to easily generate different types of rankings, including single- and multi-objective robust rankings.

Figure 6 shows the robust ranking of the algorithms with population size 100 at eight evaluation budgets. The figure shows that the rankings over time are not fixed and provide interesting insights that extend and confirm the other presented visualizations like the ECDFs.

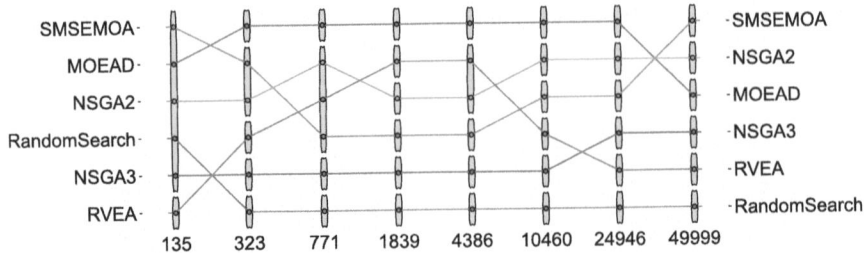

Fig. 6. Robust ranking at different evaluation times for the hypervolume indicator on all runs on all problems with population size 100. The budgets are logarithmically selected between 100 and 50 000, and the ranking order starts at the top. The significance threshold α was set for each ranking to 0.05, and 10 000 bootstrap samples were drawn. Statistically tied algorithms are within a gray box. (Color figure online)

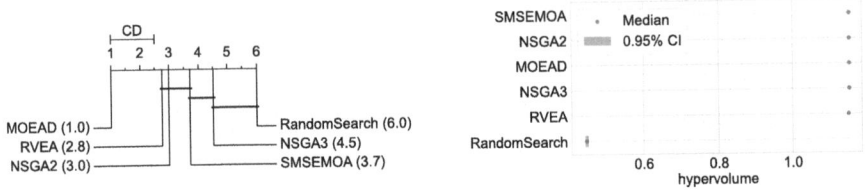

(a) Critical difference plot after 4 386 evaluations. $\alpha = 0.05$.

(b) Confidence intervals after 49 999 evaluations.

Fig. 7. Alternative ranking plots originating from the robustranking package.

Recall that robust ranking assesses (mean) overall performance. The rankings are different compared to other commonly used ranking approaches, such as critical difference plots [12]. Figure 7a shows the CD plot after 4 386 evaluations. Although the ranking order – in this example – is equal, the statistical ties are not. This is because both rankings compare different aspects: overall performance versus individual performance.

In the last ranking in Fig. 6, SMS-EMOA surpasses MOEA/D, which was in the first group in all earlier rankings. However, the confidence intervals of the bootstrap distribution in Fig. 7b show that the confidence intervals are very narrow, and the median values of the MOEAs are close to each other. This suggests that these algorithms, in their underlying samples, all tend to have converged. In turn, this indicates that the used problem instances are not extremely challenging enough for these algorithms.

As with all visualization and analytic perspectives provided in this paper, the settings of IOHinspector can be modified based on the specific goals of a user's benchmarking setup. This enables a wide range of different viewpoints on the algorithmic performances and the respective strengths and weaknesses of different algorithms in the considered portfolio.

5 Conclusions and Future Work

In this paper, we explored several aspects of benchmarking multi-objective optimization algorithms. Expanding on the existing IOHprofiler framework, we proposed software tools to simplify and support the anytime-performance comparison of multi-objective optimizers. By utilizing unbounded archives for data logging, we showcase that this anytime analysis can be achieved without modifying existing algorithms. Following the design principles of IOHprofiler, we aimed to separate decisions on the analysis side of the benchmarking pipeline from the experimental design choices during the data collection. This way, performance data can be used and re-used to answer various research questions. For example, this approach allows for changing indicators, reference points, and even ranking methodology based on the goals of the analysis.

The software presented in this work consists of two parts. The first is an update to the IOHexperimenter to enable logging multiple objectives using an unbounded archive. The second is the new IOHinspector package, which integrates a variety of multi-objective specific analysis methodologies, such as different indicators and ranking schemes, with visualizations commonly used in single-objective optimizations. As such, our IOHinspector package is not specific to the multi-objective case and can be used more broadly. To illustrate the functionality of these IOHprofiler modules, we integrated them with the popular PyMOO package. In the future, we also aim for more direct integration into other popular libraries for multi-objective optimization. In particular, integrating subset selection mechanisms to extract finite-size approximations of the Pareto front from the stored archive would be very beneficial.

For the analysis of benchmark data, we hope to encourage wider sharing of (reproducible) performance data, which could then be analyzed from different perspectives, e.g., by utilizing different indicators. While we support several commonly used indicators, we aim to expand this selection over time, specifically concerning multi-modal MOO. Finally, we hope these tools can become integrated into other types of benchmarking pipelines, such as algorithm selection and configuration scenarios, to enable the exploration of a wide variety of algorithmic design questions.

Acknowledgements. The authors from Paderborn University, University of Twente and Leiden University acknowledge support from the European Research Center for Information Systems (ERCIS). This work was also supported by CNRS Sciences informatiques via the AAP project IOHprofiler, and in part by the COST action CA22137 (ROARNET).

References

1. Audet, C., Bigeon, J., Cartier, D., Le Digabel, S., Salomon, L.: Performance indicators in multiobjective optimization. Eur. J. Oper. Res. **292**(2), 397–422 (2021). https://doi.org/10.1016/j.ejor.2020.11.016

2. Bartz-Beielstein, T., et al.: Benchmarking in optimization: Best practice and open issues. Arxiv preprint arXiv:2007.03488 [cs.NE] (2020). https://arxiv.org/abs/2007.03488

3. Beume, N., Naujoks, B., Emmerich, M.T.M.: SMS-EMOA: multiobjective selection based on dominated hypervolume. Eur. J. Oper. Res. **181**(3), 1653–1669 (2007). https://doi.org/10.1016/j.ejor.2006.08.008

4. Blank, J., Deb, K., Dhebar, Y., Bandaru, S., Seada, H.: Generating well-spaced points on a unit simplex for evolutionary many-objective optimization. IEEE Transactions on Evolutionary Computation (In press)

5. Blank, J., Deb, K.: Pymoo: multi-objective optimization in python. IEEE Access **8**, 89497–89509 (2020). https://doi.org/10.1109/ACCESS.2020.2990567

6. Brockhoff, D., Tušar, T., Tušar, D., Wagner, T., Hansen, N., Auger, A.: Biobjective performance assessment with the COCO platform. Arxiv preprint arXiv:1605.01746 (2016). https://doi.org/10.48550/arXiv.1605.01746

7. Brockhoff, D., Wagner, T., Trautmann, H.: On the properties of the R2 indicator. In: Genetic and Evolutionary Computation Conference, GECCO '12, pp. 465–472. ACM (2012). https://doi.org/10.1145/2330163.2330230

8. Cheng, R., Jin, Y., Olhofer, M., Sendhoff, B.: A reference vector guided evolutionary algorithm for many-objective optimization. IEEE Trans. Evol. Comput. **20**(5), 773–791 (2016). https://doi.org/10.1109/TEVC.2016.2519378

9. Deb, K., Jain, H.: An evolutionary many-objective optimization algorithm using reference-point-based nondominated sorting approach, part I: Solving problems with box constraints. IEEE Trans. Evol. Comput. **18**(4), 577–601 (2014)

10. Deb, K., Pratap, A., Agarwal, S., Meyarivan, T.: A fast and elitist multi-objective genetic algorithm: NSGA-II. IEEE Trans. Evol. Comput. **6**(2), 182–197 (2002). https://doi.org/10.1109/4235.996017

11. Deb, K., Thiele, L., Laumanns, M., Zitzler, E.: Scalable test problems for evolutionary multiobjective optimization. In: Abraham, A., Jain, L., Goldberg, R. (eds.) Evolutionary Multiobjective Optimization, pp. 105–145. Advanced Information and Knowledge Processing, Springer, London, UK (Jan 2005). https://doi.org/10.1007/1-84628-137-7_6

12. Demsar, J.: Statistical comparisons of classifiers over multiple data sets. J. Mach. Learn. Res. **7**, 1–30 (2006). https://jmlr.org/papers/v7/demsar06a.html

13. Dias, D.M., Jesus, A.D., Paquete, L.: A software library for archiving nondominated points. In: Proceedings of the Genetic and Evolutionary Computation Conference Companion, p. 53-54. GECCO '21, Association for Computing Machinery, New York, NY, USA (2021). https://doi.org/10.1145/3449726.3462737

14. Doerr, C., Wang, H., Ye, F., van Rijn, S., Bäck, T.: IOHprofiler: A benchmarking and profiling tool for iterative optimization heuristics. Arxiv preprint arXiv:1806.07555 (Oct 2018). https://doi.org/10.48550/arXiv.1810.05281

15. Fawcett, C., Vallati, M., Hoos, H.H., Gerevini, A.E.: Competitions in AI – Robustly Ranking Solvers Using Statistical Resampling (Aug 2023). https://arxiv.org/abs/2308.05062

16. Fieldsend, J.E., Everson, R.M., Singh, S.: Using unconstrained elite archives for multiobjective optimization. IEEE Trans. Evol. Comput. **7**(3), 305–323 (2003). https://doi.org/10.1109/TEVC.2003.810733

17. Grimme, C., et al.: Peeking beyond peaks: challenges and research potentials of continuous multimodal multi-objective optimization. Comput. Oper. Res. **136**, 105489 (2021). https://doi.org/10.1016/j.cor.2021.105489

18. Hansen, N., Auger, A., Brockhoff, D., Tušar, T.: Anytime performance assessment in blackbox optimization benchmarking. IEEE Trans. Evol. Comput. **26**(6), 1293–1305 (2022). https://doi.org/10.1109/TEVC.2022.3210897

19. Hansen, N., Auger, A., Ros, R., Mersmann, O., Tušar, T., Brockhoff, D.: COCO: a platform for comparing continuous optimizers in a black-box setting. Optim. Methods Softw. **36**(1), 1–31 (2020). https://doi.org/10.1080/10556788.2020.1808977

20. Ishibuchi, H., Imada, R., Setoguchi, Y., Nojima, Y.: How to specify a reference point in hypervolume calculation for fair performance comparison. Evol. Comput. **26**(3), 411–440 (2018)

21. Ishibuchi, H., Masuda, H., Tanigaki, Y., Nojima, Y.: Modified distance calculation in generational distance and inverted generational distance. In: Evolutionary Multi-Criterion Optimization - 8th International Conference, EMO 2015. vol. 9019, pp. 110–125. Springer (2015). https://doi.org/10.1007/978-3-319-15892-1_8

22. Ishibuchi, H., Pang, L.M., Shang, K.: A new framework of evolutionary multi-objective algorithms with an unbounded external archive. In: ECAI 2020, pp. 283–290. IOS Press (2020)

23. Jesus, A.D., Paquete, L., Derbel, B., Liefooghe, A.: On the design and anytime performance of indicator-based branch and bound for multi-objective combinatorial optimization. In: GECCO '21: Genetic and Evolutionary Computation Conference, Lille, France, July 10-14, 2021. pp. 234–242. ACM (2021). https://doi.org/10.1145/3449639.3459360

24. Jesus, A.D., Paquete, L., Liefooghe, A.: A model of anytime algorithm performance for bi-objective optimization. J. Glob. Optim. **79**(2), 329–350 (2021). https://doi.org/10.1007/S10898-020-00909-9

25. Kostovska, A., et al.: Per-run algorithm selection with warm-starting using trajectory-based features. In: Rudolph, G., Kononova, A.V., Aguirre, H., Kerschke, P., Ochoa, G., Tušar, T. (eds.) Parallel Problem Solving from Nature – PPSN XVII: 17th International Conference, PPSN 2022, Dortmund, Germany, September 10–14, 2022, Proceedings, Part I, pp. 46–60. Springer International Publishing, Cham (2022). https://doi.org/10.1007/978-3-031-14714-2_4

26. Li, M., López-Ibáñez, M., Yao, X.: Multi-objective archiving. IEEE Trans. Evol. Comput. **28**(3), 696–717 (2023). https://doi.org/10.1109/TEVC.2023.3314152

27. López-Ibáñez, M., Vermetten, D., Dreo, J., Doerr, C.: Using the empirical attainment function for analyzing single-objective black-box optimization algorithms. IEEE Trans. Evol. Comput. (2025). https://doi.org/10.1109/TEVC.2024.3462758

28. Mersmann, O., Trautmann, H., Naujoks, B., Weihs, C.: Benchmarking evolutionary multiobjective optimization algorithms. In: Proceedings of the IEEE Congress on Evolutionary Computation, CEC 2010, Barcelona, Spain, 18-23 July 2010. pp. 1–8. IEEE (2010). https://doi.org/10.1109/CEC.2010.5586241

29. Meunier, L., et al.: Black-box optimization revisited: Improving algorithm selection wizards through massive benchmarking. IEEE Trans. Evol. Comput. **26**(3), 490–500 (2022). https://doi.org/10.1109/TEVC.2021.3108185

30. de Nobel, J., Ye, F., Vermetten, D., Wang, H., Doerr, C., Bäck, T.: IOHexperimenter: Benchmarking platform for iterative optimization heuristics. Evol. Comput. m1–6 (2024). https://doi.org/10.1162/evco_a_00342

31. Preuß, O.L., Rook, J., Trautmann, H.: On the potential of multi-objective automated algorithm configuration on multi-modal multi-objective optimisation problems. In: Applications of Evolutionary Computation, pp. 305–321. Springer Nature Switzerland, Cham (2024). https://doi.org/10.1007/978-3-031-56852-7_20

32. Rook, J., Hoos, H.H., Trautmann, H.: Multi-objective ranking using bootstrap resampling. In: Proceedings of the Genetic and Evolutionary Computation Conference Companion, GECCO 2024, Melbourne, VIC, Australia, July 14-18, 2024, pp. 155–158. ACM (2024). https://doi.org/10.1145/3638530.3654436

33. Schäpermeier, L., Kerschke, P.: Reinvestigating the R2 indicator: achieving pareto compliance by integration. In: Affenzeller, M., Winkler, S.M., Kononova, A.V., Trautmann, H., Tušar, T., Machado, P., Bäck, T. (eds.) Parallel Problem Solving from Nature – PPSN XVIII: 18th International Conference, PPSN 2024, Hagenberg, Austria, September 14–18, 2024, Proceedings, Part IV, pp. 202–216. Springer Nature Switzerland, Cham (2024). https://doi.org/10.1007/978-3-031-70085-9_13

34. Schütze, O., Hernández, C.: Archiving Strategies for Evolutionary Multi-objective Optimization Algorithms. Springer International Publishing, Cham (2021)

35. Tanabe, R., Oyama, A.: Benchmarking MOEAs for multi-and many-objective optimization using an unbounded external archive. In: Bosman, P.A.N. (ed.) Proceedings of the Genetic and Evolutionary Computation Conference, GECCO 2017, pp. 633–640. ACM Press, New York, NY (2017)

36. Vermetten, D., et al.: Reproducibility files MO-IOHinspector (2024). https://doi.org/10.5281/zenodo.13843074

37. Wang, H., Vermetten, D., Ye, F., Doerr, C., Bäck, T.: IOHanalyzer: Detailed performance analyses for iterative optimization heuristics. ACM Transac. Evol. Learn. Optim. 2(1), 3:1–3:29 (2022). https://doi.org/10.1145/3510426

38. Zhang, Q., Li, H.: MOEA/D: a multiobjective evolutionary algorithm based on decomposition. IEEE Trans. Evol. Comput. 11(6), 712–731 (2007). https://doi.org/10.1109/TEVC.2007.892759

39. Zitzler, E., Thiele, L.: Multiobjective optimization using evolutionary algorithms — a comparative case study. In: Eiben, A.E., Bäck, T., Schoenauer, M., Schwefel, H.-P. (eds.) PPSN 1998. LNCS, vol. 1498, pp. 292–301. Springer, Heidelberg (1998). https://doi.org/10.1007/BFb0056872

40. Zitzler, E., Thiele, L., Deb, K.: Comparison of multiobjective evolutionary algorithms: Empirical results. Evol. Comput. 8(2), 173–195 (2000). https://doi.org/10.1162/106365600568202

41. Zitzler, E., Thiele, L., Laumanns, M., Fonseca, C.M., Grunert da Fonseca, V.: Performance assessment of multiobjective optimizers: an analysis and review. IEEE Trans. Evol. Comput. 7(2), 117–132 (2003). https://doi.org/10.1109/TEVC.2003.810758

Applications

Multi-objective Sequential Decision Making for Holistic Supply Chain Optimization

Rifny Rachman[1]([⊠]) [iD], Josh Tingey[2] [iD], Richard Allmendinger[1] [iD],
Pradyumn Shukla[1] [iD], and Wei Pan[1] [iD]

[1] The University of Manchester, Oxford Road M13 9PL, Manchester, UK
`rifny.rachman@postgrad.manchester.ac.uk`
[2] Peak AI Ltd, Manchester, UK

Abstract. This paper presents a supply chain (SC) optimization model that balances economic, environmental, and social objectives by aiming to maximize profits while minimizing greenhouse gas emissions and service level inequalities. It simulates real-world SC issues using a four-echelon facility model with variable demands from three markets. We utilize multi-objective Markov decision processes (MOMDP) through multi-objective reinforcement learning with decomposition (MORL/D), paired with weighted sum proximal policy optimization (PPO), and compare them using a non-dominated sorting genetic algorithm II (NSGA-II). The decision variables are production and delivery quantities, leading to Pareto front sets that illustrate optimal trade-offs. Key contributions include defining a three-objective SC under a MOMDP framework, introducing a Python-based SC simulation tool called Messiah, pioneering MORL/D in multi-objective SC optimization, and comparing it with PPO and NSGA-II. Our findings reveal that MORL/D achieves more balanced outcomes in optimality, diversity, and density, with enhanced hypervolume and expected utility metrics through knowledge sharing.

Keywords: Multi-objective optimization · Markov decision process · Supply chain · Reinforcement learning · Evolutionary algorithm

1 Motivation

Real-world decision-making in supply chain (SC) optimization often involves multiple echelons, facilities, routes, and interconnections, resulting in inherent complexities. These complexities are elevated when various conflicting objectives are incorporated that represent growing concerns about sustainability in economic, environmental, and social dimensions [4]. They can be achieved by optimizing the actions comprising manufacturing and delivery quantities on the

https://peak.ai/

Supplementary Information The online version contains supplementary material available at https://doi.org/10.1007/978-981-96-3506-1_18.

routes while considering observations such as demand, inventory, capacity, cumulative emission, and average service level (SL) inequality. This paper presents a case study that emulates demand fluctuations, high-dimensional actions (21 dimensions), observation spaces (49 dimensions), and operational interdependency that mimics typical SC problems encountered in practice (see Sect. 2.3). The model covers three objectives, i.e., profit maximization, greenhouse (GHG) emission minimization, and SL inequality (i.e., the cumulative gap of the demand fulfilment rate between markets [20]) minimization within a four-echelon SC network with ten facilities and non-stationary demand from three markets, constituting a commonly observed scenario by our industry partner, Peak AI Ltd. Our goal is to find an approximation of the (unknown) Pareto front (PF).

Existing studies on SC optimization predominantly employ classical and metaheuristic methods, such as evolutionary algorithms (EAs) [19]. Classical approaches like ϵ-constraint [1,3,18,22] and weighted sum [7,9] are common for simpler multi-objective SC problems. For more complex high-dimensional problems, researchers often prefer metaheuristic methods, notably population-based algorithms such as simulated annealing [12], multi-objective particle swarm optimization [31], and the non-dominated sorting genetic algorithm II (NSGA-II) [13,31]. However, these methods frequently overlook the dynamic interaction between agents and their environment. Alternatively, several studies have explored the application of reinforcement learning (RL) [28] in single-objective SC optimization based on the Markov decision process (MDP), showing improvements in profit and robustness [2,16,21,23].

Nevertheless, the application of RL in multi-objective SC scenarios is still in its infancy. To our knowledge, Shar et al. [27] are the only authors addressing this, employing multi-objective reinforcement learning (MORL) in a two-echelon serial SC network comprising a manufacturer, warehouse, and market, concentrating on reducing operational costs and GHG emissions. In addition, in this study, the SC environment is tailored for specific configurations, limiting customization. Hence, this paper makes the following contributions:

- Formally defining a multi-hierarchical, multi-facility SC problem with non-stationary demand as a multi-objective MDP (MOMDP), focusing on economic, environmental, and social performance (see Sects. 2.2 and 2.3).
- Introducing a customizable SC simulation environment in Python, named Messiah (Multi-Echelon Supply SImulation AlgoritHm) (see Sect. 4).
- Evaluating two RLs and one evolutionary algorithm: multi-objective RL based on decomposition (MORL/D), weighted-sum proximal policy optimization (PPO), and non-dominated sorting genetic algorithm II (NSGA-II) and analyzing their multi-objective optimization performance (see Sect. 4).

Subsequent sections introduce the formal definition of the SC problem, describe the methods and Messiah environment, present the experimental setup and analysis, and conclude with potential future research areas.

2   Problem Definition

This section formulates an SC network based on common real-world SC problems observed in Peak AI Ltd, featuring modified parameters for a multi-objective

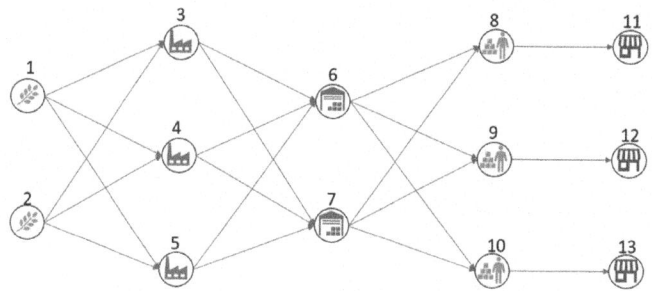

Fig. 1. An example of a four-echelon SC network will be simulated in this work. The network starts with sourcing raw material from suppliers $N^s = \{1, 2\}$, which is transported to manufacturers $N^m = \{3, 4, 5\}$, who in turn manufacture and store the products before delivering them to distributors $N^d = \{6, 7\}$. The retailers $N^r = \{8, 9, 10\}$ then receive the products and sell them on different markets $N^z = \{11, 12, 13\}$. The demand is subject to non-stationarity.

framework and incorporating multiple markets to evaluate SL inequality. The formulation is built independently from the optimization and MOMDP frameworks. An example network is presented in Fig. 1 for enhanced clarity. The variables and parameters are listed in Table 1.

2.1   Multi-objective SC Optimization Problem

We formulate the multi-objective SC problem considered here as follows:

$$
\text{Maximize} \quad Prof = \sum_t \left[\left(\sum_{i \in N^d} \sum_{j \in N^r} q^\tau_{(t-L)ij} \cdot \text{price} \right) - \left(\sum_{k \in N^m} \frac{q^\psi_{tk} \cdot c^\psi_k}{v^\psi_k} \right) \right.
$$
$$
- \left(\sum_{i \in (N^s \cup N^m \cup N^d)} \sum_{j \in (N^m \cup N^d \cup N^r)} q^\tau_{tij} \cdot c^\tau_{ij} \cdot L \right) \tag{1}
$$
$$
\left. - \left(\sum_{j \in (N^m \cup N^d \cup N^r)} I_{tj} \cdot c^\varsigma_j \right) \right], \quad \text{where} \quad i < j.
$$

$$
\text{Minimize} \quad E = \sum_t \left[\sum_{j \in (N^m \cup N^d \cup N^r)} \left(I_{tj} \cdot e^\varsigma_j \right) + \sum_{k \in N^m} \left(q^\psi_{tk} \cdot e^\psi_k \right) \right.
$$
$$
\left. + \sum_{i \in (N^s \cup N^m \cup N^d)} \sum_{j \in (N^m \cup N^d \cup N^r)} \left(q^\tau_{ij} \cdot e^\tau_{ij} \cdot L \right) \right], \tag{2}
$$
$$
\text{where} \quad i < j
$$

$$
\text{Minimize} \quad F = \frac{1}{2} \sum_{y \in N^r} \sum_{\substack{y' \in N^r \\ y' \neq y}} |SL_y - SL_{y'}| \tag{3}
$$

Table 1. Variables and parameters used in this model. Nodes i, j, and k are the facilities in the supply chain (SC) network, and period t represents the daily timestep. Variables ς, ψ, and τ denote inventory, production, and transportation activities, respectively.

Notations	Definition
q_{tij}^{τ}	Transport quantity at period t, from node i to j
q_{tk}^{ψ}	Manufacturing quantity at period t, at manufacturer k
$Prof$	Total profit of all periods
E	Total emission of all periods
F	Total SL inequality measure of all periods
SL_y	SL at node y of all periods
Rev_t	Revenue at period t
PC_t	Production cost at period t
TC_t	Transport cost at period t
IC_t	Inventory cost at period t
L	Transport lead time
I_{tj}	Inventory unit at period t, node j
c_j^{ς}	Inventory cost per unit at node j
e_j^{ς}	Emission per unit resulted from inventory at node j
c_k^{ψ}	Manufacturing cost per unit at node k
v_k^{ψ}	Yield ratio from manufacturing process at node k
e_k^{ψ}	Emission per unit resulted from the manufacturing process at node k
c_{ij}^{τ}	Transport cost per unit from node i to j
e_{ij}^{τ}	Emission per unit resulted from product transport from node i to j
$\mathbf{Q_{tj}}$	The outstanding order at node j
CE_t	The accumulated emission at period t
AF_t	The average service level inequality in period t
d_{tz}	Demand at period t, market z
Cap	Transport capacity

Subject to

$$q_{tj}^{\psi} = \sum_{i \in N^s} q_{(t-L)ij}^{\tau}, \quad \forall t, \forall j \in N^m \tag{4}$$

In Equation (5), I_{tj} is defined for j in the set N^m, which may represent a specific subset of manufacturing facilities.

$$I_{tj} = I_{(t-1)j} + q_{tj}^{\psi} - \sum_{k \in N^d} q_{tjk}^{\tau}, \quad \forall t, \forall j \in N^m \tag{5}$$

In Equation (6), I_{tj} is defined for j in the set $N^d \cup N^r$, which covers a different subset of items or conditions compared to the Equation (5).

$$
\begin{aligned}
I_{tj} = I_{(t-1)j} + \sum_{i \in (N^m \cup N^d)} q^{\tau}_{(t-L)ij} \\
- \sum_{k \in (N^r \cup N^z)} q^{\tau}_{tjk}, \quad \forall t, \forall j \in (N^d \cup N^r), \quad \text{where } i < j < k
\end{aligned}
\tag{6}
$$

$$
\sum_{k \in (N^d \cup N^r \cup N^z)} q^{\tau}_{(t+1)jk} \leq I_{tj}, \quad \forall t, \forall j \in (N^m \cup N^d \cup N^r), \quad \text{where } j < k
\tag{7}
$$

$$
SL_y = \min \left(\frac{\sum_{t=(t-L)}^{T} \sum_{x \in N^d} q^{\tau}_{txy}}{\sum_t d_{tz}}, 100\% \right), \quad \forall y \in N^r
\tag{8}
$$

where d_{tz} is the associated demand for each retailer y.

$$
0 \leq q^{\tau}_{tij} \leq Cap, \quad \forall t, \forall i \in (N^s \cup N^m \cup N^d), \forall j \in (N^m \cup N^d \cup N^r), \quad \text{where } i < j
\tag{9}
$$

$$
0 \leq q^{\psi}_{tk}, \quad \forall t, \forall k \in N^m
\tag{10}
$$

The optimization model contains 2100 decision variables: (18 delivery quantities + 3 manufacturing quantities) × 100 periods. The constraint (4) ensures that all the incoming material from suppliers is carried forward to the manufacturing process. The constraints (5) and (6) calculate the inventory in the next period depending on the previous inventory, the quantity of goods delivered, and the number of deliveries sent. The constraint (7) ensures that the amount of deliveries does not exceed the inventory level and, at the same time, guarantees that the inventory level will always be positive, as the quantity of delivery cannot be less than zero. The constraint (8) measures the SL inequality in each market, which is the percentage of demand fulfilment, ranging from 0% to 100%. The constraint (9) confines the amounts of delivery between zero and the transport capacity. Meanwhile, the constraint (10) maintains that the manufacturing amounts are not negative.

2.2   MOMDP Framework for SC: A Formal Problem Definition

A MORL agent in the SC environment operates through sequential decision-making, modeled as a finite MOMDP with periods $t = 1, 2, 3, ..., T$, representing daily decisions. A MOMDP is defined as $\langle S, A, ST, \gamma, \mu, \mathbf{R} \rangle$ [17], where at each period t, the agent observes the state $S_t = S$, such as inventory levels, order processing, and market demand. In a multi-objective SC, the state can include cumulative emissions and average SL inequality.

Given the state, the agent selects an action $A_t = \mathcal{A}(S_t)$, such as manufacturing and delivery quantities, according to a policy π_t, where $\pi_t(a \mid s)$ is the probability of action a in state s. The state transitions follow ST_t, μ represents the initial state distribution, and γ denotes discount factors. As actions are executed, the SC environment is updated, and the agent receives rewards based on multiple conflicting objectives (e.g., profit, negative GHG emissions, and negative SL inequality), represented as a vector $\mathbf{R} \subset \mathbb{R}^d$.

Unlike single-objective MDPs, MOMDPs optimize a vector of value functions $\mathbf{V}^\pi$ corresponding to a policy π [25], given by:

$$\mathbf{V}^\pi = \mathbb{E}\left[\sum_{k=0}^{\infty} \gamma^k \mathbf{r}_{k+1} \mid \pi, \mu\right] \tag{11}$$

Without known utility functions, multiple optimal value vectors may exist, forming a Pareto front $PF(\mathbf{\Pi})$, where $\mathbf{\Pi}$ is the set of all policies. A policy π is Pareto-optimal if no other policy π' dominates it:

$$PF(\mathbf{\Pi}) = \{\pi \in \mathbf{\Pi} \mid \nexists \pi' \in \mathbf{\Pi} : \mathbf{V}^{\pi'} \succ_P \mathbf{V}^\pi\}, \tag{12}$$

where:

$$\mathbf{V}^\pi \succ_P \mathbf{V}^{\pi'} \iff \left(\forall b : \mathbf{V}_b^\pi \geq \mathbf{V}_b^{\pi'}\right) \wedge \left(\exists b : \mathbf{V}_b^\pi > \mathbf{V}_b^{\pi'}\right) \tag{13}$$

2.3 MOMDP-Based SC Optimization Model

A four-echelon SC with multiple facilities, markets, and non-stationary demand is formulated based on the MOMDP framework.

State Transition Functions. State transition represents the functions moving from one state at period $(t-1)$ to the next state at period t. The state transition functions are given in Equations (14) to (17).

$$I_{tj} = I_{(t-1)j} + \sum_{i \in (N^s \cup N^m \cup N^d)} q^\tau_{(t-L)ij}$$
$$- \sum_{k \in (N^d \cup N^r \cup N^z)} q^\tau_{tjk}, \quad \forall j \in (N^m \cup N^d \cup N^r), \text{ where } i < j < k \tag{14}$$

$$\mathbf{Q}_{tj} = \{q^\tau_{(t-L+1)ij}, \ldots, q^\tau_{tij} \mid \forall j \in (N^m \cup N^d \cup N^r), i \in (N^s \cup N^m \cup N^d) \tag{15}$$
$$\text{such that } i < j\}$$

$$CE_t = CE_{(t-1)} + E_t \tag{16}$$

$$AF_t = \frac{AF_{t-1} \cdot (t-1) + F_t}{t} \tag{17}$$

State Space (S). The state represents the agents' observation of the simulation environment at a given timestep. Our SC environment uses a 49-dimensional observation space, including 11 inventory levels for raw materials and products, outstanding orders on 18 routes for two days of lead time, cumulative emission, and average SL inequality. The state at period t is defined as follows.

$$\mathbf{S_t} = \{I_{(t-1)j}, \mathbf{Q}_{(t-1)j}, CE_{t-1}, AF_{t-1} \,|\, 0 \le I_{(t-1)j}, \forall j \in (N^m \cup N^d \cup N^r)\} \quad (18)$$

Action Space (A). In our SC environment, the action space is 21-dimensional, covering manufacturing quantities from 3 manufacturers and delivery quantities on 18 routes. The actions at period t are given by:

$$\mathbf{A_t} = \{q_{tij}^\tau, q_{tk}^\psi \,|\, 0 \le q_{tij}^\tau \le Cap, \quad 0 \le q_{tk}^\psi$$
$$\forall i \in (N^s \cup N^m \cup N^d), \, j \in (N^m \cup N^d \cup N^r), \, k \in N^m, \text{ where } i < j\} \quad (19)$$

Rewards (R). The problem has three goals: maximize profit while minimizing GHG emissions and SL inequality, creating a three-dimensional reward vector. MORL agents maximize cumulative rewards with negative values for emissions and SL inequality, resulting in the reward vector $\mathbf{R_t} = Prof_t, -E_t, -F_t$.

In RL, rewards are based on objective functions (Equations (1),(2),(3)). Constraints are handled differently from optimization models. Equation (14) integrates Constraints (4) and (6), while (9) is part of the state space (Equation (18)), and the SL inequality is included in the reward calculation. Unlike optimization models, RL agents receive feedback on ongoing deliveries, cumulative emissions, and SL inequality (Equations (15), (16), (17)), which improves decision-making, a benefit not available in optimization-based models.

3 Methods

In SC practice, facilities such as suppliers, manufacturers, warehouses, and retailers are predefined, and transport routes are determined accordingly. The algorithms optimize which facilities and routes are used and to what extent. NSGA-II [11] serves as the optimization benchmark due to its wide applicability, with numerous SC studies indicating its superior performance over other multi-objective optimization methods [13,29,31]. In this study, its variable decisions are encoded as illustrated in Fig. 2 based on Sect. 2.1.

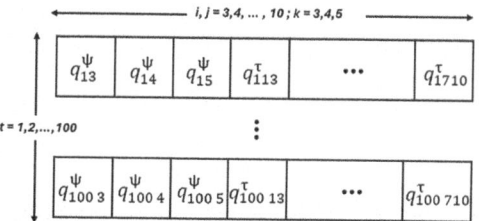

Fig. 2. In NSGA-II, an individual solution is depicted by a vector with 2100 decision variables. Each chromosome gene signifies the production and delivery amounts q_{tk}^ψ and q_{tij}^τ for each period t. Mutation and crossover apply to these solutions.

3.1   Sequential Decision Making

In contrast to NSGA-II and other optimization techniques, MDP-based methods facilitate the interaction between an agent and its environment, allowing online learning and better exploration. The agent executes an action at state t, and in response, the environment provides both an observable state and a reward, serving as feedback to the agent. The agent then uses this information to decide its next action, as demonstrated in Fig. 3 [28].

MORL Based on Decomposition. To tackle multi-objective SC problems, MDP is extended into MOMDP framework. A multi-objective SC environment has been developed to train the MORL/D algorithm [15], a population-based algorithm. MORL/D is chosen for its ability to handle multi-dimensional actions and decompose complex problems into subproblems using linear

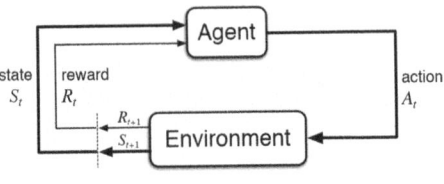

Fig. 3. Agent-environment interaction along the time steps enabling more informed sequential decision making.

scalarization. It operates as a multiple-policy approach, generating trade-off solutions for unknown user preferences. The algorithm iterates by updating policies, weights, and reference points, exchanging knowledge between subproblems to improve learning and refine the PF.

In MORL/D, policy candidates interact with the environment, and experiences are stored in buffer to improve policy performance. The best policies are retained in an external archive, and the process continues until the PF set is updated. The shared buffer facilitates cooperation across subproblems based on knowledge exchange. Meanwhile, PSA adjusts weights based on evaluations and proximity to PF solutions. When the value in an objective vector of a solution $f_j(x)$ is equal to or lower than its nearest neighbor $f_j(x')$, the weight λ_j^x is increased slightly (multiplied by δ, e.g., 1.05). Conversely, when $f_j(x) > f_j(x')$, the weight λ_j^x is reduced (divided by δ). This mechanism promotes diversity in the set of solutions [8].

Single-Objective RL with Weighted Sum. PPO [26], a single-objective RL algorithm, is leveraged for comparison. It enhances a surrogate function through stochastic gradient descent while applying clipping for stable updates, which is crucial in high-dimensional SC problems. Featuring an actor-critic architecture, PPO is known for its sample efficiency, making it apt for intricate environments. This algorithm is combined with the weighted sum method to tailor to a multi-objective environment. The selection of 21 predefined weights in this research is based on the Das-Dennis method [10] and is guided by the work of Wang et al. [31], whose study, comparable in complexity, produced 12 to 20 solutions in their PF sets. We normalize rewards to guarantee balanced preferences using the maximum and minimum values obtained from running each objective separately. The objectives are then scalarized into a single function, generating a diverse set of PFs calculated with the predefined weights.

3.2   Performance Measurements

The hypervolume [34] is frequently employed as a metric in multi-objective optimization contexts. In conjunction, we evaluate the sparsity [15], and the Expected Utility Metric (EUM) [33][1]. The sparsity calculates average squared distance between adjacent solutions $\widetilde{P}_j(i)$ and $\widetilde{P}_j(i+1)$ in front set $\mathcal{F}$, where j represents the objective index and i denotes the solution index as in Equation (20).

$$S(\mathcal{F}) = \frac{1}{|\mathcal{F}|-1} \sum_{j=1}^{m} \sum_{i=1}^{|\mathcal{F}|-1} \left(\widetilde{P}_j(i) - \widetilde{P}_j(i+1) \right)^2 \tag{20}$$

EUM calculates the expected value of the highest utility on all weights in the set Λ. Given that the utility function be a function of the value vector $\overrightarrow{v^\pi}$ and the weight vector $\overrightarrow{w}$, the EUM of the front $\mathcal{F}$ is as shown in Equation (21).

$$EUM(\mathcal{F}) = \underset{\overrightarrow{w} \in \Lambda}{\mathbb{E}} \left[\max_{\overrightarrow{v^\pi} \in \mathcal{F}} u(\overrightarrow{v^\pi}, \overrightarrow{w}) \right] \tag{21}$$

4   Experimentation

This section discusses the preliminary implementation that has been done so far. The RL experimentation operates on the Messiah simulator, a customizable SC environment that uses the Gymnasium [30] interface. This simulator necessitates node and route specifications to automatically create an SC network. The demand can be inputted as data or generated according to specified distributions. Additionally, it facilitates SC simulation using defined state transition functions.

4.1   Experimental Setup

All experiments use Python 3.11.2 on the JupyterLab platform, equipped with 128GB RAM and a 16-core CPU.

SC Environment Setup. In this SC problem, the supply from suppliers is unlimited. Demand from all markets is non-stationary: fluctuations d_{11} and d_{12} follow normal distributions ($\mu = 150, \sigma = 60$ and $\mu = 100, \sigma = 40$), while d_{13} follows a Poisson distribution ($\lambda = 200$). A product price of 20 applies across all

---

[1] EUM is not applicable to NSGA-II since it is not an algorithm based on utility. Hence, each solution is not associated with any weight.

markets, with unfulfilled demand treated as a demand loss. This scenario follows the MORL framework with a finite time horizon of $T = 100$ and a lead time of $L = 2$. The transportation capacity (Cap) is 200 in each delivery, while the manufacturing capacity is unlimited. Moreover, the values of the node-related and transport-related parameters are given in the supplementary material. The reference point for all hypervolume calculations is (-3 x 10^5, -5 x 10^5, -5 x 10^2) for the GHG emission, profit, and SL inequality, respectively.

Algorithm Setup. We use the PPO agent implementation from Stable Baselines 3 [24], and the MORL/D agent implementation from MORL Baselines 1.0.0 [14]. Both hyperparameters are given in the supplementary material. Normalization procedures are applied to enhance learning: action spaces are scaled between -1 and 1, and observation spaces are transformed to a range of 0 to 1 as suggested in the baseline.

We use 10 random seeds for each weight in PPO, resulting in 210 runs for 10 PF sets with 21 solutions each. The generalized advantage estimation method, calculated via weighted average temporal difference residuals, minimizes variance and bias. The advantage function is normalized during training for stability, preventing large values from dominating policy updates. The agent employs a multi-layer perceptron neural network, typical of actor-critic algorithms.

The MORL/D algorithm includes a reward normalization wrapper to ensure that all values in the reward vector are on the same scale. It optimizes according to the scalarized expected returns criterion [17], where the expectation values of multiple runs inform utility calculations. This paper employs the multi-policy soft actor-critic (MOSAC) method [6], which learns a set of policies in two steps, followed by an evolutionary strategy for refinement. Four training scenarios are tested: 1) without weight adaptation and shared buffer (MORL/D); 2) without weight adaptation, with shared buffer (MORL/D (SB)); 3) with Pareto simulated annealing (PSA) weight adaptation, without shared buffer (MORL/D (PSA)); and 4) with PSA and shared buffer (MORL/D (SB&PSA)). Each scenario runs with 10 random seeds, leading to 40 runs in the SC environment, following Felten et al.'s [15] approach to ensure statistical robustness.

The comparison with NSGA-II is regulated on the best possible parameters that promote convergence, taking into account computational resources. We employ NSGA-II from the Pymoo package [5] to solve our SC problem using the hyperparameters shown in the supplemental material. In this study, we perform 20 independent runs (random seeds) to obtain statistical robustness, resulting in 20 PF sets, considering the faster computation for each run and the broader gap between PF sets compared to the RL results.

4.2   Results and Discussion

This section presents the results of the experiment and their implications.

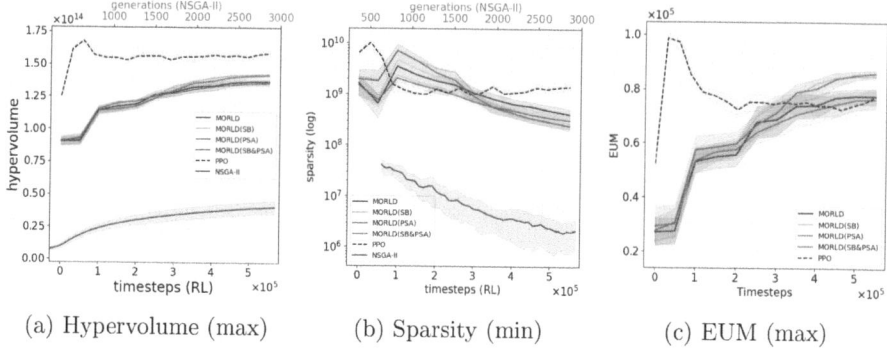

(a) Hypervolume (max)   (b) Sparsity (min)   (c) EUM (max)

Fig. 4. (a) shows multi-objective based algorithms (MORL/D and NSGA-II) demonstrate consistently progressive hypervolume convergence throughout the training while PPO immediately peaks but then decreases. Moreover, (b) presents the first two offer better density than the rest. Despite its lower hypervolume, (c) reveals that MORL/D with SB serves better EUM than PPO when converging.

Overall Performance. This section discusses the general overview of all results based on several performance indicators for multi-objective optimization. Figure 4 displays the hypervolume and sparsity of all algorithms, as well as EUMs for RL algorithms. A multi-objective model should ideally exhibit a high hypervolume, indicating extensive solution coverage and proximity to optimality, along with low sparsity, which signifies robustness [32]. The PPO algorithm has higher hypervolume values than all MORL/D scenarios, while all RL scenarios present higher hypervolume than NSGA-II. This suggests that the PPO solutions cover a larger area than the other two methods, indicating higher diversity and proximity to optimality. However, the initial spike in hypervolume and EUM, followed by a decline, suggests challenges in weight incorporation. Initially, favoring profit leads to higher hypervolume despite normalization efforts. While a few PPO solutions approach the ideal point (max profit, min GHG emissions, and SL inequality), they are sparse, diminishing the solutions' robustness.

MORL/D shows higher gradients initially, which decrease as training progresses. MORL/D with SB mechanisms outperforms other scenarios by enabling knowledge sharing across subproblems, enhancing hypervolume, and utility while maintaining solution density for robust decision-making. Balancing diversity and density is vital; dense solutions improve robustness [32], while sparse ones might offer broader coverage.

Around generation 250, NSGA-II begins to identify feasible solutions. It converges by approximately generation 3000, exhibiting a lower hypervolume than RL methods and low sparsity, which signifies a much more confined solution search area compared to RL-based techniques. This suggests an imbalance between exploration and exploitation, with a significantly greater focus on exploiting the current search area rather than exploring new ones.

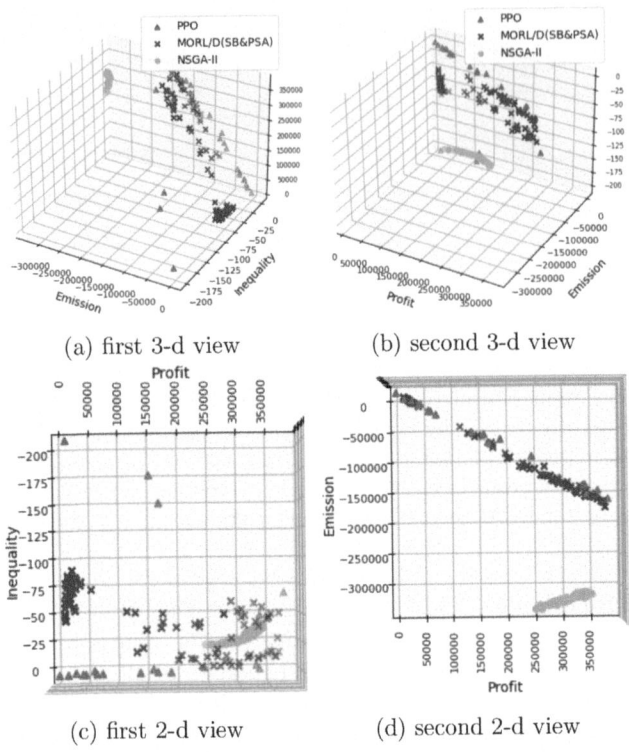

(a) first 3-d view   (b) second 3-d view

(c) first 2-d view   (d) second 2-d view

Fig. 5. MORL/D shows the most balance between diversity, optimality, and density. A few PPO solution points are close to the 'ideal point', resulting in a high hypervolume value. Nonetheless, the solutions are sparse, diminishing the robustness of the model. Meanwhile, NSGA-II solutions are concentrated in a narrow solution space.

To generate a PF set, PPO requires around 3 h and 36 min for 21 solution points, whereas MORL/D takes about 1 h and 22 min to obtain 30 to 70 points. On the other hand, NSGA-II completes the process in just 10 min for 50 to 130 points. Unlike NSGA-II, RL-based methods involve a substantial number of interactions between agents and the environment during the action search phase to update their policy. These RL methods need significant exploration to discover trade-off solutions in multi-objective scenarios, particularly in high-dimensional problems like SC.

PF Solution Sets. The experimentation results yield 10, 40, and 20 PF sets (i.e., sets of non-dominated solutions to approximate Pareto optimal solutions) for PPO, MORL/D, and NSGA-II, respectively. We select the best PF set for each method based on hypervolume and randomly choose five comparison PF sets from each algorithm to visually confirm that their coverage areas are not significantly different. Figure 5 illustrates the distribution of solutions for each best PF. The PPO PF set is the sparsest, particularly polarized in addressing

SL inequality, with values either very high or low, showing limited moderate options. Profit and emission values are more consistent, possibly due to the significant scale difference between the SL inequality and the other objectives. Normalization may not be effective given the complex environment, where PPO's solution quality heavily relies on constant predefined weights, unlike MORL/D, which updates weights during training.

In contrast, the NSGA-II PF set concentrates around lower SL inequality and higher profit, while GHG emissions are notably higher than in the other methods, suggesting a local optima trap. The conflicting relationship between profit and emission (i.e., increased profit results in higher emission) is more evident in RL-based approaches because this link is demonstrated through simple computations and weight proportions in the utility function. Meanwhile, the trade-off between profit and the SL inequality is less obvious due to more intricate calculations. Ultimately, the MORL/D PF set emerges as the most balanced solution, offering a wide range, a dense spread, and an effective integration of all objectives.

5   Conclusions

Experimentation shows that PPO achieves the highest hypervolume but has sparse solutions, while NSGA-II offers dense solutions with much lower hypervolume. In contrast, MORL/D methods exhibit decent hypervolume values with lower sparsity and higher EUM compared to PPO, signifying the most balanced solutions in terms of optimality, diversity, and density among the three techniques. The SB mechanism in MORL/D improves hypervolume and EUM while maintaining density. Future studies could involve more experimentation across various SC network architectures and, furthermore, integrate RL with meta-learning to improve training efficiency and generalization.

Acknowledgements. This study was funded by the Economic and Social Research Council (ESRC), UK Research and Innovation (UKRI), Peak AI Ltd., and the University of Manchester (Grant Reference No. ES/T002085/1).

Disclosure of Interests. The authors have no competing interests to declare that are relevant to the content of this article.

References

1. Abdolazimi, O., Salehi Esfandarani, M., Salehi, M., Shishebori, D.: Robust design of a multi-objective closed-loop supply chain by integrating on-time delivery, cost, and environmental aspects, case study of a Tire Factory. J. Cleaner Product. **264**, 121566 (Aug 2020). https://doi.org/10.1016/j.jclepro.2020.121566, https://linkinghub.elsevier.com/retrieve/pii/S0959652620316139
2. Abu Zwaida, T., Pham, C., Beauregard, Y.: Optimization of inventory management to prevent drug shortages in the hospital supply chain. Appl. Sci. **11**(6), 2726 (Mar 2021). https://doi.org/10.3390/app11062726, https://www.mdpi.com/2076-3417/11/6/2726

3. Banasik, A., Kanellopoulos, A., Claassen, G., Bloemhof-Ruwaard, J.M., van der Vorst, J.G.: Closing loops in agricultural supply chains using multi-objective optimization: A case study of an industrial mushroom supply chain. Int. J. Product. Econom. **183**, 409–420 (Jan 2017). https://doi.org/10.1016/j.ijpe.2016.08.012, https://linkinghub.elsevier.com/retrieve/pii/S0925527316301918

4. Becerra, P., Mula, J., Sanchis, R.: Green supply chain quantitative models for sustainable inventory management: A review. J. Cleaner Product. **328**, 129544 (Dec 2021). https://doi.org/10.1016/j.jclepro.2021.129544, https://linkinghub.elsevier.com/retrieve/pii/S0959652621037239

5. Blank, J., Deb, K.: Pymoo: Multi-objective optimization in Python. IEEE Access **8**, 89497–89509 (2020). https://doi.org/10.1109/ACCESS.2020.2990567, https://ieeexplore.ieee.org/document/9078759/

6. Chen, D., Wang, Y., Gao, W.: Combining a gradient-based method and an evolution strategy for multi-objective reinforcement learning. Appl. Intell. **50**(10), 3301–3317 (Oct 2020). https://doi.org/10.1007/s10489-020-01702-7, https://link.springer.com/10.1007/s10489-020-01702-7

7. Chen, Z., Andresen, S.: A multiobjective optimization model of production-sourcing for sustainable supply chain with consideration of social, environmental, and economic factors. Mathematical Problems in Engineering **2014**, 1–11 (2014). https://doi.org/10.1155/2014/616107, http://www.hindawi.com/journals/mpe/2014/616107/

8. Czyzżak, P., Jaszkiewicz, A.: Pareto simulated annealing—a metaheuristic technique for multiple-objective combinatorial optimization. Journal of MultiâĂŘCriteria Decision Analysis **7**(1), 34–47 (Jan 1998). https://doi.org/10.1002/(SICI)1099-1360(199801)7:1<34::AID-MCDA161>3.0.CO;2-6, https://onlinelibrary.wiley.com/doi/10.1002/(SICI)1099-1360(199801)7:1<34::AID-MCDA161>3.0.CO;2-6

9. Darestani, S.A., Hemmati, M.: Robust optimization of a bi-objective closed-loop supply chain network for perishable goods considering queue system. Comput. Indust. Eng. **136**, 277–292 (Oct 2019). https://doi.org/10.1016/j.cie.2019.07.018, https://linkinghub.elsevier.com/retrieve/pii/S0360835219304103

10. Das, I., Dennis, J.E.: Normal-boundary intersection: a new method for generating the pareto surface in nonlinear multicriteria optimization problems. SIAM J. Optim. **8**(3), 631–657 (Aug 1998). https://doi.org/10.1137/S1052623496307510, http://epubs.siam.org/doi/10.1137/S1052623496307510

11. Deb, K., Pratap, A., Agarwal, S., Meyarivan, T.: A fast and elitist multi-objective genetic algorithm: NSGA-II. IEEE Trans. Evol. Comput. **6**(2), 182–197 (Apr 2002). https://doi.org/10.1109/4235.996017, http://ieeexplore.ieee.org/document/996017/

12. Eskandarpour, M., Dejax, P., Miemczyk, J., Péton, O.: Sustainable supply chain network design: an optimization-oriented review. Omega **54**, 11–32 (Jul 2015). https://doi.org/10.1016/j.omega.2015.01.006, https://linkinghub.elsevier.com/retrieve/pii/S0305048315000080

13. Farrokhi-Asl, H., Makui, A., Ghousi, R., Rabbani, M.: Developing a hazardous waste management system with consideration of health, safety, and environment. Comput. Electr. Eng. **82**, 106553 (Mar 2020). https://doi.org/10.1016/j.compeleceng.2020.106553, https://linkinghub.elsevier.com/retrieve/pii/S0045790619309607

14. Felten, F., et al.: A toolkit for reliable benchmarking and research in multi-objective reinforcement learning. In: Proceedings of the 37th Conference on Neural Information Processing Systems (NeurIPS 2023) (2023)

15. Felten, F., Talbi, E.G., Danoy, G.: Multi-objective reinforcement learning based on decomposition: a taxonomy and framework (2023). https://doi.org/10.48550/ARXIV.2311.12495, https://arxiv.org/abs/2311.12495, publisher: arXiv Version Number: 2

16. Ganesan, V.K., Sundararaj, D., Srinivas, A.P.: Adaptive inventory replenishment for dynamic supply chains with uncertain market demand. In: Chakrabarti, A., Arora, M. (eds.) Industry 4.0 and Advanced Manufacturing: Proceedings of I-4AM 2019, pp. 325–335. Springer Singapore, Singapore (2021). https://doi.org/10.1007/978-981-15-5689-0_28

17. Hayes, C.F., et al.: A practical guide to multi-objective reinforcement learning and planning. Autonom. Agents Multi-Agent Syst. 36(1), 26 (Apr 2022). https://doi.org/10.1007/s10458-022-09552-y, https://link.springer.com/10.1007/s10458-022-09552-y

18. Huang, L., Zhen, L., Yin, L.: Waste material recycling and exchanging decisions for industrial symbiosis network optimization. J. Cleaner Product. 276, 124073 (Dec 2020). https://doi.org/10.1016/j.jclepro.2020.124073, https://linkinghub.elsevier.com/retrieve/pii/S0959652620341184

19. Jayarathna, C.P., Agdas, D., Dawes, L., Yigitcanlar, T.: Multi-objective optimization for sustainable supply chain and logistics: a review. Sustainability 13(24), 13617 (Dec 2021). https://doi.org/10.3390/su132413617, https://www.mdpi.com/2071-1050/13/24/13617

20. Khodaee, V., Kayvanfar, V., Haji, A.: A humanitarian cold supply chain distribution model with equity consideration: The case of COVID-19 vaccine distribution in the European Union. Decision Anal. J. 4, 100126 (Sep 2022). https://doi.org/10.1016/j.dajour.2022.100126, https://linkinghub.elsevier.com/retrieve/pii/S2772662222000571

21. Lalla-Ruiz, E., Mes, M., Voß, S.: Computational Logistics. Springer, Enschede, The Netherlands (2020)

22. Mota, B., Gomes, M.I., Carvalho, A., Barbosa-Povoa, A.P.: Towards supply chain sustainability: economic, environmental and social design and planning. J. Cleaner Product. 105, 14–27 (Oct 2015). https://doi.org/10.1016/j.jclepro.2014.07.052, https://linkinghub.elsevier.com/retrieve/pii/S0959652614007719

23. Perez, H.D., Hubbs, C.D., Li, C., Grossmann, I.E.: Algorithmic approaches to inventory management optimization. Processes 9(1), 102 (Jan 2021). https://doi.org/10.3390/pr9010102, https://www.mdpi.com/2227-9717/9/1/102

24. Raffin, A., Hill, A., Gleave, A., Kanervisto, A., Ernestus, M., Dormann, N.: Stable-baselines3: Reliable reinforcement learning implementations. J. Mach. Learn. Res. 22(268), 1–8 (2021). http://jmlr.org/papers/v22/20-1364.html

25. Roijers, D.M., Whiteson, S., Vamplew, P., Dazeley, R.: A survey of multi-objective sequential decision-making. J. Artif. Intell. Res. 48, 63–113 (2013)

26. Schulman, J., Wolski, F., Dhariwal, P., Radford, A., Klimov, O.: Proximal Policy Optimization Algorithms (2017). https://doi.org/10.48550/ARXIV.1707.06347, https://arxiv.org/abs/1707.06347, publisher: arXiv Version Number: 2

27. Shar, I.E., Wang, H., Gupta, C.: Multi-objective reinforcement learning for sustainable supply chain optimization. In: 2023 IEEE 19th International Conference on Automation Science and Engineering (CASE), pp. 1–7. IEEE, Auckland, New Zealand (Aug 2023). https://doi.org/10.1109/CASE56687.2023.10260354, https://ieeexplore.ieee.org/document/10260354/

28. Sutton, R.S., Barto, A.G.: Reinforcement Learning: An Introduction, 1st edn. The MIT Press, Massachusetts (2015)

29. Tirkolaee, E.B., Goli, A., Faridnia, A., Soltani, M., Weber, G.W.: Multi-objective optimization for the reliable pollution-routing problem with cross-dock selection using Pareto-based algorithms. J. Cleaner Product. **276**, 122927 (Dec 2020). https://doi.org/10.1016/j.jclepro.2020.122927, https://linkinghub.elsevier.com/retrieve/pii/S0959652620329723

30. Towers, M., et al.: Gymnasium. https://github.com/Farama-Foundation/Gymnasium

31. Wang, Y., Shi, Q., Hu, Q., You, Z., Bai, Y., Guo, C.: An efficiency sorting multi-objective optimization framework for sustainable supply network optimization and decision making. J. Cleaner Product. **272**, 122842 (Nov 2020). https://doi.org/10.1016/j.jclepro.2020.122842, https://linkinghub.elsevier.com/retrieve/pii/S0959652620328870

32. Xu, J., Tian, Y., Ma, P., Rus, D., Sueda, S., Matusik, W.: Prediction-guided multi-objective reinforcement learning for continuous robot control. In: III, H.D., Singh, A. (eds.) Proceedings of the 37th international conference on machine learning. In: Proceedings of Machine Learning Research, vol. 119, pp. 10607–10616. PMLR (Jul 2020), https://proceedings.mlr.press/v119/xu20h.html

33. Zintgraf, L.M., Kanters, T.V., Roijers, D.M., Oliehoek, F.A., Beau, P.: Quality assessment of MORL algorithms: a utility-based approach. In: Proceedings of the 24th Annual Machine Learning Conference of Belgium and the Netherlands (2015)

34. Zitzler, E., Thiele, L.: Multiobjective optimization using evolutionary algorithms — A comparative case study. In: Goos, G., Hartmanis, J., Van Leeuwen, J., Eiben, A.E., Bäck, T., Schoenauer, M., Schwefel, H.P. (eds.) Parallel Problem Solving from Nature — PPSN V, vol. 1498, pp. 292–301. Springer Berlin Heidelberg, Berlin, Heidelberg (1998). https://doi.org/10.1007/BFb0056872, http://link.springer.com/10.1007/BFb0056872, series Title: Lecture Notes in Computer Science

Interactive Evolutionary Reoptimization for Groundfish Survey Planning

Thomas Philip Runarsson$^{(\boxtimes)}$

School of Engineering and Natural Sciences, University of Iceland, Reykjavik, Iceland
tpr@hi.is

Abstract. This study introduces an interactive evolutionary algorithm (EA) for optimizing path planning in groundfish surveys. The approach employs interactive reoptimization to iteratively refine plans by adjusting constraints and incorporating new information, addressing the limitations of traditional optimization models and including real-world factors not initially captured. Developed with input from experienced surveyors, the method provides a practical way to refine survey plans at sea, where fast optimization is crucial. We compare the EA's performance with a mixed integer programming model applied to a groundfish survey in Iceland involving four vessels, aiming to find the shortest route while considering vessel capacity and port unloading. Results show the EA's potential in complex marine surveys, highlighting its advantages in interactive optimization and sustainable fisheries management.

Keywords: interactive reoptimization · evolutionary algorithms · planning

1 Introduction

Optimization models are simplified representations of real-world problems and inherently contain inaccuracies due to various limitations, such as approximating complex criteria, simplifying problem specifications for computational tractability, limited knowledge of the problem context, and constraints on time and resources. These inaccuracies can lead to unrealistic or infeasible solutions. Missing conditions often become apparent only after solutions are observed, and data integrity issues, such as inaccuracies or incomplete information, can further complicate the problem's formulation. For these reasons, decision makers using bespoke solvers frequently need to manually adjust their solutions. These adjustments can be complex, leading to suboptimal outcomes and often resulting in the eventual abandonment of the system. Interactive optimization approaches offer an alternative by enabling the user to adjust or enrich the model during the process, incorporating expert knowledge to better tackle real-world aspects not initially captured in the model [1]. In this paper, we employ interactive evolutionary reoptimization as our approach to refine the decision making process. By iteratively adjusting constraints or introducing new ones, we re-run the optimization to progressively improve the solution.

© The Author(s), under exclusive license to Springer Nature Singapore Pte Ltd. 2025
H. Singh et al. (Eds.): EMO 2025, LNCS 15512, pp. 275–287, 2025.
https://doi.org/10.1007/978-981-96-3506-1_19

We present an interactive evolutionary algorithm (EA) designed for conducting groundfish surveys. The initial version of the algorithm, introduced in [2], has been in use for over two decades, often relying on various workarounds. Users previously employed a trial-and-error approach, modifying survey data and resulting in suboptimal plans. To address this, we have introduced a modification that not only enhances the model but also provides a simple way for users to interactively and minimally bias the solutions. This allows them to incorporate aspects not captured by the model or its data. The approach was suggested by users, drawing on their extensive experience in surveying. For this method to be effective-especially since it is typically run on a laptop at sea-the optimization process needs to be fast. We compare the EA with a mixed integer programming (MIP) model developed for the same task. Both approaches aim to find the shortest possible route while respecting the fishing vessel's capacity limits and the need to unload at ports. A distinctive feature of the EA is its ability to determine which ports to use for unloading, whereas the MIP model requires visiting all predetermined ports at some point along the route.

The structure of this paper is organized as follows: Sect. 2 formally defines the problem and introduces the MIP model. This is followed by Sect. 3, which provides a detailed description of the EA. The comparison between the MIP model and the EA is presented in Sect. 4. Additional objectives, described in Sect. 5, are incorporated into the model to enable the user to interactively bias the search without significantly affecting the main objectives. Finally, the paper concludes with a discussion and final conclusions in Sect. 6.

2   Groundfish Survey Problem

Groundfish surveys collect data on the abundance, distribution, and biological characteristics of fish populations. This data is crucial for managing fish stocks sustainably, ensuring that fishing does not deplete them. Typically, the surveys either use a fixed station sampling or stochastic (random) sampling [3]. The idea behind using fixed stations is to create a consistent, long-term dataset by repeatedly sampling the same location at the same time of the year. Random selection of different locations, guided by statistical methods, ensures a representative sample of the area. Nevertheless, both approaches result in a set of stations for that the fishing vessel must survey. Considering the high costs associated with each day the vessel spends at sea, it is imperative for the survey leader to determine the most efficient and effective way to conduct the survey.

Determining the most efficient path through the survey stations is a complex task, influenced by several factors. By law, all fish caught must be retained and subsequently may be sold on the market, necessitating unloading within five days. Additionally, the fishing vessel's limited capacity requires regular port visits to unload the catch during the survey. The unpredictability of the fish quantities at each station further complicates the planning process. Moreover, the complexity increases when multiple fishing vessels conduct the survey, and some stations may only be accessible for towing in certain directions due to weather or other conditions.

Each station designated for trawling has defined start and end points. The selection of which point serves as the start or end can vary, depending not only on the chosen path but also on factors such as weather conditions or the unique characteristics of that particular station. Each station, denoted as i in the set $\{1, \ldots, n\}$ is, therefore, defined by a pair of points (lat_{2i}, lon_{2i}) and (lat_{2i+1}, lon_{2i+1}). To find the shortest path, a standard solver can be used by introducing the survey vessel, denoted by $i = 0$ (nodes 0 and 1). The vessel is unique in that one end serves as the starting point, and the other is the end point, with the distance between these two points set to zero, i.e. $d_{0,1} = d_{1,0} = 0$. In this scenario, the path can be defined by establishing connections between points using a variable $x_{i,j} \in \{0, 1\}$ where $x_{2i,2i+1} = x_{2i+1,2i} = 1$ define the stations. Figure 1 illustrates this notation, where the vessel is represented by nodes 0 and 1, while all other stations i and ports k are represented by nodes $(2i, 2i + 1)$ and $(2k, 2k + 1)$, respectively. Although a port does not inherently require two nodes, with $d_{2k,2k+1} = 0$, we assign two nodes to each port for consistency in the formulation. We have the conditions that one can travel into and out of any node only once:

$$\sum_{i \in \{0,1,\ldots,2n'\}} x_{i,j} = \sum_{i \in \{0,1,\ldots,2n'\}} x_{j,i} = 1 \quad \forall j \in \{0, 1, \ldots, 2n'\}$$

where $n' > n$ includes now the port nodes and the objective is to minimize the total distance travelled:

$$\min \sum_{\substack{i \in \{0,1,\ldots,2n'\}, \\ j \in \{0,1,\ldots,2n'\}}} d_{i,j} x_{i,j} \tag{1}$$

The anticipated outcome of the tours is that they will become disconnected (subtours) when returning to the same ports. The subtour elimination constraints can be dynamically generated and then incorporated into the problem-solving process using callbacks to the solver, a well-known approach used for TSP. In our implmentation the smallest subtour, containing points (i, j) in set $\mathcal{P}$, is eliminated by

$$\sum_{(i,j) \in \mathcal{P}} x_{i,j} \leq |\mathcal{P}| - 1$$

While solving the undirected version of this problem is relatively straightforward, several specific conditions necessitate adopting a directed formulation. Firstly, the towing direction at the stations may need to be specific. Secondly, due to the finite capacity C of the vessel, any fish caught must be periodically returned to port. Defining $v_{2i,2i+1} = v_{2i+1,2i} = a_i$ as the expected weight a_i of fish caught at station i. Then, the cumulative weight upon entering station

$j \in \{1, \ldots, n\}$ can be expressed by:

$$\sum_{k \in \{2,\ldots,2n\}|k \neq 2j+1} w_{k,2j} + v_{2j,2j+1} = w_{2j,2j+1}$$

$$\sum_{k \in \{2,\ldots,2n\}|k \neq 2j} w_{k,2j+1} + v_{2j+1,2j} = w_{2j+1,2j}$$

Note that the vessel's weight at the start or upon leaving a port $k \in \{n + 1, \ldots, n'\}$ will be zero. Specifically, for each port k, $\sum_{j \in \{0,\ldots,2n'\}} w_{k,j} = 0$. As a result, these flows are excluded from the sum above. In contrast, the flow from a station includes all nodes:

$$w_{2j,2j+1} = \sum_{k \in \{0,\ldots,2n'\} \setminus \{2j,2j+1\}} w_{2j+1,k}$$

$$w_{2j+1,2j} = \sum_{k \in \{0,\ldots,2n'\} \setminus \{2j,2j+1\}} w_{2j,k}$$

In these equations, the constraint $w_{i,j} \leq C x_{i,j}$ ensures that the flow is set to zero when points (or nodes) i and j are not connected and does not exceed the vessel capacity. Similarily, $v_{i,j} \leq C x_{i,j}$. This formulation effectively tracks the accumulated weight of the catch at each station in the network. The constraint employed here aligns partially with a well-known sub-tour elimination constraint commonly used in solving TSP [4]. Now the problem has now become considerably more difficult to solve.

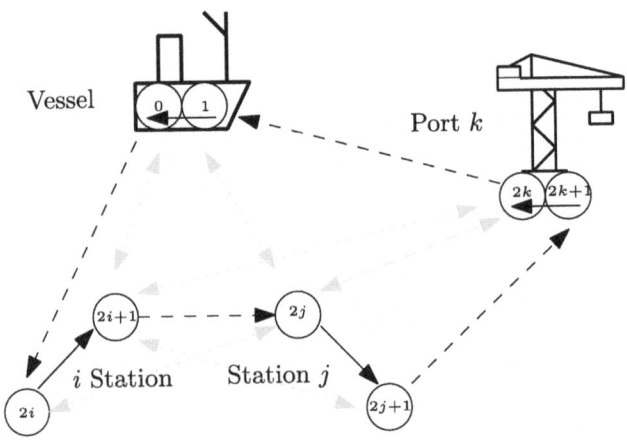

Fig. 1. An illustration of the indexed notation used in the MIP model. In the directed graph, the circles represent the nodes, with the start and end nodes labeled as 0 and 1, respectively.

If this formulation is to be successful each port must be replicated for every instance it is visited. Indeed, it is necessary to predetermine which ports will be visited and the frequency of these visits. In practical terms, it would be ideal for the solver to autonomously determine which ports to visit and the frequency of these visits. This requirement adds complexity to the standard MIP model. Reducing the number of port visits is solved by travelling to the same port in sequence. However, completely ignoring a port will require a more elaborate MIP model. Consequently, we now shift our focus to an evolutionary algorithm, that can easily incorporate this condition.

3 Evolutionary Search

A genetic algorithm developed is a variation of an algorithm developed in [2]. This path planner has been in use for over two decades without any change, but applied with numerous workarounds. The evolutionary algorithmic approach uses techniques from [5] and adapts a widely-used local search heuristic developed by [6] to tackle the TSP aspects of the problem. Present-day solvers like Gurobi [7] are capable of efficiently solving TSP problems of this size to optimality using MIP models and subtour elimination callbacks. However, when a capacity constraint is added to the vessel the MIP becomes impractical for the generic solver. The evolutionary algorithm described here is specifically designed to manage the requirement for port visits once the vessel reaches its capacity limit.

In the algorithm, each individual, denoted as ι, is represented by a sequence of integers, or genes, ranging from 1 to n'. These integers represent stations or ports, and their order in ι forms a navigational path. Each gene in this sequence can have either a positive or negative value, where the value's sign indicates the towing direction at that station. For ports, a negative sign implies that corresponding port is bypassed, and the path defined by ι continues. For example, consider integer 42 representing a port. If $\iota = [1, 4, -5, -42, 10, \ldots]$, this indicates starting at *station* 1, moving to *station* 4, entering *station* 5 from the opposite end, skipping *port* 42, and then proceeding directly to *station* 10 from *station* 5, and so on. This method of representation allows for the convenient adaptation of traditional TSP heuristics to our specific problem.

The genetic algorithm outlined in Algorithm 1 begins by generating an initial population using a randomized version of the nearest neighbor heuristic. This heuristic starts with a randomly chosen initial starting location and constructs the path in a greedy manner; however, the entry point at each station may be randomly determined. This initialization is followed by applying a modified Lin-Kernighan (LK) improvement heuristic, as referenced in [6]. The LK heuristic iteratively breaks and then greedily reconnects random station links to achieve overall path improvement. Selection of individuals is random and not strictly based on their fitness, given that they are already near-optimal due to local optimizations. In dealing with solutions that are local optima, premature convergence is a potential issue. However, diversity is preserved by replacing similar individuals with randomly initialized individuals.

Offspring are created by combining two selected parents (sampled without replacement) using the Distance Preserving Crossover (DPX) operator, as detailed in [5]. The DPX operator functions by identifying and utilizing common fragments from both parents to form an offspring, ensuring that the resulting offspring is equidistant from both parents. Initially, the offspring is not at a local optimum, necessitating the application of the LK heuristics for enhancement. After this, the offspring undergoes mutation, achieved through the 'double bridge kick move' [6] and random rotation of stations. Following mutation, the LK heuristic is applied again to refine the offspring. This newly improved offspring then replaces the worst individual in the population. This cycle of generating and improving offspring continues over several generations, until a predetermined time limit is reached.

Algorithm 1: Pseudocode for the EA (single thread)

---

1   *Initialization procedure*;
2   **foreach** *individual $\iota \in P$ (Parents)* **do**
3 | Generate ι using a randomized neighbor heuristic;
4 | Perform the modified iterative LK heuristic on ι;
5   **end**
6   *Generation loop*;
7   **repeat**
8 | *Local search improvment and evaluation*;
9 | **for** $\iota \in P$ **do**
10 | | Perform the modified LK heuristic on ι;
11 | | Evalute objective (fitness) function for ι;
12 | | Update best known path ι^*;
13 | **end**
14 | *Crossover and selection*;
15 | **for** *a random sample $\iota_a, \iota_b \in P$* **do**
16 | | ι_c = DistancePreservingCrossover(ι_a, ι_b);
17 | | Perform the modified LK heuristic on ι_c;
18 | | Improve by flipping directions on ι_c;
19 | | **if** *ι_c is better than ι_a* **then**
20 | | | Replace ι_a with ι_c;
21 | | **else if** *ι_c is better than ι_b* **then**
22 | | | Replace ι_b with ι_c;
23 | | **else if** *ι_a and ι_b are very similar* **then**
24 | | | Regenerate ι_a using initialization procedure;
25 | | **else**
26 | | | Replace the worst individual in the population with ι_c if it is better;
27 | | **end**
28 | **end**
29 | *Mutation*;
30 | **for** $\iota_d \in P \setminus \{\iota^*\}$ **do**
31 | | Select $\iota_d \in P$ with a probability 0.2;
32 | | Perform double bridge kick move in ι_d with prob. 0.2; Perform the modified LK heuristic on ι_d;
33 | | With a probability $1/n'$, flip a direction for ι_e with prob 0.3;
34 | **end**
35   **until** *convergence*;

With the integration of favorable port selection into our algorithm, our focus shifts to promoting unloading activity. This is achieved by modifying only the objective function. The new objective function, while similar to that used in the MIP model, adds a penalty factor as follows:

$$\min \sum_{\substack{i \in \{0,1,\dots,2n'\}, \\ j \in \{0,1,\dots,2n'\}}} d_{i,j} x_{i,j} (1 + \alpha m) \tag{2}$$

In this formulation, m denotes the number of times the ship visits another station while carrying a load that exceeds its capacity. The parameters α is the cost associated with surpassing the ship's capacity. This adjustment to the objective function ensures that the algorithm efficiently plans routes while also being sensitive to the capacity constraints of the ship, thereby encouraging timely unloading. Later in Sect. 5, we will demonstrate how this objective is extended to incorporate time constraints for unloading.

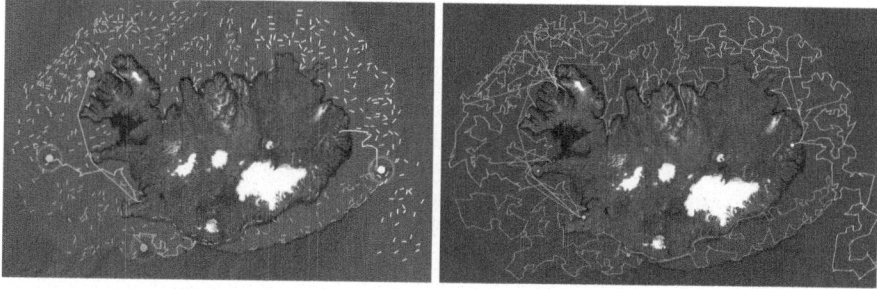

Fig. 2. The left figure shows the start of the survey conducted in spring 2023 by the four trawlers. The right figure illustrates the final entire path taken. The figures are screenshots taken from http://skip.hafro.is during the survey.

4   Computational Study

This computational study compares the evolutionary algorithm with the afore-mentioned MIP model, employing the Gurobi-11.0.3 solver that utilizes up to 4 threads. The computational tests are conducted on an AMD Ryzen 9 5950X 16-Core Processor. The evolutionary algorithm, developed in C, is also allocated 4 independent threads. The dataset for our study is derived from the groundfish survey executed in the spring of 2023, as depicted in Fig. 2. Additionally, Table 1 provides a summary of some key metrics from this survey. To avoid crossing over land, several waypoints are established to navigate between stations and ports, and the distances are recalculated using Dijkstra's algorithm [8].

This specific survey engaged four vessels, surveying distinct areas around the west, north, east and south coast of Iceland. Trawlers, each with different capacity denoted by C, were deployed in these areas. Each area is characterized by a different total number of stations n and available port options. For consistency in our analysis, we replicated the same ports as in the actual survey. This approach ensures a fairer comparison with the Gurobi solution, given that the MIP model mandates at least one visit to all selected ports. The catch data incorporated in our study reflects the actual catch for 2023, information that was, of course, unknown during the time of the survey. It's worth noting that the actual routes followed by the trawlers were subject to by various unforeseen conditions, which are not factored into our model. This will be the topic of discussion in following section.

The average time taken to travel between any two stations is approximately two hours, suggesting that a one-hour timelimit on the Gurobi solver could be plausible, particularly considering the need for frequent re-optimization throughout the survey. The results of the Gurobi solver are presented in Table 2. Comparing the incumbent solution with the historical data, the performance is quite acceptable given the large optimality gap. The last column, labeled #Ports, indicates the actual number of port visits. The number of stations are n and $n_p = n' - n$ represents the number of available port calls.

We now examine the outcomes generated by the evolutionary algorithm. The penalty factor is set to $\alpha = 0.1$. This value is sufficient for feasibility for all cases and runs. The population size of the algorithm is 30, and the number of generations was determined as eight times the sum of the number of stations and ports. Consequently, the optimization times varied: about 7 min for north, approximately 11 min for areas east and south, and notably longer, at 40 min, for the west coast area. The results from twenty independent runs of the evolutionary algorithm are presented in Table 3. In all cases the EA significantly outperforms the MIP model using Gurobi. The worst solution found is better than the incumbent solution found after one hour using four threads, with the exception of the south coast area. The south coast used a vessel with large capacity and the positions of the stations were in some sense easier to solve for both methods. The MIP model more easily solves problems with fewer port visits, achieving the lowest optimality gap of 7%. The optimality gap indicates how far the current solution is from being proven optimal.

Considering the time spent at sea, each nautical mile (nm) equates to approximately 1/10 of an hour, assuming a travel speed of 10 knots. The time saved at sea, compared to the actual voyage taken, can amount to several days. Thus, finding more efficient survey plans can result in substantial cost savings, as travel distance directly affects both time and operational expenses.

Table 1. The actual survey is conducted based on historical data, where $C_{\min}$ and $C_{\max}$ represent the minimum and maximum amounts of fish unloaded at a port, respectively.

Area	C	n	Distance (nm)	$C_{\min}$	$C_{\max}$	# Ports
West	45	164	1602	0.2	36.9	6
North	25	111	1344	10.7	24.2	4
East	60	151	1241	20.0	52.7	2
South	200	154	1209	7.4	147.6	2

Table 2. Gurobi solutions using 4 threads and one hour time limit.

Area	C	n	BestBd	Incumb	Gap	$C_{\min}$	$C_{\max}$	#Ports
West	45	164+6	1017	2117	52%	32.9	39.5	3
North	25	111+5	1029	1274	19%	7.0	23.9	3
East	60	151+3	1011	1399	28%	16.7	56.1	1
South	200	154+3	1020	1099	7%	92.7	154.4	1

5   Interactive Reoptimization

The groundfish planning is now capable of meeting the capacity constraint. However, the catch quantity remains stochastic, and the vessel may occasionally need to return to port earlier than planned. This occurred during the west coast trawl (see Fig. 2), where the catch far exceeded expectations early on. Additionally, to maintain the value of the catch, the vessel cannot stay at sea for too long. Throughout the voyage, the survey requires reoptimization due to ever changing conditions. When reviewing optimized plans, the survey leader may decide to modify conditions to discard the current best solution. For example, based on experience and long-term weather forecasts, the proposed solution might be deemed infeasible. In Fig. 3, the top path represents the best solution found for the northern area. However, due to the weather conditions in this region, the survey leader would prefer to reach a specific station (see station 11 in box 720 at the top of the figure) within the next three days. This requirement was identified only after inspecting the solution.

A flexible way to steer the solution away from the current infeasible path is to use the following time conditions, which provide the survey leader with a simple mechanism for shaping the route without significantly impacting the main objectives. The conditions can specify that a station must be:

1. reached before time t_b,
2. reached after time t_a,

Table 3. Distance statistics for twenty independent runs of the evolutionary algorithm show the average number of ports visited (excluding the final port call). All runs and threads satisfy to the capacity constraint.

Area	C	$n + n_p$	D_{min}	D_{median}	D_{mean}	D_{std}	D_{max}	#Ports (mean)
West	45	164 + 4	1130	1136	1141	9.0	1158	3.5
North	25	111 + 5	1209	1227	1225	7.3	1235	2.5
East	60	151 + 3	1094	1100	1100	3.0	1105	1.25
South	200	154 + 3	1100	1101	1101	1.0	1104	1

3. reached within the time interval $[t_a, t_b]$, or
4. avoided during the interval $[t_b, t_a]$.

This approach was suggested by the surveyors as a useful and effective strategy for interactively reoptimizing the problem.

In our example, depicted in Fig. 3, the best solution does not satisfy this new criteria, but by reoptimizing, a new plan is generated that does, as shown in the path below. This is achieved by the updated objective that now adds a further penalty factor for violating the time constraints as follows:

$$\min \sum_{\substack{i \in \{0,1,\dots,2n\}, \\ j \in \{0,1,\dots,2n\}}} d_{i,j} x_{i,j} \left(1 + \alpha(m + m_t)\right) \tag{3}$$

In this formulation, m_t denotes the number of stations that violate their time constraint. The penalty factor of the order $\alpha = 0.1$, worked well for the survey data and the number of time constraints added during the actual survey. However, further testing is needed for different survey scenarios and constraint numbers. In our example, we tested the new objective using 20 independent runs of our evolutionary algorithm. As expected, the results are slightly worse than the original unrestricted best solution, which had a distance of 1209. The new best result is 1252, with a mean and median of 1274, a standard deviation of 12, and a worst-case result of 1296. Consequently, the time at sea has increased by around 5 h.

The approach of incorporating user feedback through flexible time constraints is particularly innovative and proved to be extremely practical for our surveyors. It could be said that the users dynamically introduced multiple objectives to the problem in the form of soft constraints.

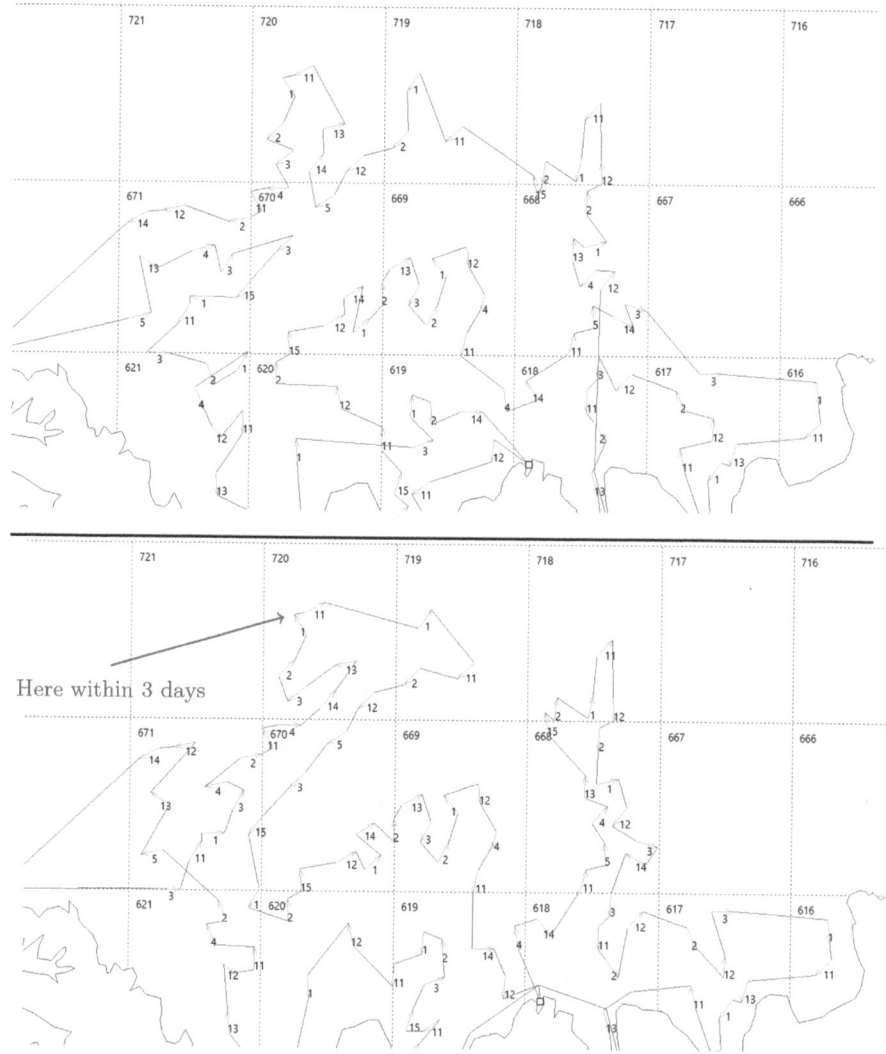

Fig. 3. The top figure displays the best solution ($D_{\min} = 1209$) found in the northern region, while the bottom figure shows a modified solution ($D = 1243$), where station 11 in box 720 at the top must be visited before day 3. Note that the towing direction for this station has been reversed when reoptimized.

6   Discussion and Conclusion

The original version of the path planner for groundfish surveys has been in use by survey leaders since 1995. This research is part of the revisions requested by the *Marine and Freshwater Research Institute* in Iceland. A key objective of our project was to explore whether modern solvers and computers could effectively address the problem using MIP models. While this approach was successful for the original problem, the extended version, which includes time and vessel capacity constraints, presents a greater challenge. These additional constraints have made it more difficult for modern generic solvers to find effective solutions. Nonetheless, efforts are currently underway to enhance the fundamental MIP model to better tackle these complexities.

The enhancements to the EA algorithm, initially developed in [2], shows considerable promise. This algorithm typically requires around ten minutes on a single thread to identify a good solution on a standard laptop computer, an attribute of significant importance considering the need for frequent reoptimization due to changing conditions at sea. Notably, the EA's capability to determine which ports to visit represents an innovative advancement. Further developments are currently in progress. We aim to incorporate all vessels into a singular optimization framework, enabling the trading of stations between vessels. Additionally, the stochastic nature of times and catches can be challenging. The evaluation of each path could incorporate simulations informed by sampling historical data or fitted distributions, a straightfoward implementation. Such advancements will provide the EA with a distinct advantage over MIP models.

In interactive optimization, fast solver response is essential, but minimizing the number of user interventions is equally important to avoid a poor user experience. If too many corrections are needed, the process can become cumbersome and detract from its advantages. Much of the work in interactive optimization has focused on comparing objective values and creating preference pairs [9,10], which often reduces user interaction to specifying preferences between objectives. While this approach has its merits, direct user insights can be more impactful when the interaction involves the solution itself rather than just the objectives. Achieving this requires more sophisticated modifications than simply adjusting preferences; it necessitates meaningful engagement with the solution, allowing users to shape it based on real-world knowledge and context.

An important aspect of our approach is the active involvement of the survey leaders in guiding how the solutions should be modified. Their extensive experience has been instrumental in shaping the interactive reoptimization strategy, including the introduction of flexible time constraints for reaching specific stations. This user-driven feedback has helped identify practical methods for steering the optimization process, allowing the solution to be refined based on real-world insights that are difficult to capture through a model alone. The ability for users to suggest adjustments and interact directly with the evolving solution ensures that the optimization remains relevant and adaptive to the actual conditions encountered at sea. This collaborative approach enhances the robustness and feasibility of the survey plans, making the optimization process more aligned with expert knowledge and operational realities.

Acknowledgment. I gratefully acknowledge the *Marine and Freshwater Research Institute* in Iceland for their invaluable contributions to this research and thank the reviewers for their insightful feedback, which helped improve the clarity of this work.

Data and code availability. The software (Win64) and data used in this study is available at the GitHub repository: https://github.com/tprunarsson/HafrallX64, which also includes the Python/C source code utilized for the experiments.

References

1. Meignan, D., Knust, S., Frayret, J.-M., Pesant, G., Gaud, N.: A review and taxonomy of interactive optimization methods in operations research. ACM Trans. Interact. Intell. Syst. (TiiS) **5**(3), 1–43 (2015)
2. Jonsson, M.T., Runarsson, T.P., Steinarsson, B.Æ.: Optimizing the sailing route for fixed ground fish survey stations, International Council for the Exploration of the Sea (1996)
3. Kimura, D.K., Somerton, D.A.: Review of statistical aspects of survey sampling for marine fisheries. Rev. Fish. Sci. **14**(3), 245–283 (2006)
4. Cook, W.J., Applegate, D.L., Bixby, R.E., Chvatal, V.: The Traveling Salesman Problem: A Computational Study. Princeton University Press, Princeton (2011)
5. Freisleben, B., Merz, P.: A genetic local search algorithm for solving symmetric and asymmetric traveling salesman problems. In: Proceedings of IEEE International Conference on Evolutionary Computation, pp. 616–621. IEEE (1996)
6. Lin, S., Kernighan, B.W.: An effective heuristic algorithm for the traveling-salesman problem. Oper. Res. **21**(2), 498–516 (1973)
7. Gurobi Optimization, LLC: Gurobi Optimizer Reference Manual (2023)
8. Dijkstra, E.W.: A note on two problems in connexion with graphs. Numer. Math. **1**(1), 269–271 (1959)
9. Branke, J.: Multiobjective Optimization: Interactive and Evolutionary Approaches, vol. 5252. Springer Science & Business Media, Heidelberg (2008). https://doi.org/10.1007/978-3-540-88908-3
10. Bin Xin, L., Chen, J.C., Ishibuchi, H., Hirota, K., Liu, B.: Interactive multiobjective optimization: a review of the state-of-the-art. IEEE Access **6**, 41256–41279 (2018)

A Multi-objective Competitive Co-evolutionary Framework with Progressive Shrinking for Wargame Scenarios

Ritam Guha[1(✉)], Ryan McKendrick[2], Bradley Feest[2], and Kalyanmoy Deb[1]

[1] Computational Optimization and Innovation (COIN) Laboratory Michigan State University, East Lansing, MI 48864, USA
{guharita,kdeb}@msu.edu
[2] Northrop Grumman Corporation, 2980 Fairview Park Drive, Falls Church 22042, USA
{ryan.mckendrick,bradley.feest}@ngc.com

Abstract. Dealing with multiple conflicting objectives in a multi-agent system is challenging, as agents' interactions complicate decision-making, especially when managing multiple Pareto-optimal fronts. In competitive co-evolutionary frameworks, not only do the objectives of each agent conflict with one another, but the agents' goals are also at odds. One such application domain is wargame strategy optimization, where the strategies of one agent must adapt based on the moves of opposing agents. Despite advancements in modern warfare, strategy analysis and decision-making are still largely manual, leaving room for great application of computational methods to automate different parts of the system. To address this, we propose a co-evolutionary optimization algorithm that integrates strategy search with interactive decision-making, allowing co-evolving populations to collaboratively identify their respective Pareto-optimal strategies. Central to this approach is a progressive-shrinking method that aligns feasible moves with those previously taken, ensuring smoother transitions. Our framework introduces a novel decision-making strategy using opposition front hypervolume improvement, particularly suited for competitive co-evolutionary contexts, combined with Penalty-based Boundary Intersection selection, to optimize strategy selections. We also examine the influence of various decision-making approaches, shrinking techniques, and parameter settings on the final results. This co-evolutionary framework, combining multi-agent interaction, evolutionary multi-objective optimization, and progressive shrinking, is not only effective for wargame strategy optimization but is also adaptable to other multi-agent conflicting systems.

Supplementary Information The online version contains supplementary material available at https://doi.org/10.1007/978-981-96-3506-1_20.

H. Singh et al. (Eds.): EMO 2025, LNCS 15512, pp. 288–302, 2025.
https://doi.org/10.1007/978-981-96-3506-1_20

Keywords: Attacker-defender system · Competitive co-evolution ·
Decision-making · Multi-objective games · Multi-agent systems ·
Progressive Shrinking

1 Introduction

In co-evolutionary optimization scenarios, where multiple agents interact, each
agent's strategy evolves in response to the other. Unlike standard optimization
problems, where objectives can be considered in isolation, co-evolutionary optimization requires both agents to continuously adapt to each other's strategies.
This challenge is amplified when the agents have conflicting objectives, transforming the problem into a competitive co-evolutionary scenario. Each agent,
while optimizing its own strategy, must also account for the actions of its opponent, making the process highly dynamic and intertwined.

One such practical application of competitive co-evolution is wargame
strategy optimization, a critical aspect of military preparation and execution.
Wargame simulations [1–3] have gained significant traction in the gaming community and military decision-making processes (MDMPs) [4]. Wargames simulate interactions between offense and defense agents, with each agent optimizing
its resources to counter the opponent's moves. While our discussion highlights
this scenario, we do not support or glorify warfare; we use wargames as an
example of a challenging multi-agent optimization problem. In military decision-
making, much of the strategy analysis and decision-making is done manually, but
this paper introduces an automated framework to assist decision-makers in optimizing and selecting strategies.

In a typical wargame, the offense agent attacks, while the defense agent pro-
tects its assets. The success of any strategy relies heavily on the opponent's
response, making it essential for both agents to co-evolve their strategies instead
of optimizing in isolation. To address this need, we propose an iterative competitive Multi-objective Co-Evolutionary (MoCoEv) optimization framework, coupled with a novel decision-making process, specifically tailored for competitive
co-evolutionary scenarios. This process utilizes opposition front hypervolume
improvement, combined with a penalty-based boundary intersection (PBI) [5]
method, customized for wargame situations. In this optimization problem, every
strategy taken by the offense or defense can be represented in terms of multiple
variables. The goal of the optimization is to co-evolve this set of variables for
both offense and defense.

In the current wargaming context, if an agent needs to shift from one strategy to another, certain "switch variables" must remain fixed across the strategies under consideration. To facilitate these smooth transitions among strategies
and further reduce problem dimensions based on variable convergence, we introduce the concept of progressive shrinking. This concept uses multiple rounds of
MoCoEv and decision-making to reduce the dimension of the problem in each
round. As we progressively reduce the variable dimension of the problem, we have
named this process progressive shrinking. Progressive shrinking serves two key

purposes: it enables agents to seamlessly transition between optimized strategies, and it significantly reduces the problem's dimensionality, making time-sensitive optimization tasks like online optimization more feasible and efficient. However, it is important to note that we do not address online optimization in this paper. The method iteratively refines the search space and decision-making process until a stopping criterion is reached, ultimately delivering more focused and adaptable strategic solutions.

In summary, the key contributions of this paper are:

- We propose a novel progressive-shrinking-based multi-objective competitive co-evolutionary optimization framework. This framework narrows the search by gradually reducing the problem's dimensionality, enabling smooth strategy shifts during execution while simplifying decision-making for planners.
- We introduce a new and generically applicable decision-making approach for multi-agent systems involving more than one Pareto-optimal front.
- The proposed system offers some flexibility in execution, allowing for a wide range of possibilities. For instance, we can choose to progressively shrink strategies on only one side, instruct the system to prioritize more defensive decisions or adjust the reference point (origin) used in the PBI process. We explore the impact of these tunable parameters to gain deeper insights into the behavior of the final optimal strategies.

The rest of the paper is structured as follows: Sect. 2 sheds light on some of the scarce existing literature related to competitive multi-objective co-evolutionary algorithms. A brief description of the wargame strategy optimization problem is provided in Sect. 3. The proposed process of intertwined multi-objective co-evolutionary optimization and decision-making is described in Sect. 4. The outcome of the application of the proposed process to the WSOP under consideration is shown in Sect. 5 and finally we conclude the paper in Sect. 6.

2   Related Studies

In recent years, co-evolutionary algorithms have gained tremendous interest in various applications of multi-agent systems [6–8]. The idea of co-evolution is inspired by similar problem-solving tasks that nature addresses in many different forms. The survival and success of different species in nature have been achieved through co-evolution among multiple species [9]. There are three types of co-evolutionary processes: cooperative [10–13], competitive [14–17] and coopetitive [18]. When two or more species evolve by cooperating to achieve their own goals, the process is called *cooperative* co-evolution. On the other hand, when multiple species evolve by competing against each other to achieve their individual goals, it is called *competitive* co-evolution. Another form of co-evolution involves species that collaborate in certain areas while competing in others. This paradigm is referred to as *coopetition* [18]. In the case of wargame strategy optimization, generally, two agents' goals are in conflict, thereby making the task a competitive co-evolution. Moreover, each agent in the wargame problem usually optimizes multiple conflicting objectives, making the overall wargame problem a lot more complicated, challenging, and interesting.

3   Wargame Strategy Optimization Problem

Wargame strategy optimization problems (WSOPs) are highly idiosyncratic, and there is no single computing model that can fully represent all types of wargames. In the Military Decision-Making Process (MDMP), wargaming is a crucial step [4], as shown in the flowchart in Fig. 1. Currently, many parts of steps 4, 5, and 6 are conducted manually by wargame specialists or analysts, creating bottlenecks. As a result, only a small fraction of the strategies or Courses of Actions (COAs) are evaluated during wargaming.

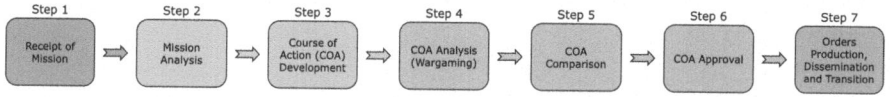

Fig. 1. Military Decision-making Process (MDMP) as outlined in [4].

This paper proposes an end-to-end automated WSOP framework that integrates steps 3, 4, and 5 using competitive co-evolutionary optimization and intertwined decision-making. We focus on a wargame involving two agents: offense and defense. The offense's goal is to maximize damage to an airbase (measured in air-to-ground missile hits) while minimizing its own costs (monetary expenses and losses of offensive lives) and imposing the highest possible costs on the defense (monetary expenses and losses of defensive lives). Conversely, the defense aims to counteract these goals, creating a direct competition between the two agents. Mathematically, the overall problem can be defined as follows:

Offense Goals:

$$\text{Minimize}_{\mathbf{x}} \left(-\text{OH}(\mathbf{x}, \mathbf{y}), \text{OE}(\mathbf{x}, \mathbf{y}) - \text{DE}(\mathbf{x}, \mathbf{y})\right),$$
$$\text{subject to } x_i \in \{x_i^{(1)}, x_i^{(2)}, \dots, x_i^{(c_i)}\}, \ i = 1, \dots, n_1. \tag{1}$$

Defense Goals:

$$\text{Minimize}_{\mathbf{y}} \left(\text{OH}(\mathbf{x}, \mathbf{y}), \text{DE}(\mathbf{x}, \mathbf{y}) - \text{OE}(\mathbf{x}, \mathbf{y})\right),$$
$$\text{subject to } y_j \in \{y_j^{(1)}, y_j^{(1)}, \dots, y_j^{(c_j)}\}, \ j = 1, \dots, n_2. \tag{2}$$

where OH, OE and DE represent `OffenseHits`, `OffenseExpenditures` and `DefenseExpenditures`, respectively; x_i and y_j denote the values of the ith offense and j^{th} defense variable, respectively; c_i and c_j represent the number of possible categorical values for x_i and y_j, respectively. The values for hits and expenses are typically derived from a high-fidelity simulation of the wargame scenario. However, in this project, we have utilized surrogate models to approximate these indicators during the optimization process. The entire process of building the surrogate models from the training data collected from the simulator is mentioned in the supplementary material.

4   Proposed Wargame Strategy Optimization Framework

The proposed framework consists of two interconnected components that work together to solve the WSOP. The first component is the optimization process, which interacts with the wargame to explore the search space strategies and identify optimized strategies for both offense and defense. The second component is the decision-maker, responsible for selecting a strategy for each side.

As mentioned before, we introduce a progressive shrinking approach where after each optimization cycle, some of the variables get fixed based on the decision-making and the optimization is re-run with reduced dimension. This ensures that the agents can freely switch from one strategy to another in the final optimized space and at the same time, the dimension reduction process narrows down the focus to smaller variations which helps in the final decision-making process. The entire workflow of this MoCoEv and decision-making is described in Fig. 2.

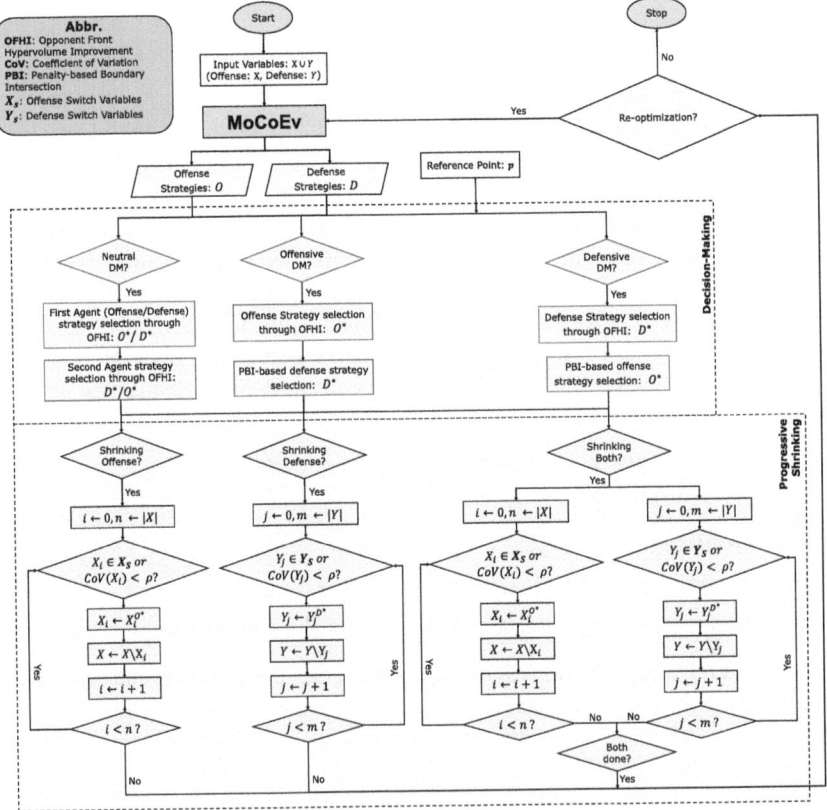

Fig. 2. The entire framework consisting of PS-MoCoEv and Co-evolutionary decision-making developed for WSOP.

4.1   Progressive Shrinking Based Multi-Obj. Co-Evol. (PS-MoCoEv)

The first phase of the process focuses on optimizing wargame strategies using MoCoEv. In this wargame, there are two agents: offense and defense. MoCoEv optimizes both agents simultaneously, considering their competitive objectives. The process works as follows: for a certain number of iterations (τ_1), MoCoEv optimizes the population of one agent based on its objectives while keeping the other agent's population fixed. During this time, the objective values for any strategy are computed by pairing it against every strategy from the fixed opponent population and computing the objective values for each pair, followed by an aggregation. In this work, we have used average-based aggregation, but median or worst-case aggregation measures can also be used. After τ_1 iterations are completed, the same process is applied to the other agent for a different set of iterations (τ_2). These cycles of improvement are applied to each agent in turn until a stopping criterion (e.g., total number of generations) is met. The optimization for each agent involves applying genetic operators to the parent population to generate offspring, followed by selecting the best solutions from the combined pool of parents and offspring. As the algorithm progresses, both agents evolve in turns, each being optimized alternately. We have used a co-evolutionary version of NSGA-II [19] as the underlying MoCoEv algorithm. A detailed description of the algorithm is provided in [20].

After the MoCoEv run is completed, an additional analysis step reduces the dimensionality of the search space by continuing with previously-taken moves leading to more focused optimization runs. In the current WSOP, if an agent wishes to transition to a new strategy, some variables (called switch variables) must remain consistent with the previously committed strategy. This step is crucial for applications like WSOP, where rapid responses are needed for strategic planning. For example, while the initial optimization and decision-making occur offline, we may need to make quick adjustments once the game is in progress. The goal is to ensure that, in the final set of optimal strategies, agents can practically and effectively make strategic shifts. At the same time, as a by-product, reduced dimensions help to narrow down the search to fewer variables, which might allow us to perform online optimization runs as well (online optimization is currently out of the scope of this paper).

To achieve this reduction, we use the decision-making process outlined in Sect. 4.2 to fix the switch variables based on automated decisions. After the initial MoCoEv run, we select one offense and one defense strategy and use their values of the switch variables to fix them. With the reduced problem dimensions, we run another MoCoEv to find optimal strategies for the simplified problem, as described in [21]. We then analyze the solutions, fix variables with a Coefficient of Variation (CoV) below a certain threshold ($\rho = 0.3$) [22], and do not use them in the next optimization phase. After each dimensionality reduction, we re-optimize using MoCoEv, progressively shrinking the search space and simultaneously reducing the number of generations needed for optimization. This method, termed Progressive Shrinking-based MoCoEv (PS-MoCoEv), can be applied to only offense, only defense, or both agents. The results of these different optimization approaches are discussed in Sect. 5.

4.2 Co-evolutionary Decision-Making

Co-evolutionary optimization problems introduce unique challenges, particularly in decision-making, where strategies for both agents must be considered simultaneously. This interdependence adds complexity to the process, making it essential to develop a decision-making approach tailored to the co-evolutionary context. We have created a novel decision-making process based on opponent front hypervolume improvement and PBI-oriented selection.

The process unfolds in two steps: selecting a strategy for the first agent and then selecting a strategy for the second agent. Suppose that we have N_1 strategies for the first agent and N_2 strategies for the second agent. For decision-making, we need to consider $N_1 \times N_2$ possible strategy combinations. When choosing a strategy for the first agent, we must evaluate it against all N_2 opposing strategies, forming a collection of N_2 objective value pairs (pairs as the problem is two-objective) for each candidate strategy. To select one strategy from the candidates, we use the concept of opponent front hypervolume improvement, which considers the entire fleet of solutions to ensure a comprehensive evaluation.

Once the first agent's strategy is selected, we focus on the N_2 strategies for the second agent. Here, the objective is to choose one of these opposing strategies based on the specific goals of the decision-making process. In this work, we explore three types of decision-making: Offensive, Defensive, and Neutral. The details of opponent front hypervolume improvement and PBI-based final selection are discussed in the following section.

Opponent Front Hypervolume Improvement. In a co-evolutionary setting, when an agent is choosing a strategy, it must evaluate how that strategy performs against all possible strategies of its opponent. This means it cannot just look at a single objective score pair, it needs to consider a range of score pairs. To address this, we propose a new approach called "opponent front hypervolume improvement" which is specifically designed for competitive co-evolutionary optimization.

Here is how it works: For the first agent, we examine all its strategies. For each of these strategies, there are multiple corresponding opponent strategies. From these strategy combinations, we determine the non-dominated front (NDF) based on the opponent's objectives, which is different from the traditional approach. We then calculate the hypervolume of this NDF and aim to improve it. Essentially, this hypervolume pushes the worst-performing points with respect to the first agent's objectives closer to the first agent's goals. A higher hypervolume indicates that the first agent performs well against most of the opponent's strategies.

Let us clarify this concept with some examples. Suppose that we are focusing on offensive decision-making. In Fig. 3, the orange circles represent all combinations of offense and defense strategies plotted in the objective space defined by

OffenseExpenditures-DefenseExpenditures vs -OffenseHits. The offense aims to minimize both objectives, while the defense aims to maximize them.

Figures 3a and 3b show the distribution of objective scores for two specific offense strategies: Offense_7 and Offense_1, respectively. The blue squares represent the objective distribution of the selected offense strategy against the defense's population of strategies. From these distributions, we can then identify the Pareto front based on the defense's objectives (maximizing both), and then calculate its hypervolume based on a reference point. According to the opponent front hypervolume improvement approach, we prefer the offense strategy that maximizes this hypervolume.

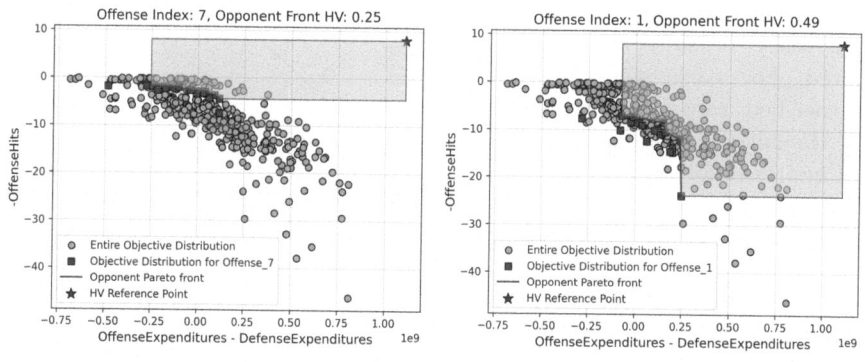

(a) The opponent front for Offense_7   (b) The opponent front for Offense_1

Fig. 3. Opponent fronts for different offense strategies.

This approach essentially means that the distribution of the objectives is increasingly pushed towards meeting offensive goals, which is ultimately advantageous for the offense. Simply put, it indicates that the chosen offense strategy is more robust against a wide range of defense strategies. In this case, Offense_1 in Fig. 3b is preferred over Offense_7 in Fig. 3a because it achieves a higher hypervolume.

The same idea can be applied to defensive decision-making in the opposing sense (the front should be identified based on offense objectives). In neutral decision-making, the order does not matter; the opponent front hypervolume improvement can be applied to both agents simultaneously. The intersection of those two fronts represents the final strategies for offense and defense. For offensive and defensive decision-making, an extra step is performed through a PBI-based selection which is described next.

PBI-Based Selection. In the case of non-neutral decision-making goals, after the first agent selects its strategy, the next step is to choose a strategy for the second agent. This process involves using a reference point ($\mathbf{p}$) and a reference angle (θ^*).

The reference point is specified by the user, and the reference angle is set to 45° for defensive decision-making and 225° for offensive decision-making, with the origin at **p**. For defense, which aims to maximize both objectives (− *OffenseHits* vs *OffenseExpenditures* − *DefenseExpenditures*), an angle of 45° is ideal. Conversely, for offense, which aims to minimize objectives, an angle of 225° is ideal. It is important to normalize both objectives before considering these angles.

We then examine the available strategies within the ranges of $[0°, 90°]$ for defense and $[180°, 270°]$ for offense. If no strategies fall within these ranges, the closest strategy (angle-wise) outside the range is selected. For each strategy within the specified range, we calculate a PBI (Penalized Boundary Intersection) metric as follows:

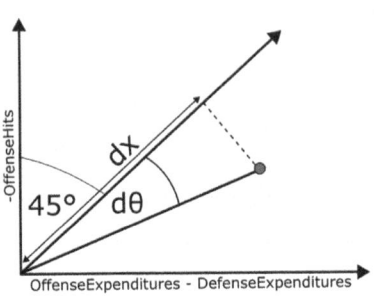

Fig. 4. illustration of the angular deviation (dθ) and distance (dx) along the reference angle used for the calculation of the PBI metric. The reference point (**p**) can be considered to be at the origin.

$$\text{PBI}(\mathbf{x}) = w_1 \times \hat{d\theta} - w_2 \times \hat{dx}. \quad (3)$$

Here, $\hat{d\theta} = \frac{|\theta - \theta^*|}{360}$ measures the normalized deviation of the current angle θ from the reference angle θ^*, and $\hat{dx}$ represents the normalized distance from the reference point **p** to the strategy point **x** along the direction of the reference angle, as shown in Fig. 4. The goal is to minimize $\hat{d\theta}$ and maximize $\hat{dx}$. Ultimately, the strategy with the lowest PBI score is chosen as the strategy for the second agent. In our work, we have used $w_1 = 0.9$ and $w_2 = 0.1$.

5   Results and Discussion

In this section, we begin by showing the results of the PS-MoCoEv run along with the decision-making process associated with it. The overall outcome depends on several key factors: the reference point used for PBI, the shrinking mechanism, and the decision-making strategy itself. To understand how changes in each of these factors affect the results, we conducted a scenario exploration study, which we describe at the end of this section.

5.1   Objectives

The objectives of the problem and the goals of the participating entities are specified in Table 1. Each objective is calculated using a surrogate model trained using grammatical evolution on high-fidelity simulation data.

Table 1. WSOP Objectives and Entity Goals.

i	Objective (f_i)	Offense Goal	Defense Goal
1	*OffenseExpenditures - DefenseExpenditures*	↓	↑
2	*OffenseHits*	↑	↓

5.2 Hyperparameters

As mentioned before, each PS-MoCoEv and decision-making run requires certain hyperparameters, which can be broadly classified into four groups: *DM strategy, Shrinking side, PBI Reference Point* and *MoCoEv algorithm paramters.* The *DM strategy* has three alternatives: offensive, defensive or neutral. The *Shrinking side* also has three options: shrinking offense only, defense only, or shrinking both. *Reference points* can be any point in the 2-D objective space suggesting the area of interest for the user. Finally, the *MoCoEv algorithm parameters* are the parameters used by the underlying NSGA-II approach like population size or number of generations.

5.3 PS-MoCoEv Round

First, we want to show the results of a PS-MoCoEv run. Any PS-MoCoEv run consists of multiple rounds. Every round is a combination of a MoCoEv run and a post-optimization co-evolutionary decision-making. Then the next round is run with a reduced variable dimension. For illustration purposes, we select a single hyperparameter configuration and discuss the outcome of the process. In this example, we have used offensive decision-making and dual shrinking strategy (shrinking both offense and defense variables) with a fixed PBI reference point of $(-5 \times 10^8, 0.25)$.

MoCoEv Run Results. After the initial MoCoEv run, the evolved strategy combinations are displayed in Fig. 5a. The black star represents the PBI reference point. In addition, Fig. 5c and Fig. 5e represent the coefficient of variation (CoV) of the offense and defense variables in the initial population of strategies, respectively. This analysis shows the degree of variation of different variables across the population of strategies. But, in the first round, we always fix the "switch variables" which are specified by our industrial collaborator. From the next round onwards, the variables with a CoV less than ρ are fixed.

Post-MoCoEv Decision-Making. In order to reduce the dimension, we need to select the values of the variables to be fixed. To achieve this, the automated decision-making process chooses one offense strategy and one defense strategy. The combination of these strategies is represented by a green star in Fig. 5a. During the preliminary round, we fix the values of the switch variables to those corresponding to the point marked by the green star. In subsequent steps, we fix the values of the variables with a Coefficient of Variation (CoV) less than ρ. This completes one round of the progressive shrinking process.

MoCoEv Re-run. After fixing the variables, the updated solutions might not be optimal based on these fixing constraints. So, following the concept of regularity in optimization as mentioned in [21,23], we perform a re-optimization using a new MoCoEv. This cycle continues until all variables have CoV beyond the ρ threshold. In this particular scenario, there were 14 rounds of MoCoEv, Decision-Making, and Re-optimization cycles. Figure 5b shows the final optimized strategy distribution in the objective space. Interestingly, what variables have been reduced in the process can be observed for both offense (from Fig. 5c to Fig. 5d) and defense (from Fig. 5e to Fig. 5f). In the scenario under consideration, we have reduced the variable dimension from 74 to 16 through 14 progressive shrinking rounds.

5.4   Effect of PBI Reference Points, Shrinking Side and DM Strategy on Final Decision-Making

The outcome of progressive shrinking is clearly influenced by the chosen hyperparameters. To explore how these settings impact the final strategy, we keep NSGA-II algorithm parameters fixed and vary other problem-specific hyperparameters. Specifically, we test different decision-making strategies-defensive, offensive, or neutral-as well as shrinking sides, focusing on offense, defense, or both. Additionally, we evaluate four distinct PBI reference points. This is not intended to determine the best set of hyperparameter values. Instead, it is an exploratory analysis to observe how varying system configurations influence the outcomes of the approach.

The final points selected after the progressive shrinking run and successive decision-making processes are presented in Fig. 6. Each plot illustrates the PBI reference point used in the study, along with the direction of the final selected points relative to the PBI reference points for various combinations of decision-making and progressive shrinking strategies. Additionally, the angles formed by the final points with respect to the PBI reference points (assuming a 2D origin at these points) are shown. The black outline in each plot represents the convex hull of the solutions found after the first MoCoEv run. In this angular representation, movements within the range of [90°, 180°] are categorized as offensive, while movements within [270°, 360°] are considered defensive. The remaining angular movements represent trade-off movements.

One key observation is that the final outcomes are highly dependent on the PBI reference points. For instance, from certain reference points, it is easier to find offensive strategy combinations (Fig. 6c) using progressive shrinking, whereas other reference points tend to facilitate defensive solutions (Fig. 6d). As expected, we generally observe more offensive movements when offensive decision-making is employed, and more defensive movements when defensive decision-making is applied. However, in some cases, offensive or defensive

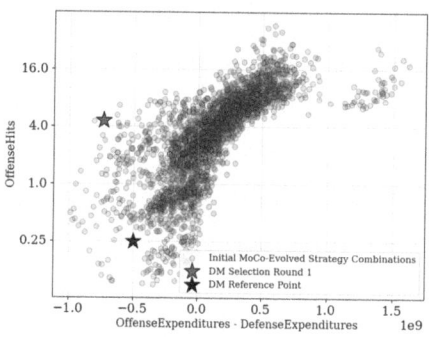

(a) Preliminary MoCo-Evolved optimized strategy combinations

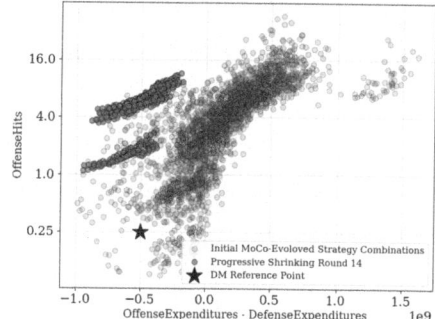

(b) Final round of MoCo-Evolved optimized strategy combinations

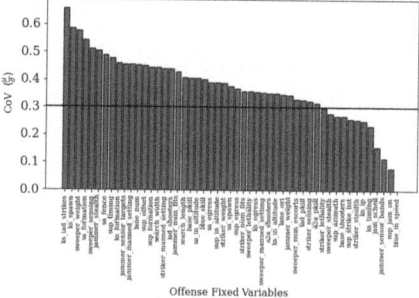

(c) The CoV for the offense variables across the population of preliminary MoCo-Evolved strategies

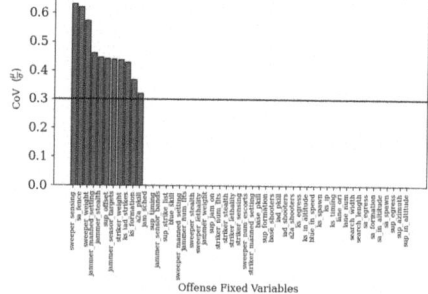

(d) The CoV for the offense variables across the population of the final round of MoCo-Evolved strategies

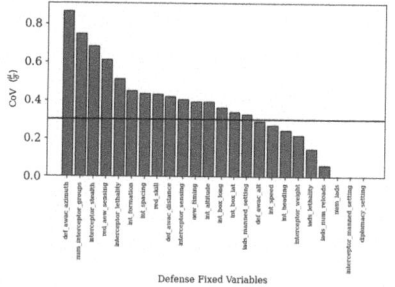

(e) The CoV for the defense variables across the population of preliminary MoCo-Evolved strategies

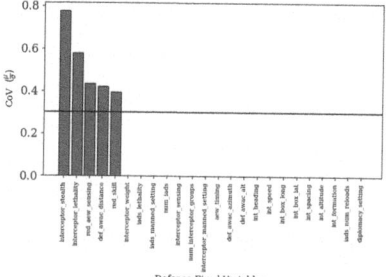

(f) The CoV for the defense variables across the population of the final round of MoCo-Evolved strategies

Fig. 5. Initial and Final round of MoCoEv run results for offensive decision-making, dual progressive shrinking and a reference point of $(-5 \times 10^8, 0.25)$.

decision-making does not lead to the corresponding offensive or defensive movements, especially when both offense and defense are involved in progressive shrinking. This suggests that the progressive shrinking process can sometimes restrict movement in the desired direction, which is intuitive, as the degrees of freedom are reduced due to the shrinking process.

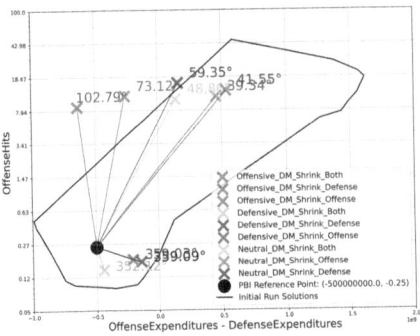

(a) Decision-making movement of selected strategy combination from a reference point of (-5e8, -0.25).

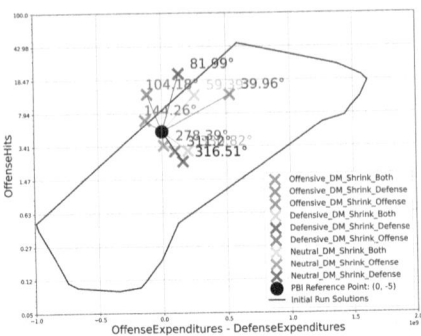

(b) Decision-making movement of selected strategy combination from a reference point of (0, -5).

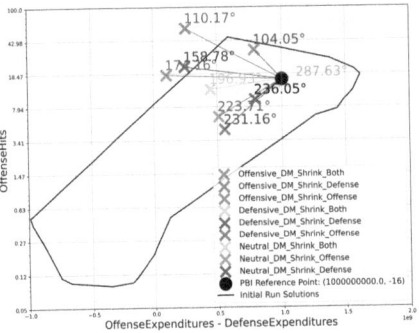

(c) Decision-making movement of selected strategy combination from a reference point of (1e9, -16).

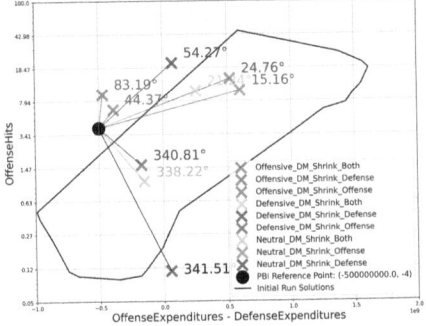

(d) Decision-making movement of selected strategy combination from a reference point of (-5e8, -4).

Fig. 6. Movement of the selected strategy combination after the entire PS-MoCoEv workflow using different PBI reference points.

6   Conclusions

In this study, we have developed a novel multi-objective co-evolutionary framework based on progressive shrinking (PS), PS-MoCoEv, for optimizing strategic wargame scenarios. The framework incorporates PS techniques alongside decision-making strategies, allowing for the co-evolution of offensive and defensive strategies in tandem for competitive wargames. Through iterative optimization and decision making, our approach reduces the dimensionality of the problem space, maintaining the practicality of already taken moves to be continued in later moves.

The results of our various optimization studies have highlighted the significance of the PBI reference points, decision-making strategies, and shrinking mechanisms in determining the final strategy outcomes. In our specific scenario, better offensive strategies have emerged more often, while in limited initial scenarios, better defensive solutions have emerged. Moreover, our results have shown the sensitivity of the progressive shrinking approach in restricting latter moves in the desired direction due to reduced degrees of freedom yielded from previous moves. The proposed PS-MoCoEv stays as a systematic, algorithmic, and automated system for wargame strategy optimization, enhancing the efficiency of decision-making in complex, multi-agent military or other similar scenarios. Future work may explore additional refinements to the decision-making process and further investigate the role of different intermediate steps for more efficient performance of PS-MoCoEV.

Acknowledgement. This research was supported by Northrop Grumman Corporation as a part of a collaboration between Computational Optimization and INnovation (COIN) Lab at Michigan State University and Northrop Grumman.

References

1. De Lima Filho, G.M., et al.: Optimization of unmanned air vehicle tactical formation in war games. IEEE Access **10**, 21727–21741 (2022)
2. Jia, Z.-X., Kiang, J.-F.: War game between two matched fleets with goal options and tactical optimization. AI, **3**(4), 890–930 (2022)
3. Ozaki, A., Furuichi, M., Takahashi, K., Matsukawa, H.: Design and implementation of parallel and distributed wargame simulation system and its evaluation. IEICE Trans. Inf. Syst. **84**(10), 1376–1384 (2001)
4. Schwartz, P.J., et al.: Ai-enabled wargaming in the military decision making process. In: Artificial Intelligence and Machine Learning for Multi-domain Operations Applications II, vol. 11413, pp. 118–134. SPIE (2020)
5. Zhang, Q., Li, H.: Moea/d: a multiobjective evolutionary algorithm based on decomposition. IEEE Trans. Evol. Comput. **11**(6), 712–731 (2007)
6. Luo, J., Cooper, J., Cao, C., Pham, K.: Cooperative adaptive control of a two-agent system. In: 2012 American Control Conference (ACC), pp. 2413–2418. IEEE (2012)
7. Li, Y., Wang, J., Liu, Z.: A simple two-agent system for multi-objective flexible job-shop scheduling. J. Comb. Optim. **43**(1), 42–64 (2022)
8. Wang, K., Gou, C., Duan, Y., Lin, Y., Zheng, X., Wang, F.-Y.: Generative adversarial networks: introduction and outlook. IEEE/CAA J. Autom. Sin. **4**(4), 588–598 (2017)
9. Russell, E.: Coevolutionary history. Am. Hist. Rev. **119**(5), 1514–1528 (2014)
10. Keerativuttitumrong, N., Chaiyaratana, N., Varavithya, V.: Multi-objective cooperative coevolutionary evolutionary algorithms for continuous and combinatorial optimization. In: Bouvry, P., González-Vélez, H., Kołodziej, J. (eds.) Intelligent Decision Systems in Large-Scale Distributed Environments. Studies in Computational Intelligence, vol. 362, pp. 288–297. Springer, Heidelberg (2011). https://doi.org/10.1007/978-3-642-21271-0_3

11. Atashpendar, A., Dorronsoro, B., Danoy, G., Bouvry, P.: A scalable parallel cooperative coevolutionary PSO algorithm for multi-objective optimization. J. Parallel Distrib. Comput. **112**, 111–125 (2018)

12. Dorronsoro, B., Danoy, G., Nebro, A.J., Bouvry, P.: Achieving super-linear performance in parallel multi-objective evolutionary algorithms by means of cooperative coevolution. Comput. Oper. Res. **40**(6), 1552–1563 (2013)

13. Garcıa-Pedrajas, N., Hervás-Martınez, C., Munoz-Pérez, J.: Multi-objective cooperative coevolution of artificial neural networks (multi-objective cooperative networks). Neural Netw. **15**(10), 1259–1278 (2002)

14. Goh, C.K., Tan, K.C., Liu, D.S., Chiam, S.C.: A competitive and cooperative coevolutionary approach to multi-objective particle swarm optimization algorithm design. Eur. J. Oper. Res. **202**(1), 42–54 (2010)

15. Meneghini, I.R., Guimaraes, F.G., Gaspar-Cunha, A.: Competitive coevolutionary algorithm for robust multi-objective optimization: the worst case minimization. In: 2016 IEEE Congress on Evolutionary Computation (CEC), pp. 586–593. IEEE (2016)

16. McIntyre, A.R., Heywood, M.I.: Multi-objective competitive coevolution for efficient GP classifier problem decomposition. In: 2007 IEEE International Conference on Systems Man and Cybernetics, pp. 1930–1937. IEEE (2007)

17. Zeng, F., Decraene, J., Hean Low, M.Y., Cai, W., Hingston, P.: Studies on pareto-based multi-objective competitive coevolutionary dynamics. In: 2011 IEEE Congress of Evolutionary Computation (CEC), pp. 2383–2390. IEEE (2011)

18. Corbo, L., Kraus, S., čić, B., Dabić, M., Caputo, A., Pellegrini, M.M.: Coopetition and innovation: a review and research agenda. Technovation. **122**, 02624 (2023)

19. Deb, K., Pratap, A., Agarwal, S., Meyarivan, T.A.: A fast and elitist multiobjective genetic algorithm: NSGA-II. IEEE Trans. Evol. Comput. **6**(2), 182–197 (2002)

20. Guha, R., Mckendrick, R., Feest, B., Deb, K.: Attacker-defender strategy optimization using multi-objective competitive co-evolution. In: Affenzeller, M., et al. Parallel Problem Solving from Nature – PPSN XVIII. PPSN 2024. LNCS, vol. 15151, pp. 351–366. Springer, Cham (2024). https://doi.org/10.1007/978-3-031-70085-9_22

21. Guha, R., Deb, K.: Compromising pareto-optimality with regularity in platform-based multi-objective optimization. IEEE Trans. Evol. Comput. **28**, 1746–1780 (2023)

22. Coefficient of variation. Accessed 27 Sept 2023

23. Guha, R., Deb, K.: RegEMO: sacrificing pareto-optimality for regularity in multi-objective problem-solving. In: Emmerich, M., et al. Evolutionary Multi-Criterion Optimization. EMO 2023. LNCS, vol. 13970, pp. 29–42. Springer, Cham (2023). https://doi.org/10.1007/978-3-031-27250-9_3

Impact of Environmental Changes on Optimized Robotics Collective Motion for Multi-objective Coverage Tasks

Reda Ghanem[1]([📧]) [iD], Ismail M. Ali[1] [iD], Kathryn Kasmarik[1] [iD], and Matthew Garratt[2] [iD]

[1] School of Systems and Computing, University of New South Wales, Canberra, Australia
{reda.ghanem,ismail.ali,kathryn.kasmarik}@unsw.edu.au
[2] School of Engineering and Technology, University of New South Wales, Canberra, Australia
m.garratt@unsw.edu.au

Abstract. Coverage tasks have garnered significant interest in recent years due to their applications in fields such as environmental monitoring, search and rescue, and robotic exploration. Swarm robotics has emerged as a promising approach to tackle these challenges, leveraging collective behaviors to enhance efficiency. However, the effectiveness of swarm algorithms often hinges on the careful tuning of parameters, which can be influenced by varying environmental features. This study investigates the impact of these features on the performance of optimized collective motion in swarm robotics for solving multi-objective coverage problems. Through a comprehensive sensitivity analysis, we evaluate how changes in parameters-such as arena size, number of robots, obstacle density, and obstacle structure-affect swarm performance in solving coverage problems. The analysis focuses on key performance metrics across multiple objectives: coverage percentage, coverage time, robot connectivity, and collision rates. Our findings provide critical insights into the adaptability of swarm algorithms, highlighting the importance of environmental context in optimizing swarm efficacy across competing objectives. These results contribute to the development of more robust and adaptive swarm-based solutions for multi-objective coverage tasks.

Keywords: Swarm Robotics · Multi-Objective Optimization · Genetic Algorithms · Sensitivity Analysis · Complete Coverage Problems

1 Introduction

Collective motion is a fascinating phenomenon observable in various natural systems, from the flocking of birds and swarming of insects to the movement of schools of fish and even molecular dynamics [2]. Inspired by these natural behaviors, numerous mathematical algorithms have been developed to address

© The Author(s), under exclusive license to Springer Nature Singapore Pte Ltd. 2025
H. Singh et al. (Eds.): EMO 2025, LNCS 15512, pp. 303–318, 2025.
https://doi.org/10.1007/978-981-96-3506-1_21

real-world challenges in swarm robotics. This field focuses on how large groups of simple, small, and often identical robots can collaboratively achieve complex tasks that individual robots cannot perform alone.

Swarm robotics systems offer significant advantages over single-robot systems, including increased efficiency, parallel operation, and redundancy. These benefits make them particularly suitable for tasks such as search and rescue, underwater inspection, and mine-sweeping [4]. Such applications fall under the category of Complete Coverage Problems (CCPs), which require thorough exploration of a target environment that may be unpredictable or hostile [15]. Successfully solving CCPs relies heavily on the coordinated motion of the swarm, governed by behavior parameters such as alignment, cohesion, separation, and obstacle avoidance.

Several approaches to CCPs have been explored, with recent innovations focusing on deploying swarming and flocking algorithms [1,3,12,13]. Existing literature emphasizes the importance of optimizing swarm behaviors to achieve high coverage efficiency. However, the influence of environmental features on these optimized strategies requires further exploration to fully understand their impact and potential for improving swarm performance in CCPs. A persistent challenge is the fine-tuning of behavior parameters for optimal performance across varying environments. Manual parameter tuning is labor-intensive and often fails to generalize across different conditions, particularly in real-time, dynamic applications where a one-size-fits-all approach is not viable [7]. Improperly tuned parameters can lead to inefficient area coverage, poor coordination, collisions, and prolonged task completion times.

This study aims to address this gap by conducting a sensitivity analysis to investigate how different environmental features impact the performance of optimized swarm algorithms in the context of multi-objective coverage tasks. Specifically, we examine how factors such as arena size, number of robots, obstacle density, and obstacle structure affect the swarm's ability to efficiently cover an area while considering multiple objectives, including coverage percentage, coverage time, robot connectivity, and collision rates. By understanding these relationships, we can enhance the design and implementation of swarm robotics optimization systems, ensuring they are adaptable to varying environmental conditions and capable of balancing competing objectives.

The remainder of this paper is structured as follows: Sect. 2 reviews related work. Section 3 outlines the proposed method for our sensitivity analysis. Section 4 presents the experimental results. Finally, Sect. 5 concludes the paper with insights into future research directions.

2   Background and Related Work

In this section, we provide an overview of the key concepts and methodologies that form the foundation of this work, including CCPs, Genetic Algorithm (GA)-based optimization, and the principles of Swarm Intelligence.

CCPs present significant challenges in sectors such as manufacturing, environmental monitoring, and autonomous logistics. Autonomous robots and vehicle swarms can efficiently tackle these challenges by mimicking the collective behaviors of social insects, such as ants and bees [11]. Key challenges in this domain include ensuring efficient area coverage, adaptability to environmental changes, scalability for large operational areas, and effective coordination among multiple robots or sensors [1]. While various direct and indirect approaches for area coverage have been explored in the literature [3,12,13], our work emphasizes the necessity of conducting a sensitivity analysis to understand how different environmental features affect the optimized robotics swarm behaviors in the context of multi-objective coverage tasks.

GAs, which draw inspiration from evolutionary principles, have proven to be powerful tools for optimizing swarm behavior by refining solutions over generations through selection, crossover, and mutation [6]. These algorithms have been successfully applied to numerous robotic tasks, including parameter optimization [3], obstacle avoidance, and motion planning [8], as well as target searching [10]. Our research pioneers the use of GA-based simulation optimization specifically for tuning collective motion parameters in swarms, focusing on balancing multiple objectives such as coverage percentage, coverage time, and collision rates. This approach enables decentralized communication and decision-making in industrial operations, such as factory automation, automated warehouse management, and autonomous delivery systems.

Swarm intelligence mimics behaviors observed in natural swarms, such as those seen in flocks of birds and schools of fish [14]. The boids model, developed by Reynolds [9], replicates collective motion behaviors in computer-based systems. Agents adhere to rules of alignment, cohesion, and separation, which enable collective motion without global knowledge of the environment [9]. Extensions of this model include obstacle avoidance and frontier search capabilities developed by Tran et al. [13]. In our approach, agent positions and velocities evolve based on these rules and forces, facilitating efficient swarm behavior tailored for multi-objective coverage tasks. Our work employs a frontier-led swarming (FLS) exploration algorithm [13] for simulating robot coverage. Further details on the simulator and algorithm will be discussed in subsequent sections.

The combination of swarm intelligence and GA-based optimization presents a powerful approach for solving CCPs in complex and dynamic environments. This work builds on existing methodologies in these fields, contributing to the development of a more efficient and adaptive solution for optimizing FLS in addressing CCPs effectively.

3 Methodology

In our previous work, we designed a frontier-led swarming simulation-optimization framework (FLS-SOF [5]) to optimize the collective motion of robots for CCPs. FLS-SOF combines three main components: (1) a GA-based optimization module for solution exploration (Subsect. 3.1), (2) a point-mass simulator for solution evaluation (Subsect. 3.2), and (3) a FLS approach for coverage [13]. Figure 1 illustrates the framework's structure.

Table 1. Decision variables in our solution encoding with ranges.

Params	Description	Range	Params	Description	Range
W_a	Alignment weight	[0, 1]	R_a	Alignment radius	$[r_d, m_r]$
W_c	Cohesion weight	[0, 1]	R_c	Cohesion radius	$[r_d, m_r]$
W_s	Separation weight	[0, 1]	R_s	Separation radius	$[r_d, m_r]$
W_{av}	Obstacle avoid weight	[0, 1]	R_{av}	Obstacle avoidance radius	$[r_d, m_r]$
W_w	Wall avoid weight	[0, 1]	R_w	Wall avoidance radius	$[r_d, m_r]$
W_f	Frontier weight	[0, 1]	R_{sh}	Share UFCO_radius	$[r_d, m_r]$

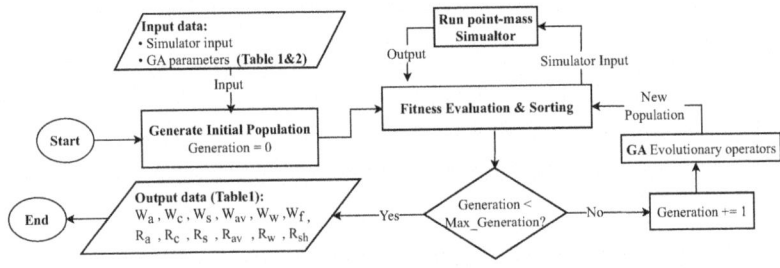

Fig. 1. Proposed simulation-optimization framework.

3.1 GA-Based Optimization Algorithm

This subsection outlines our GA-based optimization approach, which integrates FLS [13] within an evolutionary framework tailored for optimizing swarm behaviors for coverage. In a GA, an initial population of candidate solutions (P_1) is randomly generated, with each solution represented as a chromosome consisting of 12 genes/variables. Table 1 details the variables and their ranges, where r_d is the robot radius and m_r is the upper sensor range (29.7 cm and 200 cm, respectively, in this study). The population contains PS candidate solutions ($S_1, S_2, \ldots, S_{PS}$), and the GA employs real-value representation to facilitate processes such as selection, crossover, and mutation, aiming to optimize these solutions across multiple objectives.

The evaluation of candidate solutions relies on the simulation model (Sect. 3.2), where four performance metrics values are calculated to capture the multi-objective nature of the problem. Violations (V) count robot collisions with obstacles or each other and boundary breaches. Coverage Percentage (CP) evaluates exploration performance by determining the percentage of the area covered by the robots. Disconnectivity (DC) measures the extent of robot communication breakdowns during the trial, while Turnaround Time (TT) assesses efficiency by quantifying the time taken for coverage. Solutions are ranked based on these fitness values in the following order: V (ascending), CP (descending), DC (ascending), and TT (ascending). This lexicographical ranking approach allows us to identify the best-performing solution that achieves full coverage while minimizing collisions, disconnections, and time. In-depth details about our approach, including parameter settings and optimization technique, can be found in our previously published work [5].

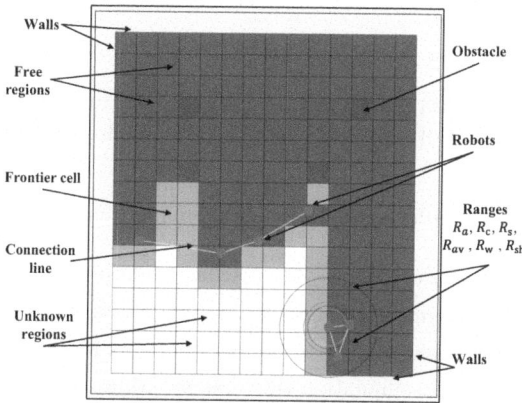

Fig. 2. A snapshot of the point-mass simulator, comprising various components, providing a visual representation of the test environment. (Color figure online)

3.2 Point-Mass Simulator

To assess the fitness of solutions in our simulation-optimization framework, we use a simulator designed to replicate the multi-objective coverage problem using FLS [13]. The simulator serves as the fitness function in the optimization process. In this study, we developed a Python simulator, $Sim_{point-mass}$, that models the robot as a step-wise movement. Figure 2 illustrates the simulation's key components, including a grid map, walls, obstacles, frontier cells, and robots.

The simulator's environment is represented as an $m \times n$ grid, where each pixel corresponds to one centimeter in the real world. Initially, all grid squares are marked as unexplored (white), but as robots explore the map, free regions are marked (green). Obstacles are marked in blue, while frontier cells (orange) represent areas robots are actively moving toward. Robots are displayed as red circles, and connection lines between robots are shown as yellow lines when they are within the communication range R_{sh}. These ranges are depicted as colored circles around the robot. To maintain clarity, Fig. 2 displays only one robot's communication ranges. The simulator is highly adaptable and supports various configurations, including different behavior weights, robot counts, obstacle counts, speeds, and grid sizes. Each robot has an unexplored-frontier-coverage-obstacles matrix (UFCO matrix). This 2D local matrix, which has the same size as the grid map ($m \times n$), is stored in the robot's local memory and represents its knowledge about the arena. The matrix contains values of 0, 1, 2, and 3, representing unexplored, frontier, explored, and obstacle cells, respectively. Robot movement is described using step movements to mimic simple step-wise or point-mass motion. Each robot has a velocity represented by $(v_{x(t)}, v_{y(t)})$ at time step t, calculated as follows:

$$v_{x(t)} = x_{2(t)} - x_{1(t)} : V_{min} < v_{x(t)} < V_{max} \tag{1}$$

$$v_{y(t)} = y_{2(t)} - y_{1(t)} : V_{min} < v_{y(t)} < V_{max} \tag{2}$$

where (V_{min}, V_{max}) represent the minimum and maximum speed, respectively, to ensure that robots operate within a specified speed range.

Table 2. Environment Configuration.

Parameter	Value	Parameter	Value	Parameter	Value
Arena width	4.40 m	Number of robots	7	Max linear speed	0.25 m/s
Arena height	4.80 m	Number of obstacles	5	Max angular speed	0.9 rad/s
Cell size	0.30 m2	Max simulation time	200 Sec.	Mini angular speed	-0.9 rad/s

3.3   Sensitivity Analysis Mechanism

This study investigates the sensitivity of environmental factors on optimized robotics swarm parameters through a series of experiments. The initial experiment tunes the FLS swarm behavior parameters (Table 1) within the experimental environment (Table 2) using our FLS-SOF to solve multi-objective coverage task. The objectives are to achieve full coverage, zero collisions, high connectivity, and minimized coverage time across two distinct scenarios. In **Scenario 1**, coverage without collective motion, aiming to maximize CP while minimizing V and TT, without considering DC. In **Scenario 2**, coverage with collective motion, targeting the maximization of CP while minimizing V, DC, and TT. These scenarios help evaluate the impact of collective motion on coverage efficiency and swarm behavior performance. These two scenarios provide critical insights into the role of DC in influencing collective motion when solving CCPs while avoiding obstacles and maintaining connectivity between robots.

Following this, we conduct four experiments to explore the impact of changing key environmental parameters-grid size, robot count, obstacle count, and obstacle positioning-on optimized FLS to solve multi-objective coverage. Each experiment consists of seven test cases in which one environmental parameter is altered. For each case, the simulation is run ten times with varying initial robot positions, enabling us to compute the mean and 95% confidence interval for all coverage performance metrics across both scenarios. Through this comprehensive testing approach, we aim to gain a deeper understanding of how these environmental variations affect the performance of optimized swarm parameters, both with and without collective motion.

4   Results and Discussions

In this section, we detail a series of experiments designed to evaluate the impact of changing environmental features on the performance of optimized collective motion for CCPs. First, we conducted an experiment to optimize the collective motion of the FLS algorithm for multi-objective coverage using our framework then we conducted a series of experiments to check the effect of changing grid size, number of robots, number of obstacles, and obstacle distribution, to assess their influence on optimized FLS algorithm.

4.1   Experiment 1: Tuning FLS Using Simulation-Based Optimization

Setup: In this experiment, the FLS algorithm was optimized for achieving full coverage and zero collisions while maintaining high connectivity, both with and without collective motion. Using the environment setting outlined in Table 2, we conducted 30 independent optimization runs. Each run, based on our recent work [5], consisted of 1000 generations with a population size of 150, a crossover rate of 0.9, a mutation rate of 0.9, and an elitism value of 5. Random seeds were varied between runs to ensure data independence, and a 95% confidence interval was used to evaluate the reliability of the results. The optimization runs were executed using the National Computational Infrastructure (NCI) with a 2.90GHz Intel Xeon Platinum 8268 CPU featuring 24 cores and 16 GB of RAM.

Results: The FLS-SOF framework successfully optimized the FLS algorithm to achieve 100% CP, zero V, and minimal TT. Without collective motion, TT was 29.91 s, while with collective motion, TT increased to 52.33 s which is expected to maintain Zero DC by making all robots keep closer to each other while exploring the environment. The detailed results, including the best run and averages across 30 runs with 95% confidence interval, are summarized in Table 3.

4.2   Experiment 2: Impact of Changing Grid Size

Setup: This experiment aims to analyze the effect of changing grid size on coverage without and with collective motion in terms of (V, CP, DC, and TT) using the best parameters produced from experiment 1. We conducted seven test

Table 3. Summary of results for Experiment 1, best and average of 30 runs with the 95% confidence interval.

	without collective motion			with collective motion			
	V	$CP(\%)$	TT (s)	V	$CP(\%)$	DC	TT (s)
Best Run	0	100%	29.91	0	100%	0	52.33
Average	0 ± 0	$100\% \pm 0$	31.34 ± 0.53	0 ± 0	$100\% \pm 0$	19.7 ± 4.71	44.097 ± 5.35

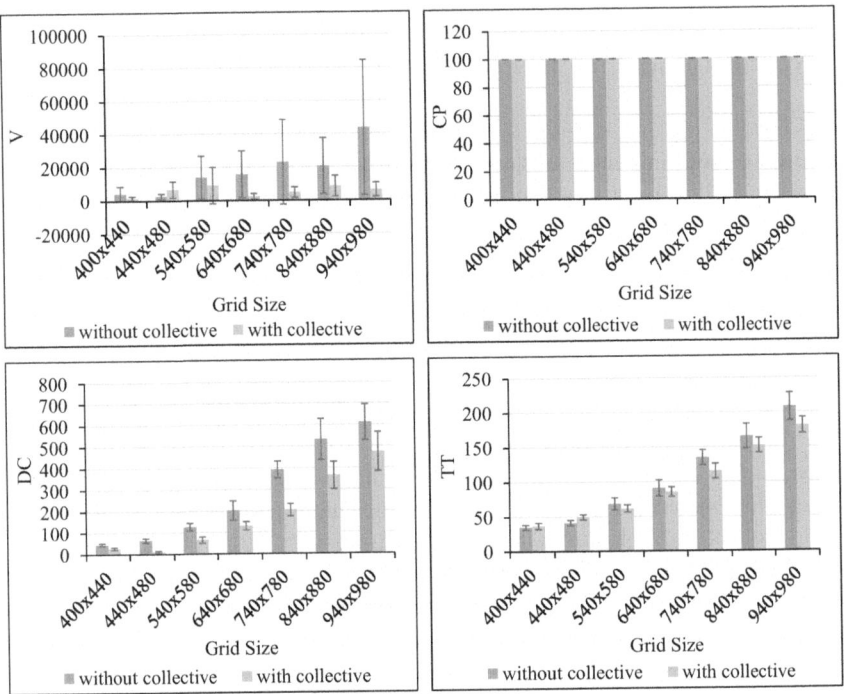

Fig. 3. Experiment 2 Performance Metric (Average with 95% Confidence Interval).

cases of changing grid size in the experimental environment (Table 2) ranging from 4×4.4 m to 9.4×9.8 m. Each case runs ten times using different starting positions for robots.

Results: The results indicate that while grid size variations did not hinder full coverage in all test cases for both scenarios, significant impacts were observed on other metrics. Specifically, V, DC, and TT were all influenced by increasing grid size. The number of collisions between robots increased, connectivity decreased, and the time required to complete coverage rose as grid size expanded. Table 4 and Fig 3 presents a comparative analysis of these results, highlighting the relationship between grid size and these key performance metrics.

Table 4. Results for coverage with and without collective motion across different grid sizes. The mean of 10 runs with the 95% confidence interval.

Grid Size	Without Collective Motion				With Collective Motion			
	V	CP (%)	DC	TT (s)	V	CP (%)	DC	TT (s)
400 × 440	4314.3 ± 4298.39	100 ± 0	45.2 ± 6.16	34.868 ± 3.48	1425 ± 1280.90	100 ± 0	27.2 ± 5.88	36.471 ± 4.80
440 × 480	2602.9 ± 1647.13	100 ± 0	63.3 ± 10.06	40.915 ± 4.17	6715.4 ± 4868.81	100 ± 0	9.4 ± 4.58	49.404 ± 3.75
540 × 580	13912.9 ± 12894.23	100 ± 0	126.2 ± 17.87	68.571 ± 8.63	8972 ± 10947.64	100 ± 0	64.6 ± 14.92	61.626 ± 5.17
640 × 680	15623.3 ± 14099.68	100 ± 0	201.8 ± 45.23	90.805 ± 11.73	2315.4 ± 1656.45	100 ± 0	130.2 ± 19.58	85.339 ± 6.78
740 × 780	22961.5 ± 25471.14	100 ± 0	391.6 ± 38.48	134.487 ± 10.98	4669.7 ± 3165.82	100 ± 0	204.4 ± 28.74	115.178 ± 10.65
840 × 880	20514.6 ± 16812.70	100 ± 0	532 ± 95.45	165.143 ± 17.70	8409.5 ± 6244.81	100 ± 0	364.3 ± 63.62	151.945 ± 10.61
940 × 980	43580.9 ± 40830.55	100 ± 0	611 ± 83.54	207.404 ± 20.12	6165.4 ± 4250.89	100 ± 0	473.8 ± 90.91	180.566 ± 11.65

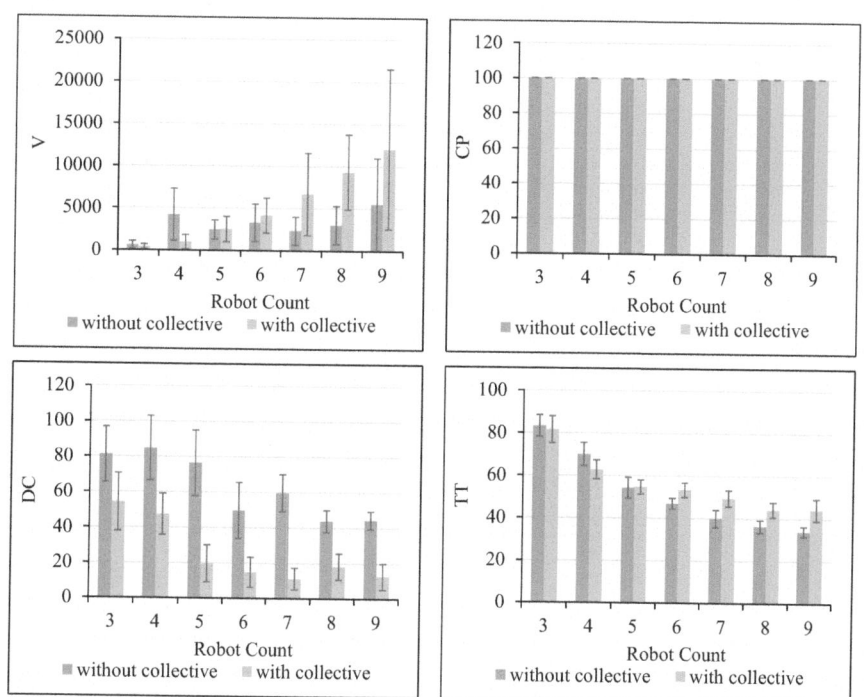

Fig. 4. Experiment 3 Performance Metric (Average with 95% Confidence Interval).

4.3   Experiment 3: Impact of Changing Robot Count

Setup: This experiment aims to analyze the effect of varying robot numbers on coverage performance in terms of V, CP, DC, and TT using the optimized parameters produced from experiment 1. Seven different robot counts, ranging from three to nine, were tested in the experimental environment described in Table 2. Each case was run ten times with random starting positions for the robots, both without and with collective motion.

Results: The results reveal that increasing the number of robots has no significant effect on CP in both scenarios, as full coverage is consistently achieved in all cases. However, V is negatively affected, as the number of collisions between robots increases with the robot count. On the other hand, DC improves as the robot count rises, indicating better connectivity. Additionally, TT shows a positive effect, with coverage time decreasing as the number of robots increases. A detailed analysis of these results highlights the relationship between robot count and these key performance metrics outlined in Table 5 and Fig. 4.

Table 5. Results for coverage with and without collective motion across various robot counts. The mean of 10 runs with the 95% confidence interval.

Robot Count	Without Collective Motion				With Collective Motion			
	V	CP (%)	DC	TT (s)	V	CP (%)	DC	TT (s)
3	617 ± 447.0	100 ± 0	81 ± 15.75	83.23 ± 5.14	399.5 ± 265.1	100 ± 0	54.2 ± 16.29	81.50 ± 6.36
4	4197.5 ± 3064.1	100 ± 0	84.7 ± 18.32	69.91 ± 5.55	968.4 ± 866.6	100 ± 0	47.4 ± 11.66	62.67 ± 4.42
5	2443.9 ± 1127.4	100 ± 0	76.4 ± 18.63	54.24 ± 4.95	2515.6 ± 1492.7	100 ± 0	19.7 ± 10.43	54.53 ± 3.31
6	3282.4 ± 2206.0	100 ± 0	49.7 ± 15.74	46.83 ± 2.52	4147.6 ± 2067.3	100 ± 0	14.8 ± 8.44	53.23 ± 3.44
7	2333 ± 1651.7	100 ± 0	59.6 ± 10.47	39.86 ± 4.06	6700.7 ± 4875.8	100 ± 0	11.2 ± 6.21	49.33 ± 3.75
8	3038.2 ± 2250.2	100 ± 0	43.8 ± 6.17	36.31 ± 2.90	9339.2 ± 4453.5	100 ± 0	18.2 ± 7.43	44.07 ± 3.52
9	5518.5 ± 5494.4	100 ± 0	44.4 ± 4.98	33.95 ± 2.31	12056.1 ± 9466.1	100 ± 0	12.7 ± 7.26	44.11 ± 5.10

Table 6. Results for changing obstacle count with and without collective motion. The mean of 10 runs with the 95% confidence interval.

Obstacle Count	Without Collective Motion				With Collective Motion			
	V	CP (%)	DC	TT (s)	V	CP (%)	DC	TT (s)
2	916.8 ± 78.64	100 ± 0	63.5 ± 7.56	39.14 ± 2.15	2979.9 ± 447.7	100 ± 0	20.2 ± 4.36	42.62 ± 3.19
3	3821.6 ± 1497.9	100 ± 0	54.4 ± 9.63	39.80 ± 1.61	3073.4 ± 784.3	100 ± 0	18.3 ± 5.29	46.12 ± 3.91
4	6223.4 ± 3142.1	100 ± 0	47.7 ± 8.35	42.19 ± 2.85	5684.3 ± 2491.2	100 ± 0	14.4 ± 5.16	48.17 ± 4.24
5	8491.5 ± 1234.3	100 ± 0	49.9 ± 9.12	42.37 ± 2.67	3177.1 ± 847.6	100 ± 0	15.7 ± 6.38	46.74 ± 4.45
6	5456.2 ± 3262.3	100 ± 0	52.3 ± 8.79	44.32 ± 1.93	7429.1 ± 1483.5	100 ± 0	17.4 ± 5.21	49.98 ± 4.14
7	1857.8 ± 1265.1	100 ± 0	54.6 ± 6.85	38.69 ± 3.10	6113.1 ± 2357.8	100 ± 0	21.7 ± 6.43	48.20 ± 3.84
8	8340.8 ± 1123.0	100 ± 0	57.0 ± 7.90	45.20 ± 2.34	4940.5 ± 1930.1	100 ± 0	14.4 ± 4.12	46.29 ± 2.76

4.4   Experiment 4: Impact of Changing Obstacle Count

Setup: This experiment investigates the effect of varying obstacle counts on coverage performance metrics through two scenarios without/with collective motion using the optimized parameters produced from experiment 1. The obstacle counts ranged from two to eight, and each configuration was assessed using the experimental setup detailed in Table 2. Each case was executed ten times, with the metrics recorded for analysis.

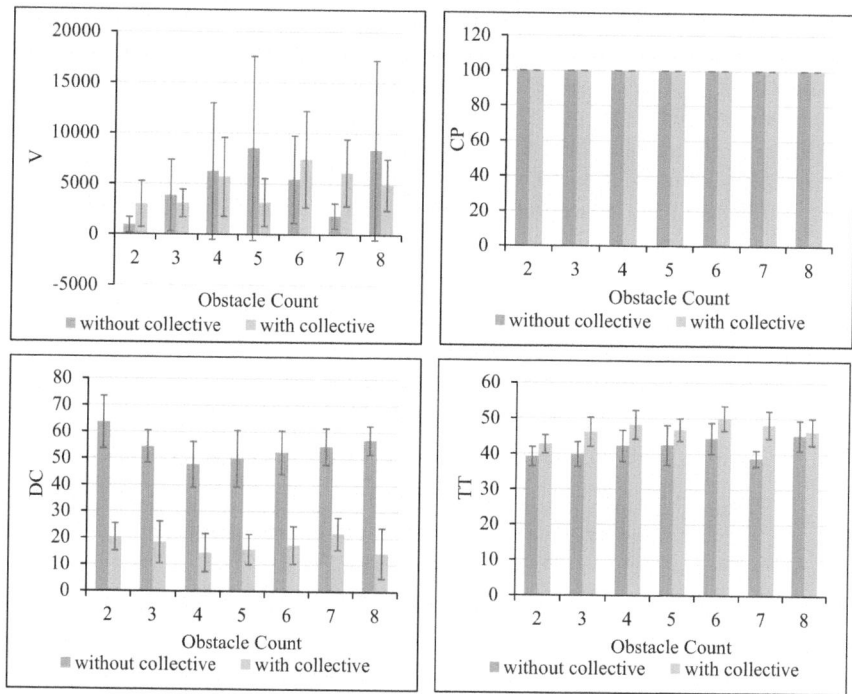

Fig. 5. Experiment 4 Performance Metric (Average with 95% Confidence Interval).

Results: The results indicate that varying the number of obstacles has no significant effect on CP, as full coverage was consistently achieved across all test cases in both scenarios. While there was no significant difference in V, a slight increase in collisions was noted with the rise in obstacle count. DC and TT remained stable, suggesting that connectivity and coverage time were maintained without significant differences. Overall, while some minor trends were observed, the primary metrics were largely unaffected by changes in obstacle counts. Table 6 and Fig. 5 presents a detailed analysis of these results, highlighting the relationship between obstacle count and the performance metrics.

4.5 Experiment 5: Impact of Changing Obstacle Positioning

Setup: This experiment investigates the impact of varying obstacle positions on the performance of the swarm both with and without the use of collective motion strategies. The best parameters derived from Experiment 1 were utilized to ensure consistency in the evaluation. Seven distinct obstacle positioning configurations were created in the experimental environment (Table 2), referred to as Structures (St1, St2, ..., St7). Each configuration was tested ten times, with robots starting from different initial positions to account for randomness and ensure that the results were not influenced by the initial conditions.

Results: The results show that changing obstacle positions had no significant effect on the CP as the roots achieved full coverage in all test cases, while slightly affecting the V by cased variations in the number of collisions. However, the differences observed were not statistically significant. Additionally, there were no significant changes in DC and TT. Overall, while some minor trends were observed, the primary metrics were largely unaffected by changes in obstacle counts. Table 7 and Fig. 6 present a detailed analysis of these results, highlighting the relationship between obstacle count and the performance metrics.

Table 7. Results when changing obstacle positions without and with collective motion. The mean of 10 runs with the 95% confidence interval.

Obstacle Position	Without Collective Motion				With Collective Motion			
	V	CP (%)	DC	TT (s)	V	CP (%)	DC	TT (s)
St1	2476.0 ± 2053.2	100 ± 0	46.2 ± 1.94	39.07 ± 10.61	4062.2 ± 2193.34	100 ± 0	20.9 ± 6.13	46.75 ± 3.92
St2	4979.1 ± 3993.16	100 ± 0	54.1 ± 3.57	42.95 ± 10.72	2746.6 ± 1616.57	100 ± 0	14.7 ± 6.96	45.46 ± 3.44
St3	9332.4 ± 6397.66	100 ± 0	55.3 ± 3.89	43.74 ± 9.25	6428.8 ± 5547.44	100 ± 0	22.1 ± 7.63	48.26 ± 3.52
St4	2272.7 ± 1678.00	100 ± 0	58.0 ± 4.06	39.85 ± 10.40	7047.4 ± 4896.60	100 ± 0	9.3 ± 3.67	49.02 ± 4.08
St5	2339.0 ± 2037.06	100 ± 0	65.1 ± 2.31	38.28 ± 13.48	6820.1 ± 5158.72	100 ± 0	16.1 ± 5.57	49.64 ± 3.93
St6	3198.4 ± 2191.25	100 ± 0	47.0 ± 2.67	40.70 ± 9.78	4028.3 ± 2346.28	100 ± 0	17.1 ± 7.50	46.16 ± 3.89
St7	2740.2 ± 2094.02	100 ± 0	57.5 ± 2.73	41.00 ± 9.66	6025.8 ± 3312.24	100 ± 0	19.8 ± 8.52	48.43 ± 4.18

4.6   Discussion

The results from the experiments demonstrate the effectiveness of our framework in optimizing FLS to solve CCPs and show how varying environmental features influence the performance of optimized collective motion in CCPs. In the first experiment, using collective motion increased TT from 29.91 s to 52.33 s, indicating that while collective behaviors improve connectivity and reduce collisions, they also slow down the overall coverage process. Despite this increase in TT, full CP was achieved, and V was minimized, suggesting that collective motion effectively maintains high coverage performance for CCPs.

The second experiment examined the impact of changing grid size on performance metrics, including V, CP, DC, and TT. The results indicated that while all test cases achieved full coverage, increasing grid size significantly affected other metrics. As grid size expanded, V increased, DC decreased, and TT rose, reflecting a correlation between larger grid areas and greater collision likelihoods, decreased connectivity, and extended coverage times. These results highlight the challenges posed by larger environments in maintaining swarm efficiency. The third experiment analyzed the effect of varying robot counts on performance. Full coverage (CP) remained consistent across all cases, but an increase in the number of robots led to a rise in V due to more collisions. Conversely, DC improved with more robots, indicating better connectivity, while TT decreased, suggesting faster coverage times. This indicates that while increasing the robot

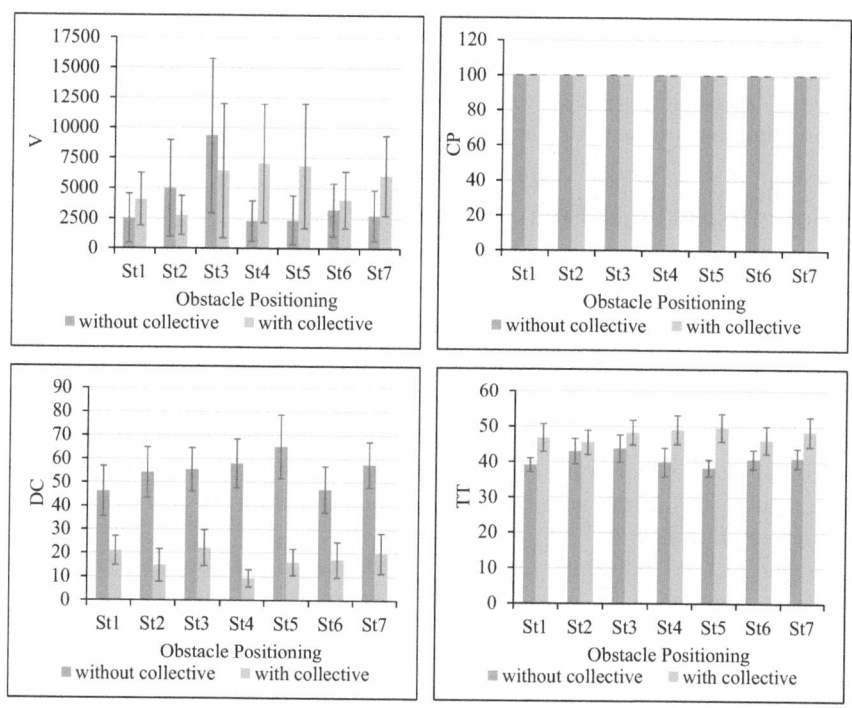

Fig. 6. Experiment 5 Performance Metric (Average with 95% Confidence Interval).

count can enhance connectivity and speed up coverage, it also raises the potential for collisions.

In the fourth experiment, the impact of varying obstacle counts was assessed. Notably, the results showed that changes in obstacle count had minimal effects on CP, with full coverage consistently achieved across scenarios. Although a slight increase in V was noted, the overall effects on DC and TT remained stable, suggesting that connectivity and coverage times were not significantly impacted. This indicates that while obstacles introduce challenges, their quantity does not critically hinder overall performance. The fifth experiment investigated how changing obstacle positioning influenced performance metrics. Similar to previous findings, CP remained at 100% across all test cases, demonstrating the robustness of coverage regardless of obstacle arrangement. While variations in obstacle positions led to slight fluctuations in V due to minor increases in collisions, these changes were not statistically significant. Moreover, no meaningful impacts were observed on DC and TT, indicating that the positioning of obstacles did not considerably affect connectivity or coverage times.

Overall, these results highlight the complex dynamics between environmental factors and swarm performance in CCPs. They underscore the necessity for ongoing exploration into adaptive algorithms capable of dynamically responding to changing environmental factors and robot configurations in real-time. This adaptability could significantly enhance the effectiveness of swarm robotics in complex coverage scenarios. The findings suggest the importance of optimizing parameters and configurations to balance coverage efficiency, connectivity, and collision avoidance across varying environments.

5   Conclusion and Future Work

In summary, this study conducts a comprehensive sensitivity analysis to explore how various environmental features-such as grid size, robot count, obstacle count, and obstacle positioning-impact robotics swarm performance in multi-objective coverage tasks. The research addresses multiple objectives, including achieving full coverage, avoiding collisions, maintaining connectivity, and minimizing coverage time. By elucidating the intricate relationships among these factors, this work contributes valuable insights into optimizing swarm robotics in dynamic environments, paving the way for future advancements in swarm behavior and performance efficiency.

The findings indicate that while the optimized FLS parameters achieve 100% coverage percentage (CP), they do not significantly vary with changes in environmental features. However, these changes substantially affect other performance metrics, including collision rates (V), disconnectivity (DC), and total coverage time (TT). Specifically, larger environments lead to increased collisions and reduced connectivity, resulting in longer times to complete coverage tasks. An increasing number of robots enhances connectivity and reduces coverage time but also raises the likelihood of collisions due to denser formations. Conversely, an increasing number of obstacles can complicate the coverage process, leading to higher collision rates while maintaining the ability to achieve full coverage. Changes in obstacle positioning have demonstrated minimal impact on coverage performance, yet they can still influence collision rates and connectivity due to variations in pathfinding dynamics. All these results underscore the intricate interplay between environmental parameters and swarm performance, highlighting the need for adaptive strategies to optimize coverage efficiency while minimizing collisions and maintaining connectivity in varying environments.

Future work will focus on developing a surrogate model to predict swarm performance metrics based on behavior parameters and environmental features. This approach aims to automate parameter tuning, thereby eliminating the need for expensive simulations each time the environment changes. Additionally, we plan to extend our framework to accommodate heterogeneous swarms, dynamic environments, and real-world hardware considerations. While we employed lexicographical ordering in our approach, we acknowledge that a Pareto-based approach could provide a more comprehensive solution that will allow for independent treatment of objectives and ensure that trade-offs between conflicting objectives are better captured. We will also explore energy efficiency measures and incorporate deep reinforcement learning techniques for real-time optimization. By automating swarm behavior tuning, our framework paves the way for advanced applications in various fields, including search and rescue, environmental monitoring, agricultural surveying, disaster response, infrastructure inspection, and autonomous exploration.

Acknowledgement. The authors would like to thank UNSW for the financial support provided through the UIPA scholarship program. This research was supported by resources from the National Computational Infrastructure (NCI Australia), funded by the Australian Government through NCRIS.

References

1. Abpeikar, S., Kasmarik, K., Tran, P.V., Garratt, M., Anavatti, S., Khan, M.M.: Tuning swarm behavior for environmental sensing tasks represented as coverage problems. In: Artificial Intelligence and Data Science in Environmental Sensing, pp. 155–178. Elsevier (2022). https://doi.org/10.1016/B978-0-323-90508-4.00001-0

2. Bahaidarah, M., Rekabi-Bana, F., Marjanovic, O., Arvin, F.: Swarm flocking using optimisation for a self-organised collective motion. Swarm Evol. Comput. **86**, 101491 (2024). https://doi.org/10.1016/j.swevo.2024.101491

3. Duisterhof, B.P., Li, S., Burgués, J., Reddi, V.J., de Croon, G.C.H.E.: Sniffy Bug: a fully autonomous swarm of gas-seeking Nano quadcopters in cluttered environments. In: 2021 IEEE/RSJ International Conference on Intelligent Robots and Systems (IROS), pp. 9099–9106 (2021). https://doi.org/10.1109/IROS51168.2021.9636217, iSSN: 2153-0866

4. Eiben, A., Nitschke, G., Schut, M.: Evolving an agent collective for cooperative mine sweeping. In: 2005 IEEE Congress on Evolutionary Computation. vol. 1, pp. 831–836, September 2005. https://doi.org/10.1109/CEC.2005.1554769. iSSN: 1941-0026

5. Ghanem, R., Ali, I.M., Abpeikar, S., Kasmarik, K., Garratt, M.: Optimizing and predicting swarming collective motion performance for coverage problems solving: a simulation-optimization approach. Eng. Appl. Artif. Intell. **139**, 109522 (2025). https://doi.org/10.1016/j.engappai.2024.109522

6. Katoch, S., Chauhan, S.S., Kumar, V.: A review on genetic algorithm: past, present, and future. Multimed. Tools App. **80**(5), 8091–8126 (2021). https://doi.org/10.1007/s11042-020-10139-6

7. Khan, M., et al.: Generating collective motion behaviour libraries using developmental evolution. In: Liu, T., Webb, G., Yue, L., Wang, D. (eds.) AI 2023: Advances in Artificial Intelligence, pp. 441–452. Springer Nature, Singapore (2024). https://doi.org/10.1007/978-981-99-8391-9_35

8. Lin, C.C., Hsiao, P.Y., Chen, K.C.: A motion planning of swarm robots using genetic algorithm. In: 2010 International Conference on Broadband, Wireless Computing, Communication and Applications, pp. 538–543, November 2010. https://doi.org/10.1109/BWCCA.2010.128

9. Reynolds, C.W.: Flocks, herds and schools: a distributed behavioral model. SIG-GRAPH Comput. Graph. **21**(4), 25–34 (1987). https://doi.org/10.1145/37402.37406

10. Tang, Q., Zhang, L., Luo, W., Ding, L., Yu, F., Zhang, J.: A comparative study of biology-inspired algorithms applied to swarm robots target searching. In: Tan, Y., Shi, Y., Li, L. (eds.) ICSI 2016. LNCS, vol. 9713, pp. 479–490. Springer, Cham (2016). https://doi.org/10.1007/978-3-319-41009-8_52

11. Thrun, M.C., Ultsch, A.: Swarm intelligence for self-organized clustering. Artif. Intell. **290**, 103237 (2021). https://doi.org/10.1016/j.artint.2020.103237

12. Tran, V.P., Garratt, M.A., Kasmarik, K., Anavatti, S.G.: Dynamic frontier-led swarming: multi-robot repeated coverage in dynamic environments. IEEE/CAA J. Autom. Sin. **10**(3), 646–661 (2023). https://doi.org/10.1109/JAS.2023.123087

13. Tran, V.P., Garratt, M.A., Kasmarik, K., Anavatti, S.G., Abpeikar, S.: Frontier-led swarming: robust multi-robot coverage of unknown environments. Swarm Evol. Comput. **75**, 101171 (2022). https://doi.org/10.1016/j.swevo.2022.101171

14. Wang, C., Zhang, S., Ma, T., Xiao, Y., Chen, M.Z., Wang, L.: Swarm intelligence: a survey of model classification and applications. Chin. J. Aeronaut. (2024). https://doi.org/10.1016/j.cja.2024.03.019

15. Zhou, X., Wang, H., Ding, B.: How many robots are enough: a multi-objective genetic algorithm for the single-objective time-limited complete coverage problem. In: 2018 IEEE International Conference on Robotics and Automation (ICRA), pp. 2380–2387. IEEE Press, Brisbane, Australia, May 2018.https://doi.org/10.1109/ICRA.2018.8461028

Author Index

The manufacturer's authorised representative in the EU is Springer
Nature Customer Service Centre GmbH, Europaplatz 3, 69115 Heidelberg,
Germany. If you have any concerns regarding our products, please
contact ProductSafety@springernature.com

Printed and bound by CPI Group (UK) Ltd, Croydon, CR0 4YY

29/04/2026

02099546-0003